AGAINST EQUALI
Readings on Economic

The compilation and publication of this set of readings has been assisted by a grant from the Foundation for Education in Economics, whose Trustees are: Professor Julius Gould, Professor Jack Wiseman and Simon Webley

AGAINST EQUALITY

Readings on Economic and Social Policy

≠

Edited by

WILLIAM LETWIN

The Macmillan Press
in association with the
Foundation for Education in Economics

M

First published 1983 by
THE MACMILLAN PRESS LTD
London and Basingstoke
Companies and representatives throughout the world

ISBN 0 333 35312 9 (hard cover)
ISBN 0 333 35313 7 (paper cover)

Typeset by
WESSEX TYPESETTERS LTD
Frome, Somerset

Printed in Hong Kong

Contents

List of contributors

PETER BAUER: Professor of Economics, London School of Economics and Political Science; sometime Fellow of Caius College, Cambridge.

KENNETH E. BOULDING: White Professor at Large, Cornell University.

JOHN CHARVET: Reader in Political Science, London School of Economics.

JAMES S. COLEMAN: Professor of Sociology, University of Chicago.

ANTONY FLEW: Professor of Philosophy, University of Reading.

THE LATE CHARLES FRANKEL: Former President, National Humanities Center, Columbia University.

THE LATE HARRY G. JOHNSON: Former Charles F. Grey Distinguished Service Professor, University of Chicago; former Professor of Economics, London School of Economics.

NATHAN KEYFITZ: Andelot Professor of Sociology and Demography, Harvard University.

WILLIAM LETWIN: Professor of Political Science, London School of Economics.

J. R. LUCAS: Fellow of Merton College, Oxford.

GEOFFREY MARSHALL: Fellow of The Queen's College, Oxford.

ROBERT NISBET: Resident Scholar, American Enterprise Institute, Washington, DC.

THE LATE GEORGE POLANYI: Former Research Officer, Institute of Economic Affairs, London.

RICHARD A. POSNER: Professor of Law, University of Chicago.

GORDON TULLOCK: University Distinguished Professor of Economics and Public Choice, Virginia Polytechnic Institute and State University.

RICHARD E. WAGNER: Professor of Economics, Virginia Polytechnic Institute and State University.

ANDREW WARD: Sometime Senior Member, Fitzwilliam College, Cambridge.

JOHN B. WOOD: Deputy Director, Institute of Economic Affairs, London.

Editor's preface

I have designed this book to challenge and to rebut egalitarianism. My own view of the matter is set out in the introductory essay. I selected the other essays because they illuminate certain issues that arise in scrutinising the egalitarian position. But I should emphasise that the inclusion of an essay in this collection is not to be interpreted as a sign that the author shares either my general opposition to egalitarianism (though many of the authors evidently do) or my particular views on any of the more specific questions which they and I discuss. In short, the essays collected here do not hew to any orthodoxy.

Although the essays are grouped in accordance with certain main topics, most of them are not narrowly confined to one of those topics but bear also on the broader issue.

The question of 'social equality' – which concerns differences of status, class, esteem and the like – receives less attention here than other aspects of equality. Reasons are suggested, nevertheless, for concluding that the claims of egalitarianism in the social sphere are as baseless as in any other and that the prospects for equalisation are more hopeless than elsewhere.

I should like to thank for their help in producing this volume the Foundation for Education in Economics, and particularly Professor Julius Gould and Mr Simon Webley.

My grateful acknowledgement is due to the authors and original publishers of the selected essays for permission to reproduce them here. The source is given at the foot of the opening page of each chapter. The variant usages of British and American English have been retained as in the original printings.

W.L.

1

The case against equality

WILLIAM LETWIN

≠

BECAUSE equality is the leading fetish of our time, because so many people endorse it as an obvious ideal, because so many have enlisted in it as a cause, without having considered its consequences, it ought to be scrutinised. This book offers a series of scrutinies, mainly sceptical, of equality as an ideal or equalisation as a practice.

Most people now believe in equality. To put it another way, most people believe that many aspects of social life should be reformed so as to get rid of inherited inequalities. That is why they support redistribution of income and wealth, within nations and among nations; why they sympathise with measures to extend powers of decision to workers as well as employers, students as well as teachers, voters as well as politicians and officials; and why they automatically assent to many similar exercises in 'democratisation', 'participation' and 'equalisation of rights'.

Most people also believe that equality as a goal is entirely self-evident, so that it neither need be nor could be justified by reasoning from any deeper principle. If that were so, one would be forced to wonder how anybody could ever oppose equality. Egalitarians accordingly tend to explain opposition as stemming from cynical efforts of favoured people to stay on top of the heap, or from the misguided and lethargic complaisance of people at the bottom of the heap. But in fact

This essay is written for the present volume as an introduction to the discussion:

For the Notes and References, see page 383 below.

there is now little such opposition to be accounted for. Most of those who stand to lose by equalisation nevertheless feel themselves compelled – by decency or religious faith, as they suppose, and most frequently perhaps by a sense of guilt – to concede that equality should by right prevail. Nor, within free democracies, is there any great mass at the bottom of the scale who are so bewitched or oppressed that they regard inequality as justified or inescapable, or so enlightened as to understand that inequality may be beneficial to themselves. Most people heartily endorse equality as a goal, some acquiesce to it reluctantly, and very few deny it outright.

This book is intended to disrupt the consensus. It calls into question the philosophical arguments which have been or might be advanced in favour of egalitarianism; points out ambiguities within the idea of equality; disputes the data which are supposed to reveal great and growing inequality; and identifies the destructive consequences which have already resulted from or may be expected from policies aimed at equalisation.

It may be alleged that this book is unbalanced, because it gives no hearing to the defendants' advocates. Such a complaint would ignore the fact that libraries, newspapers and airwaves are full of pleadings for and avowals of faith in equality, whereas the case against egalitarianism is seldom stated or heard.[1] In any event, an effort, such as this one, to stir up serious debate about a vital principle which has so widely and so long been taken for granted, goes beyond partisanship. What is said here may indeed persuade some readers that to reject equality as a goal conforms with reason even if not with fashion. At the same time, proponents of equality should be grateful to anyone who locates weak points in their armour, thus giving them opportunity to reinforce their defences. Intellectual frankness should interest everyone in a dissection of a faith which has hitherto been largely unexamined.

Egalitarianism, as a systematic doctrine, goes beyond the inarticulate public faith in the obvious goodness of equality. As expounded in political tracts, official reports, philosophical essays and other considered utterances, egalitarianism seems to rest on three ideas. (1) All persons should be equal. (2) All existing inequalities can be reduced if not utterly eradicated by action of governments or by revolutionary change in government. (3) All other political objectives must give way to equality, if any conflict arises between it and them. Full-fledged egalitarianism holds, in short, that equality is a desirable end, a feasible end, and the paramount political end.

Needless to say, the egalitarian position is seldom put quite so boldly. A simple belief that everyone should be equal in every way would seem ridiculous even in the eyes of avid egalitarians. Even they would not maintain that all human beings should be equal in height and weight, in the number of cigars they smoke, and in the frequency of their sojourns in jail. To make equality an ideal that is even remotely sensible, it must be narrowed. The most sensible limiting formula to have emerged is that people should be equal *only* in respect of certain goods which are both general and vital. The sorts of goods to which judicious egalitarians have accordingly confined their ideal are income, wealth, esteem, political power, legal rights and education. It is obviously easier for egalitarians to maintain that people should be equal in these essential respects (such as income) rather than in more particular and indifferent respects (such as consumption of strawberries). Nevertheless, as will be shown in what follows, no amount of such narrowing can give the ideal of equality a coherent and determinate content.

As to their second idea, that equalisation is practicable: here too egalitarians have tended to settle for a more confined and accordingly more defensible position. They hold that, although perfect equality is or may be unattainable, nevertheless it is always possible to move one step closer to equality. The premise which typically underlies this faith is that inequality – in all the dimensions that really matter – is made by human beings, is a product of human vice. Nature makes men equal; Man makes them unequal. This implies that social arrangements which have been fashioned badly can be refashioned so as to make them less bad. It is not, however, the moral reform of individuals (who might then bring about equalisation by private philanthropy) on which egalitarians pin their hopes, but rather enforced equalisation by government. The practical optimism of egalitarians will be shown to be intellectually unsound and politically dangerous.

As to their third idea, that equality is the paramount end of good government: liberal or democratic egalitarians frequently limit the force of this proposition by denying that equality is at all likely to conflict with the other principal ends of good government. Suppose, for instance, it were objected that equality and individual liberty necessarily clash in the context of any policy of enforced redistribution of income, inasmuch as anyone forced to pay a heavy tax is to some extent deprived of his previous liberty to spend his income as he chose. A large variety of answers is offered by egalitarians, most of which pretend to explain away this conflict of ends. One is that the deprivation of liberty on the part of the few, unwilling, rich 'benefactors' is more than offset by the enhancement of liberty on the part of the many beneficiaries – an argument which depends on the fallacy of confusing liberty to do something with ability or power to do it. Another is that property rights exist only within a framework of laws established by the state, from which egalitarians would have it follow that no person can properly be said to be deprived of his property (or denied freedom to use it as he chooses) when the laws governing property rights, which in the egalitarian view include the tax laws, are changed in a constitutional manner. Still another is that the fundamental liberty of a citizen in a democracy is his freedom to vote as he chooses, and the ancillary freedoms to discuss political questions, to belong to a party, and to criticise the government; whatever 'restrictions' the laws of a democracy may impose on a citizen are, according to this view, to be understood as voluntary obligations, entered into by each citizen through the vicarious action of his representatives, rather than as deprivations imposed on him by others. Such evasive answers are, however, quite eschewed by blunter breeds of egalitarians. They unblinkingly assert that when other ideals – liberty, stability, diversity or economic efficiency – clash with equality, those other principles must be sacrificed. I will indicate, in what follows, how the pursuit of equality jeopardises the preservation or furthering of other political goods.

How has it come about that equality now commands such widespread assent? Common among historians who lean toward egalitarianism is the thesis that equality, liberty and democracy are the first fruits of a struggle carried on for hundreds of years, a struggle by the common people against the rich, their masters. On this view, every member of the lower class who recognises his true interest demands equality; but it has taken centuries for enough of the lower class to learn this, to organise effectively for action, and to succeed partially; and the ultimate victory of equality awaits the abolition of capitalism, either by reform or revolution.

Every step of this sort of historical analysis could be shown to be an arbitrary theoretical assumption rather than an empirical finding. That every community consists fundamentally of 'classes'; that the class defines the 'interests' of its members; that the several classes are naturally at war with each other; and that perfect, stateless socialism, the reign of equality, will inevitably supersede capitalism, the reign of oppressive inequality – all these are postulates, belonging to a particular interpretation of human affairs, rather than self-evident truths or indisputable historical facts.

A proper historical attempt to explain how equality has achieved its present pre-eminence would have to investigate the diverse reasons why so many people – of the upper and middle sorts as well as the lower – have come to believe in equality. One set of reasons, certainly not negligible, is a variety of ideas which have been put forward during the past three centuries. Among these have been interpretations of Christianity which stressed the equality of all men in the sight of God; philosophical writings which, besides many other effects, made equality one of the three watchwords of the French Revolution; the doctrinal pronouncements of socialists of many varieties; and, more recently, the writings of academic social scientists, especially of certain economists and sociologists. But these are only a few of the many activities which have contributed toward bringing about the present state of affairs.[2]

A historical account that took cognisance of all the actions and circumstances which might be invoked to explain the high esteem in which equality is now held would be a very elaborate work. Valuable as this would be, nothing of the sort is attempted in this book. Occasional allusions are made to the history of equality as a goal and of equalisation as a policy, but the point of the book is to examine arguments and interpretations of fact which are in use today, rather than to trace the historical steps which brought them onto the stage.

A. Theoretical Weaknesses of Egalitarianism

In considering the arguments which have been advanced for equality, it is useful to disentangle various strands which are often interwoven in egalitarian thought. Although these strands are more or less similar inasmuch as they converge on a common conclusion, they are logically independent of one another and can therefore be scrutinised separately.*

1. *The presumption of equality*

Most people who believe in equality regard it as an obvious presumption, a self-evident starting point for thought and policy, akin to an axiom, not needing to be supported by a foundation of reasoning.

Some believers in equality suppose that their case can be made satisfactorily, or in any event quite adequately illustrated, by a parable. The parable may be put in this form. Four children sit at the tea-table presided over by their mother. When the cake is served, she *naturally* gives each child an equal piece. To give one child a larger piece than the others would be wrong unless some compelling reason justified an exceptional departure from the rule of equality. And so, say the tellers of this story, equality is the obvious presumption, the rule which ought to be followed in principle in the allocation of all the world's goods.

Like any other parable, this one achieves its persuasive force by weaving into the simple plot a series of assumptions, unstated and unrecognised, yet vital to the effect. So here the

* Some of these stands are analysed in detail in chapters 2 to 5 below.

cake stands for something which everyone wants. Moreover, in this case, the claimants are children, whose appetite for sweet things is known generally to be exorbitant. Further, being children, they are assumed to be incapable of making or buying more cake for themselves. In short, the parable introduces us, slyly, into a situation of scarcity, extreme and irremediable, where the allocation is authoritatively determined by a person assumed to be a benevolent despot.

It is easy enough to construct a parable that carries just the opposite message. A cocktail party is being given by a lavish host. Waiters circulate constantly, offering drinks and *hors d'oeuvres* of all sorts. The guests are distinguished middle-aged professionals, suave, sober and slim or slimming. When the guests leave, plenty of food and drink remains. The rule of allocation in these circumstances is that each guest consumes what he likes, and the outcome is that each guest consumes a different amount. So far from equality being the natural presumption, any effort by the host to make each guest consume the same amount would be taken as bad taste if not mad hunger for power. Instead of scarcity in the face of greed, this parable posits plenty in the presence of self-restraint.

If we wish to come closer to the circumstances in which people live most of their lives, we should think of yet another parable. It concerns a farmer who works a large plot of land and who, considering one year with another, grows an amount of grain proportional to the amount of effort he puts into seeding, weeding and harvesting. Neither a benevolent despot nor a lavish host provides for him, but he provides for himself; and within the limits set by the fruitfulness of land and climate, he can consume more or less as he chooses to work more or less.

If we now reconsider the story of the tea-table, it is clear that the mother might allocate the cake according to a large number of different criteria, each quite reasonable in itself. She might give every child as much as it likes, knowing that some like more than others. Even after all have had their fill, some cake may be left over and may spoil before the next meal; the possibility of waste is, all else being equal, a strong reason for letting people take as much as they like. If, on the other hand, there is not enough cake to go around, the mother might invoke the rule of first-come-first-served; eagerness is a traditionally accepted way of measuring desire. Of course, people who prize responsibility will be frightened by the thought that anybody should get as much as he likes; they would feel safer with a rule that people should get as much as it good for them and no more than that. To this we might retort that what feels good to a person, at least to a normal adult, is often the best evidence about what is good for him; certainly physicians often follow this rule. Again, the mother might distribute the cake according to merit, giving each child a piece proportional to the virtues which he has recently demonstrated, or proportional to her love for each. She might distribute it in accordance with her views of their different needs for nourishment, or her experience of how eating that cake affects the subsequent health of each child. In short, she can invoke numerous specific criteria within the general classes of desire, desert and need.

There is, thus, no fundamental, initial or general presumption in favour of equal shares for all. Equality would be adopted as a criterion only if the allocating authority were too ignorant, lazy or dogmatic to consider any more refined criterion. Equality would emerge, as a reasonable criterion, only if the children were equal in respect of desire, desert, need, or in some other relevant way. In short, equality is rationally defensible as a rule only when the persons in question are held to be equal, beforehand, in some predominant respect. Inasmuch as people are unequal, it is rational to presume that they ought to be treated unequally – which might mean larger shares for the needy or larger shares for the worthy. And so, the parable intended to sustain the presumption in favour of equality falls apart under critical scrutiny and seems if anything to suggest the opposite of what it intends.

2. *Identity of Essence*

The first, probably the oldest and perhaps the most persuasive, foundation for the ideal of equality is the premise that all men are essentially identical. Adherents to this line posit an essence, core or 'nature' which is present in each human being, which identifies him as human, and which, because it is durable and universal, is to be regarded as more telling than all the contingent and changeable particularities that differentiate any human individual from all others. They assert, in effect, that the fundamental similarities among men are more important than the accidental or casual differences.

Secular variants of this position have identified the essence of man as one or another of the following: his ability to reason, to converse, to govern himself by deliberate peaceable assent, to create works of beauty, or to recognise right and wrong. Whichever of these they take as their starting point, egalitarian arguments of this sort pursue the same path thereafter. They maintain that, despite superficial and accidental differences among individuals – despite even the manifest inequalities among individuals in respect of their inessential attributes – all human beings are identical in possessing the essential attribute which makes them human, and therefore all human beings are essentially equal.

In this way, all the observed differences among individuals are over-ruled by the identity alleged to be essential. Essential why? Only because it marks off the species of man from all other kinds of things. Surely an attribute that differentiates one kind of thing from another is 'important', and well worth knowing about. But that is very far from saying that what differentiates this thing from another is therefore the central, fundamental, vital, crucial aspect of this thing. What distinguishes red flowers from other flowers is their redness, yet no connoisseur of flowers would regard redness as the pivotal, uniquely telling, in short, essential characteristic of a flower. In any event, the attributes which are essential as a tool in defining human beings, that is, in differentiating men from all other beings – attributes such as the powers to reason, converse, and the like – are not therefore the attributes which are central to every branch of public policy.

Yet even if we knew man's essential nature, it would not follow that because every human being necessarily possesses it – or for want of it would be described without hesitation as abnormal, defective, or even as inhuman – all men are thereby equal. To infer equality from such identity is to commit a fallacy.

In order to identify this fallacy, it is necessary to recognise that there are two broad ways in which things can be the same. One form of sameness is the one we call equality; the other form of sameness has no necessary relation to equality.

Simple examples can illustrate this distinction. For instance, two numbers such as 3 and 5 are the same in as much as both are numbers and moreover both are integers, odd, and prime; yet 3 and 5 are clearly unequal. Bears and dogs are the same in being hairy, but we would hesitate to declare that bears and dogs are equally hairy, which might imply that they have the same amount of hair. Brahms and Bruckner could comfortably be called the same in so far as both were composers, but to call them equal composers or even equally composers would go beyond what many critics care to affirm.

Clearly two distinct varieties of sameness are present here. Although the pairs of specimens share in each instance the same attribute, they do not exhibit that attribute in the same degree. We can recognise this disjunction by labelling the first sort of sameness as 'sameness in kind' and the second as 'sameness in degree'. 'Equality' is a synonym for the latter, but not a synonym for the former.

This distinction once made, a series of implications follow, which can illuminate and rectify the discussion of equality as a principle of ethics, law and politics. (1) Things which are the same in kind, that is, the same in respect of some attribute, may be equal or unequal in that respect; though it may happen also that despite the sameness of some attribute, no meaningful statement can be made about the subjects' equality or inequality. For instance, two trees may be the same in respect of being elms, but to say that they are equally or unequally elms is meaningless, as the quality of 'elmness' does not admit of quantification. It need hardly be said that as to height, age or any number of other attributes which all elms possess, the two may be equal or unequal. (2) Things which differ in kind cannot, in that respect, be either equal or unequal. For instance, a rock and a rabbit cannot be said, without further ado, to be equal or unequal. Of course, one might say that a rabbit can run faster than a rock, and thus conclude that they have unequal powers of locomotion; but this conclusion is possible only by imputing to both the same attribute, namely 'power of locomotion', as a precondition of comparing the degrees to which they possess it. Similarly with the common cliché that men and women are unequal. Taken at face value, it is meaningless, since being of different genders, men cannot in respect of gender be either equal or unequal to women. Taking it generously, loosely enough to recognise the intended meaning, it asserts that in respect of attributes which they share, men get preferential treatment: so that, for instance, men are paid more than women, pay less for bank loans, and so on. Things can only be equal or unequal in relation to qualities which they have in common and qualities which moreover can be quantified.

In short, to say that things are the same need not mean that they are equal, and to say that things are different need not mean that they are unequal. Much discussion of equality founders on these shoals.

It follows that the attempt to deduce the equality of men from the universal presence in men of an identical essence must be dismissed as resting on the fallacy which confuses 'sameness of kind' with 'sameness of degree'. Like the numbers 3 and 5, any two men may, while being identical in kind, be unequal in any or every possible matter of degree. Although all men have a power to reason, it does not follow in the least that all men have equal power to reason, or could have, or should have. Even if we accepted that all men are identical in essence, the conclusion that they are all 'essentially equal' could emerge only by logical trickery.

A theological variation on the same theme is exposed to similar criticism. We meet it most often in the statement that all men are equal in the sight of God. Perhaps this means that all men are identical in having immortal souls; yet it appears, according to the tenets of many sects, that this will not guarantee them equal treatment, for some souls will be raised to everlasting glory while others will be condemned to eternal damnation. Perhaps it is to be understood as meaning that in God's sight we are all minuscule – though not therefore equally small; perhaps that God's infinite mercy will redeem us all, though we be unequally unworthy of redemption. Perhaps, again, God's infinite love for all men inclines Him to treat as equal souls which are strictly speaking quite unequal. No such interpretation can enable mere human beings to leap the gap between sameness of attribute and sameness of degree.

Christianity may have been a powerful influence in propagating the beliefs that underlie contemporary egalitarianism. Not that the record is unequivocal, for while various strands of Christian dogma lay some stress on equality, there are others which strongly imply the opposite: such as the doctrine of election in Calvinism; or the phrase in the Anglican catechism which instructs the child to do his duty 'in that state of life' (that status or station, as we would say) 'unto which it shall please God to call me'. Even if it were true, as it may well be, that the present vogue of egalitarianism owes much to Christian teachings, that historical truth could not be mustered as a rationally compelling argument in favour of equality. Powerful as faith is, it cannot perform the office of reason.

3. *Aboriginal Equality*

Some egalitarian positions base themselves on the premise that men are 'naturally' equal: that is, that men were equal while they lived in a 'state of nature', their original condition. That primitive paradisial equality was corrupted, according to this view, when men formed societies, for society brought in the unnatural domination and exploitation of some men by others, so engendering the malady of inequality. The cure is to reform society, so as to restore the natural, healthy condition of equality. Such, more or less, is the line promulgated by Rousseau, Marx and others, as well as by many who follow them unknowingly.

What is 'natural' in men, within this view, should be discernible by examining the condition of human beings before they have been exposed to and influenced by society. One way to do this is by examining the human individual in embryo. Such an examination, far from confirming the premised equality, reveals many differences and many inequalities among individuals. Attributes given from the moment of conception differ, and these lead to differences which accompany the individual throughout his life: among them are colouring (of skin, hair and eyes); gender; and abnormalities of structure or function, abnormalities which may be rated as defects (such as vestigial fingers) or as special blessings (such as hyper-acute hearing). Other of the differentiating attributes which accompany the individual from conception are potentialities rather than determined givens; and, although presumably nobody can fully realise all of his potentialities, nevertheless the ultimate performance of any individual is facilitated by and limited by the specific endowments with which he arrives on the scene. It is impossible therefore to maintain that all human beings are identical at the moment after conception and are made different only by their nurtures – unless one takes the radical, demonstrably false, position that all human beings are genetically identical.

One can insist on the falsity of 'natural' equality without in any way overlooking the extent to which the different concrete circumstances of each individual's life affect the way in which he shapes his life. As important, nevertheless, is the fact that individuals can exercise considerable choice as to the concrete circumstances among which they prefer to live and which they accordingly arrange to live among. To attribute differences among individuals exclusively to the mystical operations of 'Society' is to prefer faith to obvious fact: a faith frequently embraced because it yields certain desired political conclusions, particularly that men ought to be equal because they 'naturally' are equal – that is, that they would be equal if not for the distortions introduced by corrupt society.

Further to confute this faith we might point to many other differences among people which are not caused by human will, either of individuals or of communities. One such is difference of age, which carries with it many other differences, not least of which is that, all else being equal, the older one becomes (short of agedness and senility), the greater the advantages that accrue from accumulated experience. Hence the pre-eminence of older people at the tops of hierarchies, political and industrial as well as spiritual or social; and hence also the larger incomes of skilled older workers as compared with incomes of relatively unskilled younger workers in the same occupation. Other natural differences, in height, weight, musculature and other gross physical characteristics – 'natural' inasmuch as they persist despite identity of nurture – largely account for individual differences in such aptitudes as physical strength, speed and agility. Still another natural difference is in the physical details which make up a person's appearance, so that some individuals are held to be attractive, while others seem plain or ill-favoured. Although the criteria of good looks which prevail at any given place and time are laid down by social convention, and a person regarded as ugly here might be thought elsewhere to be distinctively handsome, nevertheless, in a deeper sense, differences in looks transcend social norms, because it is unimaginable that any human community should fail altogether to recognise beauty. The universal human capacity to perceive differences between individuals originates in the inherent, durable character of human beings and not in the variable standards – or, as some see it, the arbitrary and perverse standards – which prevail in one community or another.

Another way to test the proposition that men are naturally equal would be to examine the condition of adult human beings living in a 'state of nature', before they have formed society. Unfortunately this test cannot be performed empirically, because it is impossible to find human beings living in a 'state of nature'. Some peoples, it is true, are so 'primitive' that they live under forms of government which are rudimentary, sporadic and unstable; yet, though they may lack what we would call government, they do not lack community. In short, we cannot observe individuals (except for rare, dubious instances of wolf-children) who have lived outside society, isolated all their lives, regarding every other human being as an alien enemy. And therefore we can find no facts which would authorise us to assert or deny that men in a pre-social condition are naturally equal. In so far then as theorists have asserted that natural equality is the condition of men in a state of nature, they have had to rest their case on nothing more solid than pure hypothesis. It is an utterly shaky foundation, ready to be toppled by the counter-hypothesis that in a state of nature men are radically unequal.

It is true enough that society, as we know it, provides

opportunity for individuals to differentiate themselves from one another and also to make themselves unequal. Or, to drop the filmy image of 'society' in favour of terms more tangible, individuals in civilised communities (and probably in all communities) make themselves different from one another – different enough at least so that they can be recognised as themselves – and they aim to be unequal, at least in so far as some at any rate aim to earn more, run faster, act more virtuously or achieve higher office. Yet these observations do nothing to sustain the view that it is society alone or only some sorts of society which create inequality among individuals who would remain naturally equal if they could stay outside society.

Finally, even if men were naturally equal, it would not follow in the least that they should be treated equally within a society. The natural condition of things is not necessarily the most desirable or morally the superior condition. Indeed, men sensibly exert themselves to overcome or modify many natural conditions. So natural equality, even if it could be known to exist and even if it is presumed to exist, could not constitute a rationally defensible imperative for treating people equally, in any or all respects, within 'post-natural' society.

4. *Common Enterprise*

Some egalitarians maintain that men ought to be equal quite apart from whether they are or are not equal in essence or by nature. They rest their case on the view that society is a common enterprise, to which all persons contribute, and in whose benefits they are all therefore entitled to share fairly, that is equally. Each step in this argument is suspect, not to say demonstrably false.

Society is misrepresented when pictured as an enterprise. An enterprise entails entrepreneurs, who launch a project in order to accomplish a goal. But society was never launched, since human beings have never existed outside it; at no time did a number of asocial individuals, born and living in utter isolation from one another, all resolve to join together for the deliberate purpose of creating a society. Society is not a project, but simply the name we give to the fact that wherever we see human beings we see them living together in communities. Because society is not a project, it has no ends. Society may loosely be said to confer benefits on its members, with just as little reason as the sun may be said to confer benefits upon the earth. Rather it is the members of a society who confer benefits on each other by co-operative efforts. Of course, co-operation would be impossible if people lived in total isolation from one another; though conflict would also be impossible, so that a pessimist might conclude that society does more harm than good. But any such calculation is beside the point. Society is incapable of acting; it is the inevitable condition of mankind; it is not an artificial enterprise endowed with ends and purposes by individuals who could have made it or not as they chose. And, strictly speaking, society contributes nothing; the only contributors are human beings, and the only beneficiaries are human beings.

Again, to say that all persons contribute to society says either nothing or too much. If the members are thought to 'contribute' in the sense that the collective entity would vanish on the departure of all its members, then the statement resolves into a mere tautology. Without parts there can be no whole, without a whole there can be no parts; each is a necessary element in defining the others, neither 'contributes' to the other. If, however, the members are thought to contribute in the more meaningful sense that they benefit not society but each other, then the question must arise in what ways their contributions are the same. And the answer is that various individuals make contributions of different kinds, catering to the various desires, tastes, motives and purposes of different beneficiaries; some of which contributions, being the same in kind, differ in degree. These evident differences and inequalities deny the implication that, because everyone makes a contribution, everyone deserves an *equal* reward.

Here we reach the step most unwarranted of all. That the labourer is worthy of his hire, that everyone who helps should enjoy a due share of the proceeds, is a widespread belief. But the notion that only an equal share is a due share does not command the whole field. Many believe that goods produced by a common enterprise should be allocated rather according to each person's need, desire, power or general merit. The only conclusion which can encompass all these competing views is that everyone must get a 'proper' share. Proper shares differ from fair shares, as 'fair' is usually understood, namely as an approximation to 'equal'. To define equality as coextensive with fairness or justice – thus treating all that is equal as just, and all that is just as equal – does not settle the vast question of what constitutes justice but merely defines it away, and merely assumes that equality is the proper ultimate objective.

5. *Generosity*

Another view maintains that sympathy does, or certainly should, prompt each person to share his goods with less fortunate brethren. It holds that a human being armed with normal decency cannot stand by unmoved while others suffer want. The ideal of equality thus emerges as the tribute we pay to our consciences, as the inevitable consequence of a universal moral duty of every person to be generous to all others.

The premise is beyond cavil. A person lacking all impulse or power to sympathise with others would be a moral monster. But the purported inference will not hold. Compassion commands the able to help and to share when sharing helps; it does not instruct men to share and share alike in accordance with a mathematical equation. Heroes of chivalric legends who say 'your need is greater than mine' achieve inequality rather than equality; by giving all they had, they end up having less than the recipient. Lesser mortals who practise philanthropy typically end up retaining more than they have given away, yet that does not deny the authenticity of their action or its value to others.

Generosity and sympathy dictate that no man be allowed to starve in the midst of plenty. This suggests that a safety-net be provided in the form of a minimum income guaranteed to each member of the community, adequate to provide what are considered the basic necessities. Such a policy, commendable and practicable in a moderately wealthy community, may exceed the resources of a very poor community, where the effort to provide a safety-net would convert the rapid starvation of the particularly unfortunate into the slightly slower starvation of all: a dubious achievement.

In short, sincere generosity is compatible, according to the circumstances, with giving away all one has, or some of it, or none of it. To follow the rule that one should give just as much as will result in all men having equal amounts is to replace the virtue of compassion with an amoral mechanical formula, possibly as harmful in its consequences as the most vicious forms of selfishness.

6. *Envy*

Whereas some of the arguments considered above are cast in a moral mould, maintaining that equality alone can satisfy the commands of ethics or the requirements of justice, we turn now to an argument which founds the ideal of equality on convenience rather than right.

It maintains that inequality – or 'relative deprivation', a new name which combines melodrama with technicality – provokes envy among the less fortunate, and that envy corrodes the social fabric. Equality is therefore the price of social stability, because only if each person feels that the society benefits him about as much as it benefits everyone else will each desist from disruption, sabotage and sinister pursuit of his own private good regardless of harm to others.

Crucial to this position is the assertion, as a matter either of historical fact or of psychological probability, that inequality leads to envy. But historical evidence would seem to point in just the opposite direction. Five hundred years ago, when inequality was certainly more pronounced than now, envy was perhaps less deep than it is now. To go beyond 'perhaps' is impossible: it is difficult enough to assess the magnitude of envy felt by people who can be observed directly today; surmise, and inference from indirect and scanty evidence, give us evidence of only the flimsiest sort about the feelings of people long since dead. Yet popular turmoil was not a vastly more remarkable feature of late medieval Europe than it is in far less unequal societies today. Nor can cross-sectional comparisons of various societies today sustain the presumption. If one ranked all societies today according to, first, their degree of inequality and, second, their degree of social instability – tasks calling for an awesome amount of insight and subjective judgement – it might turn out that the two rankings correlated more or less closely. Yet if such a correlation emerged, which is doubtful, it would prove nothing to the purpose, since any number of other considerations might be the common causes of both inequality and social instability. The most obvious candidate would be a self-serving tyranny, which distributed goods very unequally, survived temporarily only by force of repression, and was destabilised not by envy but by outrage and hatred. Instability today results much more from such groups as dissidents in the Soviet bloc, black African nationalists, and Arab or Irish terrorists than from the 'relatively deprived' in the liberal democracies.

Psychology fails, as history does, to establish that inequality must inevitably result in envy. Some amateur tennis player may envy the world champion, but many admire him. The heights, seen from below, may inspire respect, reverence, awe, love, worship, trust, obedience or many other forms of deference, as readily as envy or disapproval.

If different individuals respond differently to a given set of circumstances, the circumstances do not *cause* any one of those reactions. If, for instance, this man loves strawberries whereas that man abhors them, it is not the strawberries which cause the one response or the other; in fact we say, if anything, that it is the 'preferences' or 'tastes' of the individual which account for his response. Similarly, since different individuals can and do respond to the superior position of others in many different ways, it cannot be maintained that inequality *causes* any one of those different responses. In short, envy is caused not by external circumstances but by something in the persons who respond enviously.

To argue that equality is an eligible cure for envy is to *assume* that inequality is evil and that envy is a natural reaction to it. If, on the contrary, inequality is natural whereas envy is corrupt, then the entire argument for equality as a cure for envy collapses. To try to eliminate envy by abolishing inequality is like trying to eliminate crime by abolishing law.

One might add further that, though envious people

continue to exist and though many societies today exhibit some social disorder, there is no reason to suppose that the envious are among the main contrivers of disorder. Many of those who refuse allegiance, who work to destroy 'the existing order', whatever it may be, seem to be moved by abstract ideas untinged by private interest, by vices other than envy, or by virtue such as they understand it to be.

7. *Democracy*

Equality is sometimes said to be the inevitable outcome of democracy, the form of government which some regard as inevitable in any community whose members are truly free. According to this view, free men will sooner or later realise that their common business must be so organised that each citizen's voice counts just as weightily as every other's; and the majority, who in any normal community are less prosperous than some few, will always use their electoral preponderance so as to redistribute income and wealth downward; from which it follows that equality is implicit in the drift of history. To put it another way: anybody who regards democracy as the best form of government must accept as desirable the policies that naturally emerge from it, among them equality.

That modern democracies have engaged in redistributive practices, direct and indirect, is not open to doubt. But is this an inevitable tendency of democracy? Here there is much room for doubt. Modern non-democratic governments also engage in redistribution, sometimes fiercer than that practised by democracies. It would seem therefore that redistribution results from the widespread belief that equality, especially equality of income and wealth, is the paramount element of justice, rather than that it results inevitably from any particular form of government.

There is no conclusive reason to believe that the majority within a democracy will always aim to level income and wealth down to their level. For one thing, the disparity of incomes *within* the least prosperous half of any industrialised community is quite considerable, with the result that those at the more prosperous fringe of the lower half may judge correctly that they have more to lose than to gain from redistribution and may therefore join in a majority of the higher-income citizens who resist redistribution. Suppose, for instance, a community of three citizens whose incomes are £4000, £5000 and £5400 respectively; on a vote to redistribute those incomes absolutely equally, the middle-income earner would do better for himself by voting against the measure (so keeping his £5000) than by voting for it (which would reduce his income to the average of £4800). The easy supposition that in democracies a majority would always have good economic reason to support redistribution is accordingly false. If people's votes were determined exclusively by a desire to get the highest possible income for themselves – the supposition made by those who believe that democracy entails redistribution – then whether a majority supported or opposed a given scheme of redistribution would depend entirely on whether the majority stood to gain or lose by it; and redistribution can go from the poor to the rich just as easily as from the rich to the poor, or it can easily go from both the rich and the poor to a majority in the middle.

But such a narrow, arithmetic view of the matter is mainly beside the point. In many modern democracies the majority party or coalition is formed less on the basis of income differentials than on the basis of ideals about how best to govern the community. Among the ideas that matter in modern democracies equality is certainly one, but another is economic efficiency. And as many instances show, the majority may believe that to give everyone the same income – or to come anywhere near giving him the same income – no matter how little or ineffectively he works is certain to destroy or severely diminish most people's incentives to work, so reducing the prosperity of each and all. Democratic majorities, in short, may and often do prefer policies that aim to raise everyone's income (as a result of general economic growth) to policies that aim to raise the incomes of some by reducing the incomes of others.

As equality is not in any way an inescapable by-product of democracy, the ardent democrat is free from obligation – suggested by the principle of love me, love my dog – to condone or endorse equality.

8. *Response to Risk*

Some, following a line of reasoning put forward by John Rawls,[3] believe that equality is a necessary implication of a psychological law which dictates men's preferences when facing situations of risk.

Suppose, as Rawls invites us to do, that a person were asked to design the distribution of income for a community of which he would then become a member; yet the designer, though authorised to determine the distribution of income, is barred from specifying his own place in it, that being determined purely by chance. He is, in effect, empowered to lay down the rules of a lottery in which he will thereafter play, but prohibited from rigging the lottery so that he would be sure to win. Under these constraints, how would a rational man design the lottery? He would, says Rawls, in effect design it in such a way that each player would be sure to win about the same amount, thus ensuring that nobody – including himself – could lose catastrophically. By analogy, only a society which conferred equal or nearly equal outcomes on all its members would be safe for all its members, and therefore a rational man would prefer it to all others.

Among various defects in this analysis, we may notice first that it does not account for the attitudes manifested by the many people who engage in lotteries. Characteristic of every lottery is that the participant pays a fee to enter; he submits to a *certain* loss in exchange for a purely *contingent* gain. Now some people gamble compulsively; and some in ignorance that the odds are against them; and many others, who are moderate and knowledgeable, do it for the rare pleasure of deliberately courting controllable risk. But in principle a lottery, if it is 'fair', is so far from being irrational from the standpoint of the subscribers that probability theorists regularly take it as an arch-case of rational behaviour. To pay £1 for one chance in a hundred of winning £100 is totally in keeping with the dictates of reason and with the tastes of millions.

Consider, in this light, the design of societies, each of which is a lottery as far as Rawls's designer is concerned, since pure chance will dictate which of the possible incomes he himself gets. Let us restrict our examination to the following four societies, identical except for differing distributions of income:

(1) All get £7500 each.
(2) Half get £5000, the other half £10,000.
(3) One per cent get £3000, 99 per cent get £7545.
(4) One per cent get £100,000, 99 per cent get £6566.

Now from the standpoint of disembodied reason, perfect rationality unembellished by any irrational preferences, all these four – and also an indefinitely large number of other – are perfectly equivalent. They are equivalent because their 'expected values'* are equal, namely £7500 in each instance; and the rational gambler, shorn of all other human attributes, pays attention to nothing but expected value. So it follows that the rational gambler, far from designing an egalitarian society, would regard it as no better or worse than an intensely unequal society. He might take the precaution, on his own behalf, of setting some lower limit below which nobody's absolute income should fall: a precaution akin to table-stakes which limit one's losses in a game of poker; but to interpret such precaution as implying a preference on the gambler's part for equality would be to overlook entirely his readiness to face the risk of loss for the chance of gain. No gambler aims at equality between himself and his co-gamblers.

But of course not everybody is a gambler. Once we leave behind the ideally rational calculator, we enter the realms of preference and are bound to notice that real human beings fall into three groups with respect to risk. Some avoid risk: they would prefer a certainty of £15 to equal chances of winning £10 or winning £20, and they tend to take out more insurance than is rational. Some are neutral: they subscribe indifferently to fair lotteries and to fair insurance. Some seek risk: they would prefer equal chances of winning £10 or winning £20 to a certainty of winning £15, and they under-insure themselves.

We may suppose, accordingly, that these will respond differently to Rawls's proposition. Those who are neutrally disposed toward risk would regard as equivalent every pattern

---

* The 'expected value' of a gamble is defined as the sum of the possible pay-offs, each weighted by the probability that it will occur.

of income distribution which yields the same expected value of income. Those who like risk would prefer a society with wide disparities of income. And only those averse to risk would do as Rawls assumes; they alone would prefer a more equal distribution of income to a less equal and hence more risky distribution. From which it follows that Rawls's argument, if it held at all, would hold only for that fraction of men who are averse to risk.

How widespread is aversion to risk? Not sufficiently widespread to be a reliable clue to what is natural in men. Human nature may be reflected at least as well by the admiration which men willingly pay to heroes and others who thrive on riskiness. Apart from heroes and outright gamblers, every investor who knowingly buys risky shares instead of blue-chips, every entrepreneur who sinks his capital in a new enterprise, every writer who labours to produce a book which may or may not sell, every student who spends years of time training for a profession which will yield to him financial rewards that are quite unpredictable – all these and many more deliberately court risk. And as most people marry, eat food which may be contaminated, carry cash in their pockets, and cross roads, it may be said that nobody could get through a normal life without accepting many risks.

It may be said, however, that there are some risks which everybody would regard as senseless, even if those risks were 'fair' in the probabilistic sense. To pay £1 for one chance in ten thousand of winning £10,000 is reasonable; to pay £1 as the fee for admission to a social arrangement in which one has 9999 chances of having no income at all during one's life-time and one chance of having an annual income of £10,000 would be drastically unreasonable, even though the expected values of the two lotteries are equal. What makes for the difference is, of course, the differing degrees to which the risk-taker can 'afford' the loss. If a loss, however large or small absolutely, had the effect of preventing the gambler from ever playing again, then the game, though remaining a fair one in a hypothetical sense, becomes potentially unfair in the practical sense. On this account it is clear that no rational person would design a social dispensation in which some persons are left either entirely without income or with incomes far too low to sustain life even briefly. A rational designer would therefore, as we have already seen, set a lower absolute limit to incomes, so providing a safety-net; but only in a drastically impoverished society would the intention to provide everyone with an absolute minimum leave no surplus to be divided, equally or unequally, according to the designer's choice. With regard to any community living beyond the margin of subsistence, the rational designer could still implement, in greater or lesser degree, his own preference as between riskiness and risklessness. And accordingly, Rawls's conclusion must be rejected: rational calculation in accordance with human nature would *not* yield an egalitarian society, since the many human beings who prefer risky undertakings to 'safe bets' would rationally create a society which offered the possibility of great rewards as well as small rewards.

Quite a separate flaw in Rawls's argument is his assumption that the designer could feasibly prescribe the *distribution* of goods in a society without thereby influencing at all the *total volume of goods* available to be distributed. Suppose that the designer faced a choice between two dispensations: one that gave every member of a community £5000, the other that gave half the members of the same community £5000 each and the other half £10,000 each. Which should he rationally prefer?

Many people would answer, as Rawls would, that the second dispensation is rationally superior, in as much as, compared with the first, nobody is worse off than before and half are better off. Sophisticated, or rather sophistical, objections may be raised to this 'natural' view.

It might be said, for one thing, that a larger income is not really better for the recipient than a smaller income. Such an assertion would rest, presumably, on some variant of the primitive idea that 'money isn't everything'. Yet giving full credit to this notion, issue could still be joined by positing a hypothetical measure of 'satisfaction' or 'happiness', and asking whether a community in which half of its members enjoyed 5000 units of happiness per year and the other half 10,000 units of happiness ought to be rationally preferred to a community in which every member enjoyed only 5000 units of happiness. Persons prepared to accept 'happiness' as a synonym for the *summum bonum*, or as a category comprehending all possible varieties of human good – spiritual as well as material, other-regarding as well as self-regarding, those accompanied by short-run pain as well as those giving short-run pleasure – must rationally affirm that the community each of whose members enjoyed either more or no less happiness is preferable. Indeed, to deny this would be to cut away the ground under Rawls's argument, for if more income (however 'income' may be defined) does not suit the recipient better than less income (all else being equal), then why should Rawls's rational designer pay the slightest attention to how much income he or anybody else gets? If more income were not better than less, it would not matter whether some people had lower incomes than others.

A second sophistical objection is that an equal distribution of income is in itself a positive good: in other words, that recipients of high incomes within an unequal society suffer sympathetic pain at the thought that others are less well-placed than themselves, while the recipients of lower incomes suffer discontent at the thought that others are better-placed. These disutilities, resulting from compassionate suffering on the one hand and envious suffering on the other hand, ought to be reckoned in as modifications on the distribution of 'private pecuniary' incomes – so say those who raise this objection. On this view, a community in which half receive £5000 and half receive £10,000 in 'private pecuniary' incomes ought to be recognised as one in which everyone's 'psychic income' is really lower than their money incomes would suggest – standing, let us say, at adjusted values of £4000 and £8000. Nevertheless, even if we accept this qualification for the sake of argument, it will not do Rawlsians much good.

For one thing, the compassionate high-income recipient could diminish his suffering by voluntarily giving away as much as he liked of his income. This possibility means that the original distribution need not be made egalitarian by edict. Moreover, if we assume that each member of the community differs in the *extent* that he suffers psychically from any specific unequal distribution, then a régime of voluntary redistribution would be rationally preferable (from the standpoint of minimising each individual's suffering) to a régime of imposed equality.

But another line of reasoning more powerfully dissolves the second objection. Let us merely transpose the discussion into 'psychic incomes', which make due adjustments for sufferings arising from inequality. What now will the Rawlsian say to the choice between two arrangements, in one of which everyone gets an all-inclusive 'psychic income' of £5000 and in the other of which half get 'psychic incomes' of £5000 and the other half get 'psychic incomes' of £10,000? He must accept the latter as superior – unless he maintains that the latter alternative is unthinkable because it represents an impossibility, logical, psychological or moral. This would be tantamount to asserting that no person, or at least no moral person, could tolerate a situation in which he received a higher psychic income than anybody else. But to assert this would merely beg the whole question at issue, for if nobody can tolerate inequality, then it could only come about by malign accident; or, if it is said that no moral person can tolerate inequality, then this is merely to assert that inequality is immoral by definition.

Having disposed of those two frivolous counters, I return to the question of whether Rawls's designer can reasonably be credited with a facility for determining the distribution of income without affecting the total income available to the community. The answer must be that he cannot. Suppose for instance, a community all of whose members receive £5000. Suppose now that one member were offered an increment of £10-worth of income in exchange for producing additional product valued at £10. Now, if he were permitted to keep the additional £10 for himself, he might undertake the additional work; but if a strict rule of equality were enforced, with the result that the incremental money income of £10 must be distributed equally among all members of the community, he might well decide that the gain accruing to himself was far too small to compensate him for the additional effort required. And if this could conceivably ever happen, it follows that the size of each person's income is not independent of the distribution of income. Accordingly, when Rawls's rational man designs a society with an equal distribution of income he is automatically, if unknowingly, designing a society such that some or all of its members are less well off than they need be in view of their tastes and productive potentials. Once alerted to this implication, rational men would respond by preferring the richer society to the equal society, provided that everyone in the richer society is at least as well-to-do as in the poorer equal society. A rational man would prefer, for instance, an arrangement in which everybody gets between (say) £7500 and £15,000 to one in which everybody gets £5000, assuming that the two were practical alternatives, so that one could move from one to another at will, merely according to whether private incentives were or were not permitted to operate.

This point can be underscored by noticing a vital distinction which tends to be overlooked simply because the thrust of Rawls's argument militates against recognising it. It is the distinction between the notions that people 'receive' certain incomes and that they 'earn' certain incomes. Rawls's rational designer might make plans about the relative incomes that each member of his projected society should 'receive', without saying anything about who would supply these receipts or how large the receipts would be in absolute measure. A government exercising perfect control over the conduct of citizens could dictate what fraction of the total output of the community should be allocated to each citizen; but, of course, as reason and experience alike tell us, the most perfectly dictatorial government cannot dictate the absolute size of the total output generated by the community – otherwise such governments could decree infinitely great accomplishments, instead of languishing, as dictatorships frequently do, at low levels of income. If, on the contrary, one thinks of a dispensation in which each person 'earns' his own income – in the precise sense that he enjoys an income equal to the marginal value product generated by his own efforts – then no Rawlsian designer, and no government however dictatorial, can determine either the absolute size of its total output or the distribution of its members' incomes. This is so because the amount of income earned by each individual will be determined by the amount of work he wishes to do and is able to do, as well, of course, as by the amount of output which the conditions of production (such as the level of technology and the supply of capital) enable his labour to generate. And it follows therefore that Rawls's doctrine applies, at most, to questions of distribution of output, as though the output to be distributed were somehow given magically or were totally insensitive to anything that the designer might do about distribution. The doctrine, in short, rests on ignoring the simple and basic fact that free rational human beings adjust the amount of work they do in accordance with incentives to work, at least one of which incentives is the possibility of increasing one's private consumption.

In short, Rawls's analysis of this point – which is far too elaborate to be dealt with comprehensively in these brief comments – is vitiated by his having assumed that all human beings do, or rationally should, avoid risk; and, secondly, that enforcing a more equal distribution of income need not depress the absolute level of everyone's income. Many human beings rationally enter risky situations and emerge from them unrepentant even if disappointed, and even those who stand most to benefit from equal distribution could rationally reject it in favour of an unequal distribution which might give them higher absolute incomes.

9. *Marginal Utility of Income*

One of the more common arguments for equality of income rests on the premise of diminishing marginal utility of income. This is the notion that if a man's income rises from £5000 to £6000 (while prices and all other relevant considerations remain constant), the additional utility provided by that additional £1000 is less than the additional utility provided by the £1000 that previously raised his income from £4000 to £5000.

Properly understood, this asserted principle must contain a kernel of truth. Income is generally desired for the sake of the consumption which it permits. And as to consumption, it seems clear that a law of diminishing utility operates. Passionately as the Englishman loves bacon and eggs for breakfast, the third helping of the morning or the sixth must be less thrilling than the first. It might be luxurious to have one's hair dressed every day rather than each week, but luxury would turn to boredom and finally exasperation as one's hair was dressed twice a day, four times a day, and at last continuously. And since the same waning of delight, followed by extinction of delight, must occur as anybody (other than an uncontrollable addict) consumes more and more of any given commodity in any given period of time, it may be concluded that the utility of money also must decline as one earns more and more of it within any given period – at least in so far as income is thought of as a means of access to consumption.

Now, taking it that the utility of income diminishes as income rises, it is easy, though fallacious, to suppose that if income were taken from the rich and given to the poor, the total utility experienced by the whole community would increase. Consider two men, one of whom earns £3000 and the other £13,000. Then shifting £1000 from the richer to the poorer increases the total utility available to the latter by more than it diminishes the utility available to the former, and so increases the total utility enjoyed by the two. Successive shifts of £1000 each have similar effect, even though the increase in utility is less marked in each successive step; and the upshot is that the total utility of the two persons is maximised at the point where redistribution has made their incomes exactly equal. It would appear to follow that equality of income throughout a community is the essential condition for maximising the total utility which the total income available could confer on the members of that community.

But this conclusion is unsustainable, for the assumptions on which it is built are questionable at the least and most probably false.

First, the diminishing marginal utility of income is deduced from the diminishing marginal utility of goods and commodities being consumed. But income has other dimensions as well. Some people, at least, regard their incomes, in part, as accolades, the most tangible honours which their superiors can bestow, the tokens which best signal to themselves and everyone else the esteem which they deserve. People who understand honour as purely relative – who consider that one is honourable only in so far as one is honoured above others – and who regard the size of one's income as a proper measure of honour, would not experience any diminishing utility of income, not at least until their incomes were high enough to exceed by a safe margin those of people whom they regard as competitors.

Again, income is wanted not exclusively to sustain consumption but also, by most people, in order to accumulate savings. One motive, perhaps the dominant one, for saving is to meet emergencies, such as illness, unemployment or accident, and especially the most common of all emergencies, that of growing too old to work. The motive for saving may be said to be prudence; many experience it as fear. And to the extent that such fear is intense – a response to eventualities that are unknown because unexperienced, and unknowable because unpredictable – the marginal utility of income may diminish little if at all. No doubt some absolute level of savings should allay the fears of any rational person; but, until a fearful person had achieved that absolute level, each increment of income might easily be regarded as just as useful as each previously acquired increment of the same size. Nor is fear the crucial consideration: rather, any emotion or rational deliberation which persuades a person to set an accumulated target of some absolute size will have the same effect of rendering the marginal utility of income constant, so far as he is concerned, at least until he has achieved his target. To recognise this is to place oneself in a position to explain many of the instances where somebody who is apparently quite well-to-do continues to work at a killing pace.

Second, the utility of income is not a fixed characteristic of each individual which attends him unchanged throughout the whole of his life. Obvious facts attest the opposite. As people age, various of their appetites and aspirations may remain stable, but others will intensify, and still others fade. Besides, the specific contents of anyone's whole array of tastes visibly changes with time. An enthusiastic traveller may convert into a stay-at-home, a spartan may move toward lavishness, a libertine toward parsimony, a miser toward ostentation; anyone who has lived in one way may move toward another way. Apart from random changes in individuals, the tastes of whole civilisations may alter with time. It may well be that the desire of Western men for material comfort – in terms of food, clothing and shelter, transportation, entertainment and leisure

– has expanded more or less constantly over the past millennium. If so, then we must conclude that the total utility of any given real income has been shifting upward from one generation to another. So even though, all else remaining fixed, it seems intuitively certain that the addition of one pound to one's income carries with it an incremental utility which is smaller than the loss of utility which would come about if one's income were lowered by one pound – nevertheless, the total utilities which any given income would yield to the same person at different points in his life are just as certainly different. Or to put it in minimal terms, since the utility of income depends on tastes, and tastes are notoriously variable, we are not entitled to assume that the utility of income is stable for any given person over time. Or, as economists might like to express it, the utility of income is not stable intertemporally.

Third, as the tastes of each individual change from time to time according to the individual's peculiar life history, it must follow that the tastes of any two individuals will differ in their composition and intensity, from which it follows in turn that the utilities experienced by any two individuals with identical incomes would not necessarily and not typically be equal. An enthusiast may get more utility from £5000 than his phlegmatic neighbour gets from £10,000; and were their incomes reversed, the enthusiast would get a total utility and marginal utility more than twice as large as the other's. The implications drawn from all this are often presented as a caution against blithely assuming identity when making interpersonal comparisons of utility. They may be put more frankly as the implication that, because people differ from one another in the intensity of their desires for income, the utility conferred on separate individuals by equal incomes must typically differ as well.

Once we reject the assumption that the utility of income is the same for all persons, then the view that redistribution of income from richer to poorer increases and ultimately maximises the community's total utility is shown to be untenable. No longer can it be said that, in a hypothetical community of two whose incomes are £3000 and £13,000, the total utility of the two persons would be improved by moving to £4000 and £12,000, and so on until each has £8000. Instead we must now admit the possibility that a redistribution *away* from equality – say toward £2000 and £14,000 – would bring about the highest total utility. And all warrant has disappeared for the view that the community's utility would be maximised at just the point where both persons had exactly equal incomes. Depending on the relative utilities of the persons in question, equality of income might be less rewarding than extreme degrees of inequality.

Fourth, even if we accepted for the sake of the argument that equality of income maximises the total utility which a given total income yields to the whole community, this would provide no moral justification for redistribution by coercion.

To be sure, if equality of income did maximise the community's total utility, that principle might be converted into a guide for voluntary conduct: a guide urging the rich man to diminish his private good for the sake of the 'public' good (defined purely as a sum of all private goods). But proponents of redistribution do not limit themselves to preaching voluntary generosity; indeed, they generally reject philanthropy as inadequate. They insist instead that the state must impose redistribution by law, because enforced redistribution is right.

But the assumed desirability of equality does not establish the rightness of enforced redistribution. One might as well maintain that the desired end of public health morally justifies the extermination of all persons who are ill. Neither does the fact that enforced distribution has been installed by democratic procedures make it morally right. One might as well maintain that the enslavement of a black minority by a white majority would be right if decided on by a democratic procedure, honouring to the hilt the rule of one man, one vote. Tyranny by a majority is not less tyrannical than tyranny by a minority; and even a democracy violates the wishes of some citizens whenever it adopts laws other than those which command universal assent. Neither the presumed desirability of an end such as equality of income, nor the presumed superiority of democratic government, can confer moral rightness on enforced redistribution.

This defect would persist even if one doubted whether the distribution of income which comes about in the absence of enforced redistribution could be justified morally. What possible principle of justice, asks the common-or-garden moralist, can make it right that an immoral pop singer should earn a hundred times more than a decent hard-working farm worker? One might, of course, answer (though far too briefly) that in as much as such pay scales emerge from voluntary bargains uncorrupted by force or fraud, they may be held to be morally innocent even if not morally commendable. But we need not maintain that the unregulated distribution of income is morally perfect in order to hold that redistributing income by coercive force is morally unfounded. Even if an existing situation is morally inexcusable, that cannot justify every and any effort to alter it. To hold otherwise would be to hold that the existence of any vice justifies any effort to extirpate it, no matter how violent or tyrannical.

Finally, it must be noted that equality is desired, within the framework of this argument, not as an end in itself, but rather as an intermediate or instrumental end: that is, as a means of achieving the ultimate end of maximising the total utility of a community. But this end (which economists call 'Pareto optimality' and the Utilitarians sometimes described as 'the greatest good of the greatest number') has repeatedly been shown to be unsustainable. For the present purpose it is enough to point out that the total utility to be maximised consists of the summed utilities of all members of the community, each of whom is treated as equal, in some fundamental respect, to all others. In short, the argument as a whole is circular, since it seeks to justify equality by reference to an end which has equality built into it as a premise.

B. Internal Contradictions of Egalitarian Policy

Having shown above that the familiar theoretical arguments in favour of egalitarianism are unsound, I shall now demonstrate that every and any egalitarian policy is internally contradictory. That is, were a government to equalise any one material dimension of life – such as pay, consumption, burden of work, or wealth – it would necessarily and inevitably create inequality in one or more of the other dimensions.

1. Suppose that the government set out to equalise pay by assuring every worker the same wage. Yet this is too vague to serve as a practicable rule. Does it mean that every worker would be paid the same rate per hour of work done? But then, if workers were allowed any freedom to choose the number of hours they worked per week, some would earn more than others per week. Does it mean that every worker would be paid the same amount annually? But then, if different workers worked different numbers of hours per year – because of ill health, breakdown of machinery or involuntary unemployment – their hourly pay would be unequal. And if they worked different numbers of years during their lives (as differences of health and opportunity would ensure), their life-time incomes would be unequal. In short, any rule imposing equality on pay per hour, day, year or life would necessarily impose inequality on pay realised during any other interval of time.

In order to avoid this paradox, an egalitarian government might arbitrarily fix on one interval of time, say one year, and equalise everyone's pay per year. To do so would achieve administrative convenience without, however, resolving the inherent contradiction. For any worker who suffered illness, absented himself from work for good reason or bad, or failed to find employment, would earn more per hour actually worked than those who laboured steadily through the year. Whether this outcome should be considered just or desirable is not at present the issue. The point is that even equality of pay, leaving aside all other dimensions of equality, is strictly unattainable because equal pay for an interval of any given dimension means, in practice, unequal pay for any longer or shorter interval.

2. Suppose that every worker were paid the same annual wage, then the potential annual expenditure per person would be unequal. At equalised annual pay of £5000, each member of a family of four in which the husband and wife both worked could afford to consume £2500 worth of goods and services, whereas the members of a family of four with only one member working could each afford to consume only £1250. This inequality of consumption potential, generated within a régime of equal pay, would of course reach its extremes in families on the one hand, in which all of the members worked, and in those, on the other hand, in which none the members worked.

Contradictions that would arise if, in order to cure this one the government undertook to equalise consumption allowances, are discussed at subsection 6 below.

3. If all workers were paid equally, they would almost certainly accumulate unequal amounts of wealth. If we assume that nobody inherits any wealth, but that different people have different prospensities to save and are permitted to save as little or as much of their earnings as they individually like, then equal pay would even within one life-time produce remarkable inequality of wealth. (See pp. 63–5 below.)

If people were permitted, as they are in capitalist economies and even in some more or less socialist economies, to invest their wealth and draw interest or dividends, then equality of income (paid for current work) would be contradicted by inequality of total income – because the equal pay that some received for current work would be enlarged, unequally, by earnings from unequal wealth.

Furthermore, if inheritance were permitted, then inequality of wealth and of income might intensify over time, even while the rule of equal pay to each worker was strictly observed.

Therefore, any thorough-going effort to equalise income would need to forbid inheritance and private saving, unless it neutralised the disequalising effect of unequal wealth by prohibiting interest, dividends and any other form of return on investment. But such prohibitions would, at the limit, be unenforceable. Even though the bulk of private saving were displaced by forced public saving, implemented by high rates of taxation, even the most oppressive taxation conceivable would not extinguish every individual's desire to save privately. Even though private gifts and bequests were declared to be unlawful, they could not be extirpated absolutely without first dissolving all families, friendships and close human associations. And even though the possibility of 'unearned' income were stopped by putting an end to all private investment in producers' capital goods, it would still be possible for people to get 'unearned' incomes in non-pecuniary form by investing their savings in consumers' capital goods. Leaving aside the question of practicality, it stands out clearly that to prevent unequal accumulation of wealth – even while earnings from work were absolutely equalised – would require continuous and all-pervasive repression.

4. If all workers were paid equally, this would entail unequal 'sacrifice' by different workers. Different sorts of work are widely regarded as being unequally burdensome. Some jobs, such as those of miners and test-pilots, are more dangerous than others. Some, such as those of night-workers and drain-cleaners, are unusually disagreeable. Some, such as those of tool-makers and psychiatrists, require particularly long and difficult training. If persons doing such jobs were paid no more than those whose work is safer, pleasanter and easier to qualify for, then equality of pay would contradict equality of effort.

Since it might be expected that where all workers are paid equally, few would volunteer to do jobs which are especially burdensome, the need to have such work done would point to forcible direction of labour. And nothing can better illustrate inequality of burden or sacrifice than the practice of conscripting people into forms of service which, though highly valuable to the beneficiaries, are repugnant to the unlucky individuals forced to perform them.

5. Suppose a government tried to resolve the foregoing contradiction by establishing a rule which equalised pay per unit of effort, burden, discomfort or sacrifice – let us say,

generally, per unit of disutility. Such a rule would immediately contradict the principle of equal income for each worker, for the income now earned by any given worker would be proportional to the disutility entailed in his work, and everyone agrees that some jobs are less agreeable than others.

But this is only the beginning of the troubles. If the difficulty of a job were measured in accordance with the difficulty experienced by any particular individual doing that job, then a person who found a job difficult because he lacked skill or energy or will would earn more per year than if he did a job for which he was better qualified or happier to do. Further, the more skill he acquired in any job, and the less difficult it thus became, the lower would be his annual income. In short, the rule of equal pay per unit of disutility would flatly contradict another possible and plausible rule: the rule of equal pay per unit of output. The former rule would encourage people to choose the work for which they were least suited.

If, on the contrary, the disutility of a job were measured without reference to how disagreeable any particular individual found it, then different workers would get the same pay for doing that job even though some found it far less demanding or disagreeable than others – a clear violation of the principle presumably embodied in the rule of equality.

Worse still, how could one realistically measure the disutility of a job, in itself or as felt by each particular person doing it? Wage rates established in free labour markets would offer no guidance on this point, because they are determined by the interplay of both demand and supply, whereas the disutility of any given kind of work affects only supply and does not exhaustively determine even that half of the picture. Nor could any sort of scientific or technical expertise answer the question objectively. Who can pretend to know exactly how much more disagreeable it is to operate a lathe at midnight than at noon? Of course, each individual can judge for himself how much extra pay it would take to induce him to exchange his present job for some other – though as such judgements involve comparison of known past conditions with predicted future conditions, they are liable to gross errors of estimation. Yet ignoring this imprecision, were an egalitarian to adopt the expressed individual tastes of each worker as the criterion for determining the pay of each individual, he would have abandoned all hope of equalising pay in any sense other than equal pay per unit of felt disutility, and he would authorise instead great inequality among the annual incomes earned by different individuals.

Any public authority charged with proportioning the pay for various jobs to the disutilities they entail could, in one sense, succeed all too easily. No matter how wrongly it decided, it would seem sooner or later to have decided correctly – because as long as workers are free to change jobs and as long as young people entering the labour force are free to choose their occupations, workers will shift out of underpriced occupations and into overpriced occupations, so that after a time workers in every occupation would or should feel that their pay fairly compensated for the disutilities of their work. Pay relativities imposed by fiat thus operate as self-confirming hypotheses, and the work of so-called expert bodies in assessing the relative disutilities of different jobs is a loose exercise in assessing loose public opinion or, worse, self-indulgence and self-righteousness passing themselves off as scientific knowledge.

6. Suppose now that an egalitarian government, having recognised that it could not achieve any sensible result by trying to equalise pay, turned instead to the strategy of equalising consumption. Suppose further that it aimed to achieve this goal by distributing an equal cash allowance to every person: man, woman or child.

This method would fail to achieve the goal. If any person saved more than another, his consumption during that period would be proportionately smaller. If any person needed to spend more on medical services than another, his consumption of all other goods and services would be accordingly smaller. A child whose education had to be paid for out of his cash allowance might be restricted to an inadequate diet. Equal consumption allowances, in cash, would fail to insure that all persons achieved an equal level of satisfaction in consumption either at any given time or through the whole of their lives: different people are not equally skilled at turning money into real utility, and the real utilities that different people experience depend in no small measure on their different temperaments, especially on their different and to some extent self-determined capacities for enjoyment.

7. Contradictions and difficulties more serious would arise if a policy were adopted of equalising consumption by conferring on each person the identical bundle of real goods. Some such thinking presumably underlies present policies of medical care free of charge to the patient, free public education, subsidised public housing and transportation, subsidised meals and foodstuffs, and the like. No doubt subsidies in kind rather than in cash are favoured by many egalitarians because they are convinced that some people would spend cash consumption allowances unwisely, buying gin when they ought to be buying medicine, buying toys rather than schooling for their children, and buying luxurious cars rather than adequate housing. No doubt it is true that some people are improvident in such ways. But subsidies in kind do not of themselves overcome such failings, and therefore it might be considered necessary to force people to use the subsidy, as the laws now force reluctant children to attend free schools. In order to be sure that people who are thoughtless, ignorant or fearful actually went to the physician at times when according to expert opinion they 'ought to', it would be necessary to establish a medical equivalent of truancy laws and truant officers. Similarly with housing and all other public services offering subsidies in kind. Indeed, the proliferation of social workers in public employment may be interpreted partly as a step in the direction of pressing people into using subsidies in kind.

Forcing everyone to use subsidies in kind does not equalise real consumption. On the contrary, there is reason to believe that the real benefits which accrue, for instance, to different pupils from attending a school, even the same school, differ in amount, and would differ no matter how schooling were organised and no matter what misguided efforts might be made to homogenise all pupils and teachers. Again, it would be difficult to say that the real benefits conferred on one patient by having his appendix removed equal or do not equal those realised by another who had an aching tooth extracted. And how much benefit is realised by a person who never uses free medical services because he is never ill, but merely benefits by the curtailment of contagious diseases?

Above all, consider the inequality of consumers' real utilities that would result if subsidies in kind were carried to their logical conclusion, and an identical bundle of goods and services were distributed to each person. Because of ineradicable differences of taste, one person would take much pleasure from his weekly mutton chop while another would eat it with loathing, if at all. One would feel that his living quarters were cramped and his clothing ration needlessly lavish; another the opposite. Assuming that each person were perfectly cognizant of what was good for himself, and supposing that barter were permitted, almost everyone could improve his situation by trading goods which he liked less for goods which he liked more but his trading partner liked less. And this certainty that trading would take place – as it does in prisons and concentration camps, where equality of consumption is aimed at by giving each inmate the identical bundle of real goods and services – proves that giving each person the same amount of money leads to a higher level of satisfaction for each person than does giving him a standard bundle of goods of equivalent monetary value. Leaving aside the small minority of people who do not properly know what they want or what is good for them, a cash allocation for consumption is best. But even then, as we have seen, an equal allocation of money would not remotely result in equalised satisfaction.

A policy of equalising consumption by distributing identical bundles of goods and services to all would founder because, contrary to what egalitarians commonly say or imply, the 'needs' of different individuals are unequal. Infants need fewer calories and more milk than stevedores. Aged people need more medical attention than young ones. Large people need more clothing than small people. And habitual smokers, drinkers, drug-takers need more cigarettes, whisky or marijuana than other people do. These last examples cast doubt on whether 'need' is an objective category at all.

What is beyond dispute is that 'needs', so far as they can be recognised at all, are extremely abstract. Everyone needs food to stay alive, but no particular foodstuff is needed by anybody. Many people throughout the world live healthy lives without ever eating beef or milk or bread. Yet even if we overlook all such problems about the nature of needs (and the resultant impossibility of specifying objectively exactly what any person, much less every person, needs), it is clear that giving every person identical consumption allowances would contradict the common understanding that different people have different and unequal needs.

8. It would seem to follow that a more appropriate egalitarian policy would be to proportion each person's consumption allowance to his needs. What would be equalised is consumption allowance per unit of need. It becomes immediately apparent that to do this would contradict equality of total consumption and of total satisfaction.

As to practical implementation: a government following this policy would be obliged to assess the true extent of each person's needs. The technical difficulty, indeed impossibility, of doing so does not require close demonstration; suffice it to say that the armies of different nations evidently hold quite varied views about the 'needs' of the soldiers whom they provision. Nor is it any answer to say, as some do, that 'needs' are 'culturally determined'; for this is to concede that 'needs' cannot be discerned by scientific knowledge, which means that they can only be determined by arbitrary discretion, exercised either by persons in authority or by respondents to public-opinion polls.

Any government that undertakes to proportion consumption allowances to 'needs' would have to add, if compelled to frank disclosure, 'and we will decide how much you need'. Greater frankness would no doubt disclose that the government's view of how much people needed – like any government's view about how much old-age pensioners need – is really in large part a decision about 'how much the country can afford'. And this reduces the whole matter to nonsense; for if need means anything, it means something contrary to how much can be afforded.

9. Equal consumption allowances for all, whether in cash or kind, would grossly contradict the principle of equal sacrifice. Those four in ten inhabitants of any economically developed country who do no work, as 'work' is normally understood, would get just as much income as the six in ten who do work. So far as the 'privileged' minority consisted of mothers and children, aged persons and others normally exempt from earning their own livings, their position might be considered morally defensible albeit unequally favoured. But we can be certain that some persons, though qualified for work by age and ability, would not work because they received the equal consumption allowance without working. They – and there is no telling how numerous they might be – would be merely the extreme instances of a predictable general tendency: once the link between work and income was severed, many people would put less effort into their labour. The burden of work would be shared most unequally as between the most conscientious and the most self-indulgent workers.[4]

Laxness of effort, condoned by this dispensation, would tend thus to reduce the community's total output and so its real income. Granted that pay is not the only incentive to work (for effort may be stimulated also by self-esteem, public honours, emulation, esprit de corps, and fear of rebuke or punishment), granted further that each individual's equal consumption allowance would rise or fall (all else being equal) according to how hard he himself worked, nevertheless much of the incentive to work hard would have vanished. Any individual worker who increased his output by working harder – supposing him to live in a country of 50,000,000 inhabitants – would improve his own consumption allowance by only one part in fifty million of the additional output. He would be subject, in effect, to a marginal tax rate of 99.999998 per cent. Conversely, and more to the point, any worker who stopped working altogether would thereby reduce the real value of his own consumption allowance by roughly 0.000002 per cent. But if many workers responded to this individually negligible penalty, each shedding his own individual burden, the equal consumption allowance of all would fall disastrously.

Similarly, equal consumption allowances would render senseless any private saving with a view to private investment.

In the absence of investment, as the community's capital stock wore out, its income would sink further and further.

Except in so far as government could replace private incentives to work and to invest by forcing or inducing individuals to act contrary to their separate, foreseeable private interests, equalised consumption allowances would result in equal economic misery. Worse still, from the egalitarian's point of view, the differential effects of coercion applied to some persons and of non-pecuniary rewards conferred on others would create new forms of inequality as the price of equalising consumption.

10. 'From each according to his abilities, to each according to his needs' is often advanced as a socialist or Marxist formula for equality. Presumably Mr Callaghan was expressing something of the same sort when he said in 1979 that the Labour Party ought to go forward under the motto, 'Need, not greed'.

As to the second branch of the formula ('to each according to his needs'): comments made above about equal income per unit of need show that this criterion of equality contradicts many others. As to the first branch of the formula ('from each according to his abilities'): it can be interpreted as the basic outline for a system of taxation. In return for giving each person an amount of income proportioned to his needs, the state will exact from each person an amount of work proportioned to his abilities.

How anyone's abilities are to be determined is left conveniently vague. Most people have many different abilities, and it should be obvious, even without cataloguing all the kinds of ability which may pertain to work, that anybody could do many different jobs. Practically speaking, therefore, it would not be any person's abilities that determined what he would be required to contribute. Instead, some official would decide *which* of any person's many abilities would be drawn into service. Of two people whose abilities enabled them to be either a prime minister or a street-sweeper (among other things), one would be recruited to run the country and the other to sweep streets. From all of which it follows that burdens, purportedly allocated equally, 'by ability', would lead to considerable inequalities of burden.

11. Confronted with such contradictions and difficulties inherent in policies which aim at equality of reward, egalitarians often take refuge in a halfway house. Their end, they say, is not to establish outright equality; rather it is to reduce inequality, to compress it within tolerable limits.

Such refuge provides no safety. Any argument which discredits a full-blown egalitarian policy, such as those considered above, applies proportionally to partial and qualified policies of the same sort. If utterly eradicating income differentials between brain-surgeons and hospital orderlies would lead to great inequalities of burden, then coercively narrowing such income differentials would still intensify the inequality of burdens, even though it did not maximise them. And similarly for each variety of egalitarian policy.

To defend halfway policies as 'moderate' is to pretend that a mitigated vice is really a positive virtue. On such reasoning, an assailant who wounded but refrained from killing his victim ought to be lauded as a benefactor. Halfway to an undesirable goal is too far by half.

12. In short, the aim of equalising income, whether in terms of earnings or consumption, is typically advanced in statements so vague as to conceal the contradictions and intolerable implications which lie just below the surface. Equalisation, along any coherent line, would inevitably bring with it unintended consequences – oppression, inequity and poverty – which would repel many advocates of equality, if they recognised those consequences, and which would reveal the dream of equality as a nightmare.*

---

* Dangers arising from redistribution are analysed in chapters 13 to 17 below.

C. Equality of Opportunity, and Equality before the Law

It may seem that an opponent of egalitarianism could not consistently support the principles that go under the names of 'equality of opportunity' and 'equality before the law'.* But this apparent difficulty is dissolved if we recognise that, in connection with these principles, 'equality' is a misnomer. What those precepts really mean is that certain rights should be enjoyed by everyone and not only by a few or many: a notion misrepresented by 'equality' but precisely conveyed by the term 'universality'.

That the demand for universality of rights came to be expressed in terms of equality is partly due to historical accident and partly to slovenly misuse of language. Though now embedded in our language, 'equality' is in this context an unfortunate term, because many people read into it the implication that everyone should possess and exercise these rights in equal degree.

Properly understood, 'equality of opportunity' means that everyone should enjoy the right to enter any occupation for which he is qualified by skill and that nobody should be denied access to an occupation arbitrarily or captiously: that is, on grounds of personal characteristics other than his ability to do the job. In so far as access to an occupation is controlled – whether by public officials, professional associations, monopolistic employers or monopolistic trade unions – that control should be exercised impartially and impersonally, which means without reference to extraneous considerations such as parentage, sex, age or religion. Insisting on this does not imply that anybody should be guaranteed whatever job he likes, when and where he likes it and independently of his skill, actual or potential. Opportunity does not mean that somebody must provide such jobs as people desire; it means rather that nobody may justly be excluded from work which he could do satisfactorily.

Similarly, 'equality before the law', properly understood, means that every citizen of a country should be subject to the

* See extensive treatment of these topics in chapters 6 to 9 below.

same laws, none enjoying special privileges, none suffering special disabilities; and that every person should have the right to a fair trial – in other words that judge and jury should studiously overlook every personal attribute of the litigants, heeding only the merits of the case made out by each of them.

Emphasised in both settings is that the right in question ought to be enjoyed by everyone, and that those who supervise the exercise of the right (such as licensing authorities, judges or their private counterparts) should use their authority or power impersonally. So far is this from implying 'equality' that it means, in at least certain critical aspects, an insistence on inequality. For it means that, among all those who may aspire to a given appointment, the one who is best qualified should get it; and it means that the litigant who puts forward the better case should win the suit. Inequality results, obviously, when some people enjoy privileged access to occupations and privileged treatment at law. But inequality results also when such rights are held universally.

A given right, though held universally in its general form, may be held in different degrees within a particular setting. Consider, for instance, a community which upholds inheritance, so that everyone in it enjoys the rights to bequeath property and to acquire property by bequest. Yet within the context of a particular will, one man's rights may be superior to another's. The residuary legatee enjoys a right to inherit which is subordinate to the rights of those to whom specific bequests have been made: he gets what is left, if anything is left, after their rights have been satisfied. His right is conditioned by theirs whereas theirs are not conditioned by his; it might be said that their rights are hierarchically superior to his; but 'inequality' would be a deceptive way of describing this relationship, especially if anyone interpreted 'equality of right' as meaning that all heirs should share out the estate equally. Moreover, only a fanatic would carry a predilection for equality so far as to maintain that nobody's right to anything should ever be subordinated to anybody else's right – in that event, bus queues would dissolve into chaos, to mention only a trivial consequence.

Again, rights may differ in duration. One man may buy a licence to fish in a stream for one day, another for one month.

We can comfortably say that those rights are unequal in respect of duration, because time is quantifiable. It would, however, be entirely misleading to say that they had 'unequal rights' if in fact both enjoyed the same constitutional right to fish.

As this example suggests, the rate at which people exercise a right is often susceptible of measurement, and one can therefore speak precisely about equality or inequality in the rates at which various people exercise a right which all of them possess. But it would promote radical confusion to infer from unequal exercise of a right that the right itself is unequally enjoyed by the persons concerned. If two citizens both enjoy the right to walk in a public park, and if one walks there often but the other never, the fact that one exercises the right more often than the other in no way alters the fact that both enjoy the identical right. Similarly, if two men enjoy the right to marry (unlike slaves who could marry only with their master's permission), the fact that one man marries three times while the other remains single does not in any way impugn the bachelor's right to marry. Again, the fact that different freemen own unequal amounts of private property does not reduce any of them to the condition of a slave who was denied the right to own private property.

'Equality' in rights is thus liable to be misinterpreted as a demand that everyone should exercise each right to an equal extent. But this is absurd. The right of free speech does not mean that anybody need talk all the time, or that everyone should talk the same amount of time, or that nobody may remain silent. To force someone to use a right because others are using it would be tyranny, and this interpretation of equality would turn all rights into duties and burdens.

Even more absurd is the implication that it is good for everyone to be alike rather than different in respect of rights – so that, for instance, if everyone were subject to total censorship, this would be taken as 'equality' and therefore regarded as better than the 'unequal' condition where all but one enjoyed freedom of speech. What matters is that certain rights should be available to be enjoyed by everyone, and this idea can best be conveyed by using the term 'universality', or, in any event, by recognising that the word 'equal' in such phrases as 'equal rights for all' is used in a special sense, meaning no more and no less than that everyone rather than a privileged few should possess certain rights.

1. What policies and actions would be required to bring about 'equal opportunity'?

Universal opportunity requires nothing more than that arbitrary exclusion should be prohibited. Simple as this precept is, the effort to put it into practice would be attended by complex puzzles. Consider, for instance, entry into the trade of taxi-driving, which is commonly regulated by an official licensing authority. In so far as the authority granted a licence to any applicant who demonstrated reasonable skill and care in driving, universal opportunity would prevail. But would it not be still better from the standpoint of opportunity to abolish the licensing authority altogether, so that any person holding a driver's permit and meeting other minimal conditions (such as adequate insurance and a safety-tested car) could carry paying passengers without going to the trouble of asking someone's permission? Again, if a licensing authority is to exist, should it be permitted to deny a licence to anyone with a criminal record? To exclude persons who have committed offences such as drunken driving might be reasonable; to exclude persons convicted of shoplifting might be arbitrary; and to exclude any ex-convict on the ground that unreliability (betokened by any crime) unfits him for taxi-driving would be a doubtful rule. The practical exercise of any licensing power raises questions no less perplexing. And yet it is hard to feel certain that all licensing – even of medical practitioners, lawyers and pilots – should be repealed forthwith in the name of facilitating opportunity.

On the other hand, certain kinds of restrictions should be lifted. There is generally no legitimate occasion for a licensing authority to limit absolutely the number of persons who may practice a trade; the effect is to guarantee a higher income to those who have entered the gates, at the expense of their customers on the one hand and of their excluded competitors on the other. Neither is there any legitimate case for a closed shop: membership of a union is as arbitrary a condition of employment as membership of a political party, religious sect or fraternal order. Nor is it acceptable that apprenticeship to a craft, apprenticeship being enforced as a precondition of practice, should be restricted to descendants of master craftsmen. A massive number of exclusionary arrangements of similar sorts exist, and they could be excised with unambiguous gains to all except those now privileged by the exclusion of others.

Yet if there is much to be done in opening opportunity by abolishing arbitrary exclusion, it is also true that too much has already been done in certain directions. Not long ago a householder in Britain was prosecuted under an equal-opportunity law because he advertised for a cook of Scottish extraction. What he should have done if, as appeared, he wanted someone who knew how to cook in the Scottish manner, was to advertise the post just that way, so opening the post to any qualified person without irrelevant reference to his or her extraction. So far, so good. But suppose the employer really wanted to have a cook of Scottish extraction about the house, because she would remind him of Highland heaths and fill his ears with the tuneful rhythms of Gaelic. 'Scottish extraction' would then be, from the employer's standpoint, one of the qualifications for the job and not a prejudicial irrelevance. Other cooks might feel offended that they were denied an opportunity merely because they were not of Scottish birth. But it is far from obvious that every cook's right to practise her craft should be given priority over an employer's desire to hire a person who suits his taste. The contrary view would be in order where the employer is a public official, not entitled to satisfy his private taste when recruiting people into public service; or where the employer is a manager, recruiting employees on behalf ultimately of many thousands of shareholders; or where the employer, being a monopolist, controls the entire supply of a certain kind of job. But where the employer is a private person, one of very many who enters a given labour market and therefore unable substantially to influence overall conditions in that market, there are good reasons for permitting him to indulge his whims and eccentric preferences. Opportunity, the right to find suitable employment, while vital, is not the highest right of all.

2. The belief that nobody qualified by skill to perform a certain sort of work should be arbitrarily excluded from doing it carries an implication which offends the susceptibilities of egalitarians. This offensive implication is that a person may legitimately be excluded from any job for want of the skill to do it satisfactorily (or to learn how to do it satisfactorily). Since everyone is more or less defective in some skills – for want of natural endowments (such as acute hearing or physical strength) or acquired training – everyone will be legitimately excluded from some and, indeed, many occupations and specific positions. By what means they should be excluded is not the issue. Whether licence to practise is restricted by law, or the adequacy of an employee's skill is determined separately and variously by each employer, or the satisfactoriness of a producer's goods or services is judged exclusively by his customers – any such means of testing competence will effectively foreclose each person from certain kinds of work, even while each person enjoys a general right to choose and pursue the opportunities which attract him. Although everyone will be legitimately excluded from some forms of work, the unskilled will be excluded from more forms and especially from work and positions which are most highly esteemed and rewarded. What offends the egalitarian about all this is that 'equal opportunity' seems inevitably to produce inequality.

For the egalitarian, the only way out of this uncomfortable paradox is the hope that people's skills can be equalised. If this could be accomplished, then freedom of opportunity would result in equality of outcome. But can people's skills be equalised? Not if a person's skills depend in substantial degree on his genetic inheritance and if the genetic inheritance of different persons is not merely different but also unequal. It has therefore become an article of faith among radical egalitarians that inequality does not stem from genetic inheritance; if they believed otherwise they would be forced to concede that inequality is in some degree or other ineradicable.

It must be admitted that it is impossible to know for certain to what extent the excellences and deficiencies of normal adults have resulted from capacities which they inherited genetically and to what extent from subsequent development of their potentials. This admitted difficulty of analysis, however, lends no credence to the radical egalitarian's view that all, or practically all, differences in the skills of normal individuals stem from differences in upbringing. Inequality of skill, in their view, results nearly exclusively from inequality of what is called the individual's 'social environment'; and from this theory follows the conclusion that 'equal opportunity' cannot be achieved unless all persons acquire bundles of skills which, even if different in composition, are equal in amount. We may remark in passing that a conscientious observer would be baffled how to tell whether persons with different skills are equally or unequally skilful. Despite this not inconsiderable difficulty, egalitarians have fostered policies which aim at equalising people's skills – as distinct from raising everyone's skills, however unequal the end result.[5] Hence British egalitarians argue that all schools should be comprehensive state schools, so that all children get identical schooling whereby all would acquire more nearly equal skills, and thus a more nearly equal start in life. Presumably the same principle would apply to higher education as well, and this no doubt explains why British egalitarians have been among the staunchest supporters of polytechnics, technical colleges and the Open University.

Yet this recipe fails to produce the desired result. Only the wilfully blind would deny that different children emerge from the same school with very unequal skills, not to mention the striking difference in average skills of children at comprehensive schools in different neighbourhoods. Obviously, say radical egalitarians, this is because children come to school from unequal home environments. And this suggests policies which would 'enrich' the education of children from 'deprived backgrounds'.

Unfortunately, experiments in enriched education, especially for black children in the United States, have disappointed their promoters. Exposure to more and presumably better education has not substantially increased the educational attainments of deprived children, so far as those can be measured by the tests that statisticians have used. Such observations can always be countered by arguing that more of the same medicine is needed to effect a cure. But a quite different conclusion is at least equally plausible. Some people could become Olympic runners if given enough good training; there are others whom no amount of training would raise anywhere near the pitch of excellence, or indeed to any acceptable level of competence – because they are too small or too big, too young or too old, too weak or simply unwilling. Is there any good reason for supposing that such differences in physical capacity are not paralleled by differences in mental capacity, and indeed in combinations of capacities (intellectual, moral and physical), in all their intricate particularity, which enter into competence for any sort of work from the least to the most exacting?

The belief that children are born with unequal capacities to acquire skill does not foreclose the decision as to how education should be allocated among them. Most would agree that every child should be taught how to read, write and do arithmetic: partly because it is difficult for any illiterate and innumerate person to look after himself; partly on the more elevated consideration that, as every normal person enjoys a capacity to reason, he should be provided with at least enough schooling to actualise that potential. It is beyond such universally stipulated minima that serious debate sets in. The broad issue is whether children are entitled to better and more education because their performance is deficient or because their performance is superior. Bluntly, is success or failure the better guide as to who should get more education? If the student's success in 'absorbing' education is his ticket of admission to more, then education will be more efficient, in the normal sense that a given input will produce higher levels of output, and educational achievement will be unequal. If on the other hand, the student's relative failure in absorbing education entitled him to extra dosage, educational effort would be relatively inefficient, while educational achievement would be somewhat (though perhaps not much) more nearly equal. Nevertheless, if genetically transmitted capacities substantially affect educability, then no system of allocating educational effort will bring about equality of skill.

From the egalitarian's standpoint, however, unequal performance of different children at school transfers attention to the unequal education or training which children receive at home before and during their time at school. Nobody can deny that it is unequal. Some parents are more intent than others that their children should submit to education and better able to train their children to welcome and take an active part in their education. In other words, whether or not educability is inherited genetically, it is most certainly inherited culturally. This being so, strenuous egalitarians ought, if consistent, to hold that as the family transmits and perpetuates inequality, the family – as an institution for bringing up infants and children – should be demolished. Let all children, from birth, be brought up in common nurseries. Although this solution is seldom met outside utopian communities and science fiction, it is part of the unspoken, because as yet unspeakable, mental baggage of a coherent egalitarian position.

But would state infant-farms really establish equality of skill? Only, for one thing, if genetics makes no difference. And here it is worth noting that differences which are explained in terms of 'cycles of deprivation', in other words as manifestly accounted for by poor upbringing, may be genetic at root. It would not be astounding – though saying it may astound – that in old and reasonably open societies, where for generations individuals have risen or fallen in rough accordance with their merits, people owe their standing in large part to their genetic endowments. If so, deprived parents transmit relatively little because they are genetically unable to do better, and deprived children suffer from genetic deprivation as the root cause of the relative poverty of their home environment. Recognising this possibility does not argue for diminishing the respect due to each human being nor for praising such personal attributes as are largely the gifts of fortune. On the other hand, it does indicate that the goal of equalised skills, even were it worthy of being set up as an ideal, would be quite unachievable, and approachable only at the cost of adopting grossly repressive policies.

It is well within our power to achieve universality of opportunity by eradicating arbitrary barriers to entry. It would be a pity if the visionary quest for 'equal opportunity' distracted us from that desirable and feasible achievement.

3. Equality before the law, understood as meaning that every person should enjoy the full benefits of due process, is now fairly well established as a constitutional principle in free democracies. Certainly, many antiquated privileges and disabilities have long since been abolished. Noblemen can no longer claim immunity from normal prosecution, wives are no longer barred from testifying against their husbands, heretics and dissenters are no longer treated as dubious witnesses. Nevertheless, trial and adjudication remain imperfect. Errors occur in particular cases, contrary to existing rules of procedure – as they always will; and some rules are overdue for remodelling – as some always will be. Nevertheless, the basic principles of fair trial are well settled, and there is widespread agreement that the rules of procedure and the rights which they confer should apply identically to every person before the bench.[6]

However, amidst this consensus as to the principles that should prevail, some voices declare that those principles are violated in practice, systematically rather than accidentally and sporadically. According to such critics, judges import biases into the courtroom: biases which stem from their middle-class upbringing, professional training, affluence and elderliness. Those biases operate to the disadvantage of the poor, ignorant, young and heterodox, thus effectively if not formally denying them fair trial. Because such allegations assume that, when a judge decides against a revolutionary, a picket, an adolescent drug-addict or a black, it is his biases which are at work rather than a fair interpretation of evidence and law, the allegations are themselves expressions of prejudice.

A somewhat subtler and more insidious variation on this theme holds that, although different judges exhibit different biases, all judges – like all human beings – are biased. Therefore an unbiased trial – the gist of due process – is unattainable. If this were intended merely to remind us that human judges do imperfect justice, there could be no dispute. Of course judges are prone to illusion, superstition, preconception, ignorance and moods – some badly so, and others less than most people, especially after opposing lawyers have done their best to inform and guide them. But bias, the heart of this critique, goes far beyond ordinary fallibility.

Bias is supposed to be an unreflective, unbidden reaction of the individual to the formative circumstances of his life. It is supposed to result from 'conditioning' imposed on the individual by his social environment. Seen in this light, man is a victim to bias rather than the maker and chooser of views. If bias operated as such critics suppose, it should be impossible to find a middle-class egalitarian, a working-class conservative or an aristocratic socialist; and the extreme variability of views which characterises individuals nurtured in similar environments, as well as the changeability of views during the course of an individual's life, should be unthinkable. We may take it, accordingly, that rough justice – a more or less good approximation to justice – is not rendered impossible by the supposedly inevitable predominance of prejudice and bias.

Another ground on which it is alleged that fair trial is practically unattainable bears more directly on equality. It is that the poor fare less well in court than the rich, because the legal advisers whom they can afford to employ are less proficient. This supposition (it is no more than that) would be difficult to test factually. An investigation would need to begin by grading litigants according to their incomes and lawyers according to their proficiency. But the incomes of litigants are not generally public knowledge and the proficiency of lawyers is a matter of subjective assessment. Moreover, poor men rarely confront rich men in court, since they have few commercial dealings with each other. To be sure, cases do arise between poor people on the one hand and their more affluent employers, provisioners, insurers and lenders; but many such cases are heard by petty-claims courts or by informal tribunals, where the quality of attorneys matters little because the facts are largely stipulated and the questions of law trivial, not to mention that when a worker appears in a case involving industrial relations he is frequently represented by an able and specialised lawyer retained by a labour union.

Most serious civil cases involving poor men, it is safe to guess, are contests between one poor man and another – and the fact that half of these poor men lose their cases is unremarkable. If one of these two poor men had more money than he does have, he might get a better lawyer (supposing that he, unlike most people, knew how to find a good lawyer); but if both of the poor men had more money, and both had better lawyers, one of them would still win and one lose.

As to criminal cases involving poor men, it might seem that the defendant is always at a disadvantage, in as much as his resources are far slimmer than those available to the public prosecutors. But this is true also for rich defendants, many of whom are indeed convicted despite being able to afford expensive advocates. And if it is pointed out that most convicted criminals come from poor families, the explanation is that most crimes are committed by poor people. Even if it were possible to establish that a higher fraction of poor defendants are convicted than of rich defendants, this would still fail to prove that the difference is accounted for by the rich defendants' having been able to buy superior legal services. In short, the allegation that the courts provide unequal protection to the poor and the rich is unproven, largely unprovable, and highly implausible.

Even were we to accept it for the sake of argument, what remedies would make sense? One would be to provide a minimally competent standard of legal service, free of charge, to anyone who requests it. This, a reasonable device for meeting the legal needs of persons who are virtually destitute, is already widely implemented (by private and public legal-aid agencies, by public defenders appointed by courts, and by actions *in forma pauperis*) and might usefully be strengthened and broadened. The opposite pole would consist of establishing a nationalised legal service on the same model as the nationalised health service. To do so would be to solve a relatively narrow problem – the legal needs of the destitute – by reform on a massive scale, with massive unpredictable side-effects. It is like setting off a nuclear bomb in order to win a skirmish between small patrols, or executing a person to stop him from singing off-key. Besides, nationalising legal services would not produce substantive equality of legal services. There would still be better lawyers and worse lawyers, and so far as the quality of a litigant's lawyer affected his chances, victory would still go to the clients of the better lawyers; though now the quality of one's lawyer would be determined by the administrative methods for allocating lawyers to clients, sometimes by bribery and corruption, by all sorts of chance, and – as now, though less than now – by the client's skill in assessing the quality of various lawyers.

In short, no conceivable reorganisation of legal practice will ever assure substantive equality of all parties before the courts. Here, as in the field of equal opportunity, the path of wisdom is to make certain, so far as we know how, that judges and juries, prosecutors and police desist from action that is personal, prejudicial or arbitrary. Where we cannot devise positive remedies whose benefits would probably outweigh their costs, we do well to restrict ourselves to negative remedies, especially when the latter are more restricted in scope, and therefore easier both to understand and to control.

D. HOW MUCH INEQUALITY IS THERE?

Enthusiasm for redistributive policies is constantly kindled and fed by the conviction that income and wealth are drastically malidistributed,* even if not as much so as in the distant past, which is supposed to have been peopled exclusively by lordly plutocrats and starving peasants. And, indeed, extreme contrasts are still visible, as between destitute vagrants and millionaire pop-stars or property speculators. Yet these extremes are obviously exceptions, which could be and indeed are dealt with by special methods for relieving absolute poverty and for taxing away windfall gains. If the great bulk of incomes fell within some quite restricted range, say between £2500 and £15,000 – as indeed they do – and most of them moreover clustered around £5000, then a reasonable observer might wonder what all the fuss was about.

The public is constantly bombarded however with allegations that the distribution of income is devilishly uneven. Underlying this conclusion is a set of facts of which the public at large are unaware and which even the best-educated members of the public do not know how to interpret correctly. On the rare occasions when the underlying facts do emerge in black and white, they most commonly take the condensed form of comparing the incomes of the most highly paid and the most

* Extended analyses of the extent and sources of economic inequality are given in chapters 10 to 12 below.

lowly paid. For instance, it might be said that the top fifth of income earners get over one-third of the national income and that the top 5 per cent get as much in total as the bottom 20 per cent. Comparing this with the presumed consequence of equality – that any 5 per cent of the labour force would earn exactly 5 per cent of the national income, any 20 per cent exactly 20 per cent and so on – the intelligent observer concludes that income is indeed distributed very unequally.

Moreover, the fact that some people, at any given moment, have higher incomes than others is taken as an infallible symptom of severe social disease. So deep-set is this presumption that most people, including many who more or less closely follow the debate, would reject as patent nonsense the proposition that a high measure of inequality would emerge from a society deliberately designed to be egalitarian. Yet it is easy to imagine just such a society and to trace its inexorable consequences.

1. Suppose a benevolent despot, dogmatically egalitarian, institutes an economic order dominated by the principle that every worker should earn the same life-time income as every other, provided only that he works from the morning of his twentieth birthday to the eve of his sixtieth birthday. A job would be available for each person; each would start at the same annual income, say £1000; and each would get an automatic rise of 4 per cent every year. Of this, 1 per cent would compensate the worker for his increased productivity resulting from accumulated experience on the job – it being one of the despot's principles that workers should be paid in proportion to their productivity, though in deference to his paramount principle of equality he declines to reward each individual worker differentially in accordance with his own individual productivity. The remaining 3 percent of the annual increase would compensate the worker for economic growth occasioned by accumulation of productive capital (all of which the workers own in common) and by improvements in technology.

Following from this thoughtful and beneficent arrangement, every worker would earn no more and no less than every other worker in his age group, and each worker would earn the same amount in the course of a full working life, though not all of them would survive to the age of sixty, the despot having been unable to reduce the death rate below one per cent for each additional year of age.

The outcome of all this, when scrutinised at any given moment, would give the misleading impression of great inequality. The workers most highly paid at any given moment, those then in their last year of work, would get nearly five times as much as the workers then just entering the labour force. The most highly paid 20 per cent of the workers would be getting among them 35 per cent of the national income, whereas the lowest paid 20 per cent would be getting barely 10 per cent. Furthermore, the best paid 5 per cent would be getting among them just as large a share of the national income as was going to the lowest paid 20 per cent. Presented without prologue, such a picture would convey a picture of desperate inequality; yet, as we have seen, it would in fact emerge from a perfectly egalitarian framework.

The lesson to be drawn from this paradox is that statistics which purport to show great inequality of income, which are almost universally interpreted as showing that, may be compatible with relatively little inequality in life-time incomes.[7] In other words, much of the inequality which they apparently disclose may be nothing other than the momentarily uneven effects of economic growth on the one hand and of mortality on the other hand.

All else being equal, inequality of income increases as people die faster, simply because fewer people survive to enjoy high incomes. To be quite precise, the share of income received by the highest income earners increases. For instance, when the death rate is 1 per cent additional year of age (and with a 4 per cent annual rise in wages), the top 5 per cent of income earners get 10 per cent of the national income; should the death rate rise to 2 per cent, they would get 11.5 per cent. As this example shows, the effect of mortality rates is not very great – nor is it unambiguous, for while the share of the highest-paid rises, so does the share of the lowest-paid. Nevertheless, some of the reduction in inequality which has been observed within the past century may be accounted for by the sharp decline in rates of mortality.

Economic growth, on the other hand, has a remarkable effect in increasing the apparent degree of inequality within the hypothetical system established by the benevolent despot. If, for instance, while the mortality rate remained at 1 per cent, the 'growth rate' (to be precise, the rate at which every worker's income rises each year) doubled from 4 per cent to 8 per cent, the share of the national income going to the upper half would increase from 69 per cent to 83 per cent. And this hypothetical conclusion lends credence to the frequent observation that the level of inequality tends to be high in economies undergoing rapid economic growth.

In short, so far as we have gone, the principal cause of economic inequality – which in this example is purely fictitious because purely temporary – is economic growth, which many welcome, rather than any unfairness inherent in the 'system'.

2. Suppose now that our benevolent despot decides to improve the productive potential of his labour force by continuing some of them – let us call them professionals – in training until they reach the age of thirty. In order to give them the same life-time income as is enjoyed by ordinary labourers, he ordains for them a higher starting salary, augmented by an automatic annual increase of 4 per cent. The professionals, in their first year of work, would earn 14 per cent more than ordinary labourers of the same age, and this differential in their favour would persist every year up to retirement at sixty. As a result, the disparity between the lowest and highest paid worker will spread, from 4½ times previously to 5¼ times now. The distribution of income at any given moment will appear to have become more unequal, despite the fact that everyone – labourers and professionals alike, those who being young now are paid little and those who being older are paid more – will have earned exactly the same life-time income by the time each one reaches the age of retirement.

This characteristic of our hypothetical state can be imputed to the real world, both empirically and normatively. Some of the apparent inequality of income observed in any country is no doubt due to the fact that certain kinds of careers curtail the span of one's working life. Apart from careers that require long training, there are careers (those of the professional athlete, aviator or stevedore) which for physical reasons end early; careers (those of the pop-star, dress designer or columnist) liable to sudden termination by a change in fashion; and many others subject to curtailment by changes in technology. Some young people thinking of entering such careers must be supposed to recognise that, unless their annual incomes are higher than in other careers, their lifetime incomes will be lower; and inasmuch as this consideration affects their willingness to enter short-lived careers, it will tend to push up their annual incomes – so creating the deceptive appearance of extreme inequality in the distribution of income. Looking at the matter from the standpoint of equity, not even an extreme egalitarian could cavil at the proposition that workers who take on jobs which necessarily restrict them to short working lives should enjoy as large a life-time income as other people and must therefore necessarily get higher annual incomes than others.

3. So far, our despot's system has provided only jobs which guarantee pre-determined annual incomes. But suppose now that he encourages some of his subjects to go into private profit-making business. Recognising the inherent riskiness of such enterprises, he guarantees them too the same life-time income as everyone else, no more and no less. But in any given year the businessman may realise a profit larger than anybody else's earned income, or no profit at all, or a loss. In any given year, that is, the incomes of businessmen will be scattered over a far wider range than the incomes of labourers and professionals: a range stretching from large negative figures to large positive figures. As a result the inequality of income will appear, when measured at any given moment in time, to have increased, despite the fact that everyone still gets the same life-time income. Once again, we may use this indication from analysis of the hypothetical model to explain and to justify some part – albeit we cannot tell how large a part – of the unequal distribution of incomes observed in real economies.

4. And now let us add a final refinement to the despot's

arrangements, supposing that he permits people to save privately and so to accumulate private hoards of wealth. But let us assume that, in order to preserve the equality of life-time income, he forbids inheritance and private investments which would return dividends to the investors.

Under these constraints, if everyone saved the same fraction of his income, then annual savings would be distributed unequally at each given moment – exactly as unequally as income. But as the amount of wealth owned by any person would consist of savings accumulated over the years, the distribution of wealth would be far more unequal than the distribution of income. And this would be so even though everyone who survived until retirement age would have accumulated exactly the same amount of wealth, amounting in fact (had they all been saving at the rate, for example, of 10 per cent) to exactly 10 per cent of their total life-time incomes.

If, as is more realistic to suppose, each person saved a greater fraction of his income as his income rose, then the distribution of wealth would become still more unequal – even though the amount of wealth accumulated by each person at the retiring age would remain strictly equal. As the adjoining Table shows, the highest paid fifth of the despot's subjects would own over one-third of the community's total wealth (if everyone saved at the same rate, which remained stable throughout their lives), or almost two-fifths of the community's total wealth (if everyone saved according to exactly the same indicated programme of rates rising in accordance with incomes).

If, as is still more realistic to suppose, some people saved hardly at all while some saved a great deal, then the distribution of wealth would be still more unequal, and it would besides cease to be true that everyone retired with the same accumulation of wealth, even though all received the same lifetime incomes.

Studies of the actual distribution of income and of wealth reveal just this pattern: that the distribution of wealth is always much more pronouncedly unequal than the distribution of income. We can say that this would be caused, in the first place, by the cumulative nature of savings and wealth, even if inheritance and 'unearned' incomes were prohibited, and even

Table 1.1 *Distribution of income and wealth*

Age	Number of persons[1]	Annual income per person[2]	Annual income of age group	Annual savings of age group at 10%	Wealth = Cumulative savings, at 10%	Annual savings of age group, accelerating	Wealth = Cumulative savings, accelerating[3]
		(£)	(£ millions)	(£ millions)	(£ millions)	(£ millions)	(£ millions)
20	1000	1000	1.00	.100	.100	.075	.075
21	990	1040	1.03	.103	.203	.088	.163
22	980	1082	1.06	.106	.309	.101	.263
23	970	1125	1.09	.109	.418	.114	.378
24	961	1170	1.12	.112	.530	.129	.507
25	951	1217	1.16	.116	.646	.145	.652
Total	5852		6.46	.646	2.206		2.038

Table 1.2 *Shares of income or wealth received by:*

	% Income	% Wealth		
		Savings at 10%	Accelerating savings[3]	Variable savings[4]
Lowest 20%	18.2	6.1	5.1	0
Lowest 40%	37.3	18.8	16.3	0
Lowest 60%	57.2	38.3	34.9	6.1
Highest 40%	42.8	61.7	65.1	93.9
Highest 20%	21.9	34.8	37.7	61.8

1. Mortality rate is 1% per year.
2. Income increases at 4% per year.
3. Savings rate accelerates at 1% per year from 7.5% to 12.5%.
4. Half of each age group saves nothing, half saves 20% of income.

if everyone who survived to retirement accumulated exactly equal fortunes; and, of course, the actual distribution of wealth is still more unequal because people with equal incomes save at different rates, because people tend to raise their rate of savings as their incomes rise, and because the outcome of investments is largely determined by chance.[8]

It remains to consider what would happen should the despot authorise inheritance and the earning of dividends by private investment. The answer is in one sense obvious. Inheritance and unearned incomes would tend to increase the inequality of income and wealth alike, not only in the momentary sense but also over people's life-times. In truth, the effects are more complex than that, since inherited capital can be dissipated as well as increased; and if we depart from the hypothetical despot's régime to look at our world, then we will encounter many instances of heirs living in genteel poverty, getting low unearned incomes from dwindling estates. We cannot confidently assume that any substantial part of the observed inequality of wealth and income is due to inheritance or to returns from investment.

5. In short, the evidence normally presented as proving that much inequality exists is illusory. It quite overlooks differences in age, length of working life, annual variability of incomes in risky undertakings, patterns of saving, success in investing, and the like. Some of what it measures are therefore differences which are purely temporary and accidental. Were adequate allowance made for these considerations, present estimates would be shown to exaggerate greatly the real degree of economic inequality in developed economies. Economic inequality, in the ethically significant sense, is far less pronounced than most people believe.

Table 1.1 considers a hypothetical community, which, for the sake of simplicity, I have assumed to consist exclusively of workers all of whom are aged exactly 20 or 25 or some year between. Every worker gets the same income as every other worker of his age; and every worker gets the same life-time income as every other, namely, £6634. The inequality of income and wealth, as they appear at the moment that this distribution describes, is expressed in the accompanying Table 1.2.

E. The meaning of Anti-Egalitarianism

Opponents of egalitarianism are commonly mistaken for proponents of inequality. Egalitarians and neutral bystanders leap, naturally if unsubtly, to that conclusion. Nor is that conclusion confuted by the thinking of most anti-egalitarians. Those whose intuitive repugnance to equality is unfortified by reasoned argument are liable to believe that, in opposing equality, they must stand for inequality: an uncomfortable stance, as few today can subscribe to inequality without feeling tainted by deficient sympathy or excessive complacency. Some others expressly endorse inequality and urge those who benefit from it to defend the *status quo* or, better, to restore the *status quo ante* – so falling into a trap, for such politics without principle, pursuing self-interest, and the self-interest of a favoured minority at that, is bound in present circumstances to strengthen the hand of egalitarians.

The imputation that opposing equality necessarily means fostering inequality puts the anti-egalitarian in a false postion, from which he can however extricate himself. The way out is by recognising himself for an anti-egalitarian, not an inegalitarian. Far from desiring inequality, he must refuse to regard either inequality or equality as ends. Policies intended to establish inequality and policies intended to establish equality he should regard alike as misguided.

1. Vital in all this is the distinction between ends of policy and by-products of policy. For a policy to claim our support, its ends must be meritorious. But its by-products need not be; sufficient if they are tolerable. We do not breathe in order to generate carbon dioxide, neither should we stop breathing in order to avoid exhaling carbon dioxide. We do not produce goods and services in order to generate inequality, neither should we curtail production in an effort to achieve equality. For the consistent anti-egalitarian, both equality and inequality count as by-products only, lacking the character of ends in themselves, because, as we have seen, no persuasive argument exists to endow them with that character.

It may be said, of course, that when the by-products of a

policy become noxious, the policy ought to be discarded despite the commendable ends it serves. So it should.

But neither equality nor inequality, to the extent we ordinarily experience, is intolerable. An anti-egalitarian may detest equality on grounds such as that it tends to be accompanied by uniformity and is therefore desired by many who hate and fear individuality, diversity and everything in human beings that makes them hard to understand and harder to control. Nevertheless, where equality or a closer approach to it came about purely as a by-product of policies aimed at ends which the anti-egalitarian judged desirable, the objection to uniformity would have no place, for no intention to produce uniformity (or equality) would have animated those policies. To insist that equalisation, occurring as a by-product, should automatically disqualify any and every policy, no matter how desirable in all other respects, would be exorbitant and self-defeating.

By contrast, a typical egalitarian detests inequality, even as a by-product, for a variety of reasons, many of which have been reviewed above. One more may be mentioned here. It is the fear that inequality feeds on itself, tending always to increase, until the day when one man will own everything and need will force all others into eternal slavery. That spectre makes egalitarians regard inequality, in any degree, even when it emerges as a by-product, as totally unacceptable. For that reason, as well as others, equality becomes for them the paramount end, the ultimate criterion of all policy. But the apprehension that any single germ of inequality will fatally contaminate a whole society is unfounded: no evidence, no argument demonstrates that inequality must always increase unless forcibly curbed. The degree of inequality that results incidentally from policies otherwise desirable can be presumed to be tolerable, in the absence of clear evidence to the contrary.

Here, as always, egalitarians will make much of persons who are absolutely destitute, ill-fed, ill-clothed, ill-housed, and unable to remedy their situation. Certainly there are such people, though the number of people officially labelled 'poor' is vastly exaggerated by the arbitrary level at which the so-called poverty line is drawn in highly-developed economies today. Certainly the plight of the really destitute should stir any decent onlooker to remedial action. Yet absolute poverty has nothing whatsoever to do with equality or inequality. If everyone were equal and equally poverty-stricken, their equality would not relieve their poverty. If only some were impoverished while others were rich, that inequality would not intensify the suffering of the poor. And the clumsiest, least sensitive and slowest way to relieve the poor would be by a policy of enforced equalisation. In short, to accept inequality as a tolerable by-product of otherwise desirable policies in no way incapacitates the anti-egalitarian from dealing with absolute poverty, a real problem deserving special attention, unlike the fictitious problem of 'relative deprivation', which is merely a sophisticated attempt to justify the intention deliberately to institute equality.

2. Another touchstone of outlooks on equality is attitudes toward the transmission of wealth by inheritance.

Testators acquire the substance of their estates by saving. People save at different rates and for different combinations of reasons. Among the common reasons, one is the wish to accumulate reserves so as to provide for one's widows, orphans and other dependants. Another is the wish to supplement income for work with income from profits and dividends. Still another is the wish to accumulate enough reserves to provide for oneself in case of illness and in the highly probable event of growing too old to work. Reasons prompting short-run savings, to pay for holidays, washing-machines, or Christmas gifts, are not significant in the present context. One very rare reason for saving, we may be sure, is in order to increase inequality.

By contrast with saving, which is deliberate even when habitual, the transmission of wealth by inheritance has a large accidental component. Though the testator usually chooses the legatees with some care, his control over how much they will get is limited by the accidents of how long he lives, how early or late he retires, how price levels move during his life, and so on. It is accordingly clear that in leaving his estate, even more than in gathering it, the testator has no intention to promote or undo inequality, and no great hope of realising such an intention were he eccentric enough to harbour it.

Quite apart from intention, it is by no means clear that inheritance must tend to increase inequality. Whether it does so or not will depend on the economic condition of heritors before they inherit, how much they inherit, and ultimately on whether they in turn spend it or pass it along. Precise and comprehensive detail about these questions is not available. Yet let us suppose, for the sake of the argument, we knew for certain that inheritance maintains and even extends inequality. What should be done about that?

For the consistent anti-egalitarian, the policy question is easy. Inheritance results from savings, and saving is desirable in as much as it swells the stock of capital, to the benefit not alone of the capital's owner but also of workers who use the capital and of consumers who use its products. Moreover, the intentions that animate saving are also commendable, in so far as people aim to look after themselves and their dependants. So, overlooking the unintended side-effects of heightened inequality, the anti-egalitarian would approve inheritance as an institution to be upheld by the laws.

The dogmatic egalitarian would readily conclude that inheritance should be abolished, because it contributes to inequality.

The moderate egalitarian would be in a quandary, supposing that the desirability of economic improvement and the desirability of individual responsibility occupied places in his hierarchy of values roughly as exalted as the desirability of equality. Most probably he would seek to resolve his quandary by following a 'middle way', which continued to recognise a legal right to devise and inherit but effectively crippled it by severe taxation. Egalitarians, dogmatic and moderate alike, would have used the side-effect – in real life a purported rather than certain side-effect – as a reason for thwarting inheritance and thus to some extent, even if not deliberately, discouraging saving. In the name of a ghost they would stifle a living thing.

3. Egalitarians of all shades are pursuing a will-of-the-wisp. They are deluded by loose thinking and utopian fantasies. Their conviction that equality is the highest good or at least one among the highest goods rests on incoherent intellectual

foundations, suffers from internal contradictions, and takes its departure from an exaggerated estimate of how much inequality exists. They are grotesquely optimistic in supposing that equality will bring in its train all the other great goods such as liberty, fraternity, wealth, justice and general virtue. Even worse, they ignore the likelihood that, if they have their way, the ultimate outcome will be a decline into widespread poverty and tyranny.

PART ONE

Egalitarianism, its theoretical weaknesses

2

Against equality again

J. R. LUCAS

≠

EQUALITY in the present age has become an idol, in much the same way as property was in the age of Locke. Many people worship it, and think that it provides the key to the proper understanding of politics, and that on it alone can a genuinely just society be reconstructed. This is a mistake. Although, like property, it is a useful concept, and although, like property, there are occasions when we want to have it in practice, it is not a fundamental concept any more than property is, nor can having it vouchsafe to us the good life. In an earlier paper[1] I argued against equality by showing that the concept of equality was confused and that many of the arguments egalitarians adduced were either invalid or else supported conclusions which were not really egalitarian at all. Many egalitarians, however, have complained that my arguments were not fair, because I had failed to elucidate the concept adequately, or because the position I attacked was not one that any egalitarian really wished to maintain, or because I had overlooked other arguments which were effective in establishing egalitarian conclusions, or because the positive counter-arguments of my own I put forward more as a matter of taste than of serious political commitment. In this paper, therefore, I want to elucidate the concept more fully, concede what I should to my critics, point out that, even so, their conclusions do not follow, and give further reasons not only for supposing that egalitarian

---

First published in *Philosophy*, Vol. 52 (1977), pp. 255–80.

For Notes and References, see page 384 below.

arguments are invalid but for discerning positive merits in some forms of inequality.

1

The concept of equality belongs, properly speaking, to the mathematical disciplines. Numbers, lengths, angles, vectors, tensors can be said to be equal to one another without any trace of metaphor. There are some attributes of men where questions of equality can be raised without any conceptual strain. We can ask whether one man is as tall as another, or we may, like Procrustes, seek to establish equality among all men in this respect. Similarly we may measure out equal weights of sugar or margarine as rations in time of war. Money is pre-eminently suitable for making comparisons with, and naturally gives rise to the questions of whether I am getting the same as you or whether your differential has been maintained, and admits the conceptual possibility of our all being paid the same. But most human attributes cannot be quantified without distortion. I cannot have as much education as you, nor as much love, nor as much happiness, because education, love and happiness are not commodities that can be measured and thus compared. One fundamental objection to egalitarianism is that it encourages people to view the good things of life in depersonalised, homogenised terms so that politicians can argue about how much should be assigned to anybody, but nobody can actually engender or enjoy them. It misconceives our human nature to see us primarily as possessors rather than as agents. Although we have feelings of pleasure and pain, and can have possessions, we are first and foremost *agents*, who do things. We are happy, we love, we are educated, in and by doing things, not in having things done to us or being given them. To talk abstractly of these goods as something that we can have is subtly to misconstrue their real nature and thus prevent our achieving them.

Few aspects, therefore, of human life can be quantified without distortion, and so the concept of equality will seldom be applicable in a strict sense: but the concept is used widely in an extended sense, and we need to see what the underlying logic of this extension is.[2] Two important types of relations are involved: *ordering relations*, that is relations which are asymmetric and transitive; and *equivalence relations*, that is relations which are symmetric and transitive. The standard examples of ordering relations are expressed by comparatives, *—er than*: e.g. *taller than*. If I am taller than you, then you are not taller than me – the relation is asymmetric; and if I am taller than you, and you are taller than Peter, then I am taller than you – the relation is transitive. Such a relationship may concern attributes, e.g. heights, but need not: we cannot really measure hardness, but can arrange things in an order of hardness: one stone is harder than another if it will scratch it but not be scratched by it, and if one thing will scratch another and that other a third, then the first thing will also scratch the third. Orderings give rise to a concept of equality. At first sight it seems simple to define two things as being, say, equally hard, if neither can scratch, or be scratched by, the other; often such a definition is adequate, but it rests on the hidden assumption that the ordering is 'complete'. An ordering is complete if any two things that can be ordered by the relation at all can be ordered with respect to each other, or, to put it another way, if the 'Law of Trichotomy' holds – thus, given any two stones, either one stone is harder than the other, or the other is harder than the one, or they are both just as hard as each other.

An example from relativity theory may help. Our ordinary, non-relativistic temporal ordering is complete: given any two events, either one comes before the other, or the other comes before the one, or they are simultaneous. In the theory of special relativity, however, a 'distant' event, that is an event outside the light-cone of another event, is neither before it nor after it nor simultaneous with it. So, too, although we may say that Kant was a greater philosopher than Wolff, and Hegel than Fichte, we may find it impossible to compare Kant with Hegel, or Wolff with Fichte.

Some social relations are ordering relations, and therefore give rise to a hierarchical system. I habitually pay respect to the Warden, the Vice-Chancellor, the Archbishop of Canterbury and the Queen, and undergraduates and college servants like to call me 'Sir', and shopkeepers and parents listen to my opinions with deference. In some societies, like ancient Egypt or modern Russia, the ordering is complete, and everybody knows his place in the hierarchy, and if of two people neither is superior to the other, then they are both social equals. But the relation of social deference does not have to be complete, and is not complete in many Western societies. There is no single all-embracing hierarchy of status, but a multiplicity of conflicting ones. Within any one of these we might be able to define social equality in terms of social deference, but outside them there will often be cases of non-comparability. If an American Congressman or a rising journalist or a successful pop-singer were to come across me, he would be as little likely to feel respect towards me as I towards him: yet it would be an unwarranted conclusion that we were, therefore, social equals. Social equality is something much more positive than a mere absence of ordering relation, and may, indeed, be compatible with a definitely ordered social system.

We need, therefore, to characterise social equality not merely negatively, in terms of the absence of some ordering relation of social deference, but positively in terms of some equivalence relation. An equivalence relation is, like an ordering relation, transitive, but symmetric, not asymmetric: if my height is equal to yours, and yours to Peter's, then mine is equal to Peter's; but also if mine is equal to yours, then yours is equal to mine, not unequal. Equivalence relations are often expressed by some phrase using the word 'same', e.g. 'the same height as'; an equivalence relation relates together all those things which have the same property. In fact, we often use equivalence relations to introduce, or even to define, properties. The concept of weight depends on our having balances, together with the facts, vindicated in experience, that if two objects exactly balance when placed in the scales, they will still balance if we interchange them, and that if two objects each exactly balance when weighed against a third, they will balance also when weighed against each other. Balancing is a symmetric and transitive relation, which therefore enables us to pick out all those things that balance with one another, and say that they are all in some respect the same, namely in respect of weight. Weight is just the property with respect to which each equivalence class is the same. Frege and Russell used a similar strategy in defining the concept of number, and in mathematics we very frequently introduce a new concept by defining first an equivalence relation, then an equivalence class, and then the property as that which all members of the equivalence class have in common. In politics the argument often goes the other way, and the fact that a number of men all have some property in common is represented as their all being equal in this respect. Instead of saying that we shall all die – which is true but not very grandiloquent – we talk of death being the great equaliser. Equality before the law does not mean that the law metes out the same sentence to us all, innocent and guilty alike, but only that we are all under the law and all answerable for our illegal acts. Many egalitarian arguments rest upon our having some one condition or aspiration or purpose in common. Often the things we have in common are important and generate valuable feelings of fellowship. But always we need to know in what respect we are the same as other people, and to what extent that similarity should override other, equally important, differences.

2

One pervasive argument for egalitarianism is the demand for justification of differences, coupled with a certain scepticism about justifications actually offered. Thus Professor S. I. Benn argues 'Egalitarians protest when . . . they see no rational justification for differentiating a particular class for the purpose of allocating certain specific privileges or burdens'. Both the issue and the standard of justification required are left to the choice of the egalitarian. Thus discrimination between the sexes has been called in question in recent years 'because, it is argued, no one has yet shown good enough reasons for thinking a person's sex relevant to the income he should earn – and the burden of proof rests on the discriminator'. But sometimes a practice is not called in question or is thought to be justified, as Benn goes on to point out: 'On the other hand, discrimination according to sex for military service has been generally accepted without much question and is usually considered well grounded: so it is rarely called an inequality'.[3] This principle, which Professor H. A. Bedau calls the *presumption of equality*[4] is clearly a powerful principle, but open to considerable objection. It is easy to ask questions, and easy not to be satisfied with the answers given. But not all questions ought to be answered, and often merely by asking a question one is committed to waiting for an answer and not dismissing it out of hand. Moreover, without considerable qualification the presumption of equality is bound to prove internally inconsistent. It cannot be a presumption we are always entitled to make, and once we have to consider whether in any particular case it is justified, its bulldozing power is already gone.

It is easy to ask questions. Job asked God to justify His treatment of him, and modern man, especially modern young man, is fond of demanding that society should justify itself to his satisfaction. But questions have to be addressed to someone, and it depends very much on the person to whom the question is addressed what sort of answer it is reasonable to expect. If you ask me, I may be able to explain why we have certain arrangements, but I cannot be called on to justify them unless I have some control over them and am therefore responsible for them. It is dangerously easy in seeking a rational justification to smuggle in an assumption of omnipotence. In our age of unbelief we tend to be 'egotheists' and to assume that we, or the State at our bidding, can arrange everything as seems best. But not everything is possible to the State, nor should it be. If we insist on the State's being answerable for all the arrangements of society, we implicitly concede to it absolute power. Unless we are totalitarians, we must be prepared on occasion to disclaim responsibility, and to refuse to offer a justification in the terms desired of some social arrangement which has attracted criticism. In an imperfect world inhabited by imperfect men, many things will go wrong, which are indubitably wrong, but which cannot be remedied except at the cost of much greater evils. Egalitarian sentiment leads easily to totalitarianism, and if we abhor totalitarianism we must be prepared on occasion to rebut the presumption of the egalitarians, and concede that not everything in our society can be justified.

There are many different limitations on the power of the State, some contingent, others essential. Often things work out badly because no one is wise enough to make them work out well. The intellectual limitations of our rulers are of immense practical importance, and sometimes, as we shall see (in sections 6–7 below), an examination of their, and our own, imperfections yields philosophical illumination. Sometimes, however, we object on a point of principle: the action complained of was an exercise of freedom, and therefore the agent cannot be called to account; or the interests involved were peripheral or illegitimate, and for that reason the issue is not justiciable: or – more difficult – the arrangements are not to be seen as the actions of anybody, and there is nobody who should be held responsible for what happened. These disclaimers of responsibility are not to be always invoked. One of the reasons for the radicals' impatience with authority is authority's tendency to brush off awkward questions with unreasonable disclaimers. Nevertheless, the tone of the discussion should change. Although we should think critically about our society, we should not be too strident in our questioning. There will be plenty of occasions when we shall have to probe and press our questions hard, and not be put off by easy evasions; but we must not assume that answers must always be forthcoming, or that nothing can be accepted unless it has been rationally justified to our complete satisfaction.

Benn is at pains to distinguish his egalitarianism from the radical egalitarianism, discussed by Bedau, which presses for the removal of all forms of differentiation. Having allowed that the conditions under attack may be contextually supplied and not explicitly stated, he protests in a footnote:

> A favorite way of discrediting the egalitarian, however, is to make it appear that he seeks to remove forms of discrimination that neither he, nor anyone else, would for a moment question. Though the Levellers were concerned only for equal political rights, for removing monopolistic privileges in trade, and for legal reforms, they were frequently accused, despite vigorous disclaimers, of wanting to level property.

But it is a perfectly reasonable counter. If the egalitarian is entitled to call any form of discrimination in question, then the anti-egalitarian can reduce the presumption of equality to absurdity by calling in question some form of discrimination the egalitarian is disposed to accept. American advocates of Women's Lib who believe that considerations of chivalry should secure them exemption from the Draft Law *are* being inconsistent if they base their claim for equal treatment on a general refusal to allow that differences of sex can ever be relevant to the treatment meted out to a citizen by the state. Often in politics criteria of relevance are difficult to determine, and we have to take into account many different considerations based on different facts. The presumption of equality, however, focuses on just one factor, and ignores all the rest.

At one time advanced educationalists get hot under the collar about inequalities of opportunity, and ask indignantly why the son of a rich man should be given a public school education while the much abler son of poor parents is denied one. No fluffy answers are accepted, and under the concentrated gaze of public scrutiny it becomes evident that what sort of education you get should not depend on who your parents are. A generation later the centre of indignation has shifted, and advanced educationalists ask indignantly why the education a boy gets should depend on the genes he happens to have inherited from his parents, and left-wing thinkers extol comprehensive schools with the aid of the same arguments that old Etonians used to use against the grammar school brigade in the days of the Butler education act. We may smile ironically, but should recognise that education is being grievously damaged and clarity obscured by a scheme of argument which presents issues in terms of a few arbitrarily selected black-and-white distinctions instead of a multitude of grey ones. The presumption of equality concentrates our attention on one distinction and leads us to ignore all the others. But whether a distinction is relevant or not cannot depend on whether the egalitarian happens to question it or not. It may be that at present no one questions the 18-plus selection for the university on the basis of academic ability. But if egalitarians aver that intellectual ability is no justification for giving one child an academic education denied to another, then I am anxious to know what, should the question of university entrance ever be raised, their answer will be. Ought I to be preparing myself to lecture on Aristotle's *Ethics* or on First-Order Predicate Calculus to people who know no Greek and cannot do Logic, but have come to Oxford in order to play rugger or row? It is, of course, a rhetorical question. But it shows the weakness of a schema of argument which depends on asking questions that are rhetorical in as much as no serious answer is sought for or listened to.

We cannot avoid every sort of distinction or discrimination. If we set out to establish equality in one respect, we shall thereby establish some other inequality in another respect. The free use of the presumption of equality is bound to lead to inconsistency. It must, therefore, be, at best, a principle of only restricted applicability, and before the egalitarian can apply it, he needs to show that the case is a suitable one for its application.

3

Egalitarian sentiments are often the vehicle for expressing positively either a demand for, or a recognition of, some underlying unity. Sometimes we are concerned to express our common humanity, and to work out its implications for our political thinking. In other cases we discover an underlying unity, find that it engenders deep feelings of fellowship which we, quite rightly, value. Arguments of the first sort, arguments from Universal Humanity as I term them, are more complicated, and deserve fuller treatment, than I originally allowed for: arguments of the second sort, peer-group arguments as I shall call them, I neglected altogether; they have great emotional appeal, but cannot, and necessarily cannot, establish all that the egalitarian wants.

Many arguments from Universal Humanity are arguments from need. They are weighty, but do not have essentially egalitarian implications,[5] and, because they are many, are none of them conclusive. The simplest and most appealing is what I might term the Oxfam argument. If my brother is in need, and I am in a position to help him, and fail to do so, then I am failing to recognise our common humanity. And in a world in which there are millions of starving people it must be wrong for anyone to have more than anyone else, because his superfluity should always be transferred to those in greater need. When there are people hungry or naked or in need of medical attention, it seems wrong to devote available resources to providing the very rich with pink champagne, or for that matter the fairly prosperous artisans of our own country with a second colour TV.

There is much force in this argument. But there are limitations to its applicability. Consider the War on Want argument. The War on Want argument, like the Oxfam argument, is concerned with human need, but holds that it is not enough simply to relieve need, and that we should, rather, devote our energies to helping people to stand on their own feet, even sometimes at the expense of meeting more immediate needs. In the long run, we cannot help them effectively, unless they will help themselves. And therefore, apart from short-term help in times of emergency, we should help them by helping them to help themselves. Their needs still have a claim on our attention and our resources; but in a less straightforward and mechanical way than the Oxfam argument would suggest. Men are not just passive patients whom we ought to do good to, in order that they may not suffer pain or deprivation or want: they are also active agents, whose nature it is to do things, and to do things on their own initiative and for their own reasons. They need liberty and opportunity as well as food and medicines; stimulus as well as satisfaction. And therefore we should, as we do in practice, acknowledge many other arguments besides the Oxfam one as weighty. We do not give all our resources to the relief of suffering and need. Let the reader consider his own gifts to charity in the past twelve months. He may well have given money to Oxfam, or to Christian Aid, or to Shelter, or to Help the Aged. But he will almost certainly have given something to a political party, or to a church, or to a theatre guild, or to a conservation group, or to pay the legal costs of someone being unfairly prosecuted by some public authority, or to some other good cause. We cherish many charities, not only those which seek to ensure that nobody will suffer from any sort of need, but also those which seek to secure by private or collective action that some one of a host of innumerable goods shall be achieved. We have many ideas of good, and many reasons for action. The Oxfam argument is one, and an important one, among them; but it is not the only one, and therefore there may be occasions when we are right to find other arguments more compelling.

Benn distinguishes from among the arguments from Universal Humanity one – *the principle of equal consideration of interests* – to which he attaches great importance, because he thinks that I have dealt with it too shortly and that it yields conclusions which are strongly egalitarian in effect.[6] It is clear that it is an important principle, and it is certainly not one I should wish to neglect. But I find it difficult to see what the word 'equal' is doing in Benn's formulation of it. Benn does not mean that any man can always claim the same treatment as any other, nor that the interests of every man should weigh equally with me. He is at pains to point out that it is perfectly possible for one man's interest to have priority over another's.[7] But then what *is* the force of 'equal'? Have I got to devote equal periods of time to listening to A and B pleading their usefulness to me? It is clear that Benn does not mean this. There are many cases where very short consideration is all that we are obliged to give to another man's interests – I need not spend long considering the claims of very distant relatives or of people who are not members of my family at all to hospitality at Christmas, and often a judge needs only a few minutes to decide that no reasonable cause of action lies on the facts presented to him.

What Benn has in mind is something very different: that there should be no non-Archimedean ordering among the members of a society, so that the interests of members of the Party always outweigh those of mere ordinary people, or that the interests of some people – blacks, Jews, wogs or levantines – are always overridden if they happen to conflict with the interests of full members of the community. Perhaps the principle can best be explained in terms of the scope of quantifiers: we want to quantify primarily over cases, not persons; justice, as we say, is no respecter of persons, although it is concerned to give full consideration to each case. What Benn wants to avoid is that there should be some people who, whatever the case, always won, or some people who, whatever the case, always lost. This, indeed, is an important principle, long acknowledged in English law, although in recent years increasingly disregarded in other areas of government activity. The tendency of official decision-makers to think that only the official point of view needs to be taken into consideration should be strenuously resisted, and Benn is quite right to insist that everyone's interests should be given proper consideration, and that the claims of those outside the government machine should not be ignored or discounted in the process of public decision-making.

The only difficulty is in describing this as giving them *equal* consideration. Benn has shown that the word is not entirely vacuous – that the principle he is propounding is more than a mere principle of consideration of interests, which would be compatible with an élitist morality which considered the interests of non-officials but never allowed them to outweigh those of the bureaucracy. But although some word is needed – I suggest 'full', 'proper' or 'due' – the word 'equal' carries misleading connotations, as Benn himself shows by linking it with the quotation from J. C. Davies: 'I am as good as anybody else; I may not be as clever or hard working as you are, but I am as good as you are.'[8] But this, although a genuinely egalitarian doctrine with characteristically untoward consequences (see section 8 below), is *not* what the principle of proper consideration of interests establishes. What the principle establishes as 'I am a man. I am not to be ignored, nor should my interests by systematically discounted'. To go further and to claim that I am *as good as* anybody else is to divorce goodness from all possible criteria, and ultimately to devalue personality. If I am as good as you no matter what you do and I fail to do, then it does not matter what you do or what I do; similarly, if my view is as good as yours, irrespective of the fact that you are clever and I am not, and you have examined the evidence and considered the arguments while I have just opined, then it means that there is no right or wrong in our thinking, and that any view is as good as any other.

A system in which on grounds of non-discrimination we can never distinguish between one view and its opposite is analogous to the 'absolutely inconsistent' systems of formal logic, where every well-formed formula is a theorem and therefore there is no point in picking out the class of theorems. To reason is to select – to select the right and reject the wrong. If you are to engage in rational argument with me, then it cannot be on the precondition that my views are just as good as yours. To reason is to lay oneself open to the possibility of being wrong, and if the egalitarian is so wedded to the principle of non-discrimination that he cannot entertain the possibility of anybody's being wrong unless everybody else is too, then egalitarianism is committed to irrationality.

4

The peer-group argument goes back to Plato. We need to treat some men – colleagues, friends, partners – as equals, peers standing in the same relation to oneself as one does to them. Although not all relations between men need be, or are, reciprocal, groups of *fellow* citizens, *fellow* officers, *fellow* rulers, played a central part in Greek social life, and still meet important emotional needs in our own society. Plato envisaged the rulers of his ideal state being so much of a peer-group that they would have everything, even wives and children, in common, so much so that the use of the first- and second-person pronouns – *I*, *me*, *my*, and *you*, *your* – should be replaced by the first person plural (*Republic*, V, 451c–469b). Likewise in the sub-ideal community for which he laid down the Laws, he is aware of the importance of fellow-feeling and peer-group behaviour (*Laws*, VI, 777d5 and XI, 919d7). We may distinguish two strands in the argument: one is that of anti-selfishness. Plato was appalled at the me-firstism rampant in Athenian society, and so he opposed to amoral self-aggrandisement the selfless pursuit of the common good. So, too, many modern egalitarians are moved primarily by a detestation of the profit-motive. But the alternatives are not exhaustive, and the dangers of corporate selfishness are no less great, indeed they are more insidious, than those of simple, individual greed. The first-person plural is still the first person, and in danger of excluding third personal outsiders. Within the group there is total equality: but the group is restricted, and there is no equality between members and non-members of the group. Plato's peers, like the peers of England, are more noticeable for the inequality which separates them from everybody else, than for the equality which does exist among them. So, too, modern denunciations of the profit-motive have been the pretext on which bureaucratic empires have been built up, and have resulted in an inequality of power which is both more unequal and more dangerous than the inequality of wealth to which objection was originally made.

The second strand of Plato's argument is less extreme. No

abnegation of self is needed to justify our enjoying the company of our fellows. It is an important part of a man's emotional life, not adequately catered for in modern society, to be among his equals. Social relationships which are 'symmetric' are undemanding. The emotional temperature is lower when I am with my pals than when I am with my girlfriend: I can relax with my colleagues in a way I cannot when I am with pupils or parishioners or the headmaster or the vice-chancellor or the bishop. Modern society fails to institutionalise provision for this need, and powerful emotions show themselves socially in football crowds and politically in demands for total fraternal equality. But the political demand is misformulated. The argument from fraternity to equality fails in two respects. It fails first because we are not all brothers. Half the human race are disqualified by sex from being even metaphorical brothers, and although the advocates of Women's Lib seem to suppose that Sorority should be the watch-word of the Sexual Revolution, it seems to me that the aspirations of most women are deeply unsisterly. Young women give few indications of seeing themselves as sisters or wanting to be treated in a sisterly fashion by the young men of their acquaintanceship, and in later years maternal and grand-maternal affection loom much larger in their life than any desire to gatecrash other people's peer-groups. It is no accident that we find Plato's treatment of sex the most repugnant part of his programme in the *Republic*. Sexual relations are essentially asymmetric, and the emotions they engender are not only intense but necessarily exclusive. In addition to the exclusive love between husband and wife, many other relationships, both within the family and outside it, are similarly asymmetric. I cannot really regard even all male men as my brethren, without misrepresenting the true state of my feelings for my father, my sons, my ancestors and my possible descendants. Similarly, the regard I have for my teachers and tutors, mentors and benefactors is necessarily asymmetric, as is the concern I feel for my pupils and possible recipients of my advice or benefactions. It is essential to society, and, as I shall argue more fully later, essential to each man's emotional fulfilment that there should be some differentiation in the structure of our society and in our social relations one with another. The full-blooded argument from fraternity to equality fails because it is founded on a premiss which is false in fact. We are not all brothers.

Fraternal feeling is none the less a good thing. It needs to be cherished and catered for, and sometimes calls for some equality in treatment or circumstance. But it neither requires, nor can endure, total equality. Fellow-feeling can exist on a basis of a recognition and mutual acceptance of differences. The tenant farmer who clapped the late Lord Halifax on the back and said, 'Tha's made a good start, lad; keep it oop', clearly did not find the difference between being a farmer and being Foreign Secretary a barrier. Other examples abound. It is not equality but justice that is essential if fellow-feeling is to flourish.[9] I can identify with you and enter into your aspirations and purposes so long as I believe that you and I are tied together by bonds of mutual respect, and that each will accord the other a consideration which we both believe will be reasonable. Equality of circumstances may conduce to fellow-feeling, but need not, and will not if in fact it seems unjust. Equal conditions often fail to engender feelings of fellowship: and even in the small, cohesive peer-group there is, and has to be, some recognition of the differences between different members.

5

I now turn to positive arguments for inequality. They are of many different kinds. Some are almost logical, opposing the principle of uniformity with that of uniqueness. Others are based on the fundamental values of liberty or justice, arguing that if these are to be observed at all in public affairs the principle of equality must to some extent be compromised. Others again are more pragmatic, arising from the practical necessities of political and social life, which in turn reflect the limited abilities and imperfect aspirations of human beings.

The argument from Universal Humanity can be called in aid of inegalitarian, as well as egalitarian, conclusions. Many inegalitarian societies show more respect for each individual man than supposedly egalitarian societies do. Marx saw merit in feudalism, in contrast to the liberal societies of his own day, because in a feudal society each man had his own place, and was respected in that place. It is better to be a bathroom attendant in an Oxford college than to be a prosperous proletarian in an amorphous plebs, because the bathroom attendant, although he occupies a relatively lowly place in the college hierarchy, nevertheless is enabled to feel that he is a valued member of that society, making a real and definite contribution to its well-being. In comparison, a modern egalitarian society can be very heartless, showing no concern for any individual as such. Although the prosperous proletarian has more money than the college servant, and although he is not obliged to regard anyone as his superior, he does not feel that he is valued for himself alone, or that society cares for anything but his cash. A society which accords respect to each man in his place is appreciated because it seems to individuate individuals in a way in which societies committed to the egalitarian ethos are unable to do. If the only social relations are transitive symmetric relations, then I necessarily stand in exactly the same relationship to society as anybody else, and therefore I can have no social position which is peculiarly my own. Since my relationship to the rest of society is the same as yours, it would not make any difference if I were replaced by you; and from this it follows that I in myself am replaceable, and therefore dispensable. In a totally egalitarian society I am always potentially redundant. I am merely a unit, not a unique individual. If I see myself as a man, with a real personality and a real contribution all of my own to make to my fellow men, then I shall reject the ethos of egalitarianism and see positive merit in a social order which acknowledges the distinctiveness of the individual and therefore the differences between men.

A status society does not have to be strictly ordered. It is compatible with there being some ordering – but the ordering does not have to be complete, and, more importantly, does not have to be all-important. What is desired is that each man should stand in regard to the rest of society in a relation which other men do not, and that this relation should itself be the ground of respect. The village cobbler performs a different function from the squire or the parson, and one that is needed, and cannot be performed, by them, however wealthy or well educated they may be. Each man wants to be respected. The egalitarian seeks to satisfy this need by ensuring that no man is ever in an inferior position *vis-à-vis* anybody else, and so insists that all social relations shall be equivalence relations. That fails to meet the need, which is much better met by allowing relations which are asymmetric but securing for each man that there is some relation with respect to which he is superior to other people. No one should be always the underdog. We can object to strictly hierarchical societies on the grounds that those on the bottom of the hierarchy – the serfs, the villeins, or the prison-camp slaves – are accorded no respect at all. But we should remedy this by having more than one hierarchy, and, in so far as any one ranking system is dominant and generally accepted as constituting *the* social order, demanding that those who are deferred to should make manifest their respect and consideration for those who render them services.

The argument can, in part, be transposed to a lower key. Two inequalities are better than one. It is better to have a society in which there are a number of different pecking orders, so that a person who comes low according to one order can nevertheless rate highly according to another. One advantage that English society used to have over American was that, whereas in America wealth was the only criterion, in England social standing was largely independent of wealth, and could, therefore, act as a corrective. More generally, it is good that there should be an athletic hierarchy besides the academic one, so that boys who are not blessed with brains may nevertheless be, and feel themselves to be, the stars of the football field. A man may not be a great success economically but still can be a big noise in the Boy Scout Association or the pigeon fanciers' club. So long as we have plenty of different inequalities, nobody need be absolutely inferior. It is only if, in the name of equality, we set about eliminating them all, that we shall succeed in eliminating many of them and thereby make those that remain far more burdensome.

Egalitarians are angered when the argument from Universal Humanity is called in aid of inegalitarian conclusions, and produce vehement counter-arguments against it. They will not accept that the college servant is really better off than the prosperous proletarian, however much happier he may subjectively suppose himself to be, because the mere fact that the society recognises a difference in status between the college servant and, say, the fellows is itself an affront to human dignity. If we differentiate at all between one man and another on account of the social functions they fulfil, then we are no longer regarding them as men but merely as performers of certain roles. The bathroom attendant may think that he is valued for himself alone, but he is wrong; he is valued merely as a cleaner of baths and lavatories, merely as a pair of hands, merely as a useful automaton and not at all as a person, a child of God, a human being, an immortal soul, the bearer of an eternal destiny.

This argument has powerful emotional appeal, but it is confused. It confuses the minimal and the maximal respect we may pay to a human being. Whatever a man does, whatever contribution he makes to our well-being, whatever his achievements, he is more than merely a doer, a contributor, an achiever, and I do not respect him properly, if I respect him merely as a doer, a contributor, or an achiever. If I am to respect him fully, I must respect him for himself, rather than merely as someone who satisfies certain specifications, just as a girl feels that she is not really loved unless she is loved for herself alone, and not her yellow hair. But only God can do that. In an imperfect world limited mortals have only limited respect for most other people. The respect which affords a basis for political argument is not a maximal respect we can aspire to but seldom achieve; rather, it is a minimal respect which we all ought to pay to everybody else. It does not exhaust the whole of political argument, but simply provides an incontrovertible starting point. I respect another man's humanity by observing a certain set of minimum conditions towards him – by not killing him, by not torturing him, by not leaving him to starve, by not depriving him of civil rights – and it is important to see these conditions as minimum conditions which must be fulfilled rather than as maximum conditions to which we should aim but which we cannot be blamed if we fail to achieve. If we set our sights too high, we shall secure nothing. It may – or it may not – be desirable that I should identify fully with the bath attendant, and seek to enable him to fulfil his potentiality in every way; but it is a fact that most people can, or at least do, identify with most other people only to a very limited extent; and if we want to ensure that there shall be nobody who is not identified with at all, we must accept the consequence that the extent to which identification is achieved will be a fairly minimal one. But better that than that we should fail to recognise another man's humanity at all.

The egalitarian argument against differentiation of function seems unrealistic. Although I may object to being regarded *merely* as the performer of a certain role, I do not normally object to being regarded as a person who *does* perform a certain role, or who has carried out certain achievements. The reason is that these roles and achievements are activities or actions of mine, and therefore manifestations of my own personal choices, and so very much part of what I essentially am. What I do is the mark I make upon the world. I am different from everybody else, and one chief way in which my being different from everybody else is made plain is in what I choose to do. Even if what I choose to do is something fairly humdrum, like cleaning baths, it nevertheless is what I have done, my own special contribution to making the world a better place. A society which differentiates between people on the basis of what they do is not denying their humanity, but emphasising a most important facet of it. This is not to say that all hierarchical societies pay respect to the human worth of all their members, any more than all egalitarian societies do. But the principle of Universal Humanity requires us to pay attention to the differences between men as well as the resemblances, and an inegalitarian society can often be showing just as much respect for the individual worth of its members as an egalitarian society does.

Professor B. A. O. Williams concedes the force of these arguments, but still maintains that only an egalitarian society would suit the true, unconditioned consciousness of every man.[10] He is right to resist the simple argument from consciousness. It is not a conclusive argument for a status society that it makes everyone happy. The slaves in the American South may have been happy, but still it is better that they should be free. A society may so condition a man's consciousness that he can form no proper view of his own potentialities, and whole peoples may be wrongly reconciled to their lot by being persuaded that it is inevitable. But it does not have to be so. Not all consciousness is false consciousness. Although we are all greatly influenced by our cultural and social environment, we can stand back and make our own critical appreciation of our society, and can consider our own position in it and make up our own minds whether we are willing to accept it or not. No society, whether hierarchical or egalitarian, will be immune from criticism or completely stable; always there will be some who are divinely discontented with their lot and who will seek to improve their own position in it or remould it to their own advantage. But that does not touch the argument from respect. Respect is not shown me by treating me merely as a transcendental *ego* or unconditioned consciousness, which, had circumstances been different, might have had very different abilities and attitudes from those I actually have. Child of my age though I am, I am what I am – a unique individual, anxious to make my own contribution to the age I live in, and to fulfil myself by filling social roles which are not just thrust on me by society but are freely accepted as giving me the opportunity of doing my bit.

Only by abstracting from all actual aspirations and activities can Williams equalise us all and extract egalitarian conclusions from the argument from respect. But respect, if it is to be respect at all, must look to the actual individual, and take account not only of what he might be, but what he actually is. And what he actually is will be different from what anybody else is, and will characteristically manifest itself in his actions: and therefore society will show respect to individuals by taking account of the different things different people do, that is, acknowledging the importance of each man's social role.

6

The argument from respect is paralleled by the arguments from liberty and from justice. Liberty requires that we let people be different, justice that we treat them differently: the one because it is for them, rather than for us, to decide what they shall do, and different men decide to do different things: the other because *all* the relevant factors should be taken into account, and these will often be different and demand different sorts of treatment. Radical egalitarians recognise the incompatibility between their ideal and the ideals of liberty and justice, and say, simply, that these ideals are less important and ought to give way when they conflict with the overriding claims of equality. Most egalitarians, however, seek to reconcile the various ideals by claiming that the uniformities they seek to ensure are compatible with the exercise of liberty and positively required by justice. They envisage a society in which each man does his own thing, but the important equalities between different people are not upset by the different things they do. It is permissible to hope for this, but not reasonable to expect it. Unless our liberties are so circumscribed that we can make choices on our own account only about matters that are essentially trivial – if we can choose our hobbies and the décor of our flats, but not our jobs or where we are to live – some of our choices will impinge on the way important affairs turn out, and will work out well or ill for us not only in our own estimation but in that of others too.

Contrary to the belief of some lovers of liberty, our values are not entirely our own but have some tendency to be shared. In any society there must be some shared values, and therefore some shared assumptions about what is to anyone's advantage or disadvantage, and so some common standards of success. This is why, although there is no necessity for social relations to be ordering relations, nevertheless a social order tends to establish itself. Although I may, in accordance with the Declaration of Independence, pursue happiness in my own way, and although many Americans have in fact set themselves idiosyncratic goals of success, nevertheless for most Americans success is to be measured in pecuniary terms. We want to succeed not only in our own eyes but in the eyes of other men too: we are competitive creatures, who value goals not because we have assessed them independently on our own account, but because others do and we want to outdo them. If we allow men liberty in things that matter, they will soon establish inequalities that signify. Hence, if we value liberty at all, we cannot abolish all inequalities, but only, at best, reduce their impact by multiplying them.

The argument from justice is more difficult. Whereas most people sense some difficulty in reconciling liberty and equality, many think that justice and equality are not only compatible, but come to the same thing. Nevertheless, justice is not equality, even though it sometimes requires that people be treated alike, as equality always does. We can see that justice is not the same as equality, because we sometimes stigmatise as unjust laws imposing 'strict liabilities', although they are evidently unobjectionable on the score of equality, since they apply to everyone without exception. If there were a law imposing the death penalty on the driver of a motor vehicle involved in a fatal accident, it would be unjust in spite of – indeed, because of – its treating all such drivers the same. We fail to do justice to the individual unless we give due consideration to the circumstances of *his* case. Equality, because it focuses attention on only a few circumstances, may well lead us to ignore some other circumstances that are relevant, and thus to be unjust.

Again, justice gives rise to certain procedural requirements, while equality is concerned only with results, not processes. Equality does not insist upon the principle *audi alteram partem: audi neutram partem* would be just as good so far as equality is concerned. Justice is much more complicated than equality. We can make sense of the tender-minded toughness that characterises the just man, if we see him as being imbued with a rational concern for the individual, which makes him unwilling to reach any decision adverse to any individual's interests, until he has considered all reasonable possibilities of not so doing, and unless he is adequately persuaded that there are reasons of an acceptable sort which require such an adverse decision to be made. This is why we require the case against a man to be tried and rejected unless it is shown to be sufficiently strong. This also is why justice is concerned not only with the final decision reached but the way in which it was arrived at, and, in particular, is concerned that no factor in favour of any individual should be overlooked or discounted.

Because justice is rational, it is subject to the requirement of universalisability, which is the hallmark of all rational decision-making. But a readiness to treat like cases alike, although a necessary feature of justice, is not a sufficient characterisation of it. It is a necessary feature of good administration, too, and even of enlightened self-interest. A modern bureaucracy could be scrupulously rational in its decision-making, and always mete out the same treatment except where circumstances warranted it, but accept, as relevant circumstances, considerations of state and of public policy, which were reasons indeed, but reasons of expediency rather than of justice. What exactly should count as reasons of justice is difficult to determine. Often it depends on convention, and often it is a matter of public agreement or general expectation rather than of abstract principle. Nevertheless, although justice may be largely conventional, it is not entirely so, and there will always be occasions where we fail to do justice to a case if we ignore certain factors, which, were equality our only guide, we should not need to take it to account. Justice does not always require that we treat different cases differently, but if we always, as good egalitarians, treat different cases the same, we can be sure that sometimes we shall commit great injustice.

The divergence of justice from equality is particularly important in economic affairs. Many people have argued against economic equality on the score of expediency, and some weight should be given to the need to provide people with adequate incentives. But for many people, particularly for members of trades unions, the question of expediency looms less large than that of justice. So long as money plays an important part in our way of life, it will be a tangible token of esteem and gratitude which ought not to be withheld from those who have done well by us and deserved well of us. Much of the current concern with differentials is concerned less with incentives than with respect. People ask for more not because there is an imbalance between supply and demand for their services – though this may well have a bearing on the readiness of employers to concede their claims – but because they think existing remuneration does not reflect the real value of what they do, and they are unwilling to acquiesce in other people putting a low valuation on their efforts. Although on occasions, under limited conditions, for set purposes, we may agree on a flat rate irrespective of effort or skill, there remains an obstinate feeling that those who have borne the heat of the day ought to be more handsomely rewarded than those who have laboured only briefly or made only a slight contribution to the success of the enterprise. Economic justice can argue in the opposite direction to economic equality.

7

Arguments from social expediency can also be urged. The argument from incentives is too well known to need elaborating here. The argument from innovation is not so well known. Professor Hayek and Lord Hailsham point out that inequality has been the means whereby economic progress has been achieved.[11] If there had not been some rich people in the early part of this century who could afford to waste a lot of money on horseless carriages, there would be no production of cars now. The argument from economic progress has become somewhat polluted with the passage of time: we can no longer feel it that important to secure that everybody has a third car or second spin-drier. Nevertheless, an important point remains. Although not all innovations are desirable, some are; and we can only discover which, if our society contains people who can afford to try out new ideas. An egalitarian society rapidly becomes wooden and immobile, because the majority of new ideas, which, when they are new, do not appeal to the majority of people, can never be put into effect.

The third argument from expediency for inequality is what I call the explosive argument. If I wanted to ensure that parcels I was sending by train should not be chucked about by the porters, it would not be enough merely to label them all fragile; but if I labelled them explosive, and let it be known that one in every thousand contained mercury fulminate, then they would be handled very carefully indeed. So, too, in affairs of our society. We can adjure officials to treat members of our society carefully but, human nature being what it is, not every official will be disposed to put himself out for awkward members of the public. There will be a tendency to treat them with scant consideration, discourtesy or even gross disregard of their rights. And most members of the public will take it lying down, and will be pushed around like sheep. But if there are some members of the public who will not only want to stand up for their rights, but are in a position to do so, the case will be very different. Although there may still be bad officials who behave like jacks-in-office, sometimes the fact will be discovered, and all officials will become anxious to avoid the sort of unpleasantness that can result from arrogant behaviour on their part. And this requires that some members of the ordinary public have the possibility of taking effective action in spite of their not having any official standing.

The best modern example is Crichel Down.* The Civil Service had been acting wrongly over a period of years; but when they sought to annex Crichel Down for their own purposes, they were resisted by a man who, because he was rich and had influential connections, was able to prevent them sweeping the issue under the carpet. He was able to fight it to a finish, which a poorer man could not have afforded to do, and in the end he won, and civil servants have been better behaved in consequence, and we all have benefited. It is therefore desirable that there should be some rich men, who can afford to fight the government on their own, and hence also on our, behalf. Of course, it is not only a matter of riches. Wealth is not always necessary or sufficient, nor is it the only desirable form of inequality for this purpose. Some John Hampdens have been successful though poor, and wealth without 'pull' would not have restored Crichel Down to its rightful owner; and we should be worried not only by what may be done to non-official members of the public, but also to non-rich ones. We want to have a number of different inequalities, some not at all evident to the official eye, which together will have the effect that in the long run any official abusing his power will be brought to book. And I for one am happy to see other people being rich or other people being influential, as part of the cost of living in a society in which officials of all sorts handle me with kid-gloves, for fear I might turn out to be rather an important person myself.

The last two arguments may seem to be practical rather than philosophical, but they reveal an important aspect of human society which in turn reflects a fundamental feature of human nature. It is difficult and costly to initiate action. If private individuals are to be able to take certain sorts of initiative effectively, they need to be rich. Not all people can be rich. If from this we infer that nobody should be rich, then we are

* The Crichel Down affair became a major political issue in 1954, leading to the resignation of the Minister of Agriculture in Churchill's administration (Ed.).

precluding private individuals from starting things on their own, and thus are conferring a monopoly of initiative power on officials. And this is dangerous and illiberal. We want there to be at least some citizens outside the state bureaucracy who not only can resist the official point of view, but can get new ideas off the ground, because otherwise we shall be not only defenceless against the bureaucratic juggernaut but soon as obsolescent as the dinosaur.

How much money is required depends on the enterprise. Any civic society or amenity group is far more effective if one of its supporters is a business man who can get things typed by his secretary or copied on the firm's Xerox. Postage, telephone calls, journeys to London to see MPs or civil servants, all cost money, and unless there are some people who do not need to count the cost very carefully, the first, critical, stages of launching a new idea will never be undertaken. Of course, at a later stage, a large number of subscriptions will more than make up for the absence of individually large subscribers – the trade unions now are not hamstrung by poverty – but this is only at a later stage. It is difficult and expensive to attract a large number of subscribers, especially if they are all equally poor and equally tight for money. The number of people anyone is likely to know in the normal course of events is limited. If some circles of acquaintanceship include one or two people who can easily part with £100, they can start a campaign for – say – enabling mothers of young children to stay with them in hospital: if the maximum possible subscription is £1, very few people know enough people well enough to touch them for £1 at the outset of a campaign which has yet to impinge on the public consciousness or prove itself as a practicable project. So too on a much larger scale, rich men are useful to have around, because they are easier to persuade to back their fancy than cautious committees or government officials. In a very different way, rich men are useful in politics, because they can afford to ignore financial inducements and will not be beholden to campaign contributors. Kennedy did not need to cheat the income tax.

Status is as important as money, and although in recent years egalitarians seem to have been less worried by social than by economic inequalities, the cases are very comparable, and the argument from the need to preserve private initiatives requires not only that there should be concentrations of economic power under the control of private individuals rather than the state, but that not every individual voice raised in protest will be disregarded. If I may be forgiven for lapsing into autobiography, let me cite an instance when I was fighting a motor manufacturer about the exclusion clauses in their guarantees, and my being an Oxford don was of crucial importance in securing the attention of a shareholders' meeting for two decisive minutes. In a finite world we cannot expect people to give adequate attention to everyone, and if everyone is to have equal attention then all will be equally ignored. Freedom of speech generates a lot of 'noise' which may well drown the significant signals unless we have some pre-set filtering devices. Many of our social institutions have the important function of telling the world at large who it is they ought to listen to. What is a university degree but this? The university certifies to all those it may concern that Mr John Smith has shown himself capable of thinking for himself, and that his opinions therefore should be treated, if not with deference, at least with some respect. If you opine that I have got myxomatosis, it will not give me pause to think, but if a doctor does, I shall act on it at once.

In a world of imperfect information we cannot take everyone for what he is really worth, and since it would be unwise to take everyone at face value, we are bound to rely on distinctions to enable us to discriminate between one man's judgement and another's, which therefore are inherently inegalitarian. It is as foolish to lament this fact as it is to worship it. If, in the name of equality, we attempt to disallow all social distinctions, we prevent people from making up their minds for themselves, and leave them all prey to the manipulators of the admass society. Better an inequality between doctors and the medically unqualified than that we should all be taken in by a plausible charlatan. But, much as we may be tempted to worship degrees or qualifications or titles or membership of select bodies, it is wrong to attach over-much importance to them. They are useful and necessary when introductions are being made, but ought not to be conclusive as to the final judgements we make. Some quacks are better than many doctors, and many of the world's most original thinkers have never held a university degree. It is always possible that, despite first appearances, the unqualified man has a sounder judgement than the expert, and the ill-bred a finer sense of what is fitting than the expensively educated. Examples abound. Snobbery is the vice that denies the possibility, and mistakes the outward appearances for the underlying fact. If we are not to be snobs, we must retain a lively appreciation that customary social distinctions may prove in any individual case utterly misleading, and be always ready to be guided by what we have discovered the individual to be really like. But in the rush of ordinary life we shall go on having to make snap judgements about people we do not really know, and must rely on socially established criteria. When the garage attendant tells me he has discovered a practicable way of obtaining energy from nuclear fusion, I shall continue to be much less interested than if a professor of physics had said the same.

We need inequality because we are limited beings only imperfectly informed. If I were God, and could look into each man's heart, I could respond to him fully and totally as the person he was: but since I am only a man, I can know only the outer man, and must of necessity judge by appearances. It makes a great difference if the man at the door is a doctor, a colleague, a former pupil, a business man or an itinerant salesman. In a very small society where everyone knows everybody else, we know who each man is, what role he plays, and therefore what response is appropriate on our part. But we do not – cannot – live all our lives within the confines of a face-to-face society, and are constantly seeking for clues to enable us to address ourselves appropriately to strangers. How many young men on seeing a pretty girl glance at the fourth finger of her left hand to see whether they should be merely chivalrous or should risk rebuff by being something more? We depend very much on various signs – in Britain very largely on accent – to indicate what the basis of social interchange is. Am I supposed to be driving a bargain with him? Or if I do not look after my own interests, can I be sure that he will not take advantage of me? The old school tie, the Oxford turn of phrase, the cavalry moustache – all play their part in informing strangers about what they may expect. As fast as one indicator is aped or falls out of fashion, another is seized upon to give us the guidance we need for the ordinary purposes of social life.

Egalitarians find all such distinctions offensive; and often, indeed, they have their offensive features. But egalitarians fail to recognise the deep social needs that give rise to such distinctions – our need to classify people in order that we may know what to expect from them and how far it is safe to relax our guard against them. Take away all outward and visible signs of friendliness and trustworthiness, and everyone will be treated as a debt-collector or high-pressure salesman. The effect of egalitarian principles is to ensure that each man is treated as every man's enemy.

Class distinctions enable a man to know where he stands. He may be better off with that knowledge – even though he stands in a low position according to most people's estimation – than without it. It depends largely on how other people treat him in the light of that knowledge. If, knowing that he is poor they are the readier to purchase his services for money, he is better off; if, knowing that he is weak, they are the readier to trample on him and use him discourteously, he is worse off. Too often today, it is the latter response that is evoked, but it does not have to be like that. We often take the offensive because of what we fear rather than because we are sure we can get away with it, and in some cultures men – like many other animals, according to the ethologists – reserve their enmity for their equals, and are remarkably forbearing to those evidently weaker than themselves.

8

We return to morality. It is forbearance and consideration of others that we want – not necessarily equal consideration, but consideration suited to the circumstances. The virtue of visible distinctions is that by indicating the sort of consideration that is appropriate they encourage us to give it. We cannot extend maximal consideration uniformly to everyone. If we are all equal, we are all competitors, since each of us, not being ready to merge his identity in Plato's ideal society, knows that sometimes he is seeking his good in rivalry with others. Few men feel willing – or can afford – to be always uncompetitive.

If only equal consideration is to be extended to everyone, then everyone must be treated equally guardedly, and there will be no occasions on which it would be reasonable to go the second mile or give the other man the best of the bargain. De Tocqueville ascribed the acquisitiveness he noted in America to the egalitarian tenor of American society; and the connection is due in part to the way in which egalitarian assumptions structure men's concepts, so as to foreclose the possibility of one's sometimes having special obligations to extend extra consideration. *Noblesse oblige* does not flourish in a climate of egalitarianism. And whatever we may think of the *noblesse*, we can ill afford to dispense with the *oblige*.

Noblesse is, in fact, inevitable. The social advantages of inequality are so great that, however equal we try to make society in some respects, there are bound to be other respects, if not money then power or prestige, in which some people are markedly better off than others. If we will admit this, we can control it. We can take steps to prevent classifications being unjust or irrelevant, or becoming obsolete, and we can encourage those who enjoy advantages to take on corresponding responsibilities. We can ensure that degrees are not awarded on a basis of self-assessment or replaced by a form of self-advertisement, and the Queen can ennoble trades union leaders and can confer knighthoods not only on rich businessmen as of yore but on those who have proved their prowess in the field of football battle. The egalitarian, because he will not allow the existence of inequalities, is unable to ameliorate them or make them work out for the benefit of all concerned. It is no accident that in societies supposedly imbued with egalitarian sentiment snobbery abounds and public relations men prosper.

Again, if we acknowledge the fact of inequality, we can adjure people to accept an inequality of obligation too. Our society is one that in fact confers great privileges on many men – perhaps deserved, but great all the same. Trades union officials, civil servants, chartered accountants, university graduates and all those in receipt of grants for higher education are very well done by, and do very well in consequence. But the fact and its concomitant obligations are not readily recognised. Pupils are surprised when I point out that a degree now is in effect a patent of nobility. The protagonists of the student movement were unable to see that *because* they were given advantages denied to other people, *therefore* their responsibilities were correspondingly different; and the reason why they were unable to see this was that they were so deeply imbued with the belief that privilege was wrong that they could not really accept the fact that they themselves were privileged, or that their being privileged could be a ground of obligation. Egalitarianism induces blindness. It not only leads us to avert our gaze from those inequalities not currently under attack, but it makes us unready to recognise in our own case benefits which perhaps, if egalitarian arguments were valid, we ought not to receive, but which, as a matter of fact, we do receive and enjoy. The rich egalitarian agrees that riches are wrong, and that the whole system ought to be changed; but meanwhile he remains rich, and he is tempted, having decided against riches in principle, not to allow the fact of his still being rich to enter into his moral reckoning. Moral reasoning is best based on facts as they are: and if, for whatever reason, there are in fact significant inequalities in our society, it is well that those who benefit most should operate with a scheme of thought which enables them to come to terms with the facts and recognise the responsibilities they engender.

Many egalitarians take a high moral line, and tell me not to set my heart on mere monetary values. Of course they are right. There are greater things in life than money, and I ought not to be too much concerned with what I earn. But nor should they. The argument cuts both ways. If I ought not to be greedy, they ought not to be envious; and if I should school myself to labour and not to hope for an additional reward, they should practise being pleased at my good fortune when I prosper, rather than belly-aching at my having done better than they. More precisely, we should distinguish two sorts of moral argument. Some are counsels of perfection, concerned largely with motives, and must be adopted whole-heartedly if they are to be acted on at all: others are binding requirements, concerned primarily with behaviour, and are better done grudgingly or for the wrong reasons than not done at all.

High-mindedness about money or any other material good falls into the former class. It may be right for me to renounce worldly possessions and devote myself to contemplation or the service of the poor: but only if I am sure that it is the thing for me, which I gladly embrace for myself and without repining. It is not for me to tell you to do it, nor for you to tell me, and it is not much good my doing it and then continuing to read the *Financial Times* and dream of dinners at the Ritz. When it comes to paying my debts, however, or giving my employees a just wage, the case is reversed. This is something you can tell me to do, and it is far better that I should do it for the wrong reasons than that I should not do it at all. If the wrongfulness of riches is urged in the former sense, there is much truth in what is said, but in the nature of the case it cannot be urged or insisted upon. If the rich young man responds like St Francis, well and good: but if he goes away sorrowful we must let him go, and cannot take it upon ourselves to remedy the one remaining thing he still lacks by relieving him of his possessions ourselves. If the latter sense is intended, then, were the wrongfulness of riches once established, it would be right to press for action; but it cannot be established. Ill-gotten gains are wrong, but it is a truism that not all gains are ill-gotten. The institution of money is defined by rules, which can be obeyed and if obeyed legitimise the acquisition of money obtained in accordance with them. Some people may have acted illegally or unjustly, and then remedial action may be called for. But it always remains possible that some have not so misbehaved, and the bare fact of having more than other people cannot of itself show that they have acquired it wrongly or ought to be deprived of it.

The argument from morality only appears to work in virtue of a confusion in modes of moral discourse. Arguments from morality can be relevant in politics, but they need to be rational arguments put forward in a dispassionate tone of voice. On a rational dispassionate view, wealth, like pleasure or power or fame, is to be seen not, indeed, as the *summum bonum*, but as a good which men often seek, and at least sometimes legitimately, and sometimes to the general benefit of society. Millionaires are like marquesses: one wants them to exist, although not to be one oneself.

Equality is the idol of the present age and, like all idols, illusory. Although it is a great thing to enjoy the company of one's equals, and although under some conditions some equalities are feasible, and well worth our striving to establish them, equality as a general goal of political endeavour is impossible to achieve, and in any case undesirable. Worse than this, the effort to establish equality everywhere has diverted the energies of many good men from more worthwhile endeavours. Because they have confused equality with humanity or with justice or with equity, men have thought that in endeavouring to establish equality they were ensuring that these other goods would be enjoyed by everyone, and have therefore been blind to the subtle ways in which our society has come to care less for men's humanity, has been less sensitive to considerations of justice, and has been more ready to countenance iniquity. Why is it that over the last thirty years our society has become more uncaring, more impersonal, more brutal? Other factors, no doubt, are also responsible, but one is our obsession with equality. It has blunted our perceptions and diverted our efforts. Instead of considering each man in his own individuality, equality has encouraged us to consider people in the mass, and in regard to those facets of their lives that can most readily be quantified and compared. If we had laboured to secure justice or humanity with half the zeal with which we have secured the more jealous god of equality, things might not have come to their present sorry pass.

3

The idea of equality as a substantive principle of society

JOHN CHARVET

≠

I AM concerned here with the idea that a principle of equality must constitute the basis of any good, just, or fully human society. A principle of equality as the basis of such a society could, however, be largely formal. It could be the principle which states that equals should be treated equally, from which it follows that unequals should be treated unequally, and this is formal because it doesn't of itself tell us how any of the particular members of a society should be treated; we first have to identify in what respects anybody is to be counted as equal to anybody else before we can say anything about how they should be treated. Such a formal basic principle of society would thus be a relatively trivial and uninteresting affair. What I am interested in is the possibility that there could be a substantive principle of equality – a principle which of itself could tell us how the particular members of a society should be treated: namely all should be treated equally.

1. A principle which tells us that all members of a society ought to be treated equally could only arrive at its conclusion

First published in *Political Studies*, Vol. 17, No. 1 (1969), pp. 1–13.

For References, see page 384 below.

that this is what ought to be done, if in the premises of the argument there is some statement about the actual equality of these men. In the arguments that I shall consider, however, it is not supposed that men are equal in such matters as their physical and mental qualities. The respect in which men are said to be equal is sometimes put in the form of an assumed actual natural equality, by which is meant that no man can naturally claim any kind of authority over any other men. In respect of authority all men are naturally equal.

The classical argument for this position, as it is found in the books of the modern political philosophers from Hobbes, proceeds by initially removing men hypothetically from all social relations, and putting them into the so-called 'state of nature'. They then assert that men in such a state must be supposed to be free and equal. And this I take to mean the following: if, having put men hypothetically in such a state, one asks: 'In virtue of what could one man claim to exercise authority over any other man?', the answer must be: in virtue of nothing whatever. In such a state nothing could count as a valid ground for one man to claim such authority. Now this is true because the hypothesis has removed the conditions in which the exercise of authority by one man over others makes sense. That is, authority only makes sense, in the context of social relations and human practices and activities, where some men, on the basis of the possession of attributes or qualities considered relevant to the carrying on of such practices and activities, can legitimately claim a superior position over others; so if one removes this context one necessarily removes the conditions in which one can talk meaningfully about authority. And so they conclude that all men are naturally in a state of equal authority towards each other, which is to say that no authoritative relations exist naturally between men.

In the beginning this argument was directed towards politically authoritative positions and concluded from its premises that political superiority, since it could not exist naturally, could only exist with the consent of all the members of society, but also that, since each man is naturally his own master – lord of himself and subject to no other – such men could only enter society on equal terms. The condition for membership of the society must be the same for all. Thus at the basis of society is an initial principle of equality that appears to be of a substantive nature. While this argument was at first directed towards political authority, it naturally leads to a more general attitude towards superior positions and the construction of a derivative principle: namely, the principle of equality of opportunity. For if one begins with the premise that no man can naturally claim a superior position over others, and yet recognises both that human abilities vary and that for human activities and practices to be carried on, superior positions will be necessary or beneficial, then one will conclude that the opportunity to attain such positions must be open equally to all. That is, that the legitimate title to the occupation of such positions must be merit alone: the possession of the natural abilities considered relevant to the carrying on of the required activities. And since the fact of possessing a pedigree of a certain kind or money of a certain amount cannot of itself give one these abilities, to admit this as a legitimate basis for a claim to exercise authority over others would be to admit that, independently of any specific activities or relations, some people had a legitimate claim to exercise authority over others, and this would be to admit something inconsistent with the premises.

Now, the principle of equality of opportunity as derived above from an initial principle of equality, together with assumptions about the desirability of differentiated positions, is also a substantive principle of society, for it specifies in what ways opportunities to attain superior positions are to be allocated between the members of society: namely, equally to all. But there is something wrong with the above argument which arises out of the initial hypothesis of a state of nature. For it is difficult to see what sense can be attached to talk about individuals in a state of nature as human beings at all, i.e., as beings possessing the attributes of humanity. We are inclined to think of humanity as essentially social, as only developing in a social context, and not possessable by individuals independently of their having entered into social relations. If this were the case, to talk about beings in a non-social state could have no relevance at all to a different type of being existing in a social condition.

However, in his article 'Justice as Fairness',[1] Rawls has attempted to reformulate the classical argument while removing the difficulty of the initial hypothesis of a state of nature. Rawls's argument is the following: instead of a state of nature we begin by assuming a number of mutually self-interested men already engaged in a well-established system of practices. From time to time individuals engaged in the practice may be expected to make complaints that they are being treated unjustly. We may then suppose that the participants in the practice discuss among themselves on what principles such complaints are to be adjudicated. Rawls asks us to imagine that they adopt the following procedure: each man is asked to propose the principles on which he would like his complaints to be judged, and that no complaints will be tried until everyone agrees on the principles by which the complaints are to be judged. It is further understood that the principles once accepted will be binding on all future occasions so that a man will not be inclined to propose principles to his immediate advantage when on future unknown occasions they may work to his disadvantage. One would expect such men, Rawls says, to agree on certain general principles which each man sees as a guarantee that his present and future interests will be protected. Now Rawls also assumes that (*a*) all participants are roughly equal in power and ability, so that no one can of himself dominate the others and (*b*) no one knows what his future position in the practice will be. Given all this, Rawls says, his men will naturally agree on equality as an initial principle – that is, that the advantages of the practice should be distributed equally. This will be so because each man, wishing to protect his interests and not knowing what his future condition will be, can only acknowledge equality as such a guarantee. But equality is only an initial principle, and assuming them to be reasonable men, they will accept that departures from such an initial position may be justified, in the sense of being beneficial to all. Departures in the direction of unequal positions will then be accepted, provided that all gain from them, and that such positions will then be accepted, provided that all gain from them, and that such positions are open to all to attain. On this argument, then, we have as an initial substantive principle of a just practice – or of a just society seen as a system of practices – equality; and equality of opportunity as a secondary derivative principle. Both these principles, however, may be over-ridden by a superior consideration, which is that departure from them makes *everybody* in the practice better off.

2. Before examining the validity of this reformulation of the classical position, I shall consider the notion of equality of opportunity as a substantive principle, for I think it can easily be seen that this notion ends in absurdity. But since it is logically derived from the initial principle of equality together with an assumption that unequal positions in human practices will be necessary and beneficial, then it would follow that either this assumption is wrong, which seems implausible, or the principle of equality, as we have it in the above arguments, must be false.

If one starts by considering the opportunity to attain superior positions in adult practices, one is rapidly led backwards into arguing that the opportunity to obtain the education that will enable one to claim superior positions should be equal for all. But one can't stop at schools, for the development of one's abilities doesn't begin there, but in the family, where being brought up by certain parents will give one an initial start over one's contemporaries less favoured in their parents. But entrance into more favoured families is not carried out on basis of merit, but on the arbitrary practice of mere birth. This, however, can be remedied by removing children from families altogether and bringing them up in State nurseries. But at this point I can couch the argument in more general terms. The principle of equality of opportunity requires that, in the development of one's natural abilities, one should not be put in an advantageous or disadvantageous position with regard to one's competitors as the result of an association with other human beings who help and encourage one to develop. Parents, teachers, friends, etc., all help or hinder one's development, and having access to those who help rather than hinder, or help more or hinder less, gives one an unfair advantage, unless the access itself is awarded on merit. But since it is absurd to suppose that one could control access adequately in this way, the only two other possibilities are: that all those through associating with whom individuals develop themselves should be equal in their capacities to help such development; or that there should be no such association at all. And both these are absurd fantasies. What I am saying is this: the principle of equality of opportunity requires that in the successful development of oneself no one should be dependent on any other human being or human practice unless this dependence is equal for all; but since it is accepted that men's abilities and capacities vary, the condition for the satisfaction of this requirement is that no one should be dependent on anyone else, and the condition of no dependence between men is that of having no society at all, and so no men.

However, it might be said that Rawls's argument doesn't require that equality of opportunity should be realised in all cases for it may be over-ruled by a higher consideration: namely, that all gain from not having equality of opportunity in particular cases. But this argument supposes that equality of opportunity in itself is a good, although it may be over-ruled by a higher good – everybody being better off. And this must be the case if equality of opportunity is to be a principle at all. But what I'm saying is that as a principle it cannot be satisfactorily formulated, i.e., formulated without incoherence or contradiction. For a complete formulation of it renders it incompatible with any form of human society, while it is being put forward as a principle of a good human society. To say: 'But we can use it without contradiction in specific areas such as entry into the civil service or education', begs the question: 'Use what?' For if you are using the principle of equality of opportunity then you are using an incoherent notion, but that you can talk sensibly and be understood in specific areas is because you need not be said to be using this principle at all, but applying the formal principle of equality – that equals should be treated equally – and providing reasons for thinking that certain distinctions hitherto made, class or money, etc., should not now be taken as constituting inequalities relevant to treating equals equally in such and such an area of human activity.

Now if the idea of equality of opportunity as a substantive principle of the just society is false, and it is logically derived, together with the reasonable assumption that human practices require superior positions, from the principle of equality, as we so far have it, then there must be something wrong with this principle of equality. What was wrong with the classical argument for equality was that it purported to be talking significantly about the human condition, while removing the context in which any such talk could be meaningful. And in fact these writers only achieve what appears to be relevant because, while removing man's social context, they leave him with attributes which he could only have developed in such a context.

3. However, the reformulation of this position by Rawls is in no better state. For, although he assumes his men to be engaged in a well-established system of human practices, and thus can legitimately allow them human attributes, he makes two further assumptions necessary for his argument which are incompatible with his initial assumption – namely, that his men are roughly equal in power and ability, and that no one knows what his future position in the practice will be. To make these two further assumptions is merely to reintroduce the state of nature by the back door. For in so far as his men are engaged in a well-established practice they will necessarily be occupying certain present positions within the practice, and have legitimate expectations as to what their future positions will be. If this were not so they could hardly be said to be engaging in a practice at all. But if they occupy such positions then some will have more power and authority within the system than others, and indeed have more or less definite future expectations of its continuity or acquisition. Such men cannot then be said to be equal in respect of power, ability and future expectations. If they are then asked to debate on what general principles claims of injustice within the system are to be adjudicated, there is no reason to suppose that they would all agree on an initial principle of equality. For at least some have established positions of authority which get their legitimacy from the accepted purposes and standards of the practice together with their possession of the required attributes for the occupation of such roles. For them to agree to

accept equality as an initial principle would be for them to agree to a principle that has no conceivable relevance to their position. Rawls wants to say that all will accept equality as a guarantee against being done down by the others, since no one knows what his future position will be. But since this cannot be true, equality cannot serve as a guarantee to those with established positions and expectations. Rawls's argument would only be true if his men engaged in the practice do not have established positions in the practice and so consequently are not engaged in the practice at all. It follows, therefore, that equality could only make sense as a principle to those in inferior positions who want to destroy the superior positions of others; and if this is all that is going on, it deserves not the slightest attention.

So Rawls's argument is merely a restatement of the classical position and rests on the validity of its starting point – a state of nature in which something significant claims to be being said about men, who have no social relations of any kind. And if the derivative principle of equality of opportunity is self-contradictory, it is because the initial principle of equality from which it is derived is self-contradictory also. For it asserts, as a basic principle to govern men's social relations, a principle which only makes sense in a condition in which men have no social relations. The contradiction within the notion of equality and its related principle, equality of opportunity, can be further brought out by considering the egalitarian argument in the more complex for that it has in the writings of J.-J. Rousseau.

4. Rousseau starts off with the traditional rigmarole about the state of nature, in which individuals possessing human attributes pursue their lives independently of each other, and so independently of all social relations. These men, Rousseau argues, cannot be supposed to be corrupt or vicious, for corruption and viciousness between men can only exist in a social context. He then provides an argument to show how with the emergence of social relations corruption accompanies it. The argument is this: in a state of nature men are conscious only of themselves and not of other human beings; they

consequently cannot compare themselves with others to see whether they are more beautiful, stronger, more able, etc. etc., than others. Once social relations develop, however, men become conscious of others as well as of themselves; but at the same time social relations only develop once men start carrying on common activities together. But carrying on common activities – such as hunting, dancing or whatever – involves standards of performance in terms of which some people can be judged superior to others. Now, since men have become conscious of others, they become conscious of themselves as occupying certain positions in relation to others through the activities they carry on together. Some men are respected more than others, and men begin to desire to achieve positions of superiority for the respect that is carried with them in the eyes of others. They then come to be concerned with the opinions that others have of them, and wish to wrest from others those opinions that most flatter them. Thus they learn to appear what they are not; deceit and lying emerge, together with pride, vanity contempt, vengeance, etc. etc. Men have become corrupt, and are henceforth involved in a struggle for power or superiority.

Now, the essence of what has gone wrong is that men have become dependent on each other by becoming dependent for their own self-respect on the opinions that others have of them. They cannot do without others, for only others can make the judgements which will provide them with the self-respect they need; and yet at the same time others constitute threats to them, because others can withhold the judgements they look for or give judgements that cannot possibly satisfy. In these circumstances individuals are left in a perpetual state of unease and restlessness, out of harmony with themselves and others, alienated; they haven't a chance of achieving happiness. If, however, this condition of humanity is to be altered, the remedy must strike at the roots of the evil: namely, at the very dependence of men on each other. One must create a form of society in which no one is dependent on any other man.

The concern for the respect of others Rousseau calls *amour propre,* which we see emerges only in a social condition. However, the *amour propre* of a man, Rousseau says, leads him to desire first place for himself – to be superior to others. But since all men desire this, and since not all can by definition be satisfied, it results in a perpetual struggle and conflict between men. In these circumstances, Rousseau says, the condition of a good society is that the *amour propre* in men be destroyed or at least suppressed, and this can be done if they substitute a demand for equality in the place of the demand for superiority. Now this is fair as equality acts as a guarantee that no one will suffer from its realisation, i.e., no one will be made inferior to any other. This equality resolves at the same time the problem of the dependence of men on each other, or the living in the opinions of others, which is the root of the problem. For equality necessarily destroys the conditions – i.e., inequality – in which the *amour propre* of a man can get a grip in his relations to others. *Amour propre* can begin to emerge and wreak its havoc only if the conditions exist in which some people can achieve superiority over others. And if *amour propre* cannot get a grip on a man's activities, then there is no scope for him to be concerned with the opinions or judgement of others, and so no possibility of his achieving or not achieving the respect of others. Thus equality, in constituting the condition which suppresses *amour propre,* constitutes also the condition which destroys the dependence of men on each other, and thus all the evils of the human situation. Man ceases to be corrupt, alienated, unhappy.

However, all this is of course an absurdity, for it involves, as the condition of the good, just or fully human society, the suppression of that element in man – namely, his *amour propre* or desire for the respect of others and of himself – which constitutes his specifically human characteristic, and requires, as the condition for the overcoming of man's alienation, the total alienation of his humanity. For, as Rousseau has shown, human society emerges only with the emergence of activities that men carry on together, which involve standards of performance and so inequalities of performance. Thus, given that men are conscious both of themselves and others, and thus of themselves in relation to others, the condition of a human society is also the condition for the existence of *amour propre* or the concern for the respect of others and of oneself in relation to others. So men in so far as they are human are necessarily dependent on each other in the manner described, and

Rousseau's argument involves the establishment as a principle of a human society, a principle which makes human society impossible.

But having argued for equality as the solution to all human problems, Rousseau then admits that distinctions within society are both necessary and permissible, provided that individuals in attaining differentiated positions do not owe their positions, either superior or inferior, to the will of any other men. That is, if inequalities are to be permitted, they must not contradict the basic principle of society, namely the non-dependence of men on each other, and this can only be so if a man is not dependent for the position he occupies on the will of any other man. And this, as we have seen, is the essential implication of the principle of equality of opportunity – that in occupying a position of a certain sort, I must not owe it to the relations I may have had with any other man: i.e., the relations must be either equal for all non-existent. But this, as we have also seen, is a fantasy. Thus, if distinctions are admitted in society, then it will necessarily be the case that dependence of men on each other will have been recreated. Consequently the admission of distinctions and of equality of opportunity as a derivative principle must necessarily contradict the basic principle from which it is derived – equality as a condition of non-dependence. And that this is possible is because the basic principle itself is self-contradictory.

5. The Rousseauan argument introduces the notion of respect, and since then people have argued from a notion of equality of respect, which is owed to all men, to an egalitarian society. So I shall now consider this argument, and in the first place in relation to the form it has in an article by Bernard Williams, called 'The Idea of Equality'.[2] Williams's argument is as follows: men are beings with purposes and intentions, who are also conscious of these. Now, in judging a man, one may do so solely in terms of his public achievements: whether he is a good administrator or academic or whatever. But clearly one can also enter into a man's own attitude or consciousness of his life: i.e., see him not only from the

external point of view, but from the internal point of view, of how he himself sees his efforts and understands his activities and performances. To treat a man in a fully human way and with respect for him, Williams says, is to adopt this internal point of view, and all men are equally owed this effort of identification. But while at first sight nothing much seems to follow from this – i.e., it would appear compatible with an hierarchical society based on birth – Williams wants to say that, in following out its implications, one is led in the direction of an egalitarian society. The consciousness a man has of his role in society, Williams argues, is the product of that society itself, and can be increased or diminished by social action. Now, what keeps stable hierarchies together is a belief in the necessity of the social orders of the society. But this will involve false consciousness, for people will not be fully conscious of the roles they actually occupy in society, but see them in a false light. Now suppose that, while the lower orders retain their false consciousness, some members of upper orders come to a clearer and truer view of their roles: i.e., they no longer see them as necessary. Then, in order to preserve the society, it will be necessary to prevent the lower orders developing the awareness of their roles that would undermine the stability of the system. Consequently an element of conscious deceit enters the system, but also an element of contempt, as the upper orders will necessarily see the lower orders as self-deceived. These elements destroy the equality of respect that is required for a just society, and so the argument leads to a demand for a socially egalitarian society.

This argument, however, rests on two notions – the notion of seeing one's role as necessary, and the consciousness one may have of one's role – which are insufficiently explored by Williams. With regard to the former notion of seeing the structure of one's society as necessary, which involves false consciousness: what has to be the case is that the members of that society take what is their social structure to be what must be. But suppose they are not aware of any other possible social structure than their own. Now, the idea of their accepting the social structure as what must be, or as necessary, becomes problematical. For it is not clear what could be meant by this, other than merely repeating that they accept their social structure with no questions asked. But merely accepting something with no questions asked or doubts raised is different from believing it to be necessary, for the latter supposes that one raises the question as to alternatives and finds no answer. But then those who merely accept something cannot be said to possess false consciousness with regard to what they accept, because there cannot be anything false in merely accepting something. One is accepting it for what it is, not for what it is not. Furthermore, the notion of necessary is relative. Nothing is necessary in itself but always in relation to something else. So that to be aware of alternative forms of society, and still assert that one's own form is necessary, would only involve falseness, if what one was asserting was that of all the possible forms of society, this one is the only possible one: i.e., necessary for human beings – which would be like pointing to a tree and saying this is the only possible tree. Whereas what one could be asserting or believing is that one's form of society was the only possible good, just or fully human one, or necessary for *them*. This may, of course, involve false consciousness, but all I want to say is that the notion of necessary won't do the work for you, and that there could be hierarchical societies based on birth and accepted by all, either as necessary or not, without false consciousness, and so without inequality of respect.

6. What is needed to get from false consciousness to egalitarianism is a much stronger notion of false consciousness. Now, false consciousness is concerned with the way in which one identifies oneself in relation to other people; and self-identification here means identifying the capacity in which one wishes to be recognised and respected by others. What I now propose to do is to consider three general ways in which a man might identify himself, and see how these might be related to the notion of false consciousness.

(1) The first case is of a man who doesn't identify himself as an individual at all, but as a mere cog in a machine, as it were – a member of an organic body that has no existence apart from the body. Now, this as it stands is incoherent, because such a man could not be said to identify himself in any way

whatsoever. For identifying oneself involves identifying oneself as an individual. So if this is going to be a possible case, one has to say that, while he is capable of seeing himself as an individual, he persists in talking and acting as though he were not. Now this would be a clear case of false consciousness because one is saying both that he has the consciousness of himself as an individual and yet refuses to recognise it.

(2) The second case is of a man who identifies himself satisfactorily as an individual, but as an individual whose identity consists in occupying a certain role in society. He is an individual peasant who never thinks of himself outside his role of being a peasant.

(3) The third case is of a man who stands back from his role and thinks of himself as someone: an individual who could be or could have been any number of things, and who merely happens to be a peasant. He doesn't identify himself with any particular role, but as a man apart from any role.

Now, if the third case is to be taken as the standard of true consciousness then the second case will have to be considered a case of false consciousness. For the peasant in the second case clearly could see himself in the manner of the third case, but refuses to do so. And it would follow from this that a social structure which prevented or discouraged individuals from identifying themselves properly as men would thereby be deficient, and if we take hierarchical societies as typically producing men of the second type of consciousness, this will constitute an argument against hierarchical societies and for egalitarian ones. So what we have to consider is whether case (3) can meaningfully be taken as the standard of true consciousness.

To decide this, consider the case (4) of a man who, while occupying a certain role, realises that he has abilities which cannot be satisfied in his existing role, and consequently feels frustrated. Such a man would, of course, no longer be a clear case of the second type, for he would no longer identify himself with his role of being a peasant, but as someone with abilities and ambitions to occupy another role. He stands back to a certain extent from his role and considers himself apart from it. Nevertheless he is not a case of the third type, for it would not follow, if this man's consciousness of himself is taken as the standard, that case (2) is suffering from false consciousness. Case (4) differs from case (2) in that he has good grounds for thinking he has abilities that could be better realised in another role, while case (2) entertains no such thought. So that, unless one were to say *a priori* that everyone has good grounds for thinking in this way, case (2) cannot be represented as suffering from false consciousness in relation to case (4). And no such assertion could be made.

So what one needs to arrive at case (3) is the notion of a man who identifies himself as a man apart from any role or any particular abilities he may have to occupy a role. In so far as self-identification is identifying the capacity in which one wishes to be recognised and respected by others, this man then desires to be identified and respected as a man and not as a role-occupier. But what would it involve to be identified and respected as a man? Clearly in the first place this would involve being recognised as a member of the species man possessing the attributes of humanity, a language speaker, who is conscious of himself and a free agent.

Now, being a free agent is what one is potentially in being a member of the species man, but not what one is necessarily, for one may refuse to recognise it or identify oneself in this respect, and this would be a variant of case (1) above – a case of false consciousness. Being a free agent, then, or being a man or human being in the sense of realising or actualising in oneself the attributes of humanity, can be seen as achieving a certain performance, which indeed all men are capable of and most men achieve to some degree. To be identified and respected as a man is to be identified and respected in one's capacity as individual free agent. But what is it to respect a man in this capacity? The answer to this lies in the notion of self-respect. For self-respect is that without which a man hasn't a chance of performing anything adequately except evil, for its loss or absence involves the loss or absence of the belief that one has the potentiality for a certain performance; and thus in the extreme case, where it is lost in relation to everything, it is the abandonment of one's humanity – one's capacity for action. To respect a man, then, in this fundamental way of respecting him in his capacity as free agent, is so to behave towards him as to help him maintain his self-respect; while not to respect him can be either to behave towards him in such a way as to try and destroy his self-respect (to beat him down, make him feel nothing, a mere worm) or (what is the more dominant mode of not respecting a man) blandly to ignore the demands of his self-respect, as though there were none – which is to ignore his humanity. But not all men can equally be given this respect, only all men in so far as they possess self-respect to some degree. For to him who possesses none, none can be given – it would be a mere meaningless gesture, for there would be nothing in him for your respect to maintain; it would be respecting him for something that he isn't. One cannot respect a child of a certain age.

If being identified and respected as a man is being identified and respected as a free agent, nevertheless free agency is not an activity on its own separable from other activities such as being an engineer, or civil servant, citizen or husband, for it clearly enters into one's performance of these roles and could only be exercised in some such specific context. Nor could one be said to be performing such roles or carrying out such activities without the activity of being a free agent. And even if one were to say free agency is primarily connected with morality or being a good man, or achieving the virtues of humanity, it is not the case either that being a good man is an activity separate from and of the same nature as the performance of specific roles mentioned above. For just as free agency enters into one's specific activities, so the activity of being a good man consists in the manner in which one carries on one's specific roles. It is to do with the relations one achieves – relations of justice, generosity, magnanimity, etc. – with those with whom one is connected through the specific roles one occupies. Thus roles and the performance of roles are a fundamental part of the human and moral world, for it is only through specific activities and relations that the activity of being a good man can be realised at all, and thus that the respect of others and of oneself can be acquired.

But then the activity of being a man or free agent and the activity of being a role-occupier of a certain sort, while different activities are nevertheless necessarily related, so that being identified and respected as a man is not something that can be categorically opposed to being identified and respected as a role-occupier of a certain sort. One does not have to stand back from one's role and identify oneself as a man apart from one's role, for all one need do is identify oneself as a man *in* one's role or roles. But then case (2) above – the man who identifies himself as a peasant and doesn't think of himself outside his role – cannot be represented as a case of false consciousness, for identifying himself as a man *in* his role is what he is perfectly capable of doing. To be a free agent is not to choose in conditions where no restrictions or dependencies exist; it is merely to act and have the courage of acting, i.e. accepting responsibility for what one is doing. But action always takes place in a specific context, and a specific context is always one full of limitations and dependencies. To see roles as restrictions on our humanity is to see what is a necessary condition of our humanity as an impediment to it. To assert case (3) above as the standard of true consciousness that a man may have of himself is to be involved in such an incoherence. For the condition of its being realised is that one does not identify with any role. Now one may still have a role, but not identifying with the role means not accepting the standards and purposes of the role as relevant criteria for judging one's life-activity, one's performances, one's being anything at all. And this means that, in so far as one carries on the role, one carries it on without reference to those aspects of it which alone can make the activity meaningful – its standards, purposes, etc. That is to say, while carrying on the role in some minimal sense, one is thoroughly alienated from it. But to lose the meaningfulness of roles is to lose the foundations of human and moral world.

Now, if this is the standard of true consciousness, those poor unfortunate persons who still identify with their roles will appear as retarded in their degree of self-conscious humanity. To raise them then to the highest standards of humanity, equality might be seen as a necessary condition. For equality as a basic and substantive principle of society destroys all traditional roles and equally alienates everybody. But now we have as the condition in which everyone can equally be respected – as a man without arrest or restriction – a condition in which all are equally alienated from the circumstances in which anyone can be respected. Once again, we have as a principle to govern a truly human society a principle which makes human society impossible.

As with other attempts to make of equality a substantive principle of society, equality of respect as a condition of the good, just or fully human society is incoherent and self contradictory, for it is only through the existence of common activities and practices, and so of roles, that a human society comes into being at all, and the species man acquires the attributes of humanity.

That throughout this argument the various forms of egalitarianism that I have considered have turned out to be self-contradictory should not be surprising. For the whole direction of egalitarianism's effort, as is clear from its origins in those totally alienated men – the free and equal men of the state of nature – has been an attempt to conceive of a man's existence as a man apart from his existing under the necessary restrictions, limitations and dependencies involved in being a member of a human society, and consequently in being a member of the human race.

4

The pursuit of equality

ROBERT NISBET

≠

IT is evident that, barring major physical catastrophe, war or some other massive cause of deflection of current social interests, the idea of equality will be sovereign for the rest of this century in just about all circles concerned with the philosophical bases of public policy. One would have to go back to certain other ages in history to find a unifying theme among intellectuals possessed of the intensity and universality we find today with respect to equality. In the past, unifying ideas tended to be religious in substance. There are certainly signs that equality is taking on a sacred aspect among many minds today, that it is rapidly acquiring dogmatic status, at least among a great many philosophers and social scientists.

Equality has all the requisites for becoming a religious – a providential – idea in our affluent age. It is simple, at least in immediate conception; it is capable of extension or application to the whole of a population, even to all mankind; it can be made to seem the very purpose of modern social and political experience, indeed a purpose contained in the bone and marrow of Western history. Finally, there is in the idea of equality that essence of permanent revolution we find in so many religious values – at least those of universal religions such as Christianity, Islam and Buddhism at the moments of their founding – when they are counterposed to the traditions and laws surrounding them.

First published in *The Public Interest*, Vol. 35 (1974), 103–20.

For References, see page 384 below.

1. Equality, not freedom, is, as Tocqueville emphasised, the *vis creatrix* of most modern social movements. Even when freedom is extolled by such movements, it is characteristically freedom to have equal shares of something – usually political power, but also, increasingly, other social, cultural and intellectual goods. Certainly, this has been true in the West since the fateful writings of Rousseau. It is noteworthy that in our own time conceptions of freedom resting on autonomy, on personal and associational immunity from supposedly popular opinion, and on the capacity for creativeness, in whatever sphere, are being pushed aside more and more by conceptions in which freedom is little more than a total social experience in which all citizens are to have equal shares.

More than any other single value, equality is the mainspring of radicalism. No other value serves so efficiently in the work of distinguishing among the varied ideologies of the present and, for that matter, of the past couple of centuries. What one's attitude is toward equality in the whole complex of social, cultural and economic goods tells us almost perfectly whether one is radical, liberal or conservative. Preoccupation with equality has indeed been the constant mark of the radical in the West for a long time. The passion for equality, first vivid at the time of the Puritan Revolution, has been the essential mark of every major revolution in the West (with the possible and mixed exception of the American) and has carried with it, often in millennial degree, the urge among its more ardent votaries to undermine, topple and destroy wherever inequality can be found.

As Tocqueville noted, equality arouses passions, at least in modern times, denied even to freedom. In substantial part, this role of equality as a motivating value is the product of the growth of large populations; the erosion of local and regional boundaries which could once conceal inequalities, or render innocuous those that had been noticed; the rise of large, legally undiversified electoral masses; and, above all, a constantly accelerating political centralisation that, by its very nature, has dissolved ancient identities and made people increasingly aware of themselves as more or less identical units. There is nothing strange, really, in the ascendant place the value of equality has in our society. 'When inequality of conditions is the common law of society, the most marked inequalities do not strike the eye; when everything is nearly on the same level, the slightest are marked enough to hurt it. Hence the desire for equality always becomes more insatiable in proportion as equality is more complete.'

There is truth, of course, in Tocqueville's words. It is not certain though, exactly how far this truth applies in American society at the present time. That the desire for equality as keystone of national social policy is great, even insatiable, among substantial numbers of intellectuals is evident enough. But among the people at large? Individuals at all levels may at times burn with the sense of injustice, may feel and struggle against the sense of dispossession, may crave more than they have, but it is far from certain that a majority, if given the clear choice, would wish for a generalised policy of equality, whether of income or anything else. There is something, after all, that appeals to the imagination, to the risk-taking sensibility, to the ever present hope of 'hitting it big', in a non-equalitarian society where channels of mobility are at least reasonably open. Beyond this, hierarchy and inequality are key elements of the social bond. We become used to these elements in nearly all forms of association, starting with family. And there is, finally, the seemingly ineradicable American respect for merit, and for goods and statuses arrived at (or which appear to have been arrived at) through merit.

There is, in sum, undoubted truth in Tocqueville's words on the place of equality, as a value, in modern populations. It does indeed bulk large, especially during times of revolution or near-revolutionary crisis. And yet, the element of truth notwithstanding, it would be hard to validate the proposition in general terms through a polling of the American people today. All evidence suggests that a very large number of Americans are indifferent, if not actually hostile, to any idea for national social policy that has substantial equalitarianism behind it.

2. This fact, this seeming indifference among the multitudes regarding inequality as such, cannot fail to have much the same effect upon our contemporary lay priests of

equalitarianism that similar indifference among pagan multitudes regarding Christian values must have had upon early missionaries. If certain crucial practices are *not* regarded as sins, if indeed there is widespread stubbornness among people in this respect, and if there is a deeply rooted reluctance to accept the new god as the sole or sovereign god, then only steps of the most heroic nature can be usefully contemplated. Thought must be given to social surgery of the most radical kind. How will it otherwise be possible to penetrate to the innermost depths of moral belief and of social tradition?

Something of this is beginning to be realised by intellectuals today, and no doubt such realisation will spread widely among intellectuals during the years just ahead. Christopher Jencks, with a candor that is still somewhat rare, tells us in the final pages of his *Inequality*: 'The crucial problem today is that relatively few people view income inequality as a serious problem.' Precisely. Or any other kind of inequality. What is desired is not so much equality of any kind as freedom, whether individual or collective, to pursue chosen ends to the limit of capacity and desire. But such freedom, even when granted by law and convention to a degree not yet attained in America, will not satisfy our intellectuals, our priests in service to the god of equality. (God is not dead; God is Equality; and this is rapidly becoming as much the case within organised Christianity as it is among descendants of Rousseau and his fellow *philosophes*.) One remembers the hard-shelled missionary in Maugham's *Rain* saying of his South Sea parishioners: 'The trouble with these people is that they will not believe in sin even when it is shown to them.' So it is with Professor Jencks's parishioners, the hungry sheep for whom he has assumed responsibility. If we want substantial redistribution, Jencks writes (in a chapter reminiscently and excitingly titled 'What Is to Be Done?'): 'We will not only have to politicize the question of income inequality but alter people's basic assumptions about the extent to which they are responsible for their neighbors and their neighbors for them.' How true. So reflected St Paul, and after him a long succession of Christian missionaries, right down to the Berrigans. So reflected Rousseau, no Christian, but no less the messianic apostle of the only true good – which in his case, as in the case of our contemporary *hommes de zèle*, was equality, no less, no more.

The problem, though, is a formidable one: convincing a population against its conscious will that it is in fact living in immorality and injustice, that its true good lies elsewhere. Left to ordinary processes of decision – even (as Jencks has shown in some detail) when these processes are based upon free public education that is more or less constantly bombarded by the equalitarian views of intellectuals able to make their way to the fore – the people still cannot be counted on to adore equality as the first of the social virtues. Respect for equality before the law, yes, though with reservations and few illusions; and respect also for reasonable equality of opportunity in education and in getting jobs suited to one's talents and desires. But for the overwhelming majority, that is about it. On the evidence of polls and surveys there is little respect for the kind of equalitarianism that matters most to intellectuals: equalitarianism that would by design sweep away the built-in inequalities of family, of inheritance, of luck, and of individual ability and aptitude. To most people legitimate equality is epitomised by equality of *opportunity* for the great diversity of tastes, talents, strengths and aspirations to be found in a population. But to a rising number of intellectuals this is the worst kind of *inequality*, for it produces, it is said, a meritocracy, which is in its own way as evil as any of the historic forms of aristocratic privilege.

Majority will – the historic foundation of democracy – cannot, then, be counted on to inaugurate the régime of equality that is desired by intellectuals. Does this have implications for the future of democracy? May we look forward to the growth of a political theory that is rooted not in majority will but instead in virtue and justice (these terms meaning, for intellectuals, equality)? The politics of virtue, from Plato to Rousseau, has rarely coincided in the past with anything easily describable as democracy.

We shall see. Present disaffection with politics, spreading alienation from the ideal of the political community and its values, and widening rents in the social fabric might easily produce a situation within the near future whereby majority will would be jettisoned along with a few other historic marks of political democracy. True, in such circumstances it would by no means follow that power in the hands of equality-oriented intellectuals would result. It might be – and on the evidence of history probably would be – power of a very different sort: power that might use the rhetoric of equality as window-dressing, as Augustus, Torquemada, Napoleon and even Hitler did, but that would surely have its mind on something else. Still, hope springs eternal in the intellectual breast.

3. The recent work that can certainly be counted on to keep hope buoyant so far as realisation of the City of Equality is concerned is John Rawls's *A Theory of Justice*.[1] I do not recall in my lifetime a book in philosophy greeted with as much praise as has been accorded this book. On both sides of the Atlantic, Rawls (who is Professor of Philosophy at Harvard University and Chairman of the Department of Philosophy there) has been hailed as author of the greatest work in ethics since Sidgwick's *The Methods of Ethics*, certainly, and quite possibly since Kant's writings on moral theory. I rather imagine that among circles of professional, genuinely informed philosophers, much of this enthusiasm for the book will shortly wane. Although it is indubitably a learned work in its way, with incontestable evidences of the author's ingenuity of argument, second and more sober readings of the book will surely come up with judgements less rapturous than those I have seen by philosophers in, say, lead reviews in the *Times Literary Supplement* (London) and the *New York Times Book Review*. But such rumination here has to do only with appreciation of the book as the work of a philosopher. It has nothing to do with the kind of appreciation that will, I am convinced, remain unabated among equality-oriented intellectuals, among those for whom *A Theory of Justice* can be regarded as the long-awaited successor to Rousseau's *Social Contract*, and as the rock on which the Church of Equality can properly be founded in our time.*

---

* Professor Rawls declares that his book is grounded in Kant's moral theory. I understand I am not alone in being very skeptical of this. For every

The essential point is, I think, that there are really two books given us under the title of *A Theory of Justice.* One is by John Rawls, philosopher. The other is by John Rawls, *philosophe.* There is, as we know, a great difference between philosophers as such and *philosophes*. It is not necessary to idealise either group to say that, whereas philosophers have as their first and over-riding goal inquiry into the nature of things – of the good, the true, the beautiful – *philosophes* have as *their* goal radical critique of a social order united with a vision of social utopia. Admittedly, *philosophes* use the works and ideas of philosophy, but they use them as handmaidens in the work of outlining the City of God while destroying the City of Man. *Philosophes* may even resemble philosophers – just as philosophers may now and then indulge in *philosophe* activity. But the difference as is known to all intellectual historians, is very great. Whatever else the *philosophes* of the late eighteenth century in France were, they were not philosophers. To have been called philosophers would no doubt have seemed the unkindest cut of all to Rousseau, Diderot, Condorcet and the others. Merely read what Rousseau thought of the 'herds of textbook authors' in his day, or note the purposes of the *Encyclopédie*.

I do not for a moment dispute Professor Rawls's claim to be a philosopher or to have written a book in philosophy. I merely suggest, on the evidence of *A Theory of Justice*, that he is also a *philosophe*, with aims and interests which would have equipped him well for the salons of eighteenth-century Paris. We live, quite evidently, in an age of *philosophes*; they are as honored by our upper class as ever they were in the eighteenth century. *Philosophes* do not like revolutions any more than wars; too many things get broken or threatened. But they love dealing with issues likely to result in revolutions and wars – issues characterised by perceptions of crisis, by conflicts of mighty abstractions, and, above all, by indictments of society united with visions of utopia. To read *philosophes* is to read about a

---

teaspoon of Kant, my own reading suggests, there are whole cupfuls of Rousseau. Strangely, though, little is said of Rousseau in *A Theory of Justice*, even though one might infer a great deal from a single remark (p. 256): 'Kant's main aim is to deepen and to justify Rousseau's idea that liberty is acting in accordance with a law that we give to ourselves.'

surrounding *ancien régime* by definition rooted in corruption, inauthenticity and tyranny, about major institutions powerless to effect reform, and about the principles of the lastingly, incorruptibly good, the social good – that is, utopia. There is a great deal of all this in Rawls. He is, without question, a lineal descendant of Rousseau.

Not, I hasten to say, in style. Rousseau may have his faults, but it would be hard to improve upon the style he adopted for his principal moral-political writings, given their objectives. He had not read much, but what he read he distilled into an oracularity that is never less than exciting to read, no matter how much one may distrust its content. With Professor Rawls it is very different. I do not know when I have read a book so dense in its rhetoric, so thicket-like in the form of its argument. One has the feeling that the book was not so much written as accumulated over the years, like some of the old mansions of the South. There is so much backing and filling, adding and subtracting of premises, introduction of assumptions where none before were necessary, and so much use of the first-person pronoun (the book must set an all-time record in this respect in the history of philosophy) that one has the feeling of Rawls as a *deus ex machina*. Books are supposed to write themselves, and the best ones do. Here the person of the author is constantly intruding, redesigning the architecture, rearranging the furniture.

In some respects, too, the book is like a palimpsest. What first hits the eye is the vast number of propositions of a more or less technical kind, along with innumerable references to other philosophical works. But if we look carefully through all of this we shall see the clear outline of another work, one not by any means separate from the first but nevertheless different: one that is in direct descent from the tracts written in the eighteenth century by the French *philosophes*. This is the work I shall largely be concerned with in what follows.

4. 'Justice is the first virtue of social institutions, as truth is of systems of thought.' That is the electrifying sentence the book opens with, after briefest preface. Its rhetorical affinity with the celebrated opening of Rousseau's *Social Contract* will be lost

to few readers. And with good reason. Just as Rousseau's exclamation about man being born free but being everywhere in chains is the axiom from which he derives an entire republic of virtue, total in its dedication to equality, so Rawls's sentence may be seen as the rock on which he builds his own community of virtue – that is, justice, itself defined as equality of the most thoroughgoing kind. The whole of *A Theory of Justice* is no more than an extension of that opening theme:

> Each person possesses an inviolability founded on justice that even the welfare of society as a whole cannot override. For this reason justice denies that the loss of freedom for some is made right by a greater good shared by others. It does not allow that the sacrifices imposed on a few are outweighed by the larger sum of advantages enjoyed by the many. Therefore in a just society the liberties of equal citizenship are taken as settled; the rights secured by justice are not subject to political bargaining or the calculus of social interests. The only thing that permits us to acquiesce in an erroneous theory is the lack of a better one; analogously, an injustice is tolerable only when it is necessary to avoid an even greater injustice. Being first virtues of human activities, truth and justice are uncompromising (pp. 3–4).

Now that is an astonishing passage and deserves to be ranked as at least a major footnote to any of the opening sections of the *Social Contract*. I dare say it would have been gladly accepted by most of the *philosophes* of eighteenth-century France, for it contains the thrilling and oracular rhetoric they loved, of devotion to the absolute individual and to the equally absolute moral community within which alone the ideal individual could realise himself without interference from intermediate institutions – institutions born merely out of history, convention and ordinary use and wont. There is also the cherished depreciation of the merely political and pragmatic in human affairs. Justice, we are told, is not a matter for those mechanisms of compromise that have been humanity's chief means of reconciling the antimonies of moral abstraction throughout history. Justice demands that the 'liberties of equal citizenship' be taken as antecedent and settled once and for all. The 'rights secured by justice' are 'not subject to political bargaining', which presumably takes care of political processes endemic in all known forms of democracy.

In fact, of course, we have no real repudiation of politics

here; only of conventional politics in favor of the politics of virtue, which is, as we know, never a relative politics but always absolute. Rare indeed is the statement of political authoritarianism in Western literature that is not built around the premise of virtue or justice – each, naturally, declared absolute, non-negotiable, and superior to all ordinary processes of 'political bargaining'. Seldom, from the time of Plato's *Republic*, has absolute authority been presented in its own name. Almost always it is authority clothed in the garments of justice, or of freedom, or of rights, with the welfare of 'the individual' held sacrosanct. I do not charge Professor Rawls with political authoritarianism; only with a Delphic intensity in the name of an absolute justice that can hardly help but suggest to many minds the sanctity of any form of power that might fulfil such justice – defined, as we shall see, as equality. It is the ineffaceable mark of every philosophy of moral absolutism to despise 'political bargaining' and to see this as necessarily inimical to the good and just society.

To return to Professor Rawls's propositions. They express, he writes, 'our intuitive conviction of the primacy of justice'. But whose conviction? There, as I have suggested, is the rub. For there is no evidence, either in our own time or in the past, that justice defined as equalitarianism would be regarded by most people, intuitively, as 'the first virtue of social institutions'. Any more than most people, either in Rousseau's or in our time, would think of themselves as born free but living in chains.

As a historian and social scientist I would not wish, myself, to declare any single virtue sovereign over all others, and capable of being intuitively arrived at. But if I were to speculate on what the majority of us would come up with 'intuitively' along these lines, I think it would not be justice, however defined. More likely it would be *protection* or *security*, followed closely by *conservation* (in the sense of perpetuation of norms and ways of life). No doubt even our remotest ancestors had, and may have occasionally snarled or fought over, rude conceptions of justice considered as fairness. And I am willing to concede that few persons, today or in the past, are likely to express a positive preference for *in*justice, once this particular value is set before them and suitably described. But to declare, as the opening line of argument in a 600-page book on morality, that justice is the virtue that will be intuitively arrived at by all human beings as primary for social institutions is to fly in the face of history and also, I would judge, in the face of sentiments regarding both security and conservation in our own day.

5. Now, how does Professor Rawls support his contention that justice – meaning 'fairness', meaning in turn equality – is the first virtue? Through comparative history, psychology, social science? Indeed not. Here we come to the *philosophe* heart of the book, the methodology through which Rawls reaches confirmation of what is for him primary and intuitive. I am going to devote most of what remains in this review to precisely this, the book's by now celebrated method of proof and of demonstration; for we have Rawls's own word for the fact that the greater part of the rest of his book, including propositions of the most radical and sweeping kind concerning social institutions, is rooted in this method: a method epitomised by what Rawls calls 'the original position' and 'the veil of ignorance'.

Before describing Rawls's method, though, I want to offer a little background for it by turning briefly to *philosophe* thought in eighteenth-century France. No reviewer I have chanced to read thus far seems to be aware of the true nature of Rawls's method of proof: a commentary no doubt on the sad decline of the history of philosophy in our time. Much is said in the reviews about Rawls's return to 'social contract' theory as the means of refuting the utilitarianism that has (on Rawls's testimony, at least) dominated moral philosophy for a century or more. But while description of Rawls's method as 'contractarianism' is perhaps not erroneous, it is far from sufficient and does not get at what is essential.

When the *philosophes* in the eighteenth century wished to 'prove' the rightness of a given value or set of values, in their larger work of annihilating the values and structures they found around them, they availed themselves of a technique widely known then as *histoire raisonnée* or, variously, 'conjectural', 'hypothetical', or 'speculative' history. This was set in sharpest contrast to the more conventional kind of history that concerned itself with actual persons, places, nations and events in the annals of mankind. Such conventional history was largely repugnant to the *philosophes*, though one or two of them did it reasonably well on occasion; for, plainly, it was not the kind of investigation from which first principles and first virtues could easily be derived by those dedicated to reformation of a social order. 'Hypothetical' history was a means of dealing with the nature and history of man as though he were liberated from all the 'corrupting' and 'distorting' influences that normally go into socialisation. It was a means of contriving – to use Professor Rawls's words – an 'original position' and a 'veil of ignorance' for man which would then make it possible to uncover the 'real' elements of man's mind and morality, and to build on these in the construction of a utopia.

Conceivably, honest and forthright critics of a social order might have said simply: 'These are the values we approve of and these are the values we intend to see woven into the fabric of the social order. All else will be obliterated.' But such forthrightness is alien to the mind of the true *philosophe*. He must always give the semblance of dealing with the roots of human nature, of demonstrating what would in fact be in force if it were not for a false consciousness that has been generated in men's minds by the corruptions, inauthenticities, tyrannics and, above all, inequalities, of a given social order.

Obviously, in such an enterprise the ordinary factual materials of history, social science and experience are useless. For how is one to extract first principles and 'first virtues' from the chronicles of Egyptians, Romans and Greeks, and from tedious annals of who ruled where and when? It is Man and Mankind, not peoples and individuals of record, that we must go to if we would reach the roots of justice or find moral levers with which to move whole worlds. And for this exciting work, as the *philosophes* knew well, there was no substitute for an imagination equipped with all the desired answers in advance and capable of 'proving' its intuitive correctness through use of a *histoire raisonnée* that would discard as irrelevant all recorded experiences of human beings and fix attention solely upon what could be cleverly assigned to a supposedly 'original position' by the *philosophe* concerned. It was precisely in this light that Rousseau, in a frequently misunderstood and often maligned sentence at the beginning of his momentous *Discourse on the Origin of Inequality*, wrote: 'Let us begin, then, by laying facts aside, as they do not affect the question.' Rousseau was only candidly admitting a practice followed by all *philosophes* from his day to ours.

Fundamentally, this *philosophe* strategy is the real core of Professor Rawls's book. He too is playing the exciting game of imagining that, through use of what he calls 'the original position' (read: state of nature), he is entering on a mode of reality denied those of us who live in the caves of contemporary social science, history and experience. He too is, in the precise sense of Rousseau's words, laying the facts aside on the ground that they do not affect the question – which indeed they do not, given the nature of the question posed by Rawls. And finally, Professor Rawls, like any sophisticated *philosophe* of two centuries ago, can say: 'We want to define the original position so that we get the desired solution' (p. 141). Naturally. That is the very essence of the *philosophe* mentality. One must never lose sight of the desired, the 'intuitive', solution, no matter what else one carries in the way of ethnological tidbits, alleged principles of psychology, apothegms of moral philosophy, even citations from Scripture, to supply ballast.*

---

*There is, though, one major difference between what Professor Rawls does and what his illustrious forerunners in the eighteenth-century did (that is, apart from ballast; Rawls favors game theory and tidbits from free market economics over ethnology, etc.). The French *philosophes* were drawing upon the best, or at least the commonly accepted social science and psychology of their day. Professor Rawls most assuredly is not. Taking refuge in something termed an 'original position' and using a 'veil of ignorance' is as far from scientific procedure as anything I can think of. Rawls seems at times to conceive of himself in the role of social scientist; there are enough references to economic theory alone to suggest this. But there is a broad gulf between what Rawls is doing in his rather simplistic use of *philosophe* method and what econometrists are involved in today in their very careful and rigorous analyses of the free market or the firm. The same has to be said of Rawls's numerous references to game theory. I am afraid the kind of game Professor Rawls is playing with imagined motivations in a hypothetical 'original position' is much more like the games philosophers might give each other for Christmas than anything easily found today in the higher reaches of mathematics and economic theory.

6. Let us move now from method to conclusion, bearing in mind, of course, that no conclusion can be other than what has been directed by the method of inquiry. 'It seems reasonable to suppose', writes Rawls, 'that the parties in the original position are equal' (p. 19). Well, yes, but then again it doesn't – at least when one thinks of the findings of ethnology and physical anthropology in the study of human behavior. Never mind, though. We are dealing here, not with facts, which have been laid aside in appropriate *philosophe* manner, but with an 'original position' so contrived as to reveal to us what human beings *would* be, *would* think, *would* do and contract for, *if* they are imagined as having been liberated from identities conferred through processes of ordinary socialisation. 'The original position', we are told, 'is the appropriate initial *status quo* which insures that the fundamental agreements reached in it are fair. This fact yields "justice as fairness" '. (p. 17). Indeed it does. We need add only that such a 'fact' will yield just about anything one desires.

It is not possible to understand the 'original position' without reference to what Professor Rawls calls 'the veil of ignorance'. What does this veil consist of?

> First of all no one knows his place in society, his class position or social status; nor does he know his fortune in the distribution of natural assets and abilities, his intelligence and the like. Nor, again, does anyone know his conception of the good, the particulars of his rational plan of life, or even the special features of his psychology such as his aversion to risk or liability to optimism or pessimism. More than this, I assume that the parties do not know the particular circumstances of their own society. That is, they do not know its economic or political situation, or the level of civilization and culture it has been able to achieve. The persons in the original position have no information as to which generation they belong (p. 137).

In sum, they don't know much of anything – anything, that is, that we are justified by contemporary psychology in deeming requisite to thought and knowledge of any kind whatever. Nevertheless, Professor Rawls is shortly going to put his happy primitives through feats of cerebration that even the gods might envy. Out of the minds of his homunculi, these epistemological zombies who don't know their names, families, races, generations or societies of origin, are going to come principles of justice and society so vast in implication as to throw all present human societies into a philosopher's limbo.

This must be said, though: Despite the parties' abysmal ignorance of the things which alone make thought possible, they are not wholly bereft. Professor Rawls assures us that his primitives in the 'original position' do know 'the general facts about human society'. He goes on: 'They understand political affairs and the principles of economic theory; they know the basis of social organization and the laws of human psychology. Indeed, the parties are presumed to know whatever general facts affect the choice of the principles of justice' (p. 137). There are those who would say they sound like certain academic intellectuals of today. There are others who would say they sound exactly like the confined neurasthenics Proust described in *Remembrance of Things Past*: able endlessly to discuss and debate monumental abstractions, but helpless when it came to the simplest duties of ordinary existence.

Such is the 'original position' and such is the 'veil of ignorance'. One's first thought is to say: Welcome to the eighteenth century! In a footnote (p. 137) Rawls seems uneasily aware that *someone* besides himself must have thought somewhere, sometime, of this device – but he can think of no one but J. C. Harsanyi, who, I infer, drew from it the wrong conclusions, inasmuch as they are pronounced utilitarian. I know nothing about the Harsanyi article referred to, but I can assure Professor Rawls that he would find much company in Parisian salons of the eighteenth century, where conceptualised primitives often strolled, in aristocrats' or *philosophes*' dress, discussing from the vantage point of the 'veil of ignorance' and the 'original position' principles of the ideal society so profound and so noble in purpose as to make surrounding culture seem base, misdirected, and obsolete.

7. I will not go into a detailed account of the principles of a just society that Professor Rawls extracts from the mouths of his happy and omniscient primitives. Those principles have been described profusely by reviewers and other admirers of the book. It will suffice to say that foremost among them are

what Rawls calls his 'two principles of justice for social institutions'. According to the first of these momentous principles, 'each person must have an equal right to the most extensive total system of equal basic liberties compatible with a similar system of liberty for all' (p. 302). That is, the principle of liberty is made prior to all else, even equality. Ostensibly, at any rate, it is made prior. A second reading of the passage just quoted might suggest that it is not so much liberty that Rawls has in mind there as equal shares in a vast, homogenised structure *called* liberty.

Prior or no, however, the first principle is utterly outweighed in mass and use by the second principle, which is that 'social and economic inequalities are to be arranged so that they are both (a) to the greatest benefit of the least advantaged, consistent with the just savings principle, and (b) attached to offices and positions open to all under conditions of fair equality of opportunity' (p. 303). And here, of course, we are out of the suburbs and in the City itself. For the book is consecrated to as radical a form of equalitarianism as may be found anywhere outside the pages of the *Social Contract*. Liberty, yes, but liberty carefully defined as a monolithic, total, practically identical experience for the entire population, something in which, by definition, people have equal shares – or else it does not exist. It was Rousseau who first perfected the technique of defining liberty in the rhetoric of equality, so as to make liberty and equality indeed virtually synonymous. Rousseau's pages abound in use of the words 'freedom' and 'liberty'. But no one with scantest acquaintance with these pages can doubt that the words have been forged on the anvil of equality – an equality that will be total, permeating, and made to reach the depths of human consciousness.

Equality is assuredly total in Rawls. From his two fundamental principles of justice – themselves derived, it must always be remembered, from the cerebrations of his conceptualised primitives in the state of nature – Professor Rawls deduces something portentously called 'the difference principle', under which 'all social primary goods' must be distributed equally throughout a society unless an unequal distribution of any of these goods is to the advantage of the least favored. By social primary goods Rawls means not only wealth and income but such things as liberty, opportunity and even 'bases of self-respect'.

Nor is it the familiar liberal concept of a merit system that Rawls proposes. Meritocracy comes in for repudiation on the ground that equality – given thrust by the two principles of justice and by the powerful and sweeping 'difference principle' – would be undermined. For obviously there are differences of strength, acuity, temperament and, inevitably, of motivation and aspiration in any group of human beings. A merit system, one based upon equal opportunity for talents and desires, would inevitably destroy that homogeneity of life Rawls seems to prize above all else. In this respect too Rawls is the child of Jean-Jacques who, directing himself precisely to the same point in the *Social Contract*, declared that the social compact (read: original position) demands that we substitute 'for such physical inequality as nature may have set up between men, an equality that is moral and legitimate, and that men, who may be unequal in strength or intelligence, become every one equal by convention and legal right'. Elsewhere in the *Social Contract* Rousseau tells us: 'It is precisely because the force of circumstances tends continually to destroy equality that the force of legislation should always tend toward its maintenance.'

That civil law should protect the weak from the strong, should, that is, guard their right to existence from arbitrary invasion or violence, goes without saying. It is, however, a very different thing to see the function of law as making equal the diversity of strengths and talents in all fields that is but a part of the human condition. I do not know how the absurd myth got started in modern thought that Rousseau urged a 'return to nature'. Nothing could be farther from the truth. He did indeed start with the concept of nature, but this was only to give even greater emphasis to his desire to create a social system so powerful, so minute and penetrating in its grasp of individuals, that a monolith of artificial equality and of equal shares of membership in an all-benign, all-knowing, and omnipotent General Will would become the basis for all life and thought.

No doubt when Professor Rawls urges upon us his revolutionary 'difference principle' he wishes us to think primarily of money and property differences. If only it were possible to limit such a principle to such matters! After all, Rawls refers in the statement of his principle to 'all social primary goods', and as one reflects on the matter, the real and far-reaching impact of the principle would be less in the sphere of money than in the world of the mind, of intellectual and cultural achievement, and in all the subtle but potent gradations of status in life which follow directly from differential achievement. On the evidence, it is not monetary differentiation – much as equalitarians like to dwell upon it – that galls and occasionally humiliates; it is rather the type of differentiation that comes from unequal intellectual and moral strengths, unequal applications of resolve and aspiration, and unequal benefactions of luck. What can we assume but that the effect of Rawls's 'difference principle' would be greatest in these respects?

I cannot help thinking that the closest we come at the present time to a manifestation of Rawls's 'difference principle' is in respect to Open Admissions and Affirmative Action in the college and university world. In each of these the ostensible and declared function is that of helping the disadvantaged on their way up in life. In both, however, what we see in fact is simultaneous destruction of standards of performance and of the hopes of those individuals *within the disadvantaged groups* whose talents and aspirations put them above the lowest common denominator of their groups. How, we are constrained to ask, is the long-run rise of any group in society helped by a principle – and, in the cases of the two programs I have just mentioned, by ongoing policies – that gives protection not so much to the least advantaged groups in the social order as to the least able, least qualified, and least motivated individuals among the least advantaged groups?

To be sure, Professor Rawls, writing in glittering abstraction from his Ivy League fastness, can point to, can take philosopher's refuge in, the fine-print clause that says 'unless an unequal distribution of any of these goods is to the advantage of the least favored'. How ingenious! But 'advantage' by whose judgement? Aye, that is the question. We will probably not go wrong if we bet that the controlling judgement will emanate from intellectuals in the world of government, foundations, and academy. At least it has been that way in all other revolutions!

8. John Rawls is clearly a learned mind, and the sources, references and allusions in his book reflect a wide diversity of reading. Even so, the omissions are massive, not to say staggering. In a work that makes liberty and equality the two sovereign virtues of social institutions, that indeed sees them intertwined in a theory of justice, the author might have thought it incumbent upon him to consider in some detail the long tradition in Western thought, beginning with Aristotle's criticism of Plato and continuing down to such minds as Tocqueville, Henry Maine and James Fitzjames Stephens, among others, that has made the *conflict between liberty and equality* its theme. There is little if any such consideration in *A Theory of Justice*, however, and one can only conclude that in this as in other respects, *philosophe* conquered philosopher, with principles reached *in scrinio pectoris* deemed sufficient unto the purpose.

So might one also expect consideration of the problem of the *contexts* of liberty in society. I refer to the kinds of contexts which a large number of historians, social scientists and philosophers have thought vital to the nourishing and reinforcement of any spirit of liberty. Professor Rawls's dedication to freedom is unimpeachable; he declares it prior in importance and lexical order even to equality. But oracularity and repetition of principle are never proper substitutes for genuine consideration of relevant circumstances and conditions. There is a long and impressive body of writings in the West which tells us that freedom needs to have roots in social differentiation, cultural pluralism, conflict of institutions, balance of power among strong social interests, and deeply based traditions – economic, religious, ethnic and other. It is difficult to see how application of Rawls's 'difference principle' could take place without destruction or substantial erosion of these – a result allowable enough if equality alone is the desired end of life, but not if equality is declared secondary to liberty, as it is so declared by Rawls. Principles are very important; but principles have consequences, and we are surely entitled in a book of this length to the author's views on both contexts and consequences.

I think most readers will find Rawls far better in his elaboration of equality, of justice as fairness, than in what he writes at great length about freedom. I believe the book would have been a better one if he had frankly abandoned his first principle of liberty, so called, and concerned himself entirely with developing the theme of equality. As I suggested above, much of the difficulty with Rawls's treatment of liberty lies in the fact that he repeatedly presents it as an overall system in which abstract individuals are to have 'equal shares'. It is impossible to conquer the belief that in Rawls as in Rousseau there is far more interest in the equal sharing of liberty than in the nature of liberty itself. I do not doubt that there are types of liberty in which equal shares may be decreed. This would appear to be as true of totalitarian governments as democratic ones. But there is a large and historically indispensable sphere of liberty – that relating to the pragmatic capacity of individuals and groups to express their essence, to fulfil chosen objectives, *to initiate, to create, and to do* – in which the thought of equal shares is plainly absurd. In *this* sphere we are forever dependent upon the talents, strengths, interests and aspirations we are in some part born with and in probably larger part recipients of during the crucial early period of socialisation. Plainly, chance, contingency, luck play a great role in liberty understood in this sense. Equality is non-existent here.

When one thinks of the implications for liberty, in the sense in which it has been known by most people for a very long time in the West, of Rawls's 'difference principle' (with its binding requirement that all 'social primary goods' must be distributed equally or, if there must be unequal distribution, in a way that it is to the advantage of the least favored), one can only confess bewilderment as to what liberty would actually consist of in Rawls's just society. I can conceive of even a despot, especially of the Napoleonic type, approving of liberty of the kind that may be parcelled out in 'equal shares'. It is, on the historical record, the kind of liberty that is *not* divisible into equal shares, that is always found in the very unequal proportions in which initiative, creativity and motivation are to be found, that has proved troubling to despots and the bureaucracies they administer.

9. As I say, we must take Professor Rawls at his word that he loves liberty and wants it to be primary in his just society. But he is not thereby absolved from the responsibility of letting us know what the difference is between liberty in a society *not* founded upon his rigorous equalitarianism and liberty in the society where all 'social primary goods', including opportunity and 'bases of self-respect', as well as income and property, must be equal or arranged to favor the underprivileged. Incessantly repeated incantations about the 'inviolability' of the person and about the absolute necessity of 'liberty of conscience' will not suffice.

There is much about liberty of conscience in *A Theory of Justice*. So is there, *mutatis mutandis*, in Plato's *Republic*, in Hobbes' *Leviathan*, and in Rousseau's *Social Contract*. Rawls shows no real awareness that *mere liberty of conscience or belief is compatible with systems of extraordinary repressiveness*. I repeat, what despotic governments have immemorially feared is not anything as private and secluded as conscience or belief, but rather those expressions of action and organisation which must by their nature always exist in highly unequal shares in any population, based as they are on unequal motivations and strengths. Rousseau's well-known antagonism toward the arts springs less, I judge, from any genuine 'puritanism' in his make-up than from the hopelessness of trying to maintain an iron equality, or justice defined as equality, in arts, letters and science.

Rousseau grants an absolute freedom of opinion and belief to his citizens in the very chapter of the *Social Contract* where he prescribes the death penalty for those who act as if they do not believe in the tenets of the Civil Religion. Of course, nothing so harsh is to be found in *A Theory of Justice*. It does come as a slight shock, though, when Rawls, following a number of pages on the sanctity of freedom of conscience (extending, *inter alia*, to civil disobedience, draft evasion and the like), concludes with the statement: 'Furthermore liberty of conscience is to be limited only when there is reasonable expectation that not doing so will damage the public order which the government should maintain' (p. 213). True, he goes on to say that such limitation must be restricted to instances where the expectation will 'be based on evidence and ways of reasoning acceptable to all'. But in large nations with excellent communications systems in the hands of their governments, that should not be a difficult matter. In fairness to Professor Rawls, he makes no Rousseauan reference to such limitation upon liberty as a means whereby individuals are 'forced to be free'. But it is worth a thought!

So is Rousseau's General Will worth a thought in any subsequent edition of *A Theory of Justice*. Rawls seems to have great trouble with the concept of majority will. One has the feeling he doesn't particularly like it – nor should he, given the outrageous preferences that democratic majorities invariably express for a social system based upon merit and achievement – but that he doesn't know quite what to do with it. What Rawls winds up doing is dissociating majority will from any of his principles of justice. That, is, whatever else this deeply embedded principle of democracy rests on, it does *not* rest on justice, as it is defined and elaborated in *A Theory of Justice*. He writes: 'It is evident from the preceding remarks that the procedure of majority rule, however it is defined, and circumscribed, has a subordinate place as a procedural device. The justification for it rests squarely on the political ends that the constitution is designed to achieve, and therefore on the two principles of justice' (p. 356). Such a statement, quite apart from whatever may lie in Professor Rawls's hopes and dreams, can serve as the basis for some tantalising *philosophe* visions of 'What Is To Be Done' when one becomes overpowered by the thought of the discrepancies between true justice and all the foibles, tastes and whims of extent majorities. No doubt, in the years ahead, it will so serve. But if so, I recommend the powerful Rousseauan distinction between the General Will (*volonté générale*), which is always and invariably right and may not at all coincide with a numerical majority, and the mere Will of All (*volonté de tous*) that is the product of a still uninstructed, wrong-thinking and untreated mass formed by the accidents of history. Near the beginning of the *Discourse on Political Economy* Rousseau even provides us with some helpful instructions on how the General Will may be ascertained in a population without bothering with voting at all.

But as Rousseau was well aware, you can't hope to achieve authentic consciousness in a people – the basis of the General Will – without taking some very radical steps. Foremost among these is eradication of the family as the unit of the social order. I have always found treatment of the family to be an excellent indicator of the degree of zeal and authoritarianism, overt or latent, in a moral philosopher or political theorist. Basically, there have been two traditions in Western thought here. In one, reaching from Plato to Rousseau, the family is regarded as an insurmountable barrier to the achievement of absolute virtue or justice in a social order and therefore is to be obliterated. In the other, reaching from Aristotle to Burke and Tocqueville, the family is declared vital to the achievement and preservation of freedom and order alike in society.

Where does Professor Rawls stand? He is well aware of the social and psychological importance of the family, and refers to it in a number of places. Let us take his final reference (p. 511) as indicative. He writes: 'The consistent application of the principle of fair opportunity requires us to view persons independently from the influences of their social position. But how far should this tendency be carried? It seems that when fair opportunity (as it has been defined) is satisfied, the family will lead to unequal chances between individuals. Is the family to be abolished then? Taken by itself and given a certain primacy, the idea of equal opportunity inclines in this direction. But within the context of the theory of justice as a whole there is much less urgency to take this course.'

I am afraid that most readers will take that last as quite unsatisfactory, even as a form of flinching. After all, 'theory of justice as a whole' notwithstanding, there is abundant evidence that the family is among the most powerful generators and reinforcers of inequality in a social order. Rawls knows this very well. He has already proclaimed his willingness to see the factors of motivation, chance and merit reduced to nullity in behalf of his cherished principle of equality. Can he, in all consistency, long neglect the family, given its demonstrable relation to inequality? Rousseau, in his

Discourse on Political Economy, was bold and consistent where Rawls is diffident. If the young are to be brought up in the bosom of equality, 'early accustomed to regard their own individuality only in its relation to the body of the State, to be aware, so to speak, of their own existence merely as part of that of the State', then they must be saved from what Rousseau refers to as 'the intelligence and prejudices of fathers'. Public authority must supplant domestic authority; the molecule of the family must be broken. But this, Rousseau suggests with characteristic ingenuity, should occasion no alarm, for the father 'would only be changing his title and would have in common, under the name of *citizen*, the same authority over his children as he was exercising separately under the name of *father*'.

Will Professor Rawls in due time find his way to this piece of radical surgery? We can only surmise that he will. Our surmise in this respect is encouraged by the final paragraph of *A Theory of Justice*, where we are urged to think, not merely big, but '*sub specie aeternitatis*', and to 'regard the human situation not only from all social but also from all temporal points of view'. And in a final sentence that arouses visions of Rousseau's legislator, Professor Rawls writes: 'Purity of heart, if one could attain it, would be to act with grace and self-command from this point of view.' Rousseau put the matter better. 'This sublime reason [he is writing about his philosopher-legislator], far above the range of the common herd, is that whose decisions the legislator puts into the mouth of the immortals, in order to constrain by divine authority those whom human prudence could not move. The great soul of the legislator is the only miracle that can prove his mission.'

5

The procrustean ideal: libertarians *v.* egalitarians

ANTONY FLEW

≠

LET me begin by distinguishing some different interpretations of equality. For not every ideal of equality constitutes a threat to liberty. On the contrary: the most fundamental of these ideals is itself essentially connected with respecting every individual's rights to *choose*, in as many respects as it practically consistent with the corresponding equal rights of everyone else.

The first basic distinction is between, on the one hand, ideals or norms and, on the other hand, facts or putative facts. The second paragraph of the American Declaration of Independence begins: *We hold these truths to be self-evident, that all Men are created equal*. . . . But it would be quite wrong on this account to discredit the Signers with some foolish belief that babies come identical, that there are no genetically determined differences of physique, of temperament and of ability. For those wise men at once glossed the phrase *all Men are created equal* with an explanation showing that this was for them a matter, not of what allegedly is the case, but of what ideally *ought* to be. The complete sentence thus reads:

> We hold these truths to be self-evident, that all Men are created equal, that they are endowed by their Creator with certain inalienable Rights, that among these are Life, Liberty, and the Pursuit of Happiness.[1]

First published in *Encounter*, Vol. 50, No. 3 (March 1978), pp. 70–9.

For Notes and References, see page 385 below.

No statement of the first (*is*) kind by itself either logically presupposes or entails any proclamation of the second (*ought*) sort. As an illustration of the nature and an indication of the significance of this first basic distinction, it is perhaps worth repeating yet once more that this necessary truth provides one of two independently decisive reasons why immoral conclusions about the propriety of discriminating either for or against individuals upon grounds of racial group membership cannot be validly deduced from premises stating only that certain racial groups are, on average, either superior or inferior to others in their natural endowments. (The second of these often neglected, yet both independently quite decisive, reasons is that nothing about the particular characteristics of a particular member or group follows from any general statement about the average of that group: you may be a dwarf or a giant or neither, and yet still happen to belong to a group which is on average either very tall or very short or neither.)[2]

When J. V. Stalin said to a visiting American Senator, 'You believe that men are equal, I know that they are not', Stalin had missed the point. What he knew, his visitor knew too. People are in fact born with very unequal potentialities. What, apparently, Stalin did not know was that the Signers were neither asserting nor presupposing a false proposition in biology or psychology. They were instead demanding that certain very general basic rights ought to be guaranteed.

The second basic distinction is between three different ideals of equality. The first and hardest to define seems to have no accepted distinguishing label – perhaps partly for those reasons. Until and unless something better is suggested, let us call this, baldly, *personal equality*. The second is usually called *equality of opportunity*, although it might be better described as fair and open competition for scarce opportunities. This is what the great French Revolution of 1789 meant by 'the career open to the talents'. The third is, by contrast with the second, *equality of outcome* or *equality of result*.

The first of these three ideals can best be introduced as a secularised version of the traditional Judaeo–Christian insistence that every soul is of equal value in the eyes of God. However much we actually do differ and perhaps should differ in other ways, we all have our lives to live and our decisions to make; and in this most fundamental respect we ought all to recognise one another as equals. As a less poetic, sexually more scrupulous poet might have written: 'A person is a person for a' that. . . .' It was this ideal, in a fully secularised form, which Immanuel Kant was expressing when he laid down 'The Formula of the End in Itself'. After taking 'rational nature' or – as we would be more likely to say – personality as 'something *whose existence* has *in itself* an absolute value', Kant's Categorical Imperative becomes:

Act in such a way that you always treat humanity, whether in your own person or in the person of any other, never simply as a means, but always at the same time as an end.[3]

Once the next two ideals have been picked out and docketed, they may seem to be unconfusably different both from the first and from each other. They are, nevertheless, quite commonly assumed to be compatible companions, even where they are not actually mistaken to be the same. Thus the editors of a recent source-book on *The 'Inequality' Controversy* write, without a qualm of historical conscience, of America's traditional 'commitment to equality of opportunity *and to equality of results*'. They really ought to know better. But they even go on to say of one of their contributors that he examines this 'concept of equality of opportunity' and 'traces the development of the concept to its logically inevitable definition as equality of results'.[4]

Yet for most people, though not for all, a large part, though not the whole of the point of equality of opportunity lies in its being opportunity to better the condition of themselves and their families; whether this is for them a matter of being better off than they are now or would otherwise be, or whether it is for them also or alternatively a matter of relativities and hence essentially of being better off in the future than (certain) others then are. For this perhaps deplorable majority the intrinsic rewards to be found in developing and using talents are as nothing compared with the further and extrinsic rewards which they hope by these means to win. Suppose that you first offer equality of opportunity; and then explain that, as a devout egalitarian of the third sort, you also propose to ensure that, whatever opportunities are or are not taken, everyone is going to be ground down and kept down to your ideal of equality of results. You will not be very warmly or widely thanked for your first offer, I think, once your second intention is fully understood. For, as Confucius really did say, without cynical exaggeration and with traditional Chinese realism: 'It is not easy to find a man who has studied for three years without aiming at pay.'[5]

It is, I suspect, mainly because they are themselves perhaps rather guiltily aware of the wide unpopularity of some of the implications of their Procrustean ideal that our contemporary egalitarians of outcome so often confound it with equality of opportunity.

One instructive method is by tripping over that favourite cliché '*life-chances*'. Jean Floud, for instance, who is much respected as a social engineer, does this in a recent article under the characteristic and revealing title 'Making Adults More Equal: The Scope and Limitations of Public Educational Policy'. She defines the key expression '*life-chances*' in a perfectly straightforward way, 'in terms of people's economic and social opportunities'. But then, like so many others, she forthwith proceeds to identify differences in educational opportunity with differences in achieved education, life-chances with actual lives. What she is talking about is correlations (reported by Christopher Jencks) between achieved education and achieved income. Yet she insists on calling differences in the former, differences in educational opportunity, while differences in the latter are correspondingly equated with differences in life-chances:

> . . . differences of educational opportunity do not explain much of the variation in individual incomes. Measures of the independent influence of educational opportunity on people's life-chance give different results.[6]

Connoisseurs of doctrinaire high-handedness will now appreciate an example of an even shorter way of collapsing this fundamental distinction; and consequently identifying the third with the second ideal of equality – equal life-chances with equal lives. 'Surely', one Swedish philosopher suggests, 'we could always define "real chance" in such a way that it becomes analytically true that if two members of a society have the same real chance to achieve equality of economic welfare, then their actual economic welfare level will be the same.'[7] Yes indeed, nothing easier. Nor more wanton and more wrong.

Personal Equality

After this briefly illustrated account of the differences between three current ideals of equality, we are now in a position to consider whether and, if so, how and how far any of these various ideals are enemies to liberty. Of the first it is obvious that the contrary is the truth. The same ideal also demands a measure of democracy, which itself in turn necessitates respect for at least the most fundamental individual liberties.

I suggest that democrats are in any case best advised to ground their – and my – convictions upon the splendid Kantian ideal to which I have just attached the colourless label 'personal equality'. To do this is to appeal – not to the false and silly doctrine that the majority is always, or even most often, right – but to the true and crucial fact that it is everyone's lives which government is governing. It is the appeal which was superbly put in the 1640s by the russet-coated Captain Rainborough in the Putney Debates of the New Model Army:

> Really I think that the poorest he that is in England hath a life to live as the greatest he; and therefore truly, Sir, I think it is clear, that every man that is to live under a government ought first by his own consent to put himself under that government; and I do believe that the poorest man in England is not at all bound to that government that he hath not had a voice to put himself under.[8]

He here, as so often, should embrace she!

The connection between democracy and certain minimum individual liberties is logically necessary. For these are those which are the preconditions of its being truly said that citizens made and implemented their decisions on how to cast their votes freely. These preconditions include, for instance, effective guarantees against intimidation. Again, it must be possible to get and to spread relevant information, to discuss issues with other people, and to organise opposition. Besides the minimal civil liberties which are in this way logically necessary to democracy it may be that other and especially economic liberties are also contingently required. For, though it is obviously possible to have a pluralist economy without democracy, there are very strong reasons for believing that a fully socialist (clause IV) setup is in practice incompatible with authentic (*i.e.*, Western: 'vote-the-scoundrels out') democratic institutions.

Certainly this contention about the economic preconditions of political pluralism is not peculiar to Milton Friedman, F. A. Hayek, and Sir Keith Joseph.[9] It has also been accepted, albeit with a somewhat sullen inertia, by such right-wing social democrats as Anthony Crosland and Roy Jenkins. And it is seen as a manifest and agreeable lesson of experience by the most powerful and persistent contemporary enemies of democracy – thus the Institute of Marxism-Leninism in Moscow sketches a programme for achieving total and irremovable Communist domination by following 'United Front' or 'Broad Left' tactics:

> Having once acquired political power, the working class implements the liquidation of the private ownership of the means of production. . . . As a result, under socialism, there remains no ground for the existence of any opposition parties counter-balancing the Communist Party.[10]

We, however, must put this question aside in order to notice that very illiberal decisions may be reached by impeccably democratic procedures. At some times and in some countries – but not, it seems, in Britain today[11] – a referendum held after a great national debate might well reaffirm legislation refusing 'the right to die' to the degradingly senile and the unrelievably ill. Similar referenda might impose and extend various choice-denying monopolies, and all manner of other legal restrictions not needed to safeguard the maximum equal freedoms of every citizen. In the words of John Stuart Mill's classic essay *On Liberty*:

> The 'people' who exercise the power are not always the same people with those over whom it is exercised; and the self-government spoken of is not the government of each by himself, but of each by all the rest.[12]

All this is as true as it is important. But what is relevant here is that no such illiberal policies are dictated by the first sort of ideal of equality. If anything it forbids them. For what is the categorical imperative never to treat anyone '*simply as a means, but always at the same time as an end*' if it is not an insistence upon everyone's equal right to make their own decisions in the light of their own chosen ends? (Kant's own attempt to derive therefrom an absolute embargo upon suicide is manifestly factitious and unsound, an unhappy product of his own too conservative first-order ethical preconceptions.)

Choice and Inequality

Unavoidable conflicts with the claims of liberty begin with the second ideal of equality: equality of opportunity. There are two complications which we need to disentangle at once. First, we need to make up our minds whether it really is equality which we are talking about, or only a minimum without a maximum. The idea of a 'welfare floor', a state-provided safety-net, is most familiar from other areas of social policy. It was indeed a main theme of Sir Winston Churchill's domestic speeches during his years as Leader of the Conservative Party.

As an ideal this is essentially different from that of a compulsory ceiling, or of anything else requiring measures to pull excellers back (notwithstanding that in practice such safety-nets are usually financed in part from progressive direct taxation). Nor is this safety-net ideal at all the same as the egalitarian ideal of state monopoly provision, provision which shall be at the same time both the minimum and the maximum, equal for all.[13] Applying these distinctions to our present area of interest it is easy to see that safety-net measures to spread and increase educational opportunity are measures to extend and to raise the floor rather than to enforce a uniform equal provision. Guided by this different ideal, and by a commitment to liberty, libertarian democrats want to defend, while their egalitarian opponents long to destroy, alternatives to and within the state system.

We also have to ask at what stage in the human life-cycle it is proposed that the desired 'equality of opportunity' should begin. There is a world of difference between, at one extreme, applying this notion to adult job applicants or to candidates for tertiary education, and, at the other extreme, applying it to newborn babies or even the freshly fertilised egg. The clashes here are with actual or possible parental liberties and they are the more serious and the more general the nearer the point of application of the ideal is put to the moment of the child's conception. The trouble is that to have been, and to be, raised in a good home is in so many ways so much an advantage. Indeed the criteria of goodness here are, for the most part, at the same time criteria of such advantage.

So, if you want to achieve ideal equality of opportunity from the very beginning, then you have to abolish the home and the family in favour of the universal compulsory comprehensive *crèche*. Failing that, your next best bet is to find ways of minimising home influences, and/or of intruding compensatory measures to offset the advantages of above-average and the disadvantages of below-average homes. Any of this must involve substantially circumscribing, if not outright abolishing, the freedom of parents to make homes, and to bring up their children as they see fit; and/or most if not all of the point of their labouring so to do.

The most extreme proposals of this kind are not at present, I believe, on any British agenda. For most of those for whom true equality of opportunity from the earliest stage is a value, it remains one value which can and has to be traded off against others. Yet the intractable inevitability of clashes between this ideal and that of the family with substantial parental rights, and duties, can be illustrated with an example which belongs to the stuff of present-day British educational politics.

Until a few years ago the stock objection to any defence of parental choice in education was to say that in this country real choice is confined to a privileged few able to afford the fat fees of private schools. Although it perhaps did too little justice to the differences between the denominational and the more secular schools within the state system – and although by overlooking the number of those who could afford such fees but preferred to spend their money in other ways it certainly under-estimated the size of this minority – this objection was still substantially correct in what it said. What were wholly wrong, and to any lover of liberty utterly obnoxious, were the supplementary suggestions: that liberties can be of value only to those who are themselves able and willing to make direct use of them; and that no one ought to be allowed to do anything which not everyone can do, or wants to do.

But now market-minded radicals associated with the Institute of Economic Affairs are plugging the idea of educational vouchers.[14] This promises a vast extension of genuine family choice either within the state sector only, or both within and outside it. To this lively liberalising idea the standard response of the wooden authoritarian Left, and of their allies entrenched in the educational bureaucracies, is to protest. First, that, since a lot of parents – and particularly working-class parents – are ignorant and indifferent, such a system, even if it were – like its American anticipators – confined to the public sector, would be bound to produce inequalities as between sump and quality comprehensives. And, second, that (since we know the previous proposition to be true) it must on no account be subjected to the experimental test which might show that a voucher system both tended to raise educational standards and pleased the public. So, when a *Daily Telegraph* editorial advocated just such an experiment, the Secretary of the Woking Constituency Labour Party wrote:

> We should worry less about 'parental choice'. . . . The voucher system, which you claim offers freedom of choice to parents, can only operate at the expense of denying children the equality of opportunity they ought to enjoy in a civilised society. Under this system we would very soon have good schools packed with the fortunate children of competent, caring parents with deprived children from disadvantaged homes languishing in sink schools.[15]

To that I want to reply that this is not, it seems, what actually is happening in those US school areas which are operating a voucher system; that in Britain we already have all too many sink schools; that under a voucher system, outstanding examples, such as William Tyndale School, would be identified, and could be reformed, more quickly; and, finally, that the supercilious, and – in the usual purely abusive sense – élitist suggestions of working-class indifference are grossly unfair to all those obviously working-class parents who during that Tyndale affair protested publicly and appeared before the television cameras. Yet my main reason for giving that quotation is to bring out that the two ideals I have described must indeed be ultimately incompatible. For people in fact are, from the beginning, incorrigibly different. So, where they are permitted to make choices, their choices will not always be in the same sense; and such differences cannot but produce, in some dimension, inequalities.

Absolute Equality?

The third kind of equality is that of outcome or results. This ideal needs to be considered in the light of a further distinction, developed by Rousseau in the second paragraph of his dissertation *On the Origin and Foundation of the Inequality of Mankind* (1755). On the one hand, Rousseau says, there is the inequality 'which I call natural or physical, because it is established by nature, and consists in a difference of age, health, bodily strength, and the qualities of mind or of the soul'. On the other there is what nowadays would be called social inequality, which 'depends on a kind of convention, and is established, or at least authorised, by the consent of men'. Most contemporary engineers of equality concentrate upon the social, while giving occasional and peripheral attention to schemes for compensating socially by starts and handicaps for whatever natural inequalities they can bring themselves to admit. But Christopher Jencks is clearly right in his protest:

> For a thoroughgoing egalitarian . . . inequality that derives from biology ought to be as repulsive as inequality that derives from early socialisation.[16]

Although this third idea of equality is today widely cherished, and cherished perhaps especially among political intellectuals,[17] it is hard to find any principled statement of which possible human differences are and are not to be condemned as inequalities – or even of why inequalities are supposed to be, as such, evil. It is also true that those who upon this ground urge in particular the reduction of (certain) differences in wealth and income rarely want to advocate an absolute equality in these respects. Bernard Shaw was very much the exception among socialists in advocating a strict equality of incomes. He remained, however, altogether typical in his inflexible refusal to set a costly personal example by surrendering his own very substantial, and therefore on his own account very unjust, surplus above average. But we must not by either of these two observations be misled to conclude that equality of outcome is not being held as a value; that it is not, that is to say, being accepted as a good in itself, good not just as a means but as an end.

Certainly there are those for whom particular egalitarian measures are solely means to other ends. In his robust exposition of *Utilitarian Ethics* Anthony Quinton, for instance, points out that:

> In most imaginable circumstances the distribution of a hundred oranges among a hundred people that will bring about the largest total utility is that in which each person gets only one. . . . [For] like most objects of desire oranges are subject to the law of diminishing marginal utility.[18]

Utilitarian Ethics

Those for whom equality is thus a means to the utilitarian end will have no inhibitions on accepting incentive inequalities which tend to maximise not just the minimum but the general welfare. But equally certainly there are now many other people for whom equality is a good in itself, perhaps even the pre-eminent or sole good. Thus on 30 December 1974 the editorialist of *The Guardian*, who presumably knows his readers, laid it on the line: 'Nearly all of us want to get through 1975 with the least damage to social equality.' Again, writing as a supporter of the Liberal Party, A. T. Peacock makes a point of first dismissing the consideration just now seen in Quinton, before proceeding to insist that Liberal support for progressive taxation is based upon 'a positive dislike of gross inequality'.[19]

Nor are the facts that people want to abolish *some* differences and not others and that even in those *some* they repudiate absolute equality sufficient to show that they are not committed to equality as a value. The first shows that for them it is a value only in certain contexts. But this limitation leaves it none the less a value. The second indicates no more than that its claims are not for them indefeasible, that trade-offs against other values may be tolerated.

'Can urban, industrial, bureaucratic societies like ours realise the promise of equality and social justice . . . without sacrificing the liberties which they have so far attained?' That was the apt question put about 'Equality' in a series of articles in *New Society* on the values proclaimed in the famous motto of successive French republics. Although the author, David Donnison, seems to have been too embarrassed to offer so much as a single illustration of the possible conflict, his conclusion was bold and correct: 'That is the central question.'[20]

Donnison is an outstandingly suitable spokesman for the socialist establishment brand of British egalitarianism. Righthand man and later successor to Richard Titmuss at the London School of Economics, eponymous chairman of the Donnison Committee and formerly member of other bodies working towards a uniform and universal system of compulsory comprehensive education, appointed to his present top Whitehall job by a Labour Minister of Health and Social Security, he has been honoured (along with Paul Streeten, Michael Young and Alex Ramsay) as one of the four great equalisers.

> Apart from any influence their writings may have had, those four must by now have planned, directed or managed several billion dollars' worth of three or four countries' capital resources, mostly to the purpose . . . of reducing inequalities. They are ambitious men at the top of severely competitive professions. . . . As far as I know each pays his taxes, takes home two or three times the average family income . . . and would work as well for a great deal less if more equal societies required that.[21]

Even the unhallowed ranks of Tuscany can scarce forbear to cheer, 'how splendid!', before proceeding, after taking careful aim, to launch an explosive missile question. Upon what grounds of principle are those four just men proposing *not* to yield up their own remaining unequal (and, we must presume, from their own account, socially unjust) excess – until and unless they shall be so compelled by law?

At the end of his original article Donnison asserts that the possible conflict between Freedom and Equality is 'the central question'. Yet it was an article remarkable for not finding need or space to make the distinctions which I have presented as being fundamental. Donnison did, however, have the grace to begin by conceding that the egalitarianism for which he was speaking is 'muddled'; and suggesting, in a usefully provocative way, that it is 'muddled because its academic spokesmen were never challenged by sufficiently tough opposition to compel them to clarify their views. . .'. Having thus originally concluded that the possible incompatibility between Freedom and Equality is 'the central question', Donnison went on two weeks later in the Correspondence columns – having perhaps been, in the meantime, shaken by the unfamiliar experience of meeting tough academic opposition – to dismiss all libertarian objectors with contempt: 'It is nonsense to tell us that nations which have more of the one necessarily have less of the other.'

Suppose that we are talking about Freedom and Equality in some purely voluntary organisation such as an Israeli kibbutz. Or suppose that we are being presented with a private moral ideal, which adherents will strive first to reach themselves, and afterwards recommend to others by example and by argument. Then there might indeed be no necessary conflict. But that is not how it is. This ideal of 'equality and social justice' is in fact one which has been approached, and which it is proposed to continue to approach, primarily, if not quite exclusively, by legal and administrative measures rather than by individual conversion and self-sacrificing self-discipline. It is also in one of its aspects, as I and others have recently been arguing, the Ideology of a New Class of social administrators – people professionally involved in (and personally advanced by) the business of enforcing it.

All this being so, the true nonsense is to pretend that there is no inverse necessary connection between imposed equality of outcome and liberties for the citizen. Of course there has to be compulsion if everyone is to be got and kept either up or down, as individually appropriate, to the officially approved average level of whatever it may be which is being equalised. No one is suggesting, surely, that those 'several billion dollars' worth of . . . resources' were the freewill offerings voluntarily made available by people who share the ideals and ambitions of the four just men?

It is equally obvious that the public provision of a welfare floor or safety net must involve some restriction of some possible liberties. For there will have to be taxes, that is to say, compulsory exactions, to pay for this too. But these exactions, these restrictions on liberty, will be modest compared with those needed to finance non-selective services available to all without any test of means. Still greater exactions must be required to finance monopoly services; in which the maintenance of the monopoly also itself inevitably involves further and different restrictions on liberty. The uniform monopoly service – admitting no element of consumer choice and hence no possibility of diversity – is at the same time and necessarily both the most constrictive of individual liberties and the most congenial to the ideal of equality of outcome.

It is, therefore, no accident that those who harbour ideals of this sort are forever pressing for always more (and never less) state monopoly in health, education, and welfare services; as well as, for that matter, over 'the means of production, distribution, and exchange'. Ralph Harris and Arthur Seldon, reviewing the first twenty years of the Institute of Economic Affairs,[22] understood well why every suggestion made by their writers for more *selectivity* and more *choice* in welfare services has run into unrelenting opposition from the Titmuss camp. For, for them, equality and not freedom or even welfare is the name of the game.

Two further observations ought to be made, especially in view of the fact that one party in these disputes is so often supposed both to have all the compassion and to be wholly disinterested. First, a selective welfare system will almost always be cheaper than a non-selective, and a state floor system cheaper than a state monopoly. So if we admit selectivity and permit choice, we can the more easily afford to provide a higher and more extensive floor. A steady opposition to such selectivity, and still more the opposition to choice, is therefore likely to be motivated by something other than a simple compassionate concern to relieve the most urgent human needs. Secondly, the expansion of non-selective and perhaps ultimately monopoly services provides more scope and more promotion for more social administrators – who then, in turn, strengthen the powerful and effective lobby pressing for still further expansion.

Who Will Equalise the Equalisers?

Apart from whatever particular limitations of liberty must be essentially involved in any particular programme for compulsory equalisation – or, for that matter, in any programme for compulsory *anything* – there are good general reasons to believe that a strenuous, sustained and extensive policy for imposing this ideal, especially in those areas which happen to be of most concern to the subjects, will as a matter of fact call for a highly authoritarian and widely repressive form of government.

I have already referred to the case for holding that a fully socialist economy must be, in practice, incompatible with a 'Western' democratic political régime, and with those minimum liberties required to make effective elections possible. Now it is precisely such a centralised, socialist, command economy which is necessary in order to make possible – though it alone will certainly not be sufficient to guarantee – the imposition and maintenance of any approved pattern of distribution. This socialist presupposition of the enforcement of 'equality and social justice' comes out very clearly in some revealing words of the chairman of a BBC series (1974) on *Whatever Happened to Equality?* (words uttered some time before his elevation to a Labour life peerage). He was confronted with:

> the idea that the state should determine everyone's rewards according to some system of fairness, and should determine prices accordingly . . . this is the acceptance of the view that there is a rational system of social justice which it is the business of the state to enforce.

John Vaizey agreed wholeheartedly: 'That's a view I should embrace very strongly. I believe that that is the way one ought to think about society.'[23]

This confession may be compared with one of the findings of a much recommended sociological study of *Class Inequality and Political Order* (1972). The author, Frank Parkin, seems to be one of those clear-headed and honest socialists who make little or no pretence of being concerned about freedom as well as equality. Parkin concludes:

> Egalitarianism seems to require a political system in which the state is able to hold in check those social and occupational groups which, by virtue of their skills or education or personal attributes, might otherwise attempt to stake claims to a disproportionate share of society's rewards. The most effective

way of holding such groups in check is by denying them the right to organise politically, or in other ways, to undermine social equality. This presumably is the reasoning underlying the Marxist-Leninist case for a political order based upon the 'dictatorship of the proletariat'. . . .

Yet there is a most remarkable, and at the same time most commonplace, deficiency in this conclusion. Nowhere in his whole book does it ever seem to cross Parkin's mind that, even in the somewhat unlikely event that such an uncriticisable and irremovable Power Élite were to subdue all temptations to appropriate massive prerequisites and privileges for its own members, still its absolute power over, and its total control of, the rest of the society must in itself constitute the greatest possible offence to any genuine ideal either of personal equality or even of equality of outcome.

So there is one key question which needs to be pressed and pressed and pressed again, not only against the Leninists but also against all the other, if milder, 'engineers of the soul', the whips of compulsory equality. (Leninists are, after all, openly committed to absolute rule by the élite vanguard; and, privately at least, never forget to ask with Lenin 'Who/whom?'.)

That one key question is: 'And who will equalise the equalisers? . . .

PART TWO

Equality of opportunity and equality before the law

6

Equality of opportunity

CHARLES FRANKEL

≠

'IT is possible', Tawney wrote 'that intelligent tadpoles reconcile themselves to the inconveniences of their position, by reflecting that, though most of them will live and die as tadpoles and nothing more, the more fortunate of the species will one day shed their tails, distend their mouths and stomachs, hop nimbly on to dry land, and croak addresses to their former friends on the virtues by means of which tadpoles of character and capacity can rise to frogs.'[1] Tawney was speaking of the notion of equality of opportunity, which has played such a central role in the defense of old-style free-enterprise capitalism. Argue with a defender of this economic system and he would have told you in the past, as he will tell you now, that the inequalities of capitalism represent the working out of equality of opportunity.

But socialists and apostles of the welfare state are also adherents of equality of opportunity. Tawney wrote the words I have quoted above [in the late 1920s], before the immense variety of programs aiming at greater equality had been introduced in Western nations, before World War II had exercised its great equalising influence on the conditions and style of life in his own country, Great Britain; and before the effort had been made to provide broad access to a great range of social goods, such as adequate health care and higher education, that had been hitherto monopolised by small,

First published in *Ethics*, Vol. 81 (1971), pp. 191–207.

For Notes and References see page 386 below.

privileged minorities. Yet through the course of this whole period, the guiding ideal, the justifying slogan, has been equality of opportunity, and the persisting complaint has been, as in previous periods, that equality of opportunity still does not exist. Similarly, a socialist may tell you that equality of opportunity has been part of the ideology by which capitalism has masked its true nature, but he nevertheless usually argues for socialism on the grounds that it alone provides true equality of opportunity. Marx's motto, at least for the transitional period of socialism that precedes the full achievement of communism, is: 'From each according to his abilities, to each according to his abilities'.

Indeed, the respect that has been paid to the principle of equality of opportunity goes beyond our own age, and even beyond the circle of believers in human equality. Unflinching antiegalitarians have apparently not been able to dispense with it. Plato defended the rigid hierarchical structure of his ideal state in part by arguing that it would be so organised that the best people in it would be selected for the most powerful positions; and Burke defended the inherited class system of Great Britain on the ground, among others, that it was an open system in which people capable of doing so rose steadily into the upper classes. In sum, democrats and antidemocrats, socialists and adherents of free enterprise, have all apparently been able to say that they believe in at least this much – that individuals sought to have a chance to go as far as their talents permit, and that it is the mark of a good society that its best people rise to the top. 'Most social systems', as Tawney said, 'need a lightning-conductor. The formula which supplies it to our own is equality of opportunity. The conception is one to which homage is paid today by all, including those who resist most strenuously attempts to apply it.'[2] All that separates the various proponents of this ideal, at any rate on the surface, is a difference of opinion over the kind of society which is best designed to achieve it. But all say that they wish to achieve it. Equality of opportunity is everybody's girl.

We probably ought not to be too surprised, therefore, that the notion of equality of opportunity has not been the subject of very much close inspection. The universal popularity of an idea usually discourages its close inspection; and if it were so inspected, it would probably not remain universally popular. Yet the key role which the notion of equality of opportunity plays in contemporary politics, law, education, and social discussion in general, invites us to look at it carefully. Indeed, its universal popularity should arouse some suspicion. Social ideas, if their meaning is at all clear, stand for some specific way of exercising power or distributing the goods of the world. They help some people more than they help others, and they represent positive threats to some people's position and possessions. If equality of opportunity is a significant ideal, there ought to be some people who are opposed to it. Or it may well be that it is a highly stretchable or ambiguous concept, which cloaks strongly divergent ideas over which people do in fact disagree. A verbal formula which everybody employs, and which therefore creates the impression of general agreement on fundamentals, is often very useful politically. But it may also prevent the clear analysis of issues and the formulation of the choices that have to be made. The peace it brings is therefore an unstable peace and one that comes at too high a price. In any case, the notion of equality of opportunity plays so central a role in the pantheon of contemporary social ideals that it clearly merits philosophical examination.

What then, do we have in mind when we speak of 'equality of opportunity'? What sort of arguments can we give to defend this ideal? Why, in fact, should we wish to defend it? And why has the ideal played so central a role in social philosophy? These questions, I believe, take us to the heart of some of the most controverted issues on the contemporary scene.

I

To pursue these questions, it is necessary first to step back from them and to review some of the problems inherent in the general ideal of equality. For the notion of equality of opportunity, although is is not itself analysed, is commonly invoked in order to resolve these problems. Let us begin by examining three versions of the notion of equality – what I shall call 'formal equality', 'fundamental' or 'basic equality', and 'distributive equality'.

1. *Formal equality*. According to Aristotle, 'Injustice arises when equals are treated unequally and also when unequals are

treated equally'.[3] This formula obviously requires that we possess rules which allow us to determine who is equal to whom and what is equal to what. Provided we have such rules, however, any set of rules will do. Thus, equality can be given a purely formal meaning. It simply calls for treating like cases alike, where 'like cases' are defined by a given system of rules. It demands that we make no further distinctions between individuals but those expressly required by the rules.

This is not unimportant, unless one thinks that a barrier against arbitrary decisions and special favoritism is unimportant. However, the reasons why many find a purely formal conception of equality inadequate are evident. It is compatible with the existence of bad rules and with highly stratified societies. If, for example, a society has rules which distinguish between its members in terms of their ancestry, the principle of formal equality remains uninfringed so long as all the members of this society are treated uniformly in accordance with these distinctions, and only in accordance with them. Indeed, if it is a fundamental rule of a society that individuals shall be assigned social positions, or given rewards and punishments, in accordance with the sovereign's caprice, then formal equality would be compatible even with capriciousness. Herodotus noticed that, in this respect, all who lived under Oriental despots were equal. Accordingly, opinions to the contrary notwithstanding,[4] formal equality, if we interpret it absolutely strictly, cannot even be defended in terms of the general importance of rules and stability in human society.

Few believers in equality, therefore, have been satisfied with a purely formal interpretation of it. They have wanted society organised not simply in accordance with rules, but with rules of a certain character. In fact, even their conception of formal equality has not been an absolutely formal one: it has been a partly substantive conception, involving the specific notion of rules that are consistent with what is known, in broad terms, as the rule of law. And beyond this, they have wished to have rules which make distinctions that are reasonable and morally defensible and that do not obscure the ways in which individuals are alike and should be treated alike.

2. '*Fundamental or basic*' *equality*. This brings us to a second

version or aspect of the notion of equality. What do we mean by 'reasonable' and 'morally defensible'? And what are the ways in which people are alike, and in which it is wrong to make distinctions between them? It is at this point that a varity of well-known assertions are made – that all men are created equal; that all have minds and consciences (or at least the potentiality of having them), and thus have certain inalienable rights, that each human being is of equal worth, in some ultimate sense, with every other because all partake in common of the quality of humanity. To analyse what is meant by such assertions, or to evaluate the arguments that have been given for them, would take me far afield. It is enough to focus here on their intent and practical consequence. They propose a policy or procedure which it is recommended we follow whenever we introduce, or attempt ot justify, any distinctions between individuals.

This policy or procedure is to treat all members of a society – or of the human race – as members of a single reference group. Accordingly, when distinctions are made between individuals a reason has to be given for these distinctions. And since the reason will involve invoking a rule of some kind, a reason has to be given for this rule. In short, the belief in the fundamental or basic equality of men shifts the *onus probandi*. Those who would treat people differently have to explain why. Those who would treat people the same are not normally subject to this requirement.

The historical consequences of this doctrine have of course been enormous. Since all established social systems in fact treat people differently, the doctrine of fundamental equality brought them all into court for trial. And in this trial, it gave the prosecution an advantage it had not hitherto possesed. A social system had to prove its innocence; the accuser did not have to prove its guilt. Thus, the process by which societies argue that their structures are legitimate also changed. What came to justify a social structure was not historical precedent but the benefits it offered individuals, not its heroic achievements in the past but its promise of future achievement. Most important of all, perhaps, the doctrine of fundamental equality made individuals the fundamental units in measuring social value. For it gave a secondary and subordinate status to all specific social groups or social hierarchies; the primary group was all individuals taken indiscriminately. Any distinctions we make between individuals, therefore, must be purely functional distinctions; they are justified only when they serve a specific purpose, and they are warranted only when they are restricted to the area in which they serve that purpose. We can distinguish between a general and a private within the army because such distinctions are necessary to an army; but when it comes to paying taxes, or the right to vote, we shall pay no attention to distinctions of military rank. Indeed, the validity of any purpose to which we appeal in order to justify treating people differently must itself be judged solely in terms of its relation to the well-being or fulfilment of individuals. We have grown so accustomed to this approach to human affairs that we do not realise how unusual it is in the record of human history.

Nevertheless, serious problems remain with this approach, even if we neglect the problem of proving its validity. As is the case with the concept of formal equality, the notion that men are fundamentally or basically (or naturally or metaphysically) equal is compatible with extreme inequalities in practical fact. All that the belief in fundamental equality requires us to do is to give good reasons for treating people unequally. But it does not say that there never are such reasons; nor does it tell us what is or is not a good reason, beyond the restriction that all reasons must refer in the end to the well-being of individuals rather than to that of groups.

Thus, it has been found to be perfectly compatible with the fundamental equality of men that business entrepreneurs should be rewarded more handsomely than dutiful ditchdiggers. The ground for this practice is the factual assertion that the entrepreneur makes a more important contribution to the general prosperity, and that the rewards offered him are necessary in order to encourage him to take the risks that go with the performance of his social function. This proposition may or may not be true, but it is certainly not self-evidently false. Similarly, laws protecting the rights of inheritance, special scholarships for the intelligent, and dachas for ballerinas have all been accepted in modern societies by people who sincerely think themselves firm believers in the basic equality of men. The fundamental rights of man seem to guarantee, in the words of the cynic, that the rich and the poor have an equal right to sleep under bridges. They may give certain basic rights to all, but they still leave men unequal in most respects; and just as much to the point, the equality they give is an equality which is not equally important to all who have it.

Thus, the ideal of equality has had to be fleshed out, to be given a more substantial embodiment than the abstract doctrine of the basic equality of all men. The fundamental rights of man as they emerged out of eighteenth-century revolutions were addressed to the removal of the special forms of legal classification and discrimination descended from the Old Regime. It is too easily forgotten by those with an Anglo-Saxon background, and particularly by Americans, that the term 'bourgeois', for example, stood not simply for a sociological category but for a quite precise, legally defined group. The assertion of universal natural rights was intended to undercut such legal distinctions. However, these universal rights left largely untouched and unregulated other kinds of difference in class, power, and economic preferment which also render men unequal. 'Grâce au capitalisme', as Henri Sée observed, 'les distinctions économiques se substituent aux distinctions juridiques.[5]

3. *Distributive equality*. There has emerged, therefore, a stronger conception of equality which argues that, in a just society, there should be, in practical terms, a more equal distribution of substantive benefits and burdens. Greater uniformity should exist not only in legal guarantees but in the actual possession of material things, in the access to immaterial goods like education which exercise a central influence on a man's destiny, and in the kind of respect and deference that build his self-image and nourish his capacities. At the very least, even if absolute uniformity cannot or should not be achieved, sharp or extreme differences in these respects should not exist between one man's situation and another's.

Needless to say, this conception of equality is a response to injustices whose reality and importance no dialectic can deny. But we must still ask some questions about it. Difficulties begin the moment one asks just what this quality is or why anyone should want it. Let us consider four.

a) The first is one which distributive equality shares with the concept of fundamental equality – namely, why should we think that making distinctions between people requires more explanation than failing to make distinctions between them? Partisans of equality commonly take the view that the rule that men should be treated alike unless there are good reasons not to do so is prima facie more plausible than other rules. But this is anything but plain. In explanation of this assumption, for example, Isaiah Berlin has written:

> The assumption is that equality needs no reasons, only inequality does so. . . . If I have a cake and there are ten persons among whom I wish to divide it, then if I give exactly one tenth to each, this will not, at any rate automatically, call for justification; whereas if I depart from this principle of equal division I am expected to produce a special reason. It is some sense of this, however latent, that makes equality an ideal which has never seemed intrinsically eccentric, even though extreme forms of it may not have been wholly acceptable to either political thinkers or ordinary men throughout recorded history.[6]

But is it true that, with respect to the example given, one would have to produce a reason only if one did not give each person an equal sized piece of cake? If we were awarding pieces of cake in relation to people's scores in a game of golf, we would have to give a reason for dividing the cake equally. Nor can we call the fact that a contest has been held a 'special' reason, of the kind that we have to invoke in order to justify departing from a principle by which we would otherwise automatically abide. There is nothing automatic about it. No one would be surprised if we gave pieces of cake to children of twelve that were twice as large as those we gave to children of two or dieters of forty. No one would think a reason was needed, if we lived in the kind of society in which such behaviour was expected, if we gave the largest piece of cake to the oldest male and no cake at all to the females. Indeed, if we did not do this, we would be asked to give a reason.

In sum, the idea that absolute equality is somehow a natural, or intellectually prior, or intrinsically uneccentric, principle, and that it is only when we deviate from this principle that we have to give justifying reasons is unwarranted. It rests on the assumption that there is some single standard set of conditions in which distributions are made. But if there are no conditions that can be regarded as *the* standard conditions, this view turns out to rest on an unargued prepossession. The concrete conditions in which distributions are made are part of what we have to know in order to know what we are going to mean by equality. And since there is no single standard set of conditions, there is no single standard meaning of equality.

b) A second difficulty is closely connected to this first one. Suppose that we give each person an equal portion of cake, but that one man complains because he just does not happen to like cake. Has he been treated equally with the others? To generalise this example, why should individuals who are different from one another be placed in similar circumstances and treated in the same way? Does this not mean that Peter, for whom these circumstances are fitting, will benefit more than Paul, to whose nature and needs they may be foreign? And is this not simply another form of inequality, since it consists in treating unequals equally? The believer in distributive equality must explain in just what way he is not denying one of the fundamental values to which the ideal of equality is attached – the value of individuality. For he seems to be employing a rule which leads to arbitrary judgements with regard to individuals – or rather to the refusal to judge individuals at all.

There is, of course, a kind of answer to this objection. It can be said that if cake is distributed and one of the recipients does not like cake, provision can be made for him to exchange it for something else of equal value. But this raises the question of what standard of value to employ. We shall now have a society in which in fact different people have available to them quite different things, although all these different things – four ounces of cake or ten minutes of Mozart, time and a half for overtime or an extra month's vacation, the pleasures of a Dry Martini or the pleasures of friendship – are somehow interchangeable on a universally satisfactory scale of measurement. That this is a state of affairs not likely to be achieved, or even approximated, in practice I do not think requires long argument.

c) Even when we simplify and restrict the notion of distributive equality, we do not avoid difficulties. It can be said – indeed, it probably should be said – that the considerations I have just mentioned are all much too abstract, that the ordinary advocate of equality knows just what he means, and that he means something much more definite. He has in mind a plain and imperious demand – namely, that some elementary human needs, such as food, shelter, and health, must be satisfied as a condition for a minimally decent human life. And the equality he seeks is simply equality with respect to the satisfaction of these needs. But at least two questions are raised by such a response.

The first is: What needs shall we include in the category of basic needs? The need for higher education? This is increasingly accepted as a basic need today, but such was not always the case. The need to visit suffering on those one hates? This is a widespread and powerful need, to the satisfaction of which, on the record, human beings have been prepared to sacrifice health, leisure, civil harmony, and even personal safety. Why, then, is it not a basic need? Yet I know of no partisan of equality who favors providing for it. He carries into the argument, even when he wishes to take care only of 'basic needs', an independent view of what these needs are. I do not quarrel with him about this. In fact, I share his position. But the question that regularly causes controversy and that the call for equality does not in itself settle, is: How do we establish the list of 'basic needs'? That it is an indefinitely expandable list is at least suggested by recent history.

Moreover, what do we have in mind when we speak of 'satisfying' a need? How far does the term 'satisfaction' go? Granted that all men need a minimal amount of food, how pleasant should the food be, how varied, how bountiful? Clearly, there are large differences in what people can enjoy, and in what they may receive, within the framework of providing a minimal amount to all. And their subjective satisfactions from receiving the same amount also differ. It appears to me, therefore, that the argument that all men should be insured of the minimal conditions of a decent life is an argument for equality only in a highly attenuated sense. It is really an argument simply for a more adequate welfare state, which is not quite the same thing. What is opposed is not inequality but human suffering and insecurity. The defense of the ideal of equality which consists in saying that it asks nothing more than universal guarantees of minimal satisfaction of basic needs really consists in abandoning the ideal of equality for the defense of something else that seems less debatable.

d) Finally, as has already become plain, distributive equality focuses on *needs*. But why should we speak of equal distribution relative to needs, rather than, for example to performance? Indeed, do not many men feel a need to be recognised for their performance? Why, then, when we speak of the requirement to satisfy human needs equally, do we overlook this need? But if this is a need, is there not a need for the recognition of human inequality? For performances differ. Once again we face the apparent implication that the call for equality is not what it seems. It is not evenhanded; it expresses a bias for some needs and some people and against other needs and other people. It seems to be, in a word, simply a demand to replace one kind of inequality with another kind.

II

So we come to the notion of equality of opportunity. For it is to this notion that philosophers and ordinary men have commonly turned to bail them out of the difficulties in which the ideal of equality, taken by itself, appears to land them. The central place that equality of opportunity occupies in the analysis and defense of equality is well illustrated in the following passage from Brian Barry's book, *Political Argument:*

> Those who wish to disparage the distributive principle of equality often seek to do so by suggesting that its adherents are committed to holding either that men *are* 'equal' in their personal characteristics or that they *ought* to be 'equal'. Then, since 'equality of personal characteristics' does not seem to make much sense it is suggested that equalitarians presumably mean 'identical' when they say 'equal'. As this idea is absurd, too, distributive equality can be conveniently dismissed as an unintelligible concept. . . . What equality 'really means' it is claimed is that some reason or other must be adduced to justify treating people differently. The incoherence, however, lies not in the concept of equality, but in the hostile formulation itself. To say that people should be equal is to say that their opportunities for satisfying

whatever wants they may happen to have should be equal. Whether or not one agrees with the claim in any particular case, it surely cannot be denied that it is a reasonably intelligible one, and one not involving any implausible prescriptions or descriptions involving uniformity or identity.[7]

To invoke the notion of equality of opportunity seems to be to take care of a number of problems. It takes account of the diversity of human wants and capacities. It answers the question as to just what it is, among all the possible goods of life, that should be equally distributed. And it explains both why inequality and difference may be accepted and what the limits to such acceptance should be in a just society. It thus appears to fill major gaps in the argument for equality.

Let us turn, therefore, and inspect this idea. Does it in fact perform these services? If we take Mr Barry's formulation of the idea, it does so only on condition that we do not take it quite literally. We must read certain limitations into it. 'To say that people should be equal,' according to Barry, 'is to say that their opportunities for satisfying whatever wants they may happen to have should be equal.' He goes on to say that, even if we do not agree with this claim, it is at least 'reasonably intelligible', and does not involve 'any implausible prescriptions or descriptions involving uniformity or identity'. But this is so, I believe, only if we silently decide that it does not mean certain things.

1. First of all, we would have to mean only *legitimate* wants. It would be quite implausible to argue, in the name of equality of opportunity, that a man who wants to torture all people over thirty ought to have an equal opportunity to satisfy this want with a man who wants, say, to support his aged parents. I recognise, to be sure, that moral standards are changing, so that, for all I know, this example may be infelicitous. Still, I take it that no one who says that men should have equal opportunities to satisfy whatever wants they may happen to have really means 'whatever wants' without qualification. We cannot accept equality of opportunity unless we accept certain moral standards, above and beyond it, which limit its field of operation.

2. The restrictions which we must silently read into the conception of equality of opportunity go beyond the notion of

morally legitimate wants. It is possible to have wants that are not in themselves morally illegitimate, but that are unrealistic. A man may want to be universally liked; he may want an economic system about which no one at all will complain; he may want a university which devotes its major energies to political activity, but which is at the same time a congenial place for skeptical dialogue and purely theoretical inquiries. Clearly, no human arrangement can give equality of opportunity to satisfy such wants. We implicitly exclude from the list of wants that people ought to have an opportunity to satisfy, I assume, those wants which no one can satisfy. Not that this prevents people from having such wants, from pushing for their satisfaction, or from demanding equality of opportunity to do so. But demands for the satisfaction of such unrealistic wants are nevertheless unacceptable. Ought implies can, and equality of opportunity does not provide an escape clause from this maxim.

3. These restrictions on equality of opportunity are fairly obvious. However, they lead to another which is less so and which suggests that the concept of equality of opportunity is somewhat more puzzling, or at any rate more complicated, than Barry's words suggest.

There are many human wants which are not unrealistic in the absolute sense we have described: conditions can be defined, that is to say, under which they could be satisfied, and these conditions are not impossible to create. However, it would be extremely costly to do so. To take an example which, unfortunately, is not at all hypothetical, consider the supersonic transport plane. It is easily possible to create conditions in which people who want to fly from New York to California in two hours will have an opportunity to do so equal to the opportunity of those who are content to make the journey in five. But is it worth it? What is the cost to the nervous systems of people on the ground, and to other social needs which have been subordinated to this one? And obviously, many other examples can be given, a good portion of them no more imaginary.

It seems to me highly doubtful, therefore, that anyone who asks for equality of opportunity can consistently mean to say that he wants a society in which people's opportunities for satisfying whatever wants they may happen to have will be equal. Human wants conflict; they are multiple and insatiable; resources, if only the resources of human time and energy, are always scarce in relation to them. Some general system of social cost accounting, which assigns different values to the satisfaction of different wants, therefore has to be employed. This represents a substantial limitation on the ideal of equality of opportunity.

4. In addition to these qualifications that have to be introduced into the conception of equality of opportunity, there is still another issue. The idea as it is normally used is ambiguous. It points in two directions. Sometimes we invoke it to condemn a situation in which people are unable to satisfy their wants, but sometimes we invoke it to condemn a situation in which they are satisfying the wrong wants, or not sufficiently ambitious ones.

Thus, it is easier for the child of a working-class family to drop out of school than for a middle-class child; but the working-class child does not suffer from inequality of opportunity in the sense we have so far been discussing it, because dropping out of school is what he wants to do. In fact, it is the middle-class child who is more likely to be suffering from inequality so defined, since there are many more in this category who want to leave school but are unable to do so. Yet most egalitarians offer such facts as these as evidence of inequality of opportunity for workers and hold that in some way it should be rectified. Their complaint, therefore, is not about unequal opportunity to satisfy the wants that people happen to have; it is about unequal opportunity to develop the right wants. Eliza Doolittle had no desire to speak the king's English; she was perfectly content speaking the English she did until Professor Higgins got hold of her. But this is precisely what proves that she did not have equality of opportunity with Professor Higgins. So there are not only moral standards and considerations of social cost that affect our notion of equality of opportunity. Cultural standards and notions of human potentialities may also be part of it.

Nor can it be argued, so far as I can see, that the notion of equality of opportunity cannot or should not be extended in this way. We do not condemn oppressive environments only because people feel oppressed inside them; we condemn them even when their victims do not feel oppressed. We do so because we think that it adds to the evil of an environment that it crushes people's power to imagine other possibilities and renders them wholly accepting of their condition. Equality of opportunity, in consequence, may quite properly lean on a conception of human or social excellence; but when it does, we cannot evaluate the demand for equality of opportunity without evaluating that conception. And it becomes different from the flatter conception of equal opportunity, conceived as opportunity to satisfy existing wants.

5. If ambiguities arise when we look at 'wants', equivalent ambiguities emerge when we focus on the notion of 'opportunity'. Indeed, its ambiguity explains, I believe, some of our bitterest social controversies.

An example will help to bring out this ambiguity. Most people would agree, I think, that it would be odd for me to complain that I never had an equal opportunity with Mickey Mantle to play center field for the Yankees. Of course, I never did have an equal chance. But the competition for center fielder of the Yankees is perfectly fair; it is based on a test of capacities for the position and nothing else; anyone may enter the competition, and, in fact, great efforts are made to see that everyone qualified does enter, and, apart from unforseeable accidents, the only thing that makes a difference is a man's ability. All that separates me from Mickey Mantle is my inability to compete with him, and since this is all that separates me, I may complain about my fate, but I cannot complain of inequality of opportunity. For when we speak of equality of opportunity to achieve something we set a man's abilities aside in estimating his chances and refer only to his chances to use them.

But much depends, therefore, on the notion of 'ability'. And here there is an equivocation. Suppose it were the case, to return to my disappointment, that I really could have competed successfully with Mickey Mantle, but that, being a city boy, I was discouraged from a very early age from doing so. My parents put other goals before me; there was not enough open space to play; my companions were an improperly motivated group who never offered me competition sufficient to challenge me, and who, in fact, often preferred to read books. Had these circumstances been different, I would have given Mickey Mantle a hard time. I had the native ability, and I was simply a victim of circumstance. If all this were the case, why could I not complain that I never had equality of opportunity with Mickey Mantle? Why, indeed, do people so tamely accept the proposition that I did have an equal chance and that the best man simply won?

We begin to see what has happened here in this extension of this example, and in my movement from a mood of resignation to one of rebellion, by noticing that we use the term 'ability' in at least two different contexts. There are contexts in which the primary desideratum is performance, here and now. In these contexts we use the term 'ability' to refer to a man's general quality of performance. And in these terms, I had an equal opportunity to show my ability with Mickey Mantle. But there are other contexts in which the primary desideratum is developmental, educational, the evoking of potentialities. And in these contexts – for example, in schools –we commonly distinguish between an individual's 'natural ability', as revealed by diagnostic tests or other means, and his actual performance. And when he performs at a level lower than his abilities we explain this in terms of his environment, or motivation, or physical health or some other factor presumably extraneous to his ability. All these factors, of course, have something to do with his total performance; they make him, in fact, unable to do better than he is doing. Yet we do not say that he does not have the ability. For in these educational contexts what we do is to distinguish between two kinds of factors involved in performance, one which is modifiable and the other which is not, except within narrow limits. And we call the latter kind of factor 'natural ability'.

Thus, just as there arise different practical conceptions of equality of opportunity depending on whether we are talking about wants as they exist or wants as they should be, so there also arise different conceptions of equality of opportunity depending on whether we are stressing performance or the development of individual potentialities. If we stress the former, we arrive at what may be called the 'meritocratic' conception of equality of opportunity. It holds that tests should be fair, that they should be open to everyone, that lack of money or other physical hindrances should not be a barrier to taking them, and that people should then be graded and rewarded in terms of their performance. So interpreted, equality of opportunity is entirely compatible with sharp hierarchical differences in society so long as there is also social mobility. It simply consists in the claim that social differentiation should be based on reasonable and objective principles, and that individuals should move up and down the hierarchy in accordance with their performance. It says nothing about the need to eliminate sharp distinctions, except insofar as this may be necessary to give everybody the same chance to compete.

Yet, clear as this 'meritocratic' conception seems, it fades at the edges when it is pushed. If it seems unfair – an inequality of opportunity – that a man should not be able to take a test for a position he wants because he cannot afford to travel to the testing place – and most advocates of meritocracy would accept this as unfair – why is it not also unfair for a man to be deprived of the opportunity to prepare himself for such a test because he cannot get the necessary education? And if it is a mark of unequal opportunity to allow a man to be deprived of an education from which he would benefit when such an education is available to others, why is it not equally an example of unequal opportunity to leave him in an environment that deprives him even of the desire to seek such an education?

Thus, we move gradually to another conception of equality of opportunity – what I think might be called the 'educational' conception. It looks upon the meritocratic approach as stilted, narrow, and coldly artificial. It condemns it for taking people simply as they are, for judging them in terms of their performance without asking what it is that makes one man perform better than another. Equality of opportunity means that men shall not be limited except by their abilities; the advocate of the 'educational' conception of equality of opportunity holds that we cannot have real equality of opportunity unless we successfully modify those aspects of the individual's situation which prevent him from performing up to the level of his natural abilities.

III

Is there any way of adjudicating between these two conceptions? Not, so far as I can see, in a wholesale manner. There is no formula that allows us to settle the matter *a priori*. We have to proceed case by case. For, if I am right in saying that these two versions of equality of opportunity emerge out of different contexts in which different purposes are primary, then each represents a potentially legitimate claim in the making of public policy. There are circumstances in which what we want and cannot compromise with is performance; we cannot put up with inferior airline pilots or brain surgeons on the ground that they are learning on the job. There are other circumstances in which searching for and nourishing talent is the primary requirement; we would think it foolish to tell an eight-year-old chess player that he could not play again because he had lost a game to a chess master. And in between, there are all sorts of circumstances in which a concern for efficiency and a concern for education are both possible. In such circumstances we have to decide how much weight we shall give to each.

However, if there is no defensible general formula that allows us to come down neatly on one side or the other, there are certain guidelines, I believe, that help us to adjudicate specific cases. I shall suggest what I think the principal ones are, for they also help us to see, I think, what the logic of the case for equality of opportunity, in either its meritocratic or education version, is.

1. One guideline is cost – not only economic cost narrowly considered, but economic cost in the broader terms of human time, energy, striving, and the probabilities of disappointment as against success. Let us go back to what we have noticed about the 'educational' interpretation of equality of opportunity. It rests, we have seen, on a distinction between the individual's 'natural' or 'inherent' abilities, which are not subject to significant modification, and other factors which are held to be modifiable. But terms like 'modifiable' and 'unmodifiable' very often express only a difference in degree, and not a difference in kind. What is the cost, for example, of changing an individual's early environment as against, say,

changing his genetic constitution? In the light of new developments in biology, it may some day be easier and less costly to change the genetic constitution of individuals. The language of 'natural abilities' is likely in these circumstances to become even fuzzier than it now is. It is possible that we shall begin to talk of an individual's 'natural abilities' in terms of those aspects of his personality which are determined by his early upbringing, rather than in terms of those that are genetically determined.

More to the immediate point, this example brings out the fact that while, in abstract principle, environmental factors are subject to modification, it is often extremely difficult to do so in practice. How do government, or the school, or organised psychological counseling, successfully intervene in methods of child-rearing affecting, for instance, the first three crucial months of the individual's life? How can the habits, fears, images of authority, and unconscious drives of the mother – or of the stand-in parents in the public institutions that might be created – be effectively changed? Despite extravagant claims, we do not really know very much about how to do this in a practical way. And what we do know indicates that it probably lies beyond our existing resources in people, funds, and general patience and goodwill. Certain limits, therefore, have to be placed on the applicability of the broad 'educational' version of equality of opportunity. We can adopt it only to the extent that we can envisage circumstances that are, for practical purposes, modifiable, and that we think are worth modifying, given the cost.

There are, therefore, general differences in the way which poor and rich societies normally construe equality of opportunity. In a poor society, at any rate one seriously committed to escaping from poverty, successful performance is urgently needed and false steps are costly. It is natural, therefore, that a meritocratic version of equality of opportunity usually takes hold in such societies, and that there should be a tendency in them to act on the principle that the race should go to the swift. This has happened in socialist societies as well as in nonsocialist ones. In richer societies, in contrast, the ampler, more educational view of equality of opportunity has a better chance to prevail. Even in a rich society, however, there are limits. If, for example, a society is able to obtain an adequate supply of first-rate mathematicians by relying on those who emerge, with no special educational effort, from the more favored classes of the population, how much should it expend to change the environment of poor people so that they make a proportionate contribution of mathematicians? The answer to this question is an open one. It involves the specification – a very difficult one – of a variety of costs on both sides of the issue: on one side, for example, the cost of maintaining an opportunity structure that limits horizons, or the cost of a socially insulated scientific élite; on the other side, the cost of undertaking experiments that may not work, or the limits on the need of the society for mathematicians, etc. These are very difficult issues to weigh, but they are examples of the kind of issue that has to be weighed when we try to determine whether the educational or meritocratic version of equality of opportunity should be stressed in a particular situation.

2. A second issue that emerges, as may already be evident, is an issue of morals, or at least of mores. The question of what is or is not modifiable, or what is or is not 'natural ability', turns, in part, on what men choose to think should be modified, and what they place beyond the realm of organised social attack. As Plato pointed out, if we really want everyone to begin at the same place, so that only 'natural abilities' control the outcome, there is one thing we must absolutely do – abolish the family and bring people up in public institutions. The family makes a more immediate difference than anything else in determining the individual's life chances. Unless we are ready to deny the institution of the family the special protections we now assign to it, only some of the inequalities associated with family origins (and, exceptional cases apart, probably not the most important) can be changed. The justification of any particular demand for equality of opportunity in the broad nonmeritocratic sense depends on whether the demand touches on fundamental matters of this sort and on the degree to which we are willing and able to do something about them.

3. A third issue has to do with the standards by which we measure either performance or ability. Let us take as an example

the volatile issue of equality of educational opportunity. It has been said with increasing frequency in Europe recently in relation to the *de facto* segregation of social classes in the schools, and with equal or greater frequency in the United States in relation to our racial problems, that equality of educational opportunity is in effect denied because, in measuring 'ability' or 'performance', we do so by standards that are culturally biased: they are bourgeois, or white middle class, or something of the sort. Accordingly, those coming from other milieux cannot usually compete successfully, and, in any case, it is an imposition to ask them to compete, since the standards in question are legitimate only in terms of social purposes that are not theirs. Equality of opportunity therefore entails, it is argued, changing the nature of the standards applied to those who are disadvantaged.

Here again the issue in one, I believe, of striking a balance. Where the needs of people in different social groups are different, and where their aptitudes lie in different areas, there is a legitimate claim that standards should be modified to take these into account. However, the degree of legitimacy of this claim is limited by the answers we give to other questions: To what extent are we willing to create an educational system that will fix most people in separate social or ethnic groups? And to what extent are the needs and aptitudes we are asked to take into account needs and aptitudes that, in the long-run, are socially and historically viable? For the argument that standards should be modified for the sole and sufficient reason that they do not fit the distinctive situation of a given group rests on at least two fallacies.

It assumes, to begin with, that all the standards employed are culturally biased. But this is not so unless we are prepared to say that there is such a thing as bourgeois mathematical logic or white middle-class astronomy. At least some intellectual disciplines are cross-cultural, and standards of performance or ability developed in relation to them are also cross-cultural in validity, even if not in their origins. Moreover, the claim that because workers and bourgeois, or black and whites, differ in cultural tastes and aptitudes in certain respects, they differ in all respects, is a non sequitur, and plainly an exaggeration.

Second, even if we agree that many tests of school performance or ability are culturally biased, which I think we must admit, this does not prove that individuals coming from different cultural backgrounds should not be measured by them. It is possible that they should be measured by them in their own interest. Ability in arithmetic, for example, is a bourgeois value. But if ability in arithmetic is useful to any citizen of an industrial society, then it is a reasonable standard to expect any citizen to meet. This does not preclude also varying educational requirements where the long-range needs of different individuals or groups are different. Nor does it preclude the criticism and correction of educational standards when these are culturally biased to no good point. But equality of opportunity remains a demand we can evaluate only if we ask: Equality of opportunity for what? . . .

7

Equality of opportunity and equality of results

JAMES S. COLEMAN

≠

THIS [*Inequality: A Reassessment of the Effect of Family and Schooling in America*] could have been an important book. Jencks and his colleagues have had the audacity to assemble and reanalyse a wide range of research on inequality, and have demonstrated a high level of technical skill in doing so. But the book misses the opportunity. To show how it comes to miss the opportunity, I must clarify at the outset certain points about inequalities in society. For it is the confusion between different meanings of inequality that leads Jencks and his colleagues to the fundamental difficulties of the book.

Inequality of Result

In every society there are occupational positions that earn different amounts of income. This income is ordinarily in money, though where income taxes are high (as in England and Sweden) or where there are ideological constraints on income inequalities (as in socialist states), a significant portion is paid in direct (untaxed) perquisites. Since these occupations are filled by persons, the differential earnings from different positions give rise to a distribution of income among persons or among families. The skewness of this distribution has historically declined in the United States, with incomes

First published in *Harvard Educational Review*, Vol. 43, No. 1 (Feb. 1973), pp. 129–37.

For Notes and References, see page 387 below.

becoming more nearly alike, though a great deal of inequality of income remains.

Thus one meaning of inequality in society is merely the differential distribution of income and other social rewards to different persons. This can be described as 'inequality of result'. The extent of inequality of result can be measured, though imperfectly, by the degree of skewness in the income distribution. The authors use (in Table 7.1) the coefficient of variation of income to measure this inequality, and show that it has declined from 1.23 in 1929 to 0.75 in 1970. They also present the share of total income held by each fifth of the population, ranging from the lowest-income fifth to the highest. The authors argue that this distribution has become very little more equal in the past twenty-five years (a claim that I will return to), and that this is the matter that concerns them. In the last chapter of the book, for example, they say, 'The reader should by now have gathered that our primary concern is with equalizing the distribution of income' (p. 261).

Inequality of Opportunity

But there is a second sense of inequality as well, one at least as familiar to most Americans as inequality in the sense above. This is inequality of access to those positions which give high income and other social rewards. Inequality in this sense is not measured by the amount of income different persons have; it is measured by the relation of a person's background to the social rewards he comes to gain. If all sons from high-income families come to have high income, and all sons from low-income families come to have low income, then there would be high inequality in this second sense. This is what is meant by 'inequality of opportunity', and it is reactions to this inequality that have been the source of recent equalising movements – for blacks, Chicanos, women, and Indians.

It should be clear that these two meanings of inequality are conceptually distinct. If there are two societies with a given degree of inequality of result, one of them might have total inequality of opportunity, via direct transmission of occupational position and wealth from father to son, while the other might have total equality of opportunity, with a son's income unrelated to that of his father. Of course, at the extreme of perfect income equality, there can be no inequality of opportunity, since there is no opportunity to do better or worse.

Now the curious aspect of this book is that the authors say in chapters 7 and 9 that they are concerned with inequality of income, and their policy proposals are directed to that inequality. But nearly all their analysis is directed to questions of inequality of opportunity. This is likely the consequence of making a book with many hands. But whatever the source of the difficulty, the result is a book that fails to study appropriately either inequalities of income or inequalities of opportunity.

A Different Book

If Jencks and his colleagues had pursued the question of why inequalities of income are as great as they are, the book would have differed in two ways from its present form. It would have started with inequality of income, and not waited until the last chapter to consider it. Much of the current book might then have been unnecessary. The questions of inequality of opportunity that they study, such as the relation of family background to income, would have been unnecessary and irrelevant. That is, much of chapters 6 and 7 would have been irrelevant. And if they found, as they argue, that income is not much related to educational attainment or cognitive skills, then there would have been no need to investigate the sources of inequality in educational attainment and in cognitive skills. That is, chapters 1 to 5 would have been unnecessary.

A second way in which the book would have differed if it had truly studied inequality of income is that it would have investigated many things it has not investigated. It would have focused not primarily on the inequalities of opportunity among persons, but on the inequalities of reward among occupational positions. These differential rewards depend on a variety of things not touched in *Inequality*: the demand for activities for which skills are scarce, and the control of entrance into highly paid positions, e.g., by professional associations or unions or credentialling systems. It would have looked for the cause of the skewness of the income distribution in societal variables, such as the rate of economic growth or level of unemployment.

It cannot be found in the individual variables that they study, such as father's occupation, for those variables are relevant to equality of opportunity, not equality of income. They would have found, among other things, a fact to negate their argument for socialism in the last paragraph of the book: that income inequality in the U.S. dropped more rapidly during the period of rampant capitalism in the early part of this century than it has dropped recently, as more and more controls have been placed on the free functioning of labor markets.

The kind of analysis the book would have engaged in, with variables defined at the societal level rather than the individual level, is exemplified by the relation between education and income. If equalising educational attainment is to lead to equalisation of income, then what should be studied is the relation, over time, between the equality of income and the equality of educational attainment. The distribution of income from 1929 to 1970 is shown in Table 7.1 in *Inequality*; the distribution of education for those age twenty-four to thirty-four in 1929 to those age thirty to thirty-four in 1970 is shown in Table 2.1 in *Inequality*. The inequalities in these two distributions are shown by the coefficient of variation, which is high when inequality is high, and low when inequality is low. The coefficients of variation for corresponding years are shown in Table 7.1 below (the correspondence chosen is the closest

Table 7.1

Year	1929	1935–36	1946	1960	1968	1970
Coefficient of variation for income	1.23	1.09	0.87	0.83	0.72	0.75
Coefficient of variation for education	0.42	0·37	0.30	0.28	0.25	0.23
Of people aged: in given year	25–34	22–31	22–31	26–35	29–33	26–30

possible for labor force participation of persons educated at particular dates, using the data Jencks presents). That for education is much lower than that for income, but both decline over time. If the coefficient of variation for each at each time is divided by that for 1929, we get the inequality at that date relative to that in 1929. The declines in inequality, as shown below in Table 7.2, are remarkably similar. Though other explanations could be offered, they suggest that increasing

Table 7.2

Year	1929	1935–36	1946	1960	1968	1970
Income	1.0	0.89	0.71	0.67	0.59	0.61
Education	1.0	0.88	0.71	0.67	0.60	0.55

equality of education does have a strong effect on increasing equality of income. The data are in direct contradiction to the authors' statements, e.g., 'Furthermore, the experience of the past twenty-five years suggests that even fairly substantial reductions in the range of educational attainments do not materially reduce economic inequality among adults' (p. 255). But the authors never carry out this kind of analysis at the societal level. Yet it, rather than the individual-level analysis they carry out, is what is relevant to the question of increasing equality of income.[1]

The Curious Notion of 'Luck'

Now none of this is to say that the book was not influenced by the professed interest in equality of income. It was, but in ways that impeded the study of what the book is mostly about, inequality of opportunity. For in their attempt to show that most income inequality is due to luck, they tried to show that it is not much related to anything else, such as family background. By minimising the importance of family background for educational attainment, for occupational status, and for income, the authors obscure the inequality of opportunity that does exist in American society.

But since most of the analyses in the book are in fact about inequality of opportunity, let me turn to those analyses. Jencks and his colleagues bring together two kinds of studies, partly using existing analyses and partly carrying out reanalyses: studies of the effects during childhood and youth of different resources, including family background, genetic endowment, and school resources on acquisition of cognitive skills and on school attainment (number of years completed); and studies of the effects, during adulthood, of family background, cognitive skills, and educational attainment on occupational status and income.

Briefly, the first kind of these studies shows that cognitive skills and educational attainment derive very little from school resources, but a great deal from family background and IQ.* The second kind of studies shows that occupational status and income are dependent both on cognitive skills and educational attainment, but not much on family background, apart from the influence of background on cognitive skills and educational attainment.

It is the results of the latter set of studies that are obscured by the need to show that income is mostly dependent on luck. This is done by a use of statistics that is unusual and, I believe, unwarranted. The use is this: studies show a given relationship between background factors and income. This leaves a certain amount of variation in income unexplained by background. The unusual twist that Jencks employs is to attribute this unexplained variation to particular other factors, luck and personality. It is this attribution, particularly the attribution to luck, which provides a major justification for policy proposals to equalise income. But if he had attributed the unexplained variation to variation in effort or other skills unmeasured by IQ tests, which is equally reasonable in the absence of positive evidence, the justification for equalising income is gone. Or if the unexplained variation were attributed to variation in income by age or to different wage levels in different regions, again the justification for equalising income is gone or greatly reduced.

There is an extremely wide variation in professional baseball players' incomes, probably unrelated to their level of education or father's occupation; but it is more related to baseball ability than luck; there is wide variability in college teachers' incomes, again little related to level of education or father's occupation, but more related to age than to luck. But the central point is that the unexplained variation in income is

* Here also they go into a question that is not relevant to the issue of income inequality, or even to the issue of inequality of opportunity, the question of how much IQ is determined by genetic endowment. What is relevant is how much change in IQ and in other capacities that increase opportunity can be brought about in children from the age that public resources can be invested in them. Here as elsewhere, Jencks has let concern with a particular question that has recently occupied investigators dissipate the central preoccupations of the book.

merely unexplained by the variables measured (father's education and occupation, own education, and a measure of cognitive skills), and cannot be attributed to something arbitrarily pulled out of a hat.

Equal Opportunity an Appropriate Goal?

The potential importance of a book on 'inequality' that treats the range of data in this one lies in the possibility of examining some fundamental questions of moral philosophy in the presence of sociological data on inequality. The recent research on the relation of school outputs to resource inputs that they review, reanalyse, and synthesise, directly raises questions about the ability of the State, even in principle, to equalise opportunity. The fact that each person begins life with a set of private resources, genetic and environmental (the first from his parents and the second largely so), means that in the absence of public resources, children have quite unequal opportunities.

What, then, can an infusion of public resources do? If the infusion is equally distributed among children with unequal backgrounds, it cannot eliminate inequality. The existing and continuing private resources, unequally distributed, must combine with the equally distributed public resources to maintain some level of inequality of opportunity. If the infusion of public resources is unequal, designed perfectly to counter the inequality of private resources, then two problems arise:

(1) To counter fully the inequality of private resources, the publicly-provided resources for the privately disadvantaged must be sufficient to provide to all children the same opportunity as held by the child with the greatest private resources, genetic and environmental. This is obviously impossible. Consequently, some decision must be made about what extra level of publicly-provided resources, below this, should be provided to the disadvantaged. But this decision is then tantamount to accepting a particular level of inequality of opportunity.

(2) If the State could be successful in fully counter-balancing differential private resources by reversely differential public resources, this would create an extreme

disincentive to parents in supplying the private resources that they currently supply unequally. This would undoubtedly reduce the overall level of resources and thus the overall level of opportunity available to the young. For the most important environmental resources for the development of the young are those expended through enormous investments of time and effort and attention by parents. It seems highly unlikely that another, more equal, social arrangement than the family could stimulate this level of personal investment in children.

For both these reasons, first because it is impossible to achieve, and second because if achieved it would lower the general level of opportunity for children, the ideal of equal opportunity is a false ideal. A society cannot make an implementable decision to create equal opportunity for all children within it. What it must do instead is to decide what level of public resources and what imbalance of public resources it should invest to reduce the level of inequality that arises from private resources. Indeed, this is what families themselves do with their different children who are differentially endowed. They determine what level of investment in extra time of parents or tutoring or physical therapy they should make to increase the opportunity of their children who are not doing well in school or are physically handicapped. They do not aim for, nor do they end up with, equality of opportunity, but instead a reduced inequality of opportunity among their children.

A third social decision that is necessary, beyond that of the level of investment of public resources and the degree of differential distribution to reduce inequality, is the type of investment of these resources for greatest efficiency. A book with data such as this one should, in addition to destroying the false ideal of equality of opportunity or equality of results, be able to give information about efficiencies of social investment. In part, this is what it attempts to do, in attempting to show that equal opportunity (defined by equal cognitive skills, equal educational level, and equal family background) does not lead to equal results (defined by income). This is the basis for its recommendation that social investments toward equalisation be made in equalising income rather than equalising opportunity.

This recommendation is compatible with a simple principle held by economists: if a greater social product is available from great inequalities in the distribution of productive resources (putting these resources in the hands of the most productive) than by a more equal distribution, then the greater inequality should exist, with the social product then redistributed to the dependent segment of the population. It then follows that everyone can be better off, because the social product is greater. This is known as the compensation principle, and was introduced by Nicholas Kaldor in the 1930s. A similar, though somewhat stronger, principle forms the basis of John Rawls's theory of justice. But the application of that principle to the decision to make social investments in inequality of result rather than inequality of opportunity is predicated on the assumption that there are no satisfactions that derive from opportunity and achievement – that all satisfactions derive from consumption of the social product. Only if money income and the consumption it allows were the source of all satisfaction would this assumption be correct. Yet we know that it is not. Much satisfaction, perhaps most, arises from the achievement of certain internally-set goals, from the capability to overcome obstacles. Only by increasing opportunity, by investing in the personal resources that provide this capability, can these satisfactions be increased.

Thus data of the sort that Jencks brings together should be directed to the question of what investment of resources is most efficient in increasing the capabilities that bring people satisfaction, both intrinsically-derived and extrinsically-derived. To answer that question, the satisfaction derived from public investments in parks, health resources, crime prevention, and a variety of other services must be included as well. But the data that Jencks examines can give a start toward an answer, within a narrower frame. When re-examined from this point of view, the data indicate that those resources which increase cognitive skills and those which increase the number of years of school completed are both effective, and about equally so, in giving the capabilities that lead to prestigeful occupations and high income. It is important to note here that the criterion is not prestigeful occupations and high income, but the capabilities that lead to them, because satisfaction derives from the exercise of those capabilities, and not only from the prestige or money awarded.

This does not mean that investment of public resources in directions other than increasing cognitive skills and level of education do not increase opportunity as well. This is one of the major defects of the existing research: cognitive skills and education level are nearly the only attributes of persons that have been studied in this way. Social skills, entrepreneurial skills, managerial capability, ability to mobilize one's resources toward an end – none of these have been measured in these studies. Thus we do not know how public investment in schools affects them, nor do we know how they affect the individual's level of opportunity to realise satisfactions.

It is not clear from the existing data just what investment of public resources is most effective in increasing cognitive skills and level of education. What is clear is that improving 'school quality' by the standard measures of quality (class size, quality of textbooks, school physical plant, teachers' experience, library size, and others) has little effect on cognitive skills. This kind of negative knowledge exists; apparently innovations in education, together with careful examination of their effects, are necessary to learn positive directions for such investment.

It should also be pointed out that preoccupation with inequality of opportunity and inequality of result in society is probably only a current preoccupation that derives from structured inequalities of opportunity for certain groups like blacks and women. When those are reduced, social attention will likely pass to other questions of social reconstruction, such as how to increase the degree of personal responsibility of persons toward particular other persons.

Nevertheless, there is now, with the existence of a large amount of sociological research on inequality of opportunity and inequality of result, and with the resurgence of interest among moral philosophers in inequality, as manifested in John Rawls's work, the possibility of serious examination of social ideals and social reality in this area. Jencks's book could have begun that examination. Its failure to do so is not lack of technical expertise, for Jencks has shown a good command of that in this book. It is instead the lack of attention to the deeper questions of moral philosophy surrounding the existence of inequality in society.

8

The idea of equality reconsidered

ANDREW WARD

≠

In his well-known article 'The Idea of Equality',[1] Professor Bernard Williams attacks as 'irrational' a society in which either medical care is distributed on grounds which include the wealth of the recipient or access to a public school education – for his and my argument assumed to be a superior kind of education – is distributed on grounds which include the wealth of the parents of pupils of secondary school age. I shall try to show that because Williams does not adequately state the principles upon which he bases his arguments, he is apparently enabled to draw substantial social conclusions from purely logical premises or from what Williams himself calls 'necessary' truths. And I shall try to show that when his principles are more clearly stated, they do not, by themselves, enable us to draw any conclusions whatsoever about the actual structure of any fair society where medical treatment and education need to be financed.

In the case of medical care, he points out, in my opinion quite correctly, that 'the proper ground of distribution of medical care is ill health: this is a necessary truth'. He then proceeds to take the case of a society where 'the possession of sufficient money becomes in fact an additional necessary condition of actually receiving treatment. . . . When we have

First published in *Philosophy*, Vol. 48 (1973), pp. 85–90.

For Notes and References, see page 387 below.

the situation in which, for instance, wealth is a further necessary condition of the receipt of medical treatment, we can once more apply the notions of equality and inequality: not now in connexion with the inequality between the well and the ill, but in connexion with the inequality between the rich and the poor ill, since we have straightforwardly the situation of those whose needs are the same not receiving the same treatment, though the needs are the ground of the treatment. This is an irrational state of affairs.'

In other words, Williams reaches the conclusion that it is an irrational state of affairs for wealth to function as a necessary condition for receiving medical care because of the 'necessary truth' that 'the proper ground of distribution of medical care is ill health'. Put more simply, Williams is able to reach the above conclusion by employing the following general principle: It is irrational to distribute medical care on any grounds other than ill health.

However, once his general principle is stated in this simplified way, it becomes more evident that the particular example which he has taken in order to illustrate the operation of this principle is only one of many possible examples. We can see this if we consider Williams's own particular example a little further. He has taken the case where, although two classes of people – the rich and the poor – have the same medical need, they do not equally receive medical care. And since part of what is meant by saying that it is irrational to *distribute* medical care on grounds other than ill health is that it is irrational that the *receipt* of medical care should depend on grounds other than ill health, it clearly follows that Williams's own particular example falls under his general principle, and hence is indeed an irrational state of affairs. But what certainly does not follow from this is that when everyone *does* receive medical care on grounds of medical need, we do not also have, on Williams's own general principle, an irrational state of affairs. The reason is that although everyone may receive medical care on grounds of ill health, the method by which the medical care is made available may still be, on grounds of inequality, an irrational state of affairs.

It is noticeable that Williams only considers a society where the possession of personal wealth is a condition of receiving medical care. He does not consider a society which runs a national health system like our own. At this point, one might object that obviously it is no part of his task to consider such a society, since, in such a society, medical care is equally available to the rich and to the poor alike. But it does not follow from this objection that in so far as Williams is interested in equality of treatment – the avowed subject of his article – he should not also have considered a society which operates a national health service like our own. For in such a society, although it is perfectly true that medical care is equally available to the rich and to the poor, it is also true that the rich pay more money (through taxes) for the upkeep of the medical system than do the poor. In other words, in a national health system like our own, the rich are paying more money for medical care than are the poor. Since it is irrational to distribute medical care on grounds other than ill health, this is an irrational state of affairs.

Now it may be said here that my argument has confused the actual availability or receipt of a good – in this case medical care – with the means of receiving or making available such a good. Thus it may be said that Williams's general principle – it is irrational to distribute medical care on grounds other than ill health – only refers to the irrationality of *receiving* medical care on grounds other than ill health; and that it does not also refer to the *means* by which this medical care is made equally available. That is, the objection is claiming that I have widened the meaning of 'distribute' in Williams's general principle so that its meaning includes a reference to the 'means of receiving' medical care, whereas, in fact, its meaning is narrower and only refers to the actual availability or receipt of medical care.

For my part, I do not see how one can talk about the irrational distribution of medical care (or any other good for that matter) without taking into account any irrationality that may exist in the means of making medical care available. But what should be clear is that my criticism of Williams's position does not depend on this verbal point. For even if it were conceded that his general principle does only make reference to the irrationality of unequal availability of medical care on grounds other than ill health, we are still left with the inequitable situation of one class of people, the rich, paying more money for the same medical care as another class of people, the poor. Yet Williams's whole thesis depends on the irrationality of treating one class of people differently from another class when the first class are not relevantly different from the second.[2] Hence when we have a situation where two classes of people are paying *different* amounts for receiving the *same* medical care (even though, on Williams's principle, the ground for receiving medical care is quite independent of the monetary position of those receiving it – and hence cannot be a relevant difference between the two classes of people), it follows that this too is an irrational state of affairs.

I conclude that it is immaterial whether or not 'the distribution of medical care' includes a reference to the 'means of making available' medical care. For whether it does or whether it does not, it still remains the case that where one class of people is paying more money for receiving the same medical care as another class of people, we are still confronted, on Williams's thesis, with an irrational state of affairs.

Precisely similar considerations apply against Williams's discussion of who should receive a superior education. He points out that 'access to this type of education is unequally distributed, because of its cost: among boys of equal promise or intelligence, only those from wealthy homes will receive it, and, indeed, boys of little promise or intelligence will receive it, if from wealthy homes; and this, the objection continues, is irrational'. But although it is irrational for a superior education to be partly, or wholly, distributed on grounds of personal wealth, it does not follow that the suggested remedies for this situation are not also irrational. Once again, because Williams only takes an example of personal wealth securing a good, he obscures this point. For the principle upon which Williams depends in order to show that it is irrational for a superior education to be wholly or partly distributed on grounds of personal wealth has nothing intrinsically to do with personal wealth. Rather he is depending on the general principle that the proper ground of distribution of a superior school education is the intellectual promise of boys and girls of school age. Admittedly, Williams also says that there could well be more dispute about whether intellectual promise is the proper ground of distribution of a superior education than there could be about the proper ground of distribution of medical care. But for the purposes of this article I am not calling into question the general principle that the proper ground of distribution of a superior education is intellectual promise. On the contrary, what I am concerned to show is that to the extent to which Williams *is* able to use this general principle to demonstrate the irrationality of securing a superior education on grounds which depend, at least partly, on personal wealth, to just that extent can this general principle be used to show the irrationality of the suggested remedies to that situation.

To maintain the principle that the proper ground of distribution of a superior education is intellectual promise is to maintain, at least, that any other ground of distribution of a superior education is irrational. This is why Williams is able to draw the more specific conclusion that it is irrational for a superior education to be distributed partly or wholly on grounds of personal wealth. I shall now consider the application of his principle against the suggested remedies for the irrational situation where personal wealth is a condition of receiving a superior education.

So far as I am aware, only two remedies have been suggested for alleviating the existing inequality. (I do not consider the possibility of dispensing with the public schools altogether. Those who advocate this course either must disagree with the assumption that the public schools give a superior education or, if they do agree with it, must bring forward some quite independent ground or grounds which, in their view, would be a sufficient reason for dispensing with the public schools altogether, e.g. the ground that they are socially divisive.) The first suggested remedy is that the cost of a public school education should be financed in the same way as the Health Service is now financed, i.e. through the existing method of general taxation. But this method of finance means that a rich person pays more for a public school education than does a poor person (as indeed he now does for a state education). Since it is irrational to distribute a superior secondary education on grounds other than the intellectual promise of boys and girls of secondary school age, this is an irrational state of affairs. The second suggested remedy is that the cost of a pupil's public school education should be financed by that pupil's local borough council. Hence the cost of the education would be borne by the local ratepayers. But since there is an obvious contingent connexion between the possession of wealth and paying higher rates – since the wealthy have larger properties – it follows that a rich person will pay more money for a superior education than will a poor person. Since it is irrational to distribute a superior secondary education on grounds other than the intellectual promise of boys and girls of secondary school age, this is an irrational state of affairs.

As in the earlier parallel case of the proper ground of distribution of medical care, it may be objected that I have widened the meaning of the 'distribution' of a superior education so that it includes a reference to the 'means of making available' a superior education, and that this is not part of its meaning. But just as before, even if this point were conceded, it still remains the case that two classes of people are paying unequal amounts for receiving the same good – in this case a superior education. Now since Williams's whole thesis depends on the irrationality of treating one class of people differently from another class when the first class is not relevantly different from the second, it follows that when two classes of people, who are not relevantly different, are paying unequal amounts for receiving the same good, this is an irrational state of affairs. And because any ground other than intellectual ability is irrelevant to the question of who should receive a superior education, it follows that a difference in wealth cannot be considered a relevant difference for treating the rich differently from the poor. Since the rich are paying more than the poor, and hence being treated differently, this is an irrational state of affairs.

Finally, I shall deal with one general objection that might be levelled against my arguments. It might be objected that if a rich person pays more for medical care or education than a poor person, this at least proportionately equalises their situations.[3] But, now, what exactly is being equalised and under what principle? What is being equalised is the respective monetary situations of a rich person and a poor person. For if more money is taken away from a rich person than from a poor person (for receipt of the same good), then the amount each has remaining is thereby proportionately equalised. But why, on Williams's thesis, should this be considered a rational state of affairs? It certainly cannot be considered so simply through the operation of the principle that for every difference in the way men are treated, a relevant social reason should be given. For it does not logically follow from this principle that everyone should possess the same amount of money. One would need to add the further premise that a relevant social reason could never (logically) be given for one person to possess more money than another. And I am not aware that anything said by Williams goes any way to substantiating that proposition. On the contrary, Williams is only concerned to argue that people's situations should be equalised unless some relevant social reason can be given for treating them differently. He is not concerned to argue that people's situations should be equalised when some relevant social reason *can* be given. And since there does not appear to be any logical objection to the proposition that relevant social reasons can be given for some people possessing more money than others (and Williams's thesis is a logical, not a moral one), it follows that logically, at least, it is not necessarily an irrational state of affairs for some people to possess more money than others. Hence, from a logical point of view, no rational reason has been given for necessarily equalising the monetary situations of the rich and the poor.

I have no wish to imply by my arguments that there cannot be genuine room for discussion about which forms of distribution of medical care and education are, in a given circumstance, fairer (or perhaps less unfair) than others. The point is, however, that some criterion of rationality or fairness, independent of any given by Professor Williams, would be needed to substantiate this. As it is, the particular examples which Williams gives of irrational discrimination are of a very one-sided type. They all depend on the rich irrationally deriving some benefit at the expense of the poor. None of them depends on the poor irrationally deriving some benefit at the expense of the rich. Yet the general principles upon which his arguments depend provide no means of differentiating the cases where the rich irrationally benefit at the expense of the poor from the cases where the poor irrationally benefit at the expense of the rich. Since the illustration of principles by one-sided examples is likely to be misleading and unfair, this is an irrational state of affairs.

9

Equality under the law

GEOFFREY MARSHALL

≠

IN an obvious, but notoriously diluted sense, a law-maker is concerned *ex officio* with promoting equality of treatment. To deal with men by general rules rather than individualised or unpredictable fiat is to treat them in at least one respect equally. But this is not to say very much, since a rule which applies equally to all may make different provisions for some as against others. This, amongst other things, would make it difficult for a modern legislative sovereign assembly to know whether it had complied with the recipe for legislative action which Rousseau prescribed in the *Contrat Social*. Rousseau there demands that the general will, besides being respectably general in its origins, must in its substance aim at generality and equality. Equality and generality of aim are exemplified in a number of ways. 'Law must be,' it is said, 'applicable to all.' It must not seek to achieve 'a merely individual or limited end'. It must not seek to 'judge an individual person or an isolated fact'. It must not purport to determine specific rights arising out of a situation not previously regulated by general agreement. It 'changes its nature when called upon to pronounce upon a particular object'. It must not lay 'a heavier burden on any one subject than on another'. And so on. 'Every authentic act of the general will lays the same

---

Chapter VII in the author's *Constitutional Theory* (Clarendon Press, Oxford, 1971) pp. 136–53.

For References, see page 387 below.

obligations and confers the same benefits on all.' The Sovereign 'knows only the nation as a whole and does not distinguish between the individuals who compose it'.[1]

Such a myopic legislator, we may suppose, would make heavy weather in our times. The lieges are not all of a lump. There are producers and consumers, officials and non-officials, farmers and manufacturers, soldiers and civilians, married men and bachelors, adults and minors. What is to be understood by treating them all alike or imposing the same burdens on all, when their situations, capacities, duties, and obligations are different and ought to be so? On the other hand, is not constitutional theory replete with dim and less dim reflections of Rousseau's specifications? No Bills of Attainder. The rule of law, not men. The equal protection of the laws.

Given, in particular cases, acceptable reasons for differences in treatment, the prescription of equality in law, as in morals, seems sometimes to fall away into an empty formality – namely that all deserve equal treatment unless good reasons prescribe otherwise. Of course, at some times and places, tautologies may strike fire. Mr Gladstone's famous truism of 1864 is an example. 'I venture to say that every man who is not presumably incapacitated by some consideration of personal unfitness or of political danger is morally entitled to come within the pale of the constitution.'[2] Lord Morley tells us that this 'thunderbolt of a sentence' threw the House of Commons into an uproar. Perhaps the House of Commons was not listening very carefully! Clearly the notion of equality, formulated as absence of disqualification, or of irrelevant discrimination, does not advance the argument very far.

1. Equal Subjection to Law

It cannot be said that there are many startling similarities between the views of Albert Venn Dicey and those of Jean-Jacques Rousseau. But one shared characteristic is an insistence on the equal application of law. By the rule of law Dicey understood, amongst other things, 'the idea of legality or of the universal subjection of all classes to one law administered by the ordinary courts'. Equality before the law, understood as the equal subjection of all classes to common rule, might at least be contrasted significantly with chaos or lawlessness, but it does not in itself imply any qualitative view about the sort of law to which all are subject. At least three senses might be given to the 'rule of law', of which this first would be the minimal sense. The three senses, or programmes, might be:

1. Everyone (equally) to be covered by, or subject to, general laws, rather than exposed to chaos, individualised commands or mob rule. Englishmen, as Dicey insisted, are ruled by the law, and by the law alone. 'A man may, with us, be punished for a breach of law, but he can be punished for a breach of nothing else.'[3] No subject of Queen Victoria in 1885, it must be admitted, would have been much astounded by this proposition.

2. Everyone (equally) to be covered by some body of law which is impartially applied without fear, favour, or anything similar, by an independent judiciary. In this sense South Africa and Rhodesia are at the present time governed by the rule of law, though some of the law in question is in substance abominable.

3. Everyone (equally) to be covered by an impartially administered body of law, which meets certain criteria of precision, equity, and justice. Professor Lon Fuller has called these conditions 'the inner morality of law'.[4] Alternatively, one might perhaps call them the ethics of legislation.

The rule of law in its English context has (like due process of law and natural justice) been mainly expounded in the senses mentioned in 1 and 2 – primarily, that is to say, as a procedural concept. The rule of law is not, in Dicey's view, violated when the King's most Excellent Majesty, by and with the advice of the Lords and Commons enacts that the Bishop of Rochester's cook be boiled to death without benefit of clergy,[5] or when the Queen-in-Parliament makes a retrospective legislative adjudication on a claim, so as to nullify, *ex post facto*, a judicial decision inimical to the Crown.[6]

Nevertheless, in two ways Dicey's doctrine was not merely procedural. The equal rule of law, as he expounded it, involves at least one substantive requirement. It must not permit overwide powers of discretionary action to be conferred on officials. It prescribes also a requirement of equal access and subjection of all private and public persons to the same judicial tribunals. It omits, however, to register the truism that the law which all citizens find when they get to the common courts may make unequal provision for some as against others. The same law that bound all could say that the Crown could not be sued, and that policemen and State officials should have powers, privileges, or legal defences not open to private citizens. At the same time, the prohibition on the creation of wide discretionary powers assumed in its original expression that there could be no valid justification for such powers, based on relevant differences between citizens and officials. Dicey's implied ideal stands rooted in a situation in which the State and its agents confront individuals in a condition of Rousseauite equipollence. A large slice of English controversy about the rule of law has been about the workability of this assumption – in effect, about the equality of public and private persons.

2. Equality of State and Individual Before the Law

It is in one way plain that the State and the individual, or the community and citizen, cannot be equals. One imposes its will upon the other. We can, however, significantly debate which community purposes require the community's agents to be given significant legal privileges not shared by private persons or collectivities. It is especially necessary to put the question in this form in the common law world, where by theory and tradition the law knows only private persons. Secretaries of State, civil servants, and policemen are equally the Queen's subjects. 'With respect to the argument of State necessity, or the distinction that has been aimed at between State offences and others, the common law does not understand that kind of reasoning, nor do our books take notice of any such distinctions.' And 'by the laws of England every invasion of private property, be it ever so minute, is a trespass'.[7] Into this framework of private rights and private law, a statutory body of public powers and public law has had to be fastened. For reasons which do not surprise us, but perhaps ought to, this has not resulted in any great growth of official privilege or discretion in the area of civil liberties. The relations of policemen with citizens are largely conducted as relations between one citizen and another. Law officers make arrests, lay informations, and prosecute offences, protected at vulnerable points by only a minimum of statutory armour. But in the field of economic and administrative relationships a different kind of transaction appears. Where the use of natural resources (and particularly land) is concerned the rules have changed. In the nineteenth century English courts may be said to have acted upon the assumption that their business was to hold an equal balance between citizens and officials. An interference with the property rights of Englishmen often gave rise to disquisitions upon the rules of natural justice (*audi alteram partem*, and no man to judge his own case). These two rules rested upon the assumption of a fairly conducted legal combat between two parties viewed essentially as equals by the arbitral tribunal. The analogy has become steadily less applicable to twentieth-century contests between the Crown and individual property-owning litigants. When governmental agencies initiate action they are conceded to be judges of the merits of their own proposals. At least one of the rules of equal judicial combat cannot apply. Indeed, its disappearance may even imperil the application of the other (*audi alteram partem*) rule. This did in fact happen in one sphere of English administrative jurisprudence, and the right to a fair hearing is only now being established as an independently valid claim of the citizen,[8] even when no longer conceived as engaged in an equal judicial contest with State officials.

Administrative justice in fact poses a dilemma. It can never be literally true that for all disputes between official agencies and individual citizens recourse should exist to an independent third party. Yet we aim to provide such recourse in a significant, if vaguely delineated, set of cases. What should define such cases? An answer sometimes suggested is roughly that official action which affects all equally, for example, raising a tax or recruiting an army, does not give rise to a dispute or a right of appeal (as distinct from political or electoral redress) whereas action affecting citizens in an individual capacity alters the case. But what is an individual capacity? A change in governmental policy or the cancellation of a defence contract may affect workers in a particular town or factory in a way not shared by the general population. But we do not admit these cases as creating a right of appeal or review. Nor without circularity can a criterion be laid down in terms of State action affecting rights rather than privileges, since the classification of a potential claim as a right will in part at least depend upon the remedies available to vindicate it. Historically the question may be put in this form. For which purposes have legislators been willing to subject governmental action to fixed rules, and for which purposes have they been inclined to leave the Government free to formulate and enforce *ad hoc* policies? Typical of the first sphere is criminal, and some social service, legislation; typical of the second, diplomacy and foreign affairs. The latter sphere is necessarily marked by inequality of citizen and State (considered as government agencies). Some advocates of administrative justice argue or imply that the sphere of fixed rules ought to be as wide as possible. But this conclusion is not obvious. The sort of equality which exists between defendants and prosecutors does not fit every possible form of public–private relationship.[9] Perhaps the only generalisation which can be made here is that the analogy breaks down wherever government is both party to an issue and a protector of some admitted general or national interest such as scarce natural resources or national security.

3. Denial of Equality

The traditional English rule-of-law man confined his concern for equality and legislative ethics to a veto upon excessive delegation of discretionary power. Predictability of action and the avoidance of procedural privilege were the values he had in mind. As a good Austinian and loyal exponent of the sovereignty of Parliament, he had no truck – at least no professional truck – with the avoidance of substantive privilege in law. Let the Queen-in-Parliament clearly place unequal burdens on one class of subjects compared with another and the subject knows where he stands. If where he stands is uncomfortable or unjust, that is no concern of jurisprudence or judges. It is a part of politics and a task for moral judgement with which legal tribunals should have as little as possible to do. The traditionalist may suspect that the question raised by the rule of equal law in the American (and Indian, German, and Japanese) sense can only be answered by a tribunal which is openly legislative. Setting this aside as mere prejudice against judicial review in any form, there remains perhaps a question whether the application of equality guarantees does not involve a creative and legislative burden greater than that which a judicial tribunal can comfortably carry.

In the jurisprudence of equal treatment, as in thinking about equality outside the law, there can be seen a certain indecisiveness about which of two positions to occupy. Argument begins with the acknowledgement that equality before the law does not require every person to be treated in the same way, but only requires similar treatment for those in similar circumstances, or an absence of discriminatory treatment except for those in different circumstances. But sometimes this view is asserted by treating equality as simply having this meaning (i.e. not to be understood as 'treating all alike'), whilst at other times it is asserted that equality cannot be absolute; that it must be balanced against other requirements; that proper classification and discrimination may take place, and that when this happens legislation may justly produce constitutional *inequalities*.

Whether we say that equality may be qualified or modified, or whether we say that acceptable departures from identical treatment do not detract from or qualify the principle of equality, the criteria upon which qualification of, departures from, or applications of, the principle take place, are obviously crucial. The notion of different situation or circumstance carries a certain ambiguity. A recent commentary on the Indian constitution explains that legislative classifications or discriminations for those in different circumstances may relate to geographical differences or differences in time.[10] Bombay may be treated differently from Madras. A reform may be introduced earlier for some than for others. It is clear, however, that the differences in situation do not consist simply in the different geographical or temporal situations themselves, but in the way these situations are evaluated and related to the legislative facts in question. The briefest excursion through equal treatment litigation reveals that this relationship and evaluation has been characterised in a number of ways. It being agreed that legislators may select different persons or groups for different treatment, since 'classification is inherent in legislation',[11] various things may be said about the conditions necessary to reconcile such classification or discrimination with the guarantee of equality. For example:

(1) That between classification and legislative objects there must be *some nexus*.
(2) That classification must be based on an *intelligible* differentiation.
(3) That classification must be based upon some *real and substantial* distinction.
(4) That classification must be *relevant* to the object of the legislation.
(5) That classification must be *rationally related* to the object.
(6) That classification must be *fairly related* to the object.
(7) That classification must not be *capricious or invidious*.
(8) That classification must not be *arbitrary*.
(9) That classification must be *reasonable*.
(10) That classification must be *just*.

These formulae are plainly not equivalent. Arranged in this way they might be seen as a series of increasingly high hurdles. Roughly speaking, and in ascending order of severity, three kinds of classification may be separated out, namely that which is intelligible, that which is relevant, and that which is just or reasonable. A distinction between two persons or classes which is intelligible or real may not be for some purposes relevant, and a distinction which is relevant to the purpose in hand may not be sufficiently relevant to be reasonable, fair, or just. The use of the word 'arbitrary' perhaps tends to conceal the difference between the second and third tests (i.e. between relevance and reasonableness) since 'arbitrary' is sometimes used to mean 'irrelevant or capricious' and sometimes to mean 'unjust or unfair'. The distinction between the two tests is important. Compare, for example, a legislative proposal to tax red-haired men, with a proposal to tax the owners of gambling clubs. In both cases the distinction between tax-worthy and un-taxworthy class is intelligible and existent. In the red-haired case the tax would fail to pass the test of both relevance and reasonableness. In the gambling case the tax would pass the test of relevance but not necessarily that of reasonableness. There might be several reasons for not thinking it reasonable. Though having a high income is a relevant reason for being taxed, one might still think the tax inequitable and unfair because other entertainments, vices, or sporting facilities were not taxed at all, or because the tax was too severe, or because one thought that the owners of gambling premises performed a service to the community.

When courts apply tests to legislative classification, it is not always clear what hurdle, higher or lower, they are requiring the impugned legislation to clear. Sometimes they seem satisfied with mere relevance; at other times more is demanded. Even if it is clear which test is being applied (though especially if it is the second) decisions are often unpredictable because of the different ways in which a large number of possible differences between persons or situations may be weighed.

Many Fourteenth Amendment cases illustrate this point. As Mr Justice Jackson said (in *Railway Express Agency* v. *New York*):[12] 'The equal protection clause ceases to assure either equality or protection if it is avoided by any conceivable difference that can be pointed out between those bound and those left free.' Yet in this case, which involved an attack on New York traffic regulations prohibiting advertisements on some vehicles but not others, a number of differences between the two classes of vehicles was pointed out. Some carried paid, others unpaid, advertisements. Some were more of a traffic distraction than others, etc. All these differences were relevant to the purposes of the regulations, but not necessarily thereby reasonable bases for the discrimination. Another feature of the prohibited advertisements mentioned in argument was that they were less of a traffic distraction than displays on Times

Square. This feature, however, was finally ignored. (It was no requirement of equal protection that all evils of the same genus be eradicated, or none at all.) Which features of the situation produced by legislative classification will strike a court as relevant and reasonable seems in many cases unpredictable. In *Goesaert* v. *Cleary*[13] Mr Justice Rutledge, Mr Justice Douglas, and Mr Justice Murphy thought that a Michigan law, prohibiting the licensing of female bartenders unless they were the wives or daughters of the male owners of a licensed victualler's establishment, made an invidious distinction between male and female owners of bars. The majority of the court, however, whilst conceding that Michigan could not 'play favourites among women without rhyme or reason', or produce 'irrational' discrimination, considered there to be a possible basis in reason (relating to the hazards of unprotected barmaids) for Michigan's action, and therefore upheld the regulation. This, perhaps, fell some distance away from a test of reasonableness. To assess that would have meant considering and weighing the counter-arguments to Michigan's belief, but this the majority were unwilling to do. The constitution did not require legislation, they said, to reflect sociological insight or shifting social standards. So, though the classification might rest, we may infer, on outmoded social standards or lack of legislative insight, Michigan could have had an intelligible and relevant, though possibly insubstantial and unreasonable, basis for its discrimination.

One of the features of the situation which is frequently rejected as decisive in equal treatment arguments is that the legislature has omitted to act in some similar situation alleged to be relevant. In an Indian case a section of the penal code was upheld, though it penalised adultery by men and not by women.[14] In Germany it has been held that the criminal punishment of male homosexuality does not violate equality by reason of not punishing lesbianism.[15] When apparently relevant features of a situation are discarded, it may be said that 'mathematical' or 'abstract' symmetry is not required by equality,[16] or that in determining the reasonableness of a classification attention may be paid to 'the established usages and customs and traditions of the people'[17] (though this consideration has become unfashionable), or that equality does not demand an attack on all evils at once. At other times, however, omission to act in some other case deemed equally evil is stigmatised. 'Sterilisation of those who have thrice committed grand larceny with immunity for those who are embezzlers is a clear, pointed, unmistakable discrimination.'[18]

It has been suggested by Indian commentators that 'frivolous' cases have sometimes been brought forward involving allegations of inequality. A sales tax on hides and skins is attacked because no tax is placed on other articles.[19] But it is not obvious why this contention is any more frivolous than any other disputes about denial of equality. Is it more frivolous than, say, the question whether a legislature would be denying equal protection if it provided for the taking over by the government of a particular firm or industry as compared with any other firm or industry? To nationalise one industry and not another – coal, but not steel – is obviously a form of discrimination. But what sort of test can be applied to the classification problem here? What foothold has an interpreter of equality between abstract symmetry and mere political preference? Is a guarantee of equality any different in its application from a guarantee of justice?

4. Equality, Privacy, and Liberty

A clash between equality on the one hand and liberty on the other occurs particularly where the equality concerned is that of access to publicly and privately supplied facilities of important kinds. The demands of equality and one sort of liberty (the liberty to supply and associate) reinforce each other. Equal treatment cases involving segregation of races or classes could equally well be argued in terms of a denial of liberty to each class to associate with each other. On the other hand, the demands of equality are potentially at odds with another sort of liberty – the liberty to withhold, withdraw, or disassociate. The United Kingdom, stepping cautiously into the field of race relations legislation, is only now encountering the clash of principles long implicit in the Fourteenth Amendment and American State and Federal anti-discrimination measures in employment, public accommodations, labour organisation, and property disposal. The boundary between what is thought just and unjust remains unsettled. There is, it is supposed, a sphere of private relationships which ought not to be subject to official enforcement provisions. The phrase 'private relationships' is, nevertheless, likely to beg questions. Here (as in the argument about the enforcement of criminal sanctions in matters of private conduct or morality) 'private' is used ambiguously both to describe a physical context ('in private') and to characterise activity as meriting immunity from public intervention. Though some matters of private morality in the second sense happen usually to take place 'in private' this second proposition is no guarantee of the truth of the first. Wife-beating or homicide within four walls is not immune from social intervention. Similarly, in arguments about discrimination, we may be told that 'it is both possible and desirable for governments to make unfairly discriminatory practices, except in the sphere of primarily private relationships, illegal'.[20] But criteria of privacy are badly needed to rescue this advice from vacuity. The limits or boundaries drawn in antidiscrimination programmes tend to be a cluster of *ad hoc* exceptions. Small businesses or housing projects below a certain size, or domestic employment, may be exempted from enforcement measures, and this is sometimes justified in terms of privacy and the right of free association. But if a right of free association or dissociation is a justifiable principle, why should it be restricted to small groups? Whether a discriminatory practice is classifiable as a private or public discrimination is not always easy to decide; and both inside and outside the law we still need a clear rationale for the extension of anti-discrimination measures from State and public operations and services in the most obvious sense into the field of communal and domestic activity. Proceeding from the certain to the less certain we might, perhaps, set out in descending order of conviction the fields in which we believe prohibition of discriminatory practices, based on race, sex, or religion, to be justified:

(1) State and governmental services.

(2) Services offered to the public generally.
(3) A service financed or subsidised from public funds.
(4) Important professions or occupations regulated or licensed by Statute.
(5) Services or occupations in which large numbers are employed.
(6) Services, provided by individuals, which are economically important or of which the supply is scarce.

What stopping points are there along this line? Obviously a principle of free choice and a policy of protecting it enters at some point. But the right to free disposal of economic resources has already suffered a serious loss of esteem, and further restrictions on it are not inconceivable if the avoidance of inequality and discriminatory practices is generally thought to be sufficiently important.

In the United States the distinction between public or state discrimination, and private or individual discrimination, has been a difficult and disputed one. It has been necessary to pursue it because the Fourteenth Amendment provides the Supreme Court with a double-edged problem. Not only does it require a decision as to whether a difference of treatment amounts to a denial of equality, but it also demands a resolution of the question whether any such denial is, or is not, the result of state action.

One thing that complicates the distinction between private and public (State or governmental) activity is the existence of quasi-governmental institutions. Many kinds of agencies, whether called boards, commissions, corporations, or authorities, as well as local government and educational bodies, are connected with, and are, in some sense or other, part of the governmental or administrative process. There may be many different tests, applicable for different purposes, to the question 'What is a public or a governmental body?' It may, for example, be necessary to delimit the 'province of government' in order to decide the proper boundaries of executive or crown privilege, or for the purpose of adjudicating on alleged libels on public officers. But it is not clear that the same tests are morally or legally appropriate to the task of distinguishing public from private discriminatory action.

Many bodies that are not directly agents of government play a part in formulating and administering public policies.[21] Other bodies pursue policies that are directly or indirectly supported, encouraged, or subsidised by the State. But if the idea of State action is spread so thinly that it is held to exist where the State uses its resources to encourage, subsidise, or licence individual activities, it becomes difficult to see where any line can be drawn between the public and private sphere. State subsidies and tax exemptions are enjoyed by almost everybody, and everything that individuals do is done, in a sense, under the law and subject to its rules.

A number of arguments have been used to extend the American Fourteenth Amendment veto on state discrimination to cover the acts of private individuals, which prima facie lie outside it. One such argument is that the states are implicated in individual discriminatory activity if they assist or enforce it through their laws or legal machinery – for example, by allowing state courts to enforce a racially restrictive covenant placed on the use of property by an individual.[22] But the argument that every use of official machinery to enforce a discriminatory act by an individual involves an endorsement of it seems too general. The mere use of trespass laws or other remedies, for example, to enforce the exclusion from private property of persons of a particular race, class, or colour, could hardly be said to involve such an endorsement. Nevertheless, some weight seems to have been given by the Supreme Court precisely to this argument. In a number of cases the Court has reviewed convictions obtained in state courts of trespassers engaged in sit-ins in restaurants, lunch counters, and department stores. In some cases local laws positively required segregation.[23] In other cases no positive requirement was made, but state involvement was inferred on the ground that the state permitted its laws to be used to enforce discriminatory exclusion. The temptation to use such an argument possibly derives from the fact that other morally relevant differences are perceived in the exclusion of particular classes of citizens from such facilities as shops or restaurants as compared with their exclusion from private homes or individual social or business arrangements. What is in issue, however, is the force of this distinction itself. *Bell* v.

Maryland[24] saw some division of opinion in the Court on the point. The majority, reversing the convictions of Negroes who had refused to leave a segregated restaurant, held that keepers of inns, public conveyances, and places of public amenity, were in a crucially different position from private householders. Private property was involved but it was 'serving the public'. Two points might be made about this use of the word 'public'. In the first place, the contrast with 'private' or 'individual' that is implied when these terms are contrasted with 'public' in the sense of 'people at large' or 'the general public' is not that which is made when 'private' or 'individual' are set off against 'public' in the sense of 'official' or 'governmental'. One cannot therefore infer from the premise that service to the 'public' is involved the conclusion that governmental or 'State' action is involved. In the second place the question to be decided about services offered to, and relationships with, the public in general is precisely what degree of choice or discrimination by individuals they may permissibly embody. Mr Justice Black, for example, in a dissenting judgement in *Bell* v. *Maryland* saw no obvious difference between the right of a storekeeper or restaurant owner to choose his guests or a property owner to choose his social or business associates.

Mr Justice Black's argument in this and similar cases was that nothing in the Fourteenth Amendment prohibited discrimination by private persons who offered goods or services, or compelled them to offer their services to the public at large without exception or restriction. This was not to assert that the constitution positively guaranteed such rights to discriminate or prevented encroachment on them by legislative action. Congress has the right to 'enforce by appropriate legislation' the provisions of the Fourteenth Amendment. Though it might seem that no such legislation could properly extend the provisions of the Amendment to actions which it did not itself embrace, there remains the possibility of legislation against private discrimination under some other head of Congressional power. When the Civil Rights Act of 1964 and its successors did place widespread restrictions on discrimination in the offering of employment and accommodation, one constitutional ground for such Federal action was found in the power to regulate inter-state commerce. In *Heart of Atlanta Motel* v. *U.S.*[25] and *Katzenbach* v. *McClung*[26] Title II of the 1964 Civil Rights Act was sustained in its application to discrimination by a hotel owner in Georgia and a restaurant owner in Alabama. In the first case it was argued that seventy-five per cent of the hotel guests were from outside the state and that, in refusing to rent rooms to Negroes the hotel was creating an impediment to inter-state travel and commerce which Congress could properly attempt by legislation to remove. In the second case the argument was more recondite. The Government made no claim that the state of Alabama supported the restaurant owner's refusal to serve Negroes in his dining room. But it was asserted that forty-six per cent of the food served consisted of meat bought from a local supplier who had procured it from outside the state, and this was held to be sufficient to place the restaurant owner within the sphere of Federal regulation.

In the matter of property sales, also, the Court has held that a state may involve itself in, and in a sense encourage and promote or endorse private action by repealing laws against discrimination in the housing market.[27] Here the dissenting minority (Harlan, Black, Clark, and Stewart JJ) criticised the majority's notion that a state could be said to be involved in or to promote discrimination by permitting the discriminatory acts of individuals. Indeed, it would seem that there is no individual act of discrimination that cannot be transmuted into 'official' discrimination if a state denies equality of treatment whenever it fails to enact and retain legislation prohibiting such discrimination.

In Britain, without the complication of states' rights or the Fourteenth Amendment, legislative prohibitions have been unambiguously applied to private discrimination; with, however, some curious inconsistencies. 'Discrimination' is defined simply as 'less favourable treatment based on colour, race, ethnic, or national origin' (with no reference to sexual or religious differences of treatment). To this provision the Race Relations Acts of 1965 and 1968 have added a jumble of exceptions permitting forms of discrimination by private householders, small employers, and firms attempting to secure a racial balance in the employment of labour. Further exception-creating provisions relate to accommodation in ships, benefits arising under charitable instruments, and employments where the attributes of persons of a particular nationality are specially related to the tasks involved. Still further oddity arises from the provisions relating to advertisement, which make it unlawful to advertise an intention to do acts which the legislation itself states to be lawful – for example an intention to offer employment to a French pastry-cook or a Finnish language instructor.

Some of the discriminatory activities treated as permissible by the legislation rest for their justification upon an implicit rationale of preserving an individual right to discriminate or exercise free choice in 'private' or domestic contexts. Others do not. Here the law reflects the moral perplexities of citizens. Equality is a matter of eliminating differences of treatment between persons, based upon irrelevant distinctions. What is hard to determine is how far majority decisions should be enforced by legal sanctions in the absence of a social consensus and, in any event, which of many individual characteristics are irrelevant for which purposes. Skin colour is the most obvious candidate for consideration as a characteristic that is almost everywhere and for almost all purposes irrelevant to the treatment which one person receives from another person. But to what extent should law and policy attempt to eliminate differences of treatment based on other human characteristics such as wealth, poverty, age, health, intelligence, or sex? An obviously relevant factor is whether a particular characteristic is counted as an endowment outside the individual's control, or an achievement for which he is responsible. Unfortunately we are not entirely certain which are which, or to what extent it is relevant that some original endowments for which individuals are not themselves responsible can be affected by their subsequent efforts. Intellectual capacity and poverty raise difficult questions here. In both Britain and America we think equality to be violated if certain legal or medical services are denied to those unable to pay for them. But we do not yet feel compelled to the same conclusion because there is not equality of access, say, to public transport, without regard to individual ability to pay the fares. Nor should we argue that the State is involved in, and endorsing, discriminatory treatment when it allows its laws to be used by private institutions to exclude those who are unable to afford the price of admission. There are a number of issues here (as equally in the disposal of property after death) on which society has not yet cleared its mind.

The application by courts and legislatures of the principle of equality illustrates, as clearly as anything could, the fact that equality is only one of a number of ends that liberal democratic communities seek to implement. Others are freedom, security, justice, and welfare. When these values clash there may be different ways of describing what is at issue. The jurisprudence of equal treatment shows how those who apply notions of equality to particular cases start out from an assumption that equality is not mere uniformity, sameness, or identity of treatment. Legislatures or societies may classify different persons or groups of persons and treat them differently, if the basis of classification meets certain requirements. Equality, it is argued, will not be violated if young and old, or rich and poor, or tentmakers and musicians, are treated differently if there are relevant differences between them and good or sufficient reasons for the differences of treatment. What the analysis of good reasons in the cases fails to bring out, however, is that if *every* departure from identity of treatment for which there are good reasons is treated as merely filling out the meaning of 'equality' properly understood, then no room is left for any recognition that some departures from identity of treatment might be better described as creating exceptions to the application of the principle of equality. The difficulty is to distinguish between the two situations. In the one a departure from sameness of treatment is undertaken out of a respect for equality, and to restore individuals to some position of comparability with others, which is regarded as having been lost or disturbed. In the other a difference of treatment reflects a deliberate and justifiable rejection of the claims of equality out of respect for the claims of some other value such as liberty or security.

There is, as we shall see, a similar temptation in legal and moral arguments about the application of the concept of liberty to argue that because 'liberty' does not mean 'unfettered licence' and because restraints on action may sometimes be justified in terms of protecting the liberty of others, that all proper restraints on freedom of action may be considered as part of the concept of 'liberty' properly so called. But if all or too many justifiable discriminations and justifiable restraints are fed into the ideas of equality and liberty in this way, the specific roles of equality, liberty, security, and justice as distinct and potentially clashing segments of morality are obscured.

PART THREE

Economic inequality, its extent and causes

10

How unevenly is wealth spread today?

GEORGE POLANYI &
JOHN B. WOOD

≠

BASIC CONSIDERATIONS

WHATEVER the trend in the distribution of wealth during the last few decades, the position today may still seem to some to be unacceptable. We have established [in the preceding discussion – Ed.] that the trend toward the wider ownership of wealth has continued steadily and continuously since the early 1930s. But the distribution may be much more even than it was, and yet still be described as 'excessively unequal'. The Labour Party has announced[1] its intention to achieve 'far greater economic equality – in income, wealth and living standards', and has proposed an annual wealth tax and a new tax on major transfers of personal wealth (gifts or inheritance). In his study of wealth ownership, with a title which might be thought to pre-judge the issues, Professor Atkinson describes the existing distribution as 'unjust', and says 'there is a strong case for the introduction of reforms in Britain designed to bring about greater equality of wealth-holding' (*Unequal Shares*, p. xix).

Various ways to do this are being proposed. New wealth

First published as chapter 2 and Epilogue of the authors' *How Much Equality?* (Institute of Economic Affairs, London, 1974), pp. 23–44, 70–7.

For Notes and References, see page 388 below.

taxes, gift taxes, and inheritance taxes are being worked out, including one which would make it necessary to record for tax purposes any transfer between individuals (including fathers and sons) of any sum over £25.[2] One might have hoped that academics in particular would first wish to establish with much more certainty the evidence on wealth distribution before discussing policy on the debatable assumption – it can be no more – that wealth is unjustly distributed, and that its ownership should be changed.

This eagerness to take up a position on wealth distribution seems to have led a number of writers to overlook the clear warning from the Inland Revenue, the source of most of the material used in the debate. In their annual statistics for 1972,[3] they repeat a warning of earlier years:

> Because of deficiencies in the data, the wealth estimates should probably not be used to derive a measure of the absolute level of the concentration of the wealth of individuals, but they can be used to show the direction in which the level is changing.

1. *The dead and the living*

Far too little attention has been paid to this warning, and even less to the way in which statistics about wealth distribution are produced through the 'mortality multiplier' method. This method is the way in which a post-mortem on the estates of dead individuals is converted into data supposed to portray the realities of a living society. Virtually all the 'facts' used by every participant in the debate have to be filtered through this statistical method, because we have no direct census or sample survey of the personal wealth of the living.[4] Under critical examination, very serious defects in the 'mortality multiplier' method are soon revealed.

In our present tax system, the only time a person's wealth has to be valued comprehensively is at death, when an assessment is made to calculate estate duty. The Inland Revenue prepares an analysis of all estates assessed for duty in each year,[5] classified by age and sex of the deceased. To estimate total personal wealth among the living, a 'morality multiplier' is applied to the assessments. The number of wealth-owners in each age and sex group and the amount of wealth are multiplied up by the appropriate mortality rate. If the number of deaths per 1000 population for a male age-group is 1 in 1000 (e.g. aged 25 to 34 in 1970), the number and value of estates in it are multiplied by 1000 to give an estimate of total wealth for the living population. Estimates of total personal wealth are thus constructed, together with analyses of numbers of owners of property in each range of wealth (as in Table 10.1 below) and of the value of each type of property[6] (e.g. houses, land, buildings, household goods, shares and other financial assets).

The method has to depend on many assumptions. One is that, in ownership of property, people who die are a representative sample of the living. The sample may however be very small, so the risk is correspondingly large that, by chance, the wealth characteristics of those who die may be unrepresentative. Thus in 1970–71 the sample of men aged 25 to 34 with property of more than £200,000 was two deaths. Since they could have added 2000 (or one-tenth) to the number of people recorded as having wealth of more than £200,000, the risk that the property of the dead may be unrepresentative of living people is serious. Professor Atkinson acknowledges: 'A wealthy young man crashing his sports car could add 1000 to the estimate of the number of people with wealth over £200,000.'

Such a chance event might well distort the supposedly representative character of wealth among people who die, and thus give an incorrect estimate of the number of rich people among the living.[7]

Estimates of the distribution of wealth are highly sensitive to whichever assumption is made about the appropriate mortality rate to be used. Some earlier estimates used general mortality rates for the whole population in each age and sex group.[8] But they did not recognise that more prosperous people tend to have lower mortality rates, so that the number of owners and amount of wealth in the higher ranges was estimated incorrectly. A correction applying 'upper-class' mortality rates to the higher wealth groups is now made and incorporated in the Inland Revenue estimates, though, of course, there is no certainty about either the social class of the deceased[9] or the appropriate correction to be applied. Professor Lydall and Mr

Tipping estimated 'upper-class' mortality rates among some younger age-groups at only about three-quarters of the general rate, so that there is scope for considerable error in estimating wealth in these cases if the correction is wrong, or wrongly applied. In addition, other factors known to have a substantial effect on mortality rates, such as whether the person is married or not, are left out of account because of lack of data.[10]

2. *Valuation difficulties*

All these problems would arise even if information about the property of people who die were complete and systematic, i.e. derived from a full survey of their assets. Estate duty assessments fall far short of that standard, because their primary purpose is to assess liability for tax, not to carry out a survey of the property of the deceased.

Information about the value of an estate is obtained only where a 'grant of representation' or probate is obtained from the High Court to enable the executors to administer the estate. Such a grant is not needed for small properties, or where the assets can be transferred without it (e.g. National Savings Certificates valued at less than £500).

Indeed, only a minority of estates are valued, and assessment is less accurate for smaller properties likely to be below the exemption limit for duty, which in 1970 was £10,000.[11] Since estates below this value comprised 84 per cent of the number assessed in 1970,[12] this is an important limitation.

Even when estates are examined thoroughly because they are expected to be liable for duty, there are substantial problems of valuation, and difficulties about double-counting and omissions. The amount of cash and personal valuables belonging to the deceased tends to be understated, either because dying people need little cash or because of evasion (e.g. relatives may have removed them). Lydall and Tipping (p. 84) considered that some types of household goods might be under-valued because of 'kind-heartedness' of official valuers; the published figures certainly seem extremely low. . . . Life assurance policies tend to be over-valued because for estate duty they are valued at the sum assured plus bonus (if any), but among the living they are worth only surrender value. A much more important source of error in the opposite direction is that many policies are omitted from estate duty statistics largely because smaller death claims are paid without requirement of a grant of representation. Consequently the number of holders of life assurance policies and their total value are substantially understated.[13]

Some assets may appear twice. Gifts from the deceased person during his life-time, for example, are counted as part of his estate if made within a specified number of years before his death (currently seven years); but they will also be counted as part of the property of the recipient, and again included in the estate duty figures when he dies. Large estates, where such transfers are more likely to be made in an endeavour to reduce estate duty, are particularly affected. The result is probably to exaggerate the apparent concentration of wealth by raising the share of wealthier adults among whom such transfers are likely to have been made.

But perhaps the most important source of error is that some types of assets are omitted altogether. Annuities and occupational and personal pensions are excluded because their benefit ceases at death. The capital value of the right to a state pension and other state payments such as unemployment and sickness benefit are also omitted. Since these omitted assets are either universally spread among all adults (notably the right to a state pension), or more widely spread than other assets (occupational pensions), and are likely to have a substantial value, the consequence is a serious under-statement of the wealth of the majority and equally therefore an over-statement of differences.

3. *How much wealth?*

These are only some of the more obvious errors and uncertainties in the figures. Without a survey of personal wealth among the living we shall never be able to judge how misleading the current discussion about wealth distribution is. But some measure of the fragility of the entire structure of discussion is illustrated by two simple observations.

First, because of uncertainties, omissions and valuation problems, no one really knows the total *amount* of net personal wealth in Britain (quite apart from its *spread*). Second, there is no agreement about the number of wealth-owners even within very wide limits.

On these two fundamental aspects, therefore – how much wealth in total, and how many own it – we are short of reliable data. One can only marvel at the way in which some academics and politicians make confident generalisations about the distribution of wealth in Britain today!

On the first, Professor E. Victor Morgan estimated[14] that in 1954 the net value of personal wealth was about £36,000 million, which included an allowance for some types of wealth omitted from the estate duty figures. On a similar basis and for the same year, Lydall and Tipping put the figure at £42,000 million, a difference of £6000 million, or one-sixth of the lower estimate. On a wider definition of omitted wealth, Lydall and Tipping reached a total for net wealth of £46,000 million in 1954, £10,000 million or 28 per cent above Professor Morgan's figure.

More recently, for 1961, Mr J. Revell estimated net personal wealth in Great Britain by the estate duty method at £63,500 million, or 16 per cent higher than the Inland Revenue estimate (£54,900 million). For the UK, his estimate from estate duty information accounted for about 84 per cent of the total of personal sector assets, as assessed from other information.[15] It seems that the Inland Revenue estimate was only about three-quarters of the total of personal wealth as assessed by independent valuations of the various types of assets.

The current figures are also open to uncertainty. Thus Professor Atkinson has estimated that the inclusion of occupational pension rights (together with property settled on a husband or wife or held in discretionary trust) would add 15 per cent to the Inland Revenue total of estimated wealth.[16] If we were to add an allowance for the unknown amount of wealth belonging to people with small properties omitted from the estate duty figures plus the value of state pensions, it seems possible that omitted wealth could be about one-third of the recorded total. This would mean that in 1970, when the total net personal wealth indicated by Inland Revenue data was some £97,000 million, about £30,000 million should have been added to the figures. A major part of this missing wealth is either distributed evenly among all adults of the same age-group (value of the right to state pensions) or is likely to be more evenly distributed (e.g. occupational pensions) than the total of recorded assets. The inclusion of this further wealth would therefore substantially alter the general picture, and show that wealth is much more widely dispersed than popular discussion at present understands.

4. *Under-valuation of 'popular' assets*

Apart from the omission of some largely 'popular' types of wealth, the valuation of particular assets also tends to under-value or under-represent assets which are widely held, and therefore under-estimates total wealth and its dispersal among the majority.

Houses

For instance, Professor Lydall and Mr Tipping noted that compared with the results of the 1954 Oxford University Institute of Statistics savings survey, the value of houses and other premises seemed to be substantially understated in the Inland Revenue estate duty estimates.[17] For 1961, using estate duty information, the value of dwellings in the UK was put at £11,100 million compared with an estimate of £16,600 million (or about 1½ times) from national accounting information.

It seems that the value of houses may still be under-estimated. For 1970, the Inland Revenue wealth estimates showed a total of some £29,000 million as the value of residential buildings (homes). In contrast, an estimate based on housing statistics gives a total of about £46,000 million (9.27 million owner-occupied dwellings: average price of all dwellings £4975). It seems that in 1970 the value of homes owned may have exceeded the Inland Revenue estimated by more than 50 per cent.

Since a house is the major asset for people of moderate means, this apparent under-valuation in the Inland Revenue estimates is important in understanding the degree of equality in the distribution of wealth. Indeed, it may be asked whether the degree of understatement of the value of housing and other 'popular' assets may not invalidate the entire data about wealth distribution.

Life assurance

For life assurance, Lydall and Tipping found that the estimate from estate duty statistics of total sums assured amounted to less than £900 million in 1954 for persons with estates of more than £2000. But since the published total of sums assured was nearly £8000 million, this estimate of assurance for people with more than £2000 seemed much too small. For 1960, Mr Revell found that the estate duty estimate of life assurance policies was less than half the value of sums assured recorded in life office statistics: about £6500 million compared with £14,500 million.

Cash and household goods

A further source of what the Inland Revenue describes as 'bias' in the estimates,[18] though not perhaps large, is the under-valuation of cash in the home, which may be an item of relatively more importance for people of modest means[19] than for the wealthy.

A more important item which seems to be under-valued in the Inland Revenue estimates is 'household goods', a term which includes all the contents of a house (appliances, silver, china, linen, furniture, etc.) and motor-cars. For 1961, Mr Revell's estimate using estate duty data was 10 per cent higher than the Inland Revenue figure for Great Britain; but even on this higher estimate the estate duty total for the UK was only about half the value of household goods as independently assessed (£2100 million on estate duty basis compared with £3900 million using a national accounts estimate.

For 1970 the Inland Revenue's estimated value was £3500 million, equivalent to an average of only about £200 per household. Since this is a gross figure before deducting liabilities, it seems impossibly low in a society where about one-half of households have a car. The exclusion of assets among people who are not assessed for duty is one reason;

Table 10.1 *Ownership of durable goods and homes: Great Britain, 1956 to 1972*

1. Durable Goods

Per cent of households owning:	1956 %	1966 %	1970† %	1972† %
	Trade estimates	AGB	FES	
Television set	40	88	91	93
Washing machine	19	59	65	66
Refrigerator	9	47	66	74
Central heating	*	19	30	37
Motor-car		45‡	52	53

* negligible
† UK
‡ *Social Trends*, No. 4, HMSO, 1973.
Sources: 1956: Trade estimates; 1966: AGB Home Audit; 1970–72: Family Expenditure Surveys.

2. Homes

Owner-occupied dwellings (GB):	1956	1966	1970	1972
	Department of the Environment			
Number (000)	4850	8320	9270	9790
Proportion of total dwellings (%)	32	47	50	51

Source: Housing statistics, Dept. of the Environment.

another is that the second-hand value of goods as assessed for estate duty is less than their value to the living. The key figures for durable goods and homes given in Table 10.1, however, illustrate trends in ownership which must be inadequately reflected in the official estimates.

The major bias in the Inland Revenue estimates seems to be towards the under-statement both of the total amount of wealth and of those types of wealth which are particularly widely spread among the majority. Omissions of relatively 'popular' types of wealth,* of the entire property of small wealth-owners, and the under-valuation of the property of people of modest

* Omitted wealth also includes property settled on a husband or wife or held in a discretionary trust (above, p. 234), which is likely to be particularly important among higher wealth groups. But the estimates by Professors Atkinson and Day correcting for this and other omissions show that on balance 'popular' assets predominate among missing wealth, and the effect of the correction is to increase equality (below, pp. 245–7).

means which, though assessed, is not thoroughly valued because it is unlikely to become subject to duty, all help to account for this bias. In conclusion, it should now be obvious that such figures as are available cannot be assumed to give a satisfactory answer to the question 'How much wealth is there?'

5. *How many wealth-owners?*

Not only do we lack a reliable figure for the total amount of wealth; we also do not know the number of people who own it. Inland Revenue statistics (based on estate duty figures subjected to the 'mortality multiplier') suggest that only 17 million adults in 1970 had any personal wealth at all. If that were truly the picture, it must follow that about 24 million had none.* This at any rate is the statistical basis for the 'concentration' analysis of wealth distribution as usually quoted (share of top 1 per cent, etc. – Table 10.3), because in the absence of information on 'missing' wealth, property can be assigned only to the 17 million adults officially estimated as being owners. In Table 10.2 this figure is contrasted with a Stock Exchange survey initiated in 1965 which estimated that 33 million adults (21 and over) owned some form of wealth. The contrast is all the more interesting as the Stock Exchange sample was restricted to financial assets, and omitted houses and other physical assets which would have brought in more people.

The Inland Revenue estimates of wealth-owners again appeared to be low for the more 'popular' types of financial assets. The Stock Exchange estimates for 1965 of numbers of owners of life assurance, national savings certificates and premium bonds, and post office and trustee savings bank accounts, were two or three times the Inland Revenue estimate. But for the more 'upper-class' types of financial

* i.e. assuming that the total of 'potential' wealth-owners is the number of adults in Great Britain aged 15 and over (some 41 million in 1970) and also that people with no recorded wealth of the type included in the estimates have no wealth. The latter assumption is known to be incorrect, but is normally made in analyses of the wealth distribution because of ignorance about the wealth of people not shown as owners in the official estimates.

Table 10.2 *Estimated number of wealth-owners: Great Britain, 1965 and 1970*

	Stock Exchange Survey Adults aged 21 and over	Inland Revenue Estate Duty Estimates Adults aged 15 and over	
	1965	1965	1970
	No. (mill.)	No. (mill.)	No. (mill.)
Owners of:			
Life assurance	23	11	11
National Savings Certificates and Premium Bonds	21	7	7
Quoted Stocks and Shares	2½	2½	2½
Post Office and Trustee Savings Bank Accounts	20	9	6
Shares and Deposits in Building Societies	4	2½	4
Total:			
Persons owning Wealth[1]	33	18	17

[1] In the Stock Exchange survey the total is for people owning financial assets (money saved or invested). In the Inland Revenue estimates it includes owners of all types of property. Numbers owning individual assets add to more than total owners because a person may own several types of assets.

Sources: Stock Exchange survey of ownership of financial assets (money saved or invested), 1965, and *Inland Revenue Statistics*.

assets (company stocks and shares, shares and deposits in building societies) the Inland Revenue and Stock Exchange estimates were much closer. In particular, for quoted stocks and shares the two estimates approximately coincided. This under-representation of the property of small owners and the more accurate coverage of the property of richer people is confirmed by the Inland Revenue: 'Most of the deficiencies . . . [in the estimating process] apply progressively more to the lower ranges of net wealth than to the higher'.[20]

From the Stock Exchange inquiry it seemed that about 90 per cent of adults aged 21 and over had some property in contrast to only 41 per cent of adults aged 15 and over, as implied by the Inland Revenue estimates.

Evidence that on a household basis the proportion of wealth-owners is at least double the Inland Revenue figure for adults is given by the 1954 Oxford University Institute of Statistics survey. According to this sample survey, nearly 80 per cent of 'income units' in Great Britain (consisting of a single person or a couple and their dependants) had some property in 1954.[21] Since in the past 20 years the extent of ownership has substantially increased (e.g. home ownership nearly doubled from 28 per cent in 1953 to 51 per cent in 1972) it seems likely that at present well over 80 per cent of households have some property.

Whether there are under 20 million or over 30 million wealth-owners is not known, therefore. What is important in the debate on wealth distribution is to acknowledge this ignorance, and to recognise the severe limitations of the estate duty data which are the only source of knowledge about the distribution of personal wealth. In 1970, out of 639,000 deaths, assessments for duty were made in only 290,000 cases (less than half), and about the other 349,000 (presumed to be small properties) no information is available. These 349,000 people will certainly have left *some* property, but their assets would have been recorded in the figures as nil. On such a narrow and misleading foundation, one cannot build reliable estimates of either the number of owners or the amount they own. Despite the confident claim implied in the title of his book, Professor Atkinson admits: '. . . the estate duty statistics only provide adequate coverage of the upper part of the wealth distribution. This means that total wealth is likely to be under-estimated, which *leads in turn to an overstatement of the share of the top wealth-holders*'. (Our italics.)

6. *How many 'potential' owners?*

Moving on from the difficulties of estimating the total amount of wealth and the numbers who now own it, there is the further question of how to measure the number of people who are 'potential' owners, i.e. who might own it.

Finding, for example, that the official estimates for 1970 (Table 10.3) show 17 million owners of wealth, we might say that only one-third of the total population of Great Britain (54 million) has any wealth at all. But this conclusion is clearly unrealistic. Of the 54 million, about 13 million are children under 15; and they are unlikely to be wealth-owners.

Consequently some assumption has to be made about the number of people who *are* potential owners. If, as in Table 10.3

we follow the assumption made by the Inland Revenue that the total of 'potential' owners is the number of adults aged 15 and over, there is a total of some 41 million adult 'potential' owners in 1970. Since, on the Inland Revenue estimates, 17 million (41 per cent) own property, the balance of 24 million must have none. But it is this same total of 41 million adults which is used in the concentration analysis to show the proportion of total wealth owned by the wealthiest 1 per cent, 5 per cent, etc. of adults. This is the origin of the widely quoted but misleading statistic that the wealthiest 10 per cent of adults own 70 per cent of the total personal wealth (lower part of Table 10.3).

The statistic is misleading, first, because the property of

Table 10.3 *Estimated distribution of personal wealth: Great Britain, 1970*

Inland Revenue data

Range of Wealth £	Adults aged 15 and over No. (000)	Amount of Wealth £000 million
Over 200,000	19	8
100–200,000	40	5
50–100,000	132	8
20– 50,000	524	16
10– 20,000	1,049	14
5– 10,000	3,217	23
1– 5,000	8,189	21
Up to 1,000	3,924	2
Total: Wealth-owners	17,094	97
No Wealth	24,152	—
Total: Adults	41,246	97

Shares of Top 1 per cent, etc.

Our estimates

Proportion of Adults Top:	Range of Wealth More than: £	No. (000)	£000 million	% of total wealth
1%	28,000	412	30	31
5%	8,900	2,062	54	56
10%	5,600	4,125	68	70

Source: Inland Revenue Statistics 1972, Table 86, and our estimates. Wealth values are net of liabilities.

married women is often included with that of their husbands in the wealth estimates since that is often the way in which it is legally held. How far this is so is unknown; but to the extent that it prevails married women should be excluded from the total of 'potential' owners. If *all* their wealth were held by their husbands the total of adults who are potential owners would fall by some 14 million (the number of married women) to 27 million, and the share of total wealth held by the wealthiest 10 per cent would, by this adjustment alone, fall from 70 per cent to about 62 per cent in 1970.

Secondly, age differences within the adult population aged 15 and over are clearly important. Some people are much more likely to be potential owners than others, simply because they are older. Since the estimates of wealth distribution reflect the assets held by a cross-section of adults of various ages at a point in time (1970), it would be unrealistic to regard all of them as equally likely to be owners or to own the same amount. That would be to say that the 15-year-old office boy is expected to own as much as the 65-year-old company chairman (and having started off with the same wealth, should never add to it).* The same point would apply to other jobs or professions – civil servant, broadcaster, politician, sports star.

A substantial proportion of the adults shown in Table 10.3 as having no wealth will be under 25 years of age.† There are about 8 million young people between 15 and 24, few of whom have yet had time to amass much in the way of possessions, but they are conventionally counted among those having no, or negligible, wealth and are, in this way, part of the 'evidence' about 'unequal shares'. If young people under 25 were excluded from the total of potential owners the share of the wealthiest 10 per cent of adults would fall still further.

If young people are living independently, their inclusion in the figures for distribution of wealth, though statistically correct, is misleading as it increases the apparent degree of 'unfairness'. If they live at home as dependants, they share in

---

* Below, pages 243–5, for further discussion of age difference effects.

† About half the total of people of all ages who appear on the estate duty estimates to have no wealth (37 million including children) are under 25. (*Inland Revenue Statistics, 1972*, p. 156.)

the wealth of the family. Including them as independent units (because the wealth statistics relate to individuals, not to families) simply exaggerates the measure of concentration.

As with married women who may be wrongly counted as independent potential owners, the unrealistic inclusion of young people still dependent on their families as if they were potential owners follows from the basic defect of the wealth estimates: that they derive from assessments of the wealth of *individuals*, not of *families*. But we do not have information about the wealth of families, which would be more realistic for the analysis of wealth distribution. As the Inland Revenue concedes: '. . . the notion of concentration [degree of inequality] is more meaningful in relation to the wealth of households rather than of individuals, but the figures are not available in that form'.[22]

7. *Age differences and inequality*

Age differences also affect the general pattern of wealth-holding because older people obviously tend to have more wealth, which again falsifies the picture of wealth concentration popularly quoted. For 'inequality' between older and younger people is not what is usually meant when the distribution of wealth is described as 'unjust'; it reflects the normal life cycle in which a person may at one period of his life be poor and later hold substantial property.

Incomes rise with age and out of higher incomes a larger proportion is saved;[23] in addition, the income from the return on the savings (which may itself be re-invested) will have had time to rise. Older people therefore tend to have substantially more property than younger. Thus, for 1954, Professor Lydall and Mr Tipping found that the average net wealth of adults in Great Britain aged 75 and over was seven times that of the 20–24 age-group. Professor Atkinson has argued that these differences do not provide a major explanation of the degree of concentration in wealth distribution, because there is substantial inequality within age-groups (p. 51). But his analysis of shares of wealth in each age-group in 1963–67, to support his view, also shows that, apart from the youngest group where concentration is high because many young people have little or no wealth, the degree of concentration among males (who own nearly two-thirds of total wealth recorded in the Inland Revenue estimates) rises systematically with age. According to his estimates for 1963–67, the share of the top 10 per cent of male wealth-owners increased through the age ranges from 63 per cent among males aged 35–44 to 75 per cent among those aged 85 and over. Similarly, a sample survey of American families ('consumer units') for 1962 showed that, apart from the youngest group (under 35), where many had little wealth, and which accounts for only a small part of total personal wealth, the highest concentration was among people aged 65 and over.[24]

The data used in Professor Atkinson's analysis for 1963–67 (as also by Lydall and Tipping for 1954) show how higher average wealth among older people gives a larger proportionate share of total wealth than its share of the total of adults to each succeeding higher age-group (Table 10.4). Adults aged 25–34 were about 20 per cent of total adults, but accounted for less than 12 per cent of total personal wealth. Thus the ratio of their share of total wealth to their proportion

Table 10.4 *Wealth and age: Great Britain, 1963–67*

Age Group of Adults	Proportion of Total Adults aged 25 and over* %	Proportion of Total Personal Wealth %	Proportion of Wealth as % of Proportion of Adults %
	Popn. statistics	Atkinson	
25–34	19.8	11.8	60
35–44	21.2	15.9	75
45–54	20.4	20.2	99
55–64	19.2	24.8	129
65–74	12.4	16.6	134
75–84	5.8	8.8	152
85 and over	1.2	1.9	158
Total	100.0	100.0	
Below 55	61.4	47.9	78
55 and over	38.6	52.1	135

* 1965

Source: A. B. Atkinson, 'The Distribution of Wealth and the Individual Life Cycle', *Oxford Economic Papers*, July 1971, p. 249, and population statistics.

of total adults (shown as a percentage in the last column of the Table) was 60 per cent.

With increasing age this percentage rises, and the wealth ratio of people aged 85 and over was 158 per cent of their population ratio. The lower section of the Table shows that the wealth-to-numbers ratio among people 55 and over is about 1 ¾ times that of people less than 55.

This disproportionate share of total personal wealth among older people* is bound to increase the wealth concentration. It is clearly misleading, therefore, to use this concentration analysis which reflects a cross-section of people of different ages as an indicator of the degree of supposed injustice. Allowance must be made for age differences as a cause of differences in wealth.

8. *Amended estimates*

At this stage the reader may conclude that the analysis of wealth distribution as generally presented is indeed more misleading than helpful and will be surprised that so little attention has been paid to the shortcomings of the statistics. If there is one conclusion that emerges with certainty, it is that there is no foundation for the widely quoted claim by Professor Atkinson that 'over a quarter of total personal wealth in Britain is in the hands of the richest 1% of the adult population and as much as three-quarters belongs to the top 10%'.

As we have suggested, the main result of the errors and omissions and the uncertainty about the number of potential wealth-owners is that the concentration analysis exaggerates the degree of differences in wealth.

The true extent of concentration in wealth holding cannot be judged. But an attempt by Professor Atkinson to correct the figures for some types of omitted wealth (though incomplete) gives an indication of the extent of the exaggeration. His

* Among holders of financial assets in Great Britain, a survey conducted in 1968 by the British Market Research Bureau for the Building Societies Association found that people aged under 45 accounted for only one-third (31 per cent) of the total value of investments although they comprised just over half (53 per cent) of the total adult population (aged 16 and over).

estimates for personal wealth in Britain in 1963–67, together with partial amendments, are summarised in Table 10.5.

Before Professor Atkinson's adjustments, the wealthiest 1 per cent of adults are shown as owning one-third and the wealthiest 10 per cent nearly three-quarters of total personal wealth.* The first adjustment was to include an estimate for 'missing' personal wealth. An estimated £750 per man and £250 per woman was added for small estates where no valuation is available. A further addition was made for the estimated value of occupational pension rights, annuities, and property settled on a surviving husband or wife or held in discretionary trusts. These items, also omitted from the estate duty statistics, were assumed to be distributed in the same way as recorded wealth. The result, shown in the second column of Table 10.5, is to reduce the share of the top 10 per cent from nearly three-quarters to two-thirds.

Table 10.5 *Adjusted distribution of personal wealth: Great Britain, 1963–67 (Adults aged 25 and over)*

as presented by Atkinson

	Per cent of Total Personal Wealth		
	Unadjusted	Adjusted for 'missing' personal wealth	Adjusted for 'missing' wealth plus state pensions
	%	%	%
Owned by:			
Top 1%	32	29	22
5%	58	54	41
10%	73	67	52

Source: A. B. Atkinson, *Unequal Shares*, p. 14, and 'The Distribution of Wealth and the Individual Life Cycle', *Oxford Economic Papers*, July 1971, p. 252.

This is a marked reduction, although the full effect of adding missing wealth is still understated. No allowance is made for probable under-valuation of the major part of properties which, though assessed for estate duty, are not inspected closely because they are expected to be below the limit of

* The figures, therefore, do not allow for age differences, or the position of married women, discussed in the text.

liability for tax. Furthermore, the amount attributed to people excluded altogether from the estate duty figures for wealth they left is necessarily arbitrary and almost certainly under-estimated. In theory, omitted estates might have been worth up to £5000,* so the allowance of £750 for men and £250 for women is clearly nominal. In addition, the procedure of allocating some of the missing wealth (occupational pensions, etc.) in the same way as wealth is recorded in the estate duty estimates must incorporate the same bias inherent in these figures. Finally, there is no correction for wives and other dependants of the owners of wealth being included among the 'property-less'. So even before going further, the adjusted figure of 67 per cent ought to be still further reduced.

A much more substantial adjustment, reducing the share of the top 10 per cent from two-thirds to roughly half, is shown in the third column of Table 10.5 which allows for the value of the right to state pensions. The value of the expected benefit, calculated on estimated life expectancy and discounted at 5 per cent, is equally spread among all adults of a given age-group. Its inclusion has a substantial equalising effect on wealth distribution.

The outcome of these adjustments is to reduce the share of the top 10 per cent from 73 to 67 per cent on adding missing personal wealth conservatively valued, and to 52 per cent after allowing for the value of state pensions. Even now, the figures are not age-standardised, and do not allow for the usual accumulation of wealth between the ages of 25 and 65. These estimates related to the mid-1960s, since when the concentration of wealth has been reduced further.[25] Professor Alan Day has estimated[26] that in 1973, after making these and other corrections, the share of the top 10 per cent in personal wealth was reduced to 41 per cent.

9. *A revised conclusion*

In view of the shortcomings of the original data, and if these adjusted estimates are even approximately correct, we suggest that statements about the alleged 'excessive' degree of

* The exemption limit was raised to £15,000 in 1972.

concentration of wealth ought to be altogether much more tentative, and ought also to acknowledge the dispersion that has already taken place. In the opening statement of the theme of his book Professor Atkinson asserts that 'One of the most marked inequalities in our society is that in the distribution of wealth. The evidence available shows that . . . as much as three-quarters belongs to the top 10 per cent'.

Even his own revisions of the estimates show that this statement clearly requires considerable amendment. We suggest that the amendments do not go far enough. Admittedly we have only limited knowledge about the ownership of wealth, and the number of potential owners to which wealth data should be related, so that it is doubtful whether we can arrive at a realistic assessment of 'shares' at all. What is certain is that published estimates greatly exaggerate the concentration of wealth. Even partial corrections suggest that the share of the wealthiest 10 per cent is nowhere near three-quarters, is probably less than half – and may be about 40 per cent – and even that degree of concentration does not allow for wives and other dependants of wealth-owners. If every person included in the top 10 per cent had only one unrecorded dependant, the formula would be reduced to 20 per cent of the people owning 40 per cent of the wealth.

10. *Further adjustment*

There is no reason why the process of correction should end with the inclusion of 'missing' private wealth and the value of state pensions. State pensions are certainly a large item in social service expenditure, but in 1970 they accounted for only about one-sixth of the total (£1800 million out of £10,000 million). The balance of over £8000 million included other social security cash benefits (unemployment and sickness benefit, family allowances, supplementary benefits, etc.) and benefits in kind, such as state education, national health service and local authority housing.

Council housing is particularly important as it now forms about one-third of the country's housing stock. None of this is included in personal wealth, and council tenants on death are not assessed to estate duty on their accommodation. What is omitted is a capital value which would reflect the benefit to the tenant of the difference between the state-subsidised rent he paid and the market rent.

Nearly all such benefits are either provided equally to everyone, or means-tested to favour lower-income groups. If we could take account of the capital value of the right to receive them, it is obvious that the distribution of wealth would look much more egalitarian. And there is no logical reason why *any* social service spending should be excluded when the right to state pensions has correctly been counted as part of personal wealth. The problem is to value them, and the danger is that these items, which largely give rise to 'human' wealth (increasing a person's well-being and future income) may be neglected for just this reason. As Professors Bauer and Prest have observed, discussions about wealth may not be soundly based partly because of 'the belief that only those aspects of reality are significant which can be quantified, whether genuinely or spuriously'.[27]

To illustrate the magnitudes involved we quote one example – education. For the United States it has been estimated that the value of investment in education is about two-thirds of the total value of national capital in tangible form (reproducible physical assets).[28] If the same proportion is applied in the UK, the value of educational capital invested in the population in 1970 would be about £80,000 million.

Conditions in Britain are different and higher education is less widespread. Nevertheless the figure suggests that educational capital is of the same order of magnitude as all personal wealth. If we were able to assess the capital value of all state social benefits it would easily exceed the value of all the tangible personal wealth whose distribution is currently under discussion. And since most social benefits are equally available among all adults, acknowledging their value would reduce substantially the share of the wealthiest adults in total private *and* social personal wealth.

Whether or not they can be quantified, the very large public expenditures on social benefits available to all have significantly narrowed the differences in wealth. Since such public 'human' investment is to a large extent a substitute for private saving by the majority to provide for retirement, sickness and education, its exclusion presents an incomplete and misleading picture of wealth distribution.

Professor James Meade has observed: 'there can be no doubt that the great expansion of the first stages of education in the last half century has been an equalising factor of the greatest importance . . .'[29] An analysis of the distribution of property which omits this 'important form of capital' is in his view 'very incomplete if not positively misleading'.[30]

Professor Atkinson referred to 'human' wealth such as education, but decided that 'this particular aspect of wealth is not one to which I can do justice in this book', so omitted it (p. *xx*). In ignoring growth in 'public' education as well as in other forms of social expenditure, he leaves out of the account a major part of the process of spreading wealth in Britain over the past few decades.

11. *Public and private wealth*

In terms of measurable 'non-human' assets, the general impression is that personal property is by far the most important item in the national wealth, but this impression is based on a particular way of assessing the relative sizes of the main wealth sectors. As Table 10.6 shows, there are two ways to measure shares of national wealth. In the value of physical assets (land, buildings, plant and equipment, etc.) shown in the first column of Table 10.6, the personal sector accounted in 1966 for only one-third of national wealth. The value of physical assets of companies and the public sector (including nationalised industries) is jointly about double that of the personal sector; and the public sector alone has assets almost equal to those of personal wealth. But in terms of net worth, shown in the right-hand column of the Table where the net value of financial assets is added to that of physical assets, the personal sector is predominant, with three-quarters of total national wealth.

Net worth, therefore, as usually quoted in analyses of the shares of wealth between sectors (for example by Professor Atkinson) suggests that personal wealth is by far the most important. As the middle column of Table 10.6 indicates, however, this is because the personal sector has a large positive financial balance – reflecting the lending of money to companies and the public sector through holdings of shares, government securities, etc. – while companies and the public sector have a correspondingly large negative financial balance.

Table 10.6 *Personal and public wealth: United Kingdom, 1966* as presented by Revell and Roe

	Physical Assets		Financial Assets (net value)	Total: Net Worth	
	£000 m.	%	£000 m.	£000 m.	%
Personal Sector	46	33	59	105	75
Companies	51	37	—22	29	21
Public Sector	41	30	—35	6	4
Overseas			— 2		
Total	138	100		140	100

Source: J. Revell and A. R. Roe, 'National Balance Sheets and National Accounting', *Economic Trends*, HMSO, May 1971.

Consequently, a net worth analysis of wealth by sectors gives a misleading picture of the degree of economic power or control over the use of resources exercised by personal wealth. For although the personal sector is largely the ultimate provider of finance, it does not necessarily follow that the individual lenders or investors effectively control the physical resources which are mainly in the company and public sectors. How far this is so depends on the extent to which shareholders control the management of companies and holders of government securities control the use of resources in the public sector. In the public sector, in particular, virtually no such power is exercised by the bond holders; and the analysis of physical assets leads to the same conclusion as our rough estimate of the value of mainly socially-provided 'human' capital (education): that the size of publicly-controlled wealth is in practice probably about equal in importance to that of private wealth.

The evidence assembled in Sections 1 and 2 [of the original publication – Ed.] leaves no room to doubt that the oft-repeated slogans about the extent of inequalities of wealth are based on partial statistics which provide a false picture of the changing real world. In the mouths of politicians and popular broadcasters, such misleading claims may charitably be attributed to ignorance and propagandist zeal.

It is less easy to excuse academic writers who have lent spurious authenticity to a presentation that is not only at variance with everyday observation but does not withstand exposure to easily available information.

Some Wider Issues

So far we have been trying to assess the facts – or lack of them – rather than discuss their wider implications. Since we have repeatedly drawn attention to defects in the statistical sources and to the shortcomings of the methods on which popular discussion insecurely rests, there seems to be little scope for generalisation. In any event, the present monograph is an interim report, and it is hoped to present a fuller study in a further report.

Nevertheless the analysis in the preceding sections suggests some provisional conclusions. For instance, we have criticised attempts to show that there has been no change in the spread of wealth over the years. It seems to us irrefutable that wealth and income have become much more evenly spread during the last 40 years. Commonsense observation of everyday life seems to support this view.

That this spreading of wealth, first observed over 20 years ago by Miss Kathleen Langley,[31] and later by Professor Lydall and Mr Tipping with estimates extended to the mid-1950s,[32] should once more be disputed is remarkable. Yet in the widely quoted study by Professor Atkinson (already the basis for misleading programmes on 'educational' television),[33] the author repeatedly asserts that changes in wealth represent 'in part' rearrangement of wealth within wealthy families or, more strongly, 'the redistribution of wealth over this century has not been between the rich and the poor, but between successive generations of the same family'.

A possible clue to understanding the reasons for this resistance to all the evidence of the wider dispersal of wealth may be found in a quotation from Karl Marx's *Das Kapital* at the head of chapter 3 of Professor Atkinson's book: '. . . the progress of capitalist production . . . lays open in speculation and the credit system a thousand sources of sudden enrichment'. This enrichment Marx attributed to exploitation of the workers, whose living standards must, he said, always decline. In the significant sentences which follow (not quoted by Professor Atkinson), Marx continues:

> Moreover, the capitalist gets rich, not like the miser in proportion to his personal labour and restricted consumption, but at the same rate as he squeezes out the labour-power of others and enforces on the labourer abstinence from all life's enjoyments.

What may lie behind the reluctance to acknowledge the evidence about the dispersal of wealth we see all around us could therefore be the need to sustain the Marxist thesis that under capitalism the workers must become progressively more impoverished. As the contrast becomes more conspicuous (and more widely understood) between the massive increase in the standard of living of ordinary people in the West compared to the negligible improvement in the Soviet Union, we may therefore expect that people influenced by the Marxist view will be forced to ever more elaborate arguments in attempts to deny the obvious.*

1. *How much inequality?*

Not only is there insufficient data to support doctrinaire critiques of the supposed concentration of wealth; the debate about the 'fairness' of distribution is further impeded by the lack of any clear lead from the critics about how much 'inequality' there should be. Although there is a presumption that in principle absolute equality should prevail,† this can hardly be sustained as a cogent criterion. Professor Atkinson

* A particularly bizarre example is the inaugural lecture by Professor M. Morishima given at the London School of Economics in November 1973, in which the rate of exploitation of workers in the capitalist system is validated by mathematical economics. There is not a single reference to economic conditions as they have developed or now exist in any country in the world.

†'. . . the basic principle [is] that the distribution should be equal' (*Unequal Shares*, p. 79).

himself has shown that age differences alone can produce a wide range of differences in wealth ownership. In a society in which incomes vary only with age and everyone inherits an equal amount of wealth, the top 10 per cent of adults might still own 30 per cent of personal wealth, largely through the accumulation of savings through life.[34]

Older people tend to have higher incomes; their experience and training have had time to yield their full reward. An American survey has thrown some light on the importance of age and savings in leading to differences of wealth. In 1963 it was found that income in US families headed by a person in the age-group 45–54 was about a quarter above the average for all ages, while in the age-group 18–24 it was only about 70 per cent of the average. People in middle age had *on average* about 1¾ times the income of those in the youngest adult age-group.[35] This source of 'inequality' is all the larger since such differences are wider for higher-income groups (e.g. the ratio between the earnings in middle age of an industrial manager and his starting pay is much higher than for a manual worker).

Moreover, people with higher incomes save a larger proportion of them. This is a further factor leading to 'inequality'. The same US survey report showed that in 1960 urban families with average incomes saved about 2½ per cent of them, while those with about three times the average income saved 23 per cent, almost 10 times more as a proportion of their higher incomes. This combination of higher incomes and a larger percentage of them saved, meant that of a sample of families in 1960–61, the top income group, accounting for only 2 per cent of the families, held 44 per cent of the total annual savings.[36]

Similarly, among the different age-groups the higher income of older people resulted in disproportionately higher savings. Thus among families headed by a person in the age group 45–54, which in 1963 had about 1¾ times the income of families in the youngest (18–24) adult age-group, the *proportion* of income saved was about three times, and the *amount* saved about five times, that of the youngest adult age-group.[37] In the US it is likely that the main reason for the concentration of wealth is not inheritance, but differences in accumulation through savings during life-time.

If such a degree of departure from strict 'equality' is accepted as permissible, being based on the 'deserved' reward of life-time accumulation, what degree of 'inequality' is 'excessive'? With equal incomes and equal inheritance, the wealthiest 10 per cent of adults might still own 30 per cent of total wealth. If so, excessive 'inequality' must presumably exceed this degree of concentration. If we further accept that incomes in practice must be unequal to reward varying skills, this will produce wider differences in wealth, and the share of the top 10 per cent might well be around 40 per cent without being 'unfair'. Yet that is roughly what the incompletely amended figures for the existing wealth distribution in Britain already show.*

2. *How much is too much?*

So how much is too much? One definition of the 'ideal' distribution is Professor Atkinson's statement that the case for more equality rests on social justice and on the acceptance of 'the basic principle that the distribution should be equal unless departures from equality can be justified according to what are considered relevant criteria.'

The 'ideal' that everyone should have equal incomes and equal property, unless a departure from this 'norm' can be specially justified, may be logical but it is unhelpful in practice. As Professor Atkinson himself says: 'This statement as it stands is not particularly strong, since its force turns on the definition of "relevant" criteria.'

It is also a surprising statement to be made by an academic economist. It is as if there were no such reality as a market for labour in which the forces of demand and supply are matched (however roughly) so that the consumer's requirements for the whole range of goods and services are met by allocating the available supply of labour between conflicting demands for it.

---

* i.e. the amended estimate by Professor Alan Day for 1973, including partial correction for omitted wealth and under-valuation of some 'popular' assets (above, p. 247). Some part of the existing degree of concentration is due to unequal inheritance. Nevertheless the comparison quoted here suggests that it is probably no more than could result from equal inheritance and life time accumulation in a society with unequal incomes.

All the realities of everyday life are ignored: on the supply side there are undeniably wide differences in intelligence, skills, aptitudes and other human qualities such as effort, strength, reliability; just as on the demand side there is a wide range of job opportunities – from cabinet ministers to cabaret singers, fitters to florists, plasterers to potato-growers. What are the 'relevant criteria' by which society can judge the relative remuneration of these occupations, except through a labour market in which supply and demand tend to move into balance and relative wages as part of this mechanism tend to reflect the relative value of the marginal product of each type of labour?

It would be unrealistic not to take account here of an apparent paradox in public opinion. In most fields of endeavour, apart from business, superior talent and pre-eminence are freely acknowledged and indeed generally welcomed. In art and sport outstanding ability is recognised and applauded not reluctantly but eagerly. No one thinks it 'unfair' that there are ballerinas as well as a corps de ballet, prima donnas as well as singers in the chorus, stars and 'bit' players, teams at the bottom and at the top of the football league (and even four divisions).

In business, it seems, the successful man (though judged by the very same criteria of consumer demand) may expect no similar regard; his achievement is viewed with suspicion. Commentators and some academics explain to the public that his wealth is not the result of his skill and his effort, but has been in some way extracted from other people and therefore at their expense. It is clear that in commercial life, as elsewhere, people differ widely in their aptitudes and abilities. Unless such differences in contribution to the wealth of the nation are acknowledged, we pursue a false egalitarianism, which tries to reward unequal contributions equally.

If differences in income and wealth due to differences in abilities, or to saving/spending habits or to age, are all 'acceptable', then only 'inheritance' remains as the source of 'unfairness'.

Before examining inheritance we must point to a major cause of inequality which is seldom discussed though it was a preoccupation of earlier economists who were concerned with monopoly incomes, exclusivity and restriction of entry. A simple but striking example explains the point. By 1974 some London daily newspapers were having to pay £8000–£9000 a year to their compositors. This high salary in no way reflected the skill involved or the small number of people able to undertake the job, but rather the restriction of entry into the printing industry, the long drawn out apprenticeship and the bargaining power of the printing union. The job is one which can be learned with a far shorter period of training than imposed by the union in Britain and could, in practice, be done by a competent shorthand typist or any other keyboard operator. In Russia, for instance, the composing rooms at *Pravda* and *Izvestia* are largely staffed by women who undertake six months' training. So union power maintains for one group an income of £9000 for doing a job which other people would be happy to do (since it would improve their position) at £4000. This is a powerful cause of inequality and 'unfairness' in incomes.

Other examples include the docks and wherever the level of wages has been artificially maintained by restriction of entry, including many of the professions. Similarly women are often denied the opportunity to enter better paid jobs by restrictions on entry in a wide range of occupations. Their incomes are therefore depressed and this in turn accentuates the degree of inequality.

3. *Inheritance and inequality*

It appears, however, from the emphasis on 'merit' in the discussion, that the real target of criticism is wealth from inheritance rather than from saving out of higher income. Inheritance, says Professor Atkinson, cannot be justified by 'deserts': 'A person who has inherited £1 million has not foregone consumption earlier in life to acquire it—he has not, to use Locke's phrase, "mixed his labour with it" . . . Heirs cannot be said to inherit through any "merit" of their own.' What proportion of the largest fortunes is inherited is not known; nor do we know what proportion of total personal wealth is held by people with fortunes of £1 million or more, which seem to be the focus of disapproval.

A rough estimate of the amount involved can be derived from

the 1970 figures of wealth distribution (Table 10.3). The top wealth group, with more than £200,000, held a total of some £8000 million, which, though it includes the property of people with less than £1 million, may be used as an approximate measure of the total wealth of people with large fortunes. Of this £8000 million about £4000 million was wealth in excess of £200,000. Part of it (perhaps one-fifth)* will be wealth from lifetime accumulation and not from inheritance, so that the 'excessive' wealth due to large inherited fortunes, which is the main target of criticism, is likely to amount to about £3000 million, or 3 per cent of total personal wealth.

The egalitarian proposition resolves itself therefore into an allegation that about 3 per cent of personal wealth held by the richest is indefensible because it is 'excessive' wealth derived mainly from fortunes from inheritance. It is evidently wrong for the top 10 per cent of wealth-owners to have 70 per cent (on the usual false calculation of shares of total personal wealth), but it would be acceptable for them to have 67 per cent (on the same basis)! If this is all that is meant, the case should be restated to indicate that the objection is not to the spread of wealth as such, but only to its apex – a relatively minor aspect.

Apart from doubts whether, on various alternative assessments and interpretations, the wealthiest 10 per cent own 70 per cent, 50 per cent or 40 per cent of total personal wealth, a shift of the order of 3 per cent is less than has already occurred over the past five years through the spontaneous process of 'levelling-up' as the incomes and savings of the majority rise. As this process is still in its early stages by comparison with the USA, further spreading of wealth may reasonably be expected to take place without deliberate government action.

---

* A study of a sample of top wealth-leavers in 1965 showed that about one-fifth of sons leaving £100,000 or more had fathers who left less than £5000 (at 1956–57 prices): C. D. Harbury and P. C. McMahon, 'Inheritance and the Characteristics of top wealth leavers in Britain', *Economic Journal* (September 1973), Table II. If these are regarded as 'self-made men' and assuming that their average property is the same as that of people with mainly inherited wealth, the same proportion of one-fifth can be used as an approximate measure of the proportion of wealth accumulated during their lifetime by top wealth-owners.

Five years may seem a long time in which to achieve further redistribution. But it seems that confiscation is not proposed (because this would inhibit saving by accumulation, which is approved). What is proposed is reform of taxation on inherited wealth (including taxes on gifts) along lines which would gradually spread inherited wealth more widely, or measures simply to impoverish 'the rich' to enrich the state, and thus to add to the concentration of power, which history suggests is at least as objectionable as the private concentration of wealth. Apart from the damage which might be done to incentives and to savings (neither of which are limited to the desire to accumulate during one's life-time), it is arguable that the quality of cultural life and the degree of political freedom, which benefit from large private wealth-holdings independent of the state or corporate business organisations, would also be put at risk.

CONCLUSION

The main conclusion thus seems to remain that the egalitarian thesis, in terms of a general condemnation of differences in wealth and incomes, is unproven and misleading. The advocacy of 'equality' and exploitation of what are unavoidable (and arguably desirable) differences by the emphasis on virtually meaningless statistics such as 'the top 10 per cent own 70 per cent' arouses expectations which cannot be fulfilled, and which few advocates of more equality would themselves support. In this sense, the case presented is a deformed picture of British society, but one which makes it easier for politicians and commentators to invoke the latent feelings of envy present in most societies at most times.[38]

Above all, it would seem that the statistics on which popular discussion rests are too weak for the purpose to which they are put. The Inland Revenue warns against attempting to use estate duty information to give a picture of the concentration of wealth. The warning is ignored; and very selective use is made of clearly defective data. To believe that 10 per cent of the adult population owns 70 per cent of the wealth it is necessary, it would seem, to believe such insupportable propositions as:

(1) 24 million adults own nothing at all.
(2) in the years 1965–70 the number of wealth-owners *fell* by 1½ million (from 18.6 million to 17.1 million).
(3) anyone whose wealth exceeded £5600 in 1970 is in the top 10 per cent, and anyone with more than £28,000 is in the top 1 per cent.
(4) the value of the contents and motor-car of the average British household is only £200.

In short, the available statistical information was not intended, and cannot be used, to give an accurate picture of the spread of wealth in contemporary society.

In a further report we hope to discuss the statistics it would be desirable to collect, and perhaps go some way to fill the gaps by a field survey of the living, for a more accurate judgement on the spread of wealth and income.

11

The stability of inequality

KENNETH E. BOULDING

≠

THE stability of inequality is a source of distress to all sensitive egalitarians. This stability is particularly distressing in the face of measures which are designed to reduce inequality. In the United States, for instance, there is a strong egalitarian bias, which de Tocqueville pointed out many years ago, in the political and social spirit of the society, but in spite of this the relative distribution both of income and of capital has exhibited remarkable stability, at least in the last 25 years. Figure 1 shows this almost unbelievable stability in the relative income shares. Figure 2 suggests a similar stability in the distribution of capital, though it is harder to get complete data on this; of course if we include human capital, the situation becomes much more complicated.

Quantitative evidence on inequality around the world is hard to get. Several recent studies (for example, see Adelman and Morris, and Chenery) suggest that economic development in the poor countries usually increases inequality and it is only the rare case which diminishes it. On a world scale the fact that economic development has been so largely confined to the temperate zone in the last 100 or 200 years has meant an enormous increase in world inequality. The temperate zone has drawn ahead whereas the tropics have stayed behind.

Socialism, a large part of the impulse for which has come out of political demands for equality, has turned out to be very

---

First published in *Review of Social Economy*, Vol. 33, No. 1 (April 1975), pp. 1–44.

For References, see page 390 below.

FIGURE 1 PERCENTAGE SHARE OF AGGREGATE INCOME RECEIVED BY EACH FIFTH OF FAMILIES AND UNRELATED INDIVIDUALS U.S.A., 1947–1972

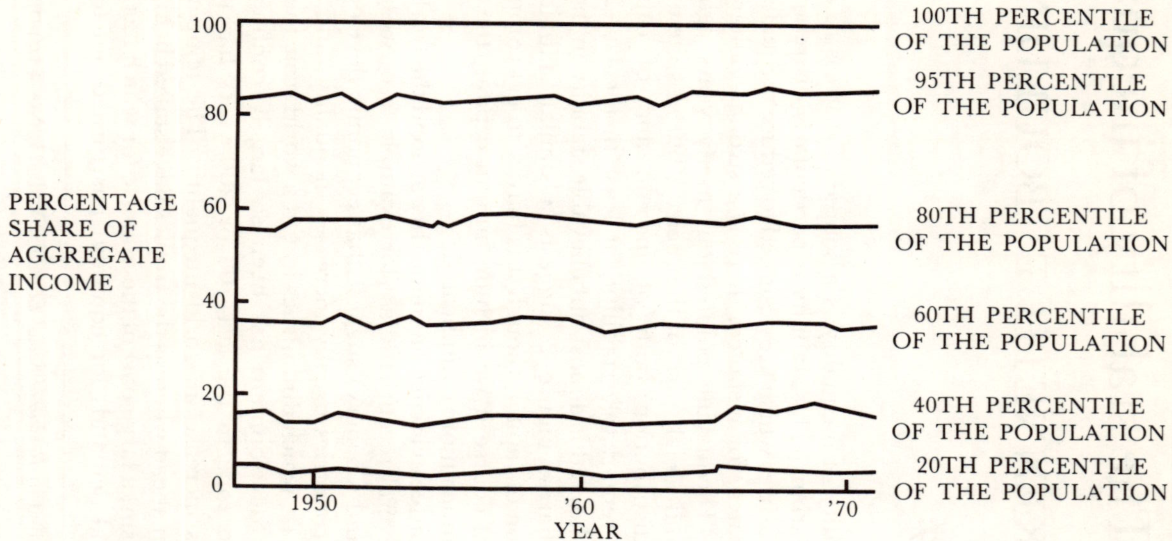

Source: U.S. Bureau of the Census *Current Population Reports*, Series P-60, No. 85, 'Money Income in 1971 of Families and Persons in the U.S.' (Washington, DC, Government Printing Office, 1972).

FIGURE 2 SHARE OF WEALTH BY RICHEST 0.5 PER CENT OF POPULATION U.S.A., 1922–1969

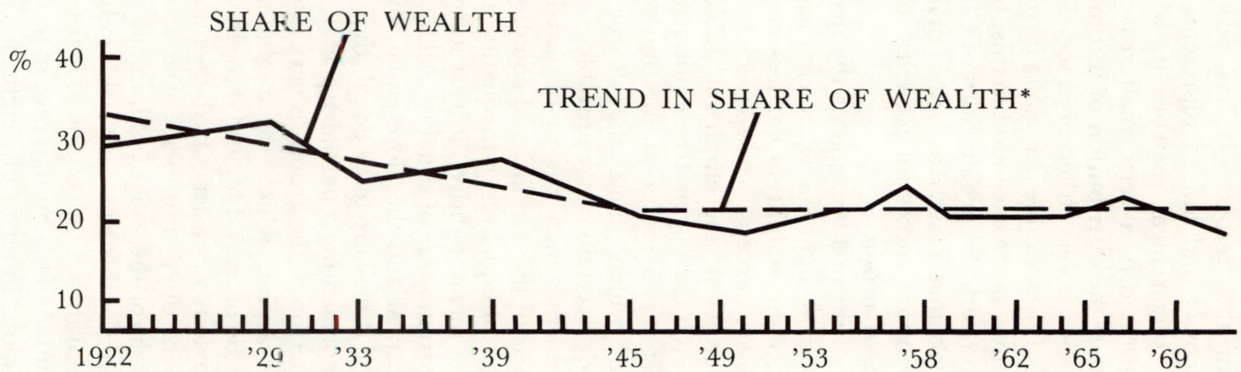

* IRS ESTIMATE

Source: James D. Smith and Stephen D. Franklin, 'The Concentration of Personal Wealth, 1922–1969', *American Economic Review*, 64, 2 (May 1974).

disappointing in this respect. It has produced enormous inequalities of power and indeed represents a retrogression, politically, into oligarchical societies in which all political power is concentrated in a very small group. It is doubtful, also, as to whether the distribution of income outside the top 1/1000 of population is very different in socialist countries than it is in countries of comparable per capita income which are not socialist. China may be an exception to this, but this may have a good deal to do with the peculiarities of Chinese culture, as reflected in the fact that Taiwan as well as mainland China has been one of the more successful societies in moving toward equality in terms of income.

The stability of inequality suggests the need for theoretical models which throw light on what characteristics of social dynamics produce this stability. One does not have to go to an equilibrium theory except as a special case of general dynamics. Nevertheless, the empirical stability of inequality suggests that even if there is no true equilibrium of inequality, there are at least very strong equilibrating constraints on the dynamic system which make the degree of equality or inequality outside a certain range unstable.

The first problem which has to be faced in constructing theoretical models of the dynamics of equality or inequality is the measurement of equality or inequality itself. By equality we clearly do not mean identity, at least in social systems, for identity is the extreme case of equality. All hydrogen atoms are presumably identical and therefore equal; human beings are not identical, and if they are to be equal, they must be equal in some variable representing a partial aspect of the system which constitutes the person or the group. A very interesting question is how far this aspect, which we might call the 'equality variable', has to be measurable, and if so, in what degree. The problem is obviously easier if the equality variable is measurable in cardinal numbers. We can, for instance, measure the height or the weight of humans with considerable accuracy and express this as a cardinal number of centimetres or grams, or even inches or pounds. Then we can establish a cardinal distribution of the human race in terms of the equality variable in question. In terms of weight, for instance, we vary from the tiniest premature baby to the fattest circus freak, a range, let us say, from 1 lb to 1000 lb. The distribution is almost certainly unimodal, although one doubts that it conforms to a normal distribution – it has some skewness and maybe some flatness at the top. Weight distribution would be a function of the age distribution because weight is a function of age. It may be a function of the income distribution, as rich people tend to be fatter, although this relationship is likely to be weak. The inequality in weight can be expressed by any of the standard measures: standard deviation, Gini index and so on.

Equality in weight would be an absurd ideal. On the other hand, it is by no means absurd to rank various distributions according to their preferability. There may be too many skinny people and too many fat people. Whether a ranking by a simple measure of equality or inequality would be adequate is an important question, and one certainly cannot rule out the possibility that of two distributions with the same Gini index, we would rank one higher than the other, for instance, if one had fewer extreme cases than the other. Even in this case the problem of the evaluation of variety is a real one. Do we really want a world in which all people of 25 are exactly the same weight or the same height? The answer is: 'Probably not.' On the other hand, we probably also do not want a world in which half the people weigh 100 lb at maturity and the other half 500 lb. Bimodality always seems to create trouble, and while we cannot assume either that we do not prefer more trouble to less, at least this is something which has to be valued in its own light.

We could push the problem back a little further and ask ourselves: Would there be any dynamic instabilities in different degrees of inequalities of weight, let us say, in a biological species, leaving aside for the moment the complications introduced by the growth in weight from the infant to the adult and considering only adult members of the species? It seems likely that within a single species there is a fair degree of equality. Absolute equality would be unstable, simply because of random variation in the factors which affect the adult weight in the individual. This problem is related somewhat to the stability of age distributions. If we plant a forest of identical trees on the same date, all the trees would be of the same age and this would be unstable even if they were left alone. The instability might be so great indeed that the species would become extinct on reaching the age of death. On the other hand, if it were capable of seeding itself, there would be a new generation of somewhat diverse ages and we would end up after a long time with a forest of somewhat like a normal age distribution as between seedlings, young trees and old trees. There are obviously strong equilibrating constraints directed toward a certain degree of inequality both of age and, of course, of age-related weights.

The role of sexual selection in raising or lowering equality in a species is a fascinating problem which would require some pretty complicated models for solution. Such a selection may move the whole species toward the tastes of the female or whoever is the discriminating factor. This is why sexual selection could easily lead to extinction, for the tastes of the selector, whether male or female, are not necessarily those which increase the probability of survival. We might have a situation, however, which perhaps is not wholly unrealistic in the case of the human race, in which a mutual sexual selection operates to create inequality, in which the successes from the point of view of selective preference mate with each other; then the failures also mate with each other. This principle may be important in the distribution of beauty, even in the dynamics of the distribution of wealth and income. One suspects that the more random is the mating process, the more the species moves toward equality, as the gene pool is randomly distributed among the members of the population. The selective elements which introduce nonrandomness, whether this is sexual selection or even isolation, tend to generate inequality, and if this proceeds far enough, we get two species instead of one.

It would be interesting indeed to work out a computer model on various assumptions about the rich only marrying the rich and the poor only marrying the poor, and seeing what this does to the distribution of the gene pool in the human race. Under some perhaps extreme circumstances this might result in the development of two different species incapable of cross-reproduction. The fact that this has not happened in the history of the human race, in spite of a great deal of separation and differentiation, tells us something about the human gene pool, but I am not quite sure what. It certainly suggests that common genetic elements in different segments of the human race are far more important than those elements which produce differences. Still, genetics cannot be ruled out altogether, but our ignorance about human genetics and the impact of the distribution of the gene pool is a real handicap to us, both in the understanding of social dynamic processes and in their control.

The evolutionary impact of preferences outside sexual preference, such as preference for different kinds of foodstuffs, has been very little studied by the biologists, although the possibility of this having evolutionary impact is by no means negligible. Natural selection obviously selects the preferences of those species which survive, at least toward increasing the probability of survival. A cow which did not like grass or a lion which did not like meat would probably not contribute much to the gene pool after a generation. In social systems, however, preferences of many kinds are of great importance, although even here they may be adverse to survival. Selection must exert some long-run influence in selecting preferences, however these are generated, which have favorable effects on survival probabilities. Societies which have exhibited strong preferences for destroying their own children are seldom around for the anthropologists to study. Similarly, many societies may have become extinct because of rigid food preferences which could not adapt themselves to a changing environment.

In social evolutionary dynamics preferences for equality, or inequality, may have an impact which is far from negligible, but we know very little about the nature of the functions which relate equality preferences to survival probabilities. This would indeed by a fascinating problem for historical research. Was it, for instance, the very strong equality preferences of pre-Columbian, North American Indians which prevented them from forming larger societies, and hence left them exposed to European invaders? How far were the dominant techniques of the Europeans derived from their ability to form large-scale organisations of a hierarchical character which cannot be formed if the preference for equality is too high? Perhaps these questions are too unanswerable to be worth raising. One has the uneasy feeling that while it would save us a lot of trouble to brush them aside, our real understanding of social dynamics may depend on finding some kind of answer to them.

As we move into social systems, the problem of the measurement of equality and inequality becomes much more difficult. The question which we raised earlier as to whether the concept of equality or inequality requires a cardinal measure becomes of considerable importance. In the case of things like income or even wealth, we do have a cardinal measure of sorts in terms of money values of some kind, although, as every economist knows, these are very imperfect surrogates for the thing they are supposed to measure, and the appearance of cardinality is largely a fraud. I am inclined to think that all cardinality is rather a fraud, even in a thing like weight, for although we can easily measure the difference between a person who weighs 180 lb and one who weighs 181 lb, the significance of this weight number depends on its distribution among the various organs and structures of the body. Whereas one person, shall we say, growing from 150 lb to 180 lb may simply be filling out and developing a better physical apparatus, another going from 150 lb to 180 lb may simply be getting fat. Even in such things as weight, therefore, the significance of cardinality may not be any better than it is in things like measures of real income or GNP.

Wherever what we are measuring implies complex structure, then cardinality may be an illusion. On the other hand, the measurement of equality and inequality by ordinal numbers is a problem, simple as it seems, which, as far as I know, has never been solved. Consider, for instance, the problem of the measurement of the degree of equality of status in society. Status is a property of the person which can be measured very easily in ordinal terms, in the sense that we can quite frequently rank the people of society in order of status, but it makes no sense at all in terms of cardinal numbers. Does a Supreme Court judge have 1856 times the status of the Vice-President? On the other hand, simple number ranks are also inadequate as a measure of status and equality, unless perhaps we can also rank the differences between the ranks. Is the difference between an assistant and an associate professor greater than the difference between associate and full professor? We might even find some agreement in answer to a question like that. It is certainly not a nonsensical question and may be part of people's perceptual apparatus.

Even 'ranked ranking' does not really answer the question, however, of the measurement of the equality of status. Suppose we had two societies with 20 status ranks, where most people could identify the rank of themselves and of any other person, and even could rank the differences between the ranks. In one society the difference between the statuses might still be small, and in another it might be large. With an equal number of ranks one society might be relatively equal in status and another very unequal. Perhaps we could use mobility between statuses as the measure of status inequality and status difference. This won't do either, however, because we can certainly postulate increased mobility without any change in the status difference. What looks like a very simple question here turns out to be a conceptual problem of great difficulty. One has an intuitive feeling that Britain, for instance, is a society with much greater inequality of status than the United States. One has a similar intuitive feeling that the status differences in the Soviet Union between, let us say, the élite of the Communist party and the Baptists is very high. It is very disturbing when one finds a concept as meaningful as that of status difference which seems to be so completely intractible to measurement or indexing. One would like to see a rather major effort devoted to this problem.

When we come to inequality of income and wealth, economists, especially, are much more at ease in using cardinal numbers, though even here the existence of an unknown function relating, let us say, income to utility is a bit of a skeleton at the feast. No one would defend the proposition that a man with $100,000 a year is ten times as well off as a man with $10,000 a year and a hundred times as well off as a man with $1000 a year. Diminishing marginal utility of income is a famous principle in economics which is used constantly, for instance, in defense of progressive taxation, but the problems of measurement of utility are even greater than they are in the case of status. Economics, indeed, must be almost unique in the sciences in having an optimum criterion in the field of distribution which is wholly satisfactory in every respect except operationality. This is the principle, of course, that the ideal distribution is that in which the marginal utility of income, or whatever it is that is distributed, is equal for all parties in the distribution, so that taking a dollar from A and giving it to B would harm A just as much as it would benefit B. The only awkward question is: How do we know? And the only answer is, I suppose, that we guess and that we embody these guesses in some kind of process of political decision-making.

The problem of how much each party has of some distribution variable may be difficult, but at least in things like income and wealth there are partial solutions, which are almost certainly better than nothing. A much more difficult question is: How do we identify the parties among whom the distribution is to be made? This is a question which is usually simply taken for granted in most discussions of the subject, but the more one thinks about it, the more difficult it seems to become. Suppose we take, for instance, the famous question, distribution among the generations. It is possible to imagine a society, as has been suggested many times, in which the measure of riches, whatever it is, increases with age, so that all the young people are poor and all old people are rich. In any one year the Gini index looks horrible and indicates an extremely inegalitarian society, but over the life cycle everybody has exactly the same income. Nevertheless, of two societies which had exactly the same income over the total life of each person, participating in them, and in which these incomes were equal, one could have an unequal distribution of the life span and another an equal distribution, and again the question arises: Which is preferred?

Here again, economic theory is suggestive. We can postulate an optimum (preferred) distribution over an individual life span which also determines the personal saving-borrowing pattern. There is even a fair amount of formal theory about this, suggesting, for instance, that the saving-borrowing patterns would be directed toward equalising the distribution over the life span according to the principle of diminishing marginal utility of income, simply because if this function is constant over the life, then each period should have approximately equal income. If we have a very unequal distribution of the life span, so that we are poor when we are young and rich when we are old, it would be advantageous to borrow when we are young and pay back when we are old, how much depending on the rate of interest and our internal subjective rate of time preference, or our 'rate of impatience', as Irving Fisher would call it. Complicating the picture further is the possibility of discounting for uncertainty, which will also affect intertemporal transfers simply because uncertainty increases exponentially as we move forward into the future. There seem to be wide differences in preferences here. On the one hand, there are the impatient who take the cash and let the credit go, enjoy life while they are young and don't think about old age. On the other hand, there are the puritans who are anxious to diminish future uncertainty by youthful thrift, for having is a good deal more certain than getting.

The problem becomes even more difficult if we include the generations not now living. What, for instance, should be our distributional response to posterity? There are wide differences here in the values of different societies and different individuals. Some people and societies have a strong sense of community with the generations of the future. People deny themselves in the present for the benefit of their unborn grandchildren because their personal indentity is so closely bound up with that of the family. There is a very interesting associated phenomenon here which might be described as 'recipient's guilt', or 'grantee's guilt'. Being the recipient of a one-way transfer for which we have given nothing in return can easily be destructive to the identity, and hence creates what might almost be described as a sense of unrequitedness. It is this which induces what I have called 'serial reciprocity' (Boulding, 1973) – A makes a grant to B which makes B feel uncomfortable and perhaps of lower status, or guilty, and B relieves this feeling by making a grant to C, who in turn has to make a grant to D, and so on. Inter-generation grants are very much of this character. Every generation has inherited a great deal from its ancestors, which is a grant which cannot be requited by turning it into an exchange. There is no way to repay our ancestors directly for what they have done for us, and this creates a kind of subterranean guilt which perhaps can only be relieved by doing something for our descendants. How far this extends into the future, however is a moot question. Should we economise on the use of oil now so that human beings 200 years from now might have things a little easier? These are very tricky questions, indeed, and yet they are involved in equality preference. We cannot simply dismiss them even though they are extremely difficult to answer.

Perhaps we could divide the dynamics of equality problem into two parts which correspond roughly to supply on the one side and demand on the other. On the supply side we have all those innumerable complex processes of society which change the degree of equality, or perhaps we should say the degrees of equality, in their innumerable dimensions and measures. Oddly enough, nobody has produced a very satisfactory explicit model of these processes and one would think that computer modelling of the general dynamics type would be extraordinarily helpful in this regard. We start off with a distribution as it exists, say, on Monday, and we ask ourselves what events will change this in ways to produce the distribution of Tuesday. The first process is simply births and deaths between Monday and Tuesday; individuals will be born and some will die. Those who are born will start off with some kind of inheritance, some of which may be explicit, but most of which will be implicit, depending on the family into which they are born. We could almost postulate that each baby born comes into the world with a certain capital value, which would be much larger in the case of a baby born to a middle-class American family than it would be to a baby born to a poor Haitian peasant.

Those who die have capital value, some of which may simply disappear at the moment of death, as when an active young person with a high chance of a rich future is accidently killed, some of which, however, will be heritable, particularly in the form of claims to physical capital. These inheritances have to be distributed among the inheritors, whoever they may be, and the dynamics of equality obviously depends on the rules which the distribution of inheritance follows. Under primogeniture the object is to preserve inequality, mainly in order to prevent the breakup of large units of land, and it is interesting that the 'égalité' of the French Revolution referred much more to equal distribution of estates on inheritance than it did to political equality. Perhaps the greatest force making for dynamics leading toward inequality is the fact that inheritance goes almost wholly to the family, this being the major integrative unit of society. A little bit goes outside the family in the shape of foundations, but probably this is quite small, and some of this is collected for public purposes through inheritance taxes, although this again is relatively small in most societies. This means that the inheritances tend to concentrate on a relatively small phylum of the human race as it spreads out through space-time.

Besides inheritance, of course, the other factor in social relations which is fundamental to the dynamics of equality is differential lifetime saving or accumulation. A person's capital stock at any one moment is equal to what has been inherited plus what has been accumulated during the lifetime. Accumulations may be negative, of course, in which case the capital stock declines. The main factor leading to inequality in the distribution of wealth, outside of the restricted range of inheritance, is the principle that it is easier for the rich to save than it is for the poor. Income is a function of total capital stock including the value of human capital possessed or to some extent controlled by the person, control being important because it may increase the net rate of return on what is actually possessed, that is, on the net worth. The very poor cannot save at all as their incomes are equal to subsistence, and if they tried to consume below their income, they would simply die. For the very rich, saving is easy; in fact they have difficulty consuming their income, especially if the mores of society are rather puritanical and there is not much fashion for conspicuous consumption as there was, say, in the time of Louis XIV. Conspicuous consumption, oddly enough, may lead to greater equality, as it prevents the saving of the rich. On the other hand, in so far as it diminishes the total of saving, it will diminish the rate of growth of the whole society.

The demand for equality operates mainly to try to affect these parameters of the dynamic system which constitute the supply. One could think of the elasticity of the supply of equality as the amount which is produced in response to a given change in demand for it. This supply may be quite inelastic. The inertia of the inequality-producing institutions is so large that even a great deal of demand for equality may not produce much change in the amount, but only perhaps in the costs of getting it, just as a rise in demand for Rembrandts increases their price but does not increase their quantity. It is clear, however, that the supply of equality is not wholly inelastic, simply because there has been a movement, at least over the last 200 years, in this direction in a good many different variables.

How much the rise in equality is due to changes in the demand for equality itself and how much is due to very real changes in the supply as a result of society's simply getting richer is hard to say. The early stages of 'development' always seem to produce inequality, mainly because the distribution of the ability to develop may be very unequal, so that we get a pattern in which a small group in society gets richer and the vast majority do not. This seems to be the typical pattern of the urban revolution and the development of civilisation 5000 years ago, and it is all too typical of many poor, but developing societies today.

Beyond a certain point in development, however, productivity increases so much that equality becomes almost inevitable. Equality depends to some extent on the product mix itself in a society. A society which produces automobiles sufficient for only 10 per cent of its population will inevitably be highly unequal – 10 per cent of the people will have them and 90 per cent will not, no matter how the society is organised. A society which produces an automobile for every family can hardly help distributing them fairly equally, for there is no point in a rich man having 100 automobiles. Adam Smith's vision of the 'invisible hand' arose out of his perception that, even though a Highland chieftain might command all the food produced in the clan, he couldn't possibly eat it all and had to divide it moderately equally among the stomachs of the whole clan (Smith). Development itself, therefore, may increase the supply of equality and it may also, of course, increase the demand as people become more aware of their own relative condition as a result of developing information systems. On the other hand, it must also be faced that there is also a real demand for inequality, otherwise we would not have lotteries. Rokeach's studies (Rokeach, 1968 and 1973) of value priorities in a sample of American people suggest that equality as as abstract ideal is not very high on a scale of relative values, and its position is relatively unaffected by status. This suggests perhaps that many people prefer a society in which there is some chance of being rich to one in which there is no chance of being rich, although how far the chances of being rich can be offset by the chance of being poor is hard to say.

All these considerations suggest that the concept of a moving equilibrium of inequality is by no means absurd as an intellectual construct and that it may be quite helpful in interpreting the actual movements of society. The equilibrium is probably a range rather than a point. How far it changes in response to changes in demand or in supply is a rather open question. Revolutionary changes require very peculiar circumstances of societal breakdown and are apt to be rare. Evolutionary and political change, especially in democracies, may also depend on accidental circumstances which may not have high probability. The political demand for equality may not be a mere summation of individual demand for it. It depends on the accidents of political rhetoric and competing alternatives. Thus, the failure both of the welfare proposals of the first Nixon administration and of the McGovern campaign suggest that the political demand for equality in the United States is very ineffective, and that the virtually proportional and nonprogressive character of the American tax system may not be wholly an accident. Involuntary redistribution can only be achieved if those who gain are more powerful politically than those who lose. In a democracy this means it is hard to redistribute away from 51 per cent of the people, and if people's fears of redistribution are excessive, a minority of the people can easily veto redistribution. It may well be, therefore, that changes in supply are historically more important in creating equality than changes in demand, and that egalitarians pay far too much attention to the demand for equality and not nearly enough to the supply.

12

Equality and economic theory

HARRY G. JOHNSON

≠

IT is a well-known fact about the economics profession and the economically literate fringe, here and in other countries, that the emphasis of concern about the economic system has shifted dramatically from questions of efficiency and economic growth to questions of equity of income distribution and 'the quality of life'. In the advanced industrial countries of 'the West', at least until the energy crisis and the beginnings of the current recession, this shift manifested itself in a mixture of antipathy toward what used to be called 'the rat-race', indignation about the values and methods of the competitive or capitalist system, and alarm about 'the environment' and specifically the threat of exhaustion of natural resources by depletion in the service of high and rising standards of living. In the less developed countries, the previous objective of rapid economic growth, to be obtained by any possible policy for stimulating industrialisation, has been supplanted by insistence on the priority of an equitable distribution of income over growth. (Some of the most vociferous of the current critics of 'the capitalist system' for its failure to secure equity in income distribution, incidentally and not unexpectedly, are the very same people who twenty-odd years ago used to berate capitalism for its failure to provide as rapid economic growth

Presented as the C. Woody Thompson Memorial Lecture (April 1975) to the Midwest Economics Association conference in Chicago; and first published in *Nebraska Journal of Economics and Business*, Vol. 14 (1975), pp. 3–17.

as communist planning was assumed to be able to do. In that respect, all that has happened is that Mao and China have replaced Stalin and Russia as the clinching proof of capitalism's social failure.)

The transfer of popular economic attention from efficiency and growth to equity and grace as criteria of capitalist performance and demonstrations of the need for changed policies, possibly – and in the minds of some, necessarily and as an added bonus – including bloody revolution in which the good guys will win as always, was to some extent predictable from both economic sociology and the history of our subject. One might predict, sociologically, that significant numbers of members of a successful elite governing class, conscious of their privileged position and not convinced of the social-instrumental justification for that position, would feel guilty enough to support policies for making the distribution of income more equal and less dependent on the performance of function. The educated classes are the privileged in contemporary society; and, as Schumpeter argued in his *Capitalism, Socialism and Democracy*, the intellectual and not the alienated worker is the Achilles heel of capitalism – as Marxist activists are well aware. Historically, the last period of sustained interest in equality of income distribution as a major social goal was the period of flowering of English neo-classicism in the late nineteenth century, and specifically the work of the 'Cambridge School' of Marshall and Pigou. That concern reflected on the one hand the success of British capitalism in combination with the rigidity of the British class system in creating the appearance that the problem of affluence and growth had been solved, so that distribution was the important socioeconomic problem still to be overcome; on the other hand the dissenting-Protestant, non-Church-of-England-establishment branch of the British version of the Christian tradition, with roots going back to the Cromwellian revolution and the 'Leveller' and 'Digger' democratic sects.

The social outlook, and more formally the welfare economics, of the 'Cambridge School', made a deep impression, through maternal influence, on the social views of John Maynard Keynes, in the form of such opinions as that England was an economic democracy in which any man of ability could pull himself out of the common herd, that capitalists ought to have some reward but would be quite content to work mostly for pleasure rather than money, and that what the workers want – or at least should have – is not higher real wages but more playing fields and better and more secure working conditions (one can detect more than the traces of the same attitudes in the writings of Joan Robinson). The concern with the goal of equality of income distribution has remained into modern times a distinguishing feature of economics in Britain and in other locations influenced significantly by British socio-economic thinking, often without appreciation of either the phase in the evolution of British social structure that gave economic egalitarianism in that country its distinctive and now somewhat fossilised form, or of the transient character of the phase of the industrial revolution in which Britain seemed so predestinedly and permanently ahead of her competitors that the possibly seriously deleterious effects of the pursuit of equality of income distribution on efficiency, international competitiveness, and economic growth could be dismissed or disregarded. It should be noticed, on the side of technical analysis, that Edgeworth's early demonstration in *The Hedonical Calculus* that egalitarianism could not be supported logically by the then-prevailing philosophy of utilitarianism was quietly ignored, and that the shocking initial impact made by Lionel Robbins's demonstration, in *The Nature and Significance of Economic Science*, that egalitarianism required interpersonal value judgments that could not be given a scientific foundation – which led to the development of modern or 'the new' welfare economics – has had little lasting effect, except on the curricula in some economics departments, the crucial point having been quietly converted into a great difficulty that must be stared firmly in the face and passed by in silence.

In parallel fashion, one might have predicted that the United States, having apparently achieved a position of effortless eternal affluence – high and automatically rising standards of living – having been assured of the permanence of this happy state by two of its deepest thinkers (Walt Whitman Rostow and John Kenneth Galbraith), and been cushioned against recognition of reality both by various elements in

American Revolutionary mythology and by the 1920s change in the American immigration laws that gave the mass of the American population a protected position of access to the fruits of American technological leadership as producer-rentiers rather than consumers, should have experienced a marked shift of emphasis from production to consumption and from growth to sharing. Similarly, one might have expected (though more speculatively) that engagement in a war of the Viet Nam type would shatter confidence in the mythology of American democratic superiority, and with it unquestioning American belief in the virtues of the American enterprise system; and that the intellectuals of other countries would be quick to convert domestic American dissatisfaction with the American system into a philosophy of anti-Americanism, disguised thinly as ostensibly intellectually-dispassionate criticism of the capitalist or competitive system.

It is not all that surprising, therefore, that the attention of professional and amateur economists has swung back from income production toward income distribution. The study of income production and augmentation is a mundane and arduous task, with no splendid rewards to be earned, except when the normal processes of automatic growth are disrupted by policy errors of a simple, obvious, and easily reversible kind The notable exception was the great depression of 1929, which made possible the intellectual glories of the Keynesian Revolution; but on the whole, positive economics offers 'no such thing as a free lunch'. Income distribution is a far more socially exciting concern entirely; and it enables its student to appeal to philosophical and moral considerations – 'justice' and 'equity' and 'fairness' – which are inherently non-quantifiable and hence can easily be assigned infinite quantitative importance by contrast with the penny-pinching and cheese-paring quantities with which positive economics concerns itself.

What is surprising, extremely disappointing, and has the potential for the ultimate destruction of the politically free and economically affluent society we are accustomed to, is the virtual absence, from current demands for and controversies about economic equity, of any impact whatsoever of elementary economic theory, let alone the developments that have occurred during the past third of a century of empirically oriented theorising about people in their roles as consumers of goods and suppliers of labor services over time in conditions of affluence. From the point of view of the professional and scientifically committed economist, the great gap thus revealed between academic and popular economic understanding is disturbing and discouraging, to an extent depending on the relative strength in individual academic motivation, of 'the instinct of workmanship' (as Veblen called it) and 'the price system', which in academic terms can be interpreted as the personal appeal of satisfying scientific curiosity on the one hand and the desire to produce a socially esteemed and privately profitable intellectual service on the other. Even more disturbing and discouraging is the propensity of colleagues academically qualified by training and career appointment to throw their professional scientific equipment overboard in order that their craft may ride higher and more visibly on the wave-crest of popular opinion. I myself am fairly phlegmatic about and not much concerned with the question of whether economics is immediately socially useful in solving the current problems of society as society itself conceives them; but I recall being much impressed, and saddened, by A. C. Pigou's valedictory lecture as Professor at Cambridge, in which, having spent his life in the belief that the study of economics was justified by the social fruit rather than the scientific light it provided, only to see his country just before his retirement adopt the protective tariff against which he had campaigned in his youth, he was forced to console himself with the thought that perhaps a little light is worth having after all.

I shall, however, abandon further discussion of this professional economic aspect of the current popular concern about equity, since it could lead only into a discussion of the current demand for 'relevance' in economics teaching and research – a demand which in my experience invariably amounts to an effort to force economists to lend their voices and scientific prestige to propaganda in support of the demander's political program. (The experience referred to, it may be worth noting for its irony in juxtaposition to current demands for relevance, began with an undergraduate student effort to force the faculty at the University of Toronto to change the course content to knowledge and techniques more directly relevant to the winning of the war against Hitler, which demand was indirectly designed to put pressure on the Canadian government to support Stalin by launching a 'second front' against Germany.) But it seems worthwhile to offer some more general observations on the phenomenon, albeit in the form of a few rather disjointed and tentative remarks rather than a completely integrated social theory, before proceeding to my main theme of what current economic theory has to contribute to understanding of the issue of equity.

First, it is symptomatic of the deeply conservative character of social culture, of its strong dependence on the use of social myths and social stereotypes to represent and permit popular thought about the contemporary social world, and of the consequential long lag in the adjustment of intellectual concepts about society to social reality, that current concern about social equity is so closely identified with ideas about the nature of the economic system that date from the nineteenth century, and particularly from a historical phase or sub-phases in the evolution of the British economy and society. More concretely, the general 'liberal' concepts of and concern about equity in income distribution – to use the word 'liberal' in its general American rather than European sense – reflect the late nineteenth-century British society as a society recently emerged from feudalism and still assigning a great deal of political and social power to landed wealth; and an industrial economy organised on the bases of non-corporate, strongly family-based enterprise and employing a technology emphasising material capital in the form of machinery which both competed directly with mere unskilled labor-power and provided the *sine qua non* co-operant required for labor skill and ingenuity to earn superior economic rewards. Material property as the source of economic power and social prestige, the concentration of property in families, and the preservation of that concentration through inheritance, obviously both raised questions of equity among individuals, and suggested that, since non-human property was the key source of opulence, rectifying inequality among persons through wealth and income redistribution would have little if any deleterious economic consequences. At the same time, the pragmatic argument for inequality in terms of the need for a warrior class supported by the agricultural surplus through rents, and the moral argument for inequality in terms of 'the divine right of kings', had been steadily eroded by the much earlier development of the nation-state, its success in gradually establishing law and order within its own domain, and the secularisation of government in the transition from absolute monarchy to representative democracy (which in Britain before 1868 meant bourgeois democracy, not popular democracy). The minority Marxist-radical concern with inequality, for its part, goes back for its depiction of the nature of modern industry still farther, to the early nineteenth century and the effects of the 'agricultural revolution' prior to the 'industrial revolution', and the associated population explosion, in creating vast masses of displaced formerly independent agricultural tenants and laborers, forced to earn their living by virtue of their labor power alone, through sale of their services in a buyer's market dominated by the owners of the machinery necessary to put their labor to profitable use in the production of cheap industrial products. Neither picture of the industrial and capitalist system represents the economic and social reality of today, as J. K. Galbraith has argued in a series of important books whose wise insights have unfortunately largely been disguised by their wisecracks. This is especially so in the United States, which has no past history of feudalism, little of government by landed aristocracy, and none of surplus labor (but rather the reverse). But popular ideas about society, and about how society should be reformed, are as already mentioned characterised by a very long cultural lag – and very rarely indeed have they been updated by the commanding analysis of a brilliant social scientist, as shown by the gigantic status of Smith, Ricardo, Marx, and Keynes as the four horsemen of economics – not the four horsemen of the Apocalypse, but the four horsemen of an unbeatable football line-up – and the social memory of Ricardo's contribution is becoming steadily fainter, as is the associated description of economics as 'the dismal science' (actually more due to Malthus), to the point where Ricardo is remembered mostly by Marxists as the only classical economist Mr Marx thought well of.

Second, current discussion of the equity of the competitive system and the inequality of income distribution associated with it demonstrate the depth to which at least popular thought about society remains penetrated by Christian concepts, even among those who pride themselves on their presumed liberation from religious beliefs. Liberal social views, again in the American sense of 'liberal', are based rather obviously on the supreme commandment of the New Testament, 'Love thy neighbor as thyself' – even if the neighbor shuns the intimacy as an invasion of his privacy. Radical and Marxist views, on their part, are derived from the Old Testament – also preferred by bigoted and violent fundamentalists – with its emphasis on the superiority of 'the chosen people', its callousness toward the murder, plague and pestilential persecution of 'the unwashed', its grim warning that 'the Lord thy God is a jealous god', its assumption of special knowledge acquired by the ownership of sacred books and logical disputation about their meaning – sometimes reinforced by actually reading them – and its use of prophesy to stimulate social action by the assurance that the action merely conforms to God's will. The most important general point about the dominance of ultimately religious concepts in thinking about social reform is that religion is a consumption and not a production activity – it contributes only prayers for the success of the producers' efforts against the hazards of nature and the benign neglectfulness of God himself, while claiming its material tithe from the harvest. I do not in saying this intend to commit myself on the basic question of which is more important, making the living, or making the living worthwhile, but only to point out that society may be badly advised indeed to take its advice on economic morality from parasites on the social surplus, whatever their claims for moral entitlement to that position and the complementary role as adviser may be – religious calling, noble birth, a good education, youthful self-confidence, or the study of social science. More neutrally, and from the standpoint of social science itself, it is an interesting question why popular social policy discussion remains a religious activity in a secular society, and what the implications are for how societies actually believe and behave in contrast to how social science would prescribe that they believe and behave (if 'prescription' is a fair word for the assumption that society will use rationally the knowledge made available by scientific study and research).

Third, the form of current concern about inequality of income distribution raises some obvious questions and suggests some further generalisations for the newly emerging and to some extent interdisciplinary specialisation of the economic theory of government, as well as more generally for political science. One thought along these lines concerns the short time-horizons of elected governments, and their consequent attentiveness to the short-range interests of the existing adult voting population in their existing occupations, a myopia which meshes with the tendency of humanity, with short lifespans and much shorter spans of post-adolescent, pre-elderly-and-retiring, mature adult participation in the social governing process, to concentrate on inequality in the distribution of current income and wealth among currently existing adult members of society to the disregard or heavy discounting of longer-run effects on the amount and distribution of future income and wealth among future generations of citizens. The political process pays little heed to the old American saw 'from shirtsleeves to shirtsleeves in three generations', or in Britain to the fact that, just before the system of hereditary peerages was replaced by life peerages, very few of the members of the House of Lords indeed could trace their titles back beyond the late nineteenth century. Everyone here must be to some extent familiar with the inegalitarian career of Jacqueline Bouvier Kennedy Onassis; but where are the descendants of Doris Duke, Barbara Hutton, and Gloria Vanderbilt of nineteen-thirties notoriety; and who in this room has ever heard of the Palmer family that built this House, and of the regal Mrs Potter Palmer who bossed the society of Chicago in its pre-World War I prime as Mayor Daley bosses the politics of the city today (for that matter, who remembers who was the boss in Mrs Potter Palmer's time)?

Another thought, intruding into basic political theory and

hence only ventured tentatively, concerns one of the many well-known 'dilemmas of democracy', which may be stated as follows. The fundamental argument for democracy is that no alternative system of government by an individual, an elite, or even a numerical majority but not the totality of the citizens of a state, can be trusted to treat with respect, and as protected by rights, the ambitions, efforts, aspirations, and acquisitions of those not entitled to political representation. (It is this problem, incidentally, which is making the nation-state increasingly an anachronism in the governmental system of an interdependent world.) Democracy is necessary for the preservation of personal (human) freedom. But government has been increasingly extending itself into the economic sphere; and in so extending itself it counterposes to the rights of property, and specifically the right of the owner of property to the enjoyment of the income of property, an alternative system of rights in property and its use based not on ownership, acquisition, and accumulation of property, but on existence as a human being and the associated right to vote, including voting about the disposition of other people's property. In short, the justification for democratic government is that people must have equal political rights as *persons*; the dilemma is that they use these political rights to demand equal economic rights over property, though as property-owners (as distinct from human beings) they are by no stretch of the imagination equal. In other words, democracy requires either a convention drawing a clear line (if this is possible) between political activity as concerned with people and economic life as concerned with capital; or else it presupposes a society of independent farmer-capitalist-workers, as in the Jeffersonian concept of democracy, or a slave-owning society in which the slaves don't count as deserving but deprived democrats, as in Greek democracy.

I turn now to the positive question posed in my title, what contemporary economic theory has to say about economic equity, and more concretely about inequality or apparent inequality in the distribution of wealth and income. Much of this could be put, from one point of view, in terms of the necessity for accurate measurement of what it is that gives grounds for complaint on grounds of equity, and the crude, misleading, and downright erroneous information conveyed by measurement based on the usual statistics on the distribution of income and wealth. From an alternative point of view, economic theory stresses the proper application of the concepts of gross value of sales, gross income, and net income, and of income and capital; choice between alternatives yielding income (properly defined) in alternative forms, some of which do not and some do pass through the market and are therefore received as income; choice between alternatives of varying risk of outcome, and of preferences averse to or favoring risk; preferences between current consumption and future consumption, and particularly preferences about economic self-improvement; the relevance of the human life-cycle and family-formation cycle, and associated time-profiles of capacity to render productive services on the one hand and consumption needs (or expenditure needs – the presence of consumers' durables together with imperfect capital markets makes it necessary to distinguish expenditure and consumption) on the other, together with their implications for the optimum distribution of the wealth portfolio between human and non-human capital; the importance of publicly provided consumption and publicly provided capital; the influence of imperfections in capital markets, especially human capital markets and the possibilities of market substitutions between human and non-human capital; and, last but certainly not by any means least in the modern world, the distorting influences of taxation systems that omit entirely certain kinds of activity usually lumped together as 'leisure' but actually entailing a considerable variety of non-marketed activities, and discriminate in favor of or against the possession of certain kinds of capital and the enjoyment of income from it.

Right at the outset, there is a problem of the human unit to which the argument and analysis refer: is it the individual, the family unit, the individual over his lifetime, the family over its lifetime as such, or the family regarded as a sort of human inventory lasting over generations, the identities of units in the stock changing over time without the inventory itself changing? The gradual processes of social change with advancing affluence, in conjunction with the myopia of the democratic political process itself, have narrowed the perspective of political discussion to the point almost of regarding every living human being of every possible age as entitled to an equal income, a standard of egalitarianism that no economist could regard as a reasonable basis for organising a viable economic system. Yet without some definition of the socially relevant unit, the discussion of equity must remain imprecise, and hence offer ample temptations for the self-interested assertion that while everyone ought to be equal, one's own sub-group ought to be more equal than others. In other words, the ambiguity is certain to invoke application of a principle I presented to this Association fifteen years ago under the description of Johnson's Law of Social Intransitivity – which is, that everyone has good reasons for thinking himself better than everybody else.

Turning to the question of measurement, and accepting for the time being that the standard is current individual or family income as conventionally-measured, there is a well-known problem of allowing for the fact that certain consumption expenditures really should be assigned to the cost of living (or of earning an income) rather than to the standard of living (the income earned). The problems involved received a great deal of now-forgotten attention during the early days of national income accounting, particularly in the writings of Simon Kuznets; they pose a perennial problem for any welfare system, especially with regard to the variation of rents with location; and they pose a difficult problem for the interpretation of urban-rural measured income differentials, especially in the modern context of the alleged 'income gap' between the developed and the developing countries, since much of the process of economic development involves urban agglomeration and the cost of transportation and distribution of food and other goods that in subsistence or near-subsistence agriculture are immediately available without incurring such costs, or at costs not passed through the market. Inequalities in conventionally measured income will in some measure, and perhaps in large part, correspond to differences in cost of living conceived of in this broad sense.

This is the problem of gross sales value versus gross income.

The difference between gross and net income arises as soon as we recognise that productive contribution and consumption needs stretch over time, though they become increasingly serious as productive contribution increasingly requires education and training and a sacrifice of present income opportunities for the sake of larger income later. Correct theory would require definition of labor income as current wages minus both interest on past investments in the creation of the 'human capital' contribution to the earning of the wages, and of the costs involved in both the support of the worker in retirement and the production of replacements in the form of bearing and rearing children.

Turning to questions of differences of individual preferences, economics has long recognised differences in preferences concerning non-wage-income aspects of employment, including working-place amenities, physical aspects of work, social approval or disapproval of the activity, and the balancing of cash reward and time available for leisure. Adam Smith was particularly sapient on this issue, and Marshall characterised the relevant considerations in the concept of nonpecuniary advantages and disadvantages. Everyone in this room knows that one of the attractions of the academic life is its long holidays, another its substantial freedom to arrange the programming of one's own work; its non-pecuniary disadvantages are often seen as comprising the necessity of devoting time to talking to ignorant students, spending time and unpaid effort on administration, and turning out a very poorly specified and arbitrarily evaluated product called 'original research contribution'. Freedom of choice between alternative careers mixing monetary and non-monetary rewards in different proportions is bound to produce apparent differences among equals when returns are measured by only one yardstick, 'money income'.

A further dimension of the problem of choice familiar to classical and neo-classical economists, one which has been clarified by more recent work on the analysis of choice under uncertainty, concerns the fact that differences in aversion to or fondness for risk will lead to differing choices among occupations differing in risk, and that since statistics can only observe the outcomes of risky choices, not the *ex ante* risks themselves, incomes measured *ex post* will in this respect produce the appearance of inequality, possibly great inequality, among individuals when in fact they have had complete equality so far as the range of available opportunities is concerned.

The problem of the effects of choice on measured income distribution becomes still more subtle when one introduces the possibility of choice with respect to opportunities differing in the investment in the creation of human capital they require and the total apparently wage-income returns they offer to labor and human capital combined in the services of the human individual. Differences in preferences as between present and future consumption, and between the use of own labor time for what may be called 'unproductive consumption' and 'productive consumption' (or consumption and investment), in some cases requiring also imperfection of capital markets using human production power as collateral, will necessarily (if investment in human capital is at all rational) produce considerable differences between the wage-receipts of anthropologically equal physical specimens, which on a superficial view represent gross inequality among persons but instead represent the outcome of free choices by initially equal individuals. In this connection, the concept of human capital and investment in it merely uses technical economic concepts to analyse phenomena described differently in social and religious-moral terms – such as the social concepts of a 'good family background' and 'a bad family' and the semi-religious approval of a commendable father of a family as 'a good provider'.

This brings us to consideration of the biological and social life-cycles of the human individual and the family unit, which have important implications for the supply of labor by the household, and the time-patterning of the level of rewards at different stages of the individual's working and family life. Thus the typical upward trend of earnings rates with age until some point in middle age reflects both the accumulation of experience and the accumulation of family consumption requirements up to that phase in life – the two different considerations are difficult to disentangle due to the fact that, though people often wish they could be older or younger than they are, they have little effective choice but to pass through life as biology prescribes, so that the time-distribution of lifetime earnings can be fairly arbitrarily determined. But variations of earnings with age obviously imply that measurements of income distribution not differentiated by age and education period will obviously give the appearance of inequality, whereas with correct economic analysis there is actually equality of opportunities.

The roles of the biological and family-formation cycles in creating apparent inequality according to popular standard measures of the latter has many aspects. One that is worth special comment here is the fact that rational management of human capital in relation to the individual and family life-cycles requires disinvestment in human capital and investment in material capital as life advances. The relevant economics include the once hotly debated notion of 'keeping capital intact' in arriving at the proper definition of income and wealth, and the economics of conservation and of depletable resources, which have acquired urgent interest as a result of 'environmentalism' and more recently the energy crisis. Some relevant points here are, first, that statistics of the distribution of wealth are likely to show a misleading degree of concentration and apparent inequality – especially as 'wealth' is invariably statistically defined to include only a selection of easily marketable assets, to the exclusion of both personal consumption capital and capitalisable future labor income, and public capital yielding a monetary or real income to the citizen as a right but not capitalised into his net worth. Second, the association of age and seniority with the possession of marketable assets and personal consumption capital unencumbered by debt, though usually identified resentfully as evidence of the economic power of the old and the inequality imposed by the capitalist system on the young, in fact reflects the declining total economic and social power of the aging, as evidenced by their typically declining overall net worth position and the gradual transition from active participation in the production process to rentiers dependent on the decision-making ability and productive power of people younger than themselves.

I have just mentioned the provision of goods by means of

public capital in which citizens have property rights by virtue of citizenship or residence, but which is not included in personal net worth by standard statistical conventions. Both the provision of consumption goods by public production and the provision of such goods by public capital investments, including both privately appropriable goods and 'public goods' in the technical sense of the term, available by right of citizenship or residence, constitute an income or consumption flow for the individual and as such should be counted as an asset included in the individual's net worth; but by statistical convention it is not, with the result among other things that many already-implemented policies for increasing equality of opportunity and of income simply are counted as having zero effect on social inequality. This point is made forcefully in a recent critique of studies of inequality of wealth in Britain by George and Priscilla Polanyi, who maintain correctly that individual wealth should include the capital value of rights to free education, health care, and social and retirement benefits, and should not be defined to include only stock-market assets and landed property. Since these rights are far more equally distributed than the assets just mentioned – whose choice obviously involves a certain degree of personal preference – the usual statistics give a quite distorted picture both of the degree of inequality and the extent to which real inequality has been reduced by social policy.

Finally, we come to the distorting influence of taxes and tax-avoiding choices on measured inequality. One would expect, as a general principle of economic behavior, that competition and equalisation of marginal net private returns would result in distorted tax systems designed to penalise high incomes and the ownership of great wealth but affecting certain types of occupations and of asset ownership differentially, being passed on to the consumer (at least to a significant extent) in the form of higher prices. This alone would tend to produce a tendency for measured inequality of gross-of-tax income distribution to increase, and for inequality of net-of-tax income to be relatively little affected by egalitarian fiscal income-redistribution measures. Analysis here is complicated and difficult, though, because we are referring to statistical measures of observed inequality that attempt to condense changes in magnitudes and frequencies of observations into a single summary number whose construction itself may have little connection with the moral questions on which it seeks to provide quantitative information.

These are only a few broad observations on the lines on which contemporary economic theory indicates that questions of inequality of distribution of income and wealth should be approached, oriented primarily to identification of whether there is a problem and what the nature of the real problem may be. The approach does, however, have some important implications for policies concerned with inequality or alleged inequality. Shortage of time prevents me from discussing the matter in detail here: I have developed a fuller analysis in a number of previous publications.

First, to be consistent with both the principle of individual freedom and personal responsibility, and the requirements of efficient economic organisation (which incidentally includes bureaucratic centralised economic management equally with the competitive enterprise system), policy should concentrate on providing equality of *opportunity* rather than equality of measured-income *ex post* results. Many liberals and radicals, including many economists, are completely inconsistent on this score, in the sense of advocating both policies promoting *ex ante* inequality of opportunity and access and policies promoting *ex post* equality of measured outcomes. A standard homely example is the tendency of many educators to advocate greater equality of educational opportunity for students, while approving of teachers' pay scales that drive the best teachers toward the best universities with the best, most easily teachable, students. Greater equality of opportunity for students would require that a teacher suffer a severe financial loss in moving from a mediocre university with mediocre students exacting to teach, to a university whose admission procedures ensure that even the most incompetent and careless teacher can have first-class graduates whose subsequent worldly success he can contemplate with quite unjustified pride.

Second, there is an important distinction to be made – and which is made albeit cumbersomely in various income and wealth tax systems – between high incomes earned by the individual's or family's own efforts, or partially earned that way, and high incomes earned as a result of luck, in some sense, or more theoretically manageably by inheritance. The standard difficulty with inheritance tax is of course the implied penalty on the aspiration to improve the opportunities for one's family. An equally important practical difficulty is that, due to the state's greed for revenue, the tax is usually based on the amount left by the testator rather than the amounts received by the heirs – though the issue is correction of inequality among the still living rather than the recently dead – and the state uses the capital it receives through such taxation for consumption rather than the maintenance of capital intact. My own feeling is that too much tends to be made of inequalities of inheritance of property, now that a land-based economic system has been succeeded by a technological-innovation-based economic system, and that on a reasonable perspective over, say, three generations, inequalities due to this source tend to be ironed out as new families replace the old in productive success.

The *third* and final point is that once one begins to think at all seriously about inequality among people, one is up against a problem that my former colleague Frank Knight liked to emphasise and which he believed insuperable: the passing on through biological inheritance of genes favorable or unfavorable to economic success, and through family inheritance of a variety of personality characteristics favorable to economic success such as determination and persistence, and honest and logical thinking or the converse. Equality of inheritance of the capacity to exploit opportunity could only be secured by scrapping both the family as an institution and the freedom of selection of a mate for purposes of procreation. That might be an improvement, but one cannot envisage either radicals or conservatives accepting its implications. An important part of the reason is, as various social philosophers have claimed, that radicalism and conservatism are both 'inherited' in the broad sense used here.

PART FOUR

Redistribution, its ailments

13

The egalitarian imperative

RICHARD E. WAGNER

≠

AS a source of revenue, transfer taxation is relatively unimportant. In 1976 transfer taxation accounted for only $5 billion out of total revenues of $300 billion. The primary support for transfer taxation derives from the belief that it is a valuable means of promoting equality in the distribution of wealth. Supporters of transfer taxation believe that the normal outcome of a market economy is increasing inequality in the ownership of wealth and the receipt of income; transfer taxation is seen as a mechanism for offsetting this presumed cumulative process. This chapter explores from several perspectives the egalitarian imperative that has dominated the literature on transfer taxation.

Inequality in Static Perspective

Few topics seem as capable of arousing the passions of intellectuals as the distribution of income and wealth. The basic facts concerning inequality would appear to be quite simple. The lowest fifth of families in terms of income earns just over 5 per cent of the income earned by all families, while the second-lowest fifth of families earns just below 12 per cent. By contrast, the highest fifth of families earns over 41 per cent, while the second-highest fifth earns nearly 24 per cent. The distribution of wealth, though documented less extensively than the distribution of income, seems to be even more

First published as chapter 2 in the author's *Inheritance and the State* (American Enterprise Institute, Washington, DC, 1977), pp. 23–38.

For Notes and References, see page 390 below.

unequal. It has been estimated that the highest 20 per cent of families in terms of wealth own over 70 per cent of total net family wealth, while the lowest 20 per cent own practically nothing.[1]

There are many reasons why figures on the distribution of income and wealth exaggerate the degree on inequality. A proposition that goes back to Adam Smith is that there will be a general tendency in a market economy for income differentials among employments to be such that the net advantages of various employments are equalised.[2] If employments differ in their non-monetary returns and in the monetary expenses of entering and pursuing them, they will need to differ in their monetary returns as well. Occupations that require long and expensive training before one can earn a livelihood will require higher monetary returns than unskilled occupations just to compensate for the greater cost of entry. Occupations with working conditions that are generally regarded as disagreeable will offer higher returns than occupations in which working conditions are generally regarded as agreeable. In a setting in which people were free to choose among occupations, there would exist an inequality in measured income necessary to offset opposing inequalities with respect to other relevant characteristics.

A few observations on this point seem in order. The relation between age and income is but one factor causing the data to exaggerate the degree of inequality. A lifetime profile of a person's income will typically start low, rise until it peaks during the middle years, then fall off during the retirement years. Suppose all persons have identical income profiles over their lifetimes. If the incomes of persons of different ages are merged to produce a distribution of current income, inequality will appear despite the perfectly equal distribution of lifetime income. This is not to say that all observed income differences are due to such life-cycle considerations, of course, but only that the figures usually ignore such considerations and so exaggerate the amount of inequality.[3]

It is also widely recognised that nonpecuniary differences among occupations cause the statistics on the distribution of income to overstate the extent of inequality. Much of the inequality in the distribution of money income is necessary to offset an opposing inequality in the distribution of nonmonetary forms of income and monetary expenses of earning income. Other things being equal, if people prefer to live in less populous rather than more populous areas at equal wage rates, they will live in more populous areas only if they are compensated by higher wages. Generally, the higher the educational requirements for entering an occupation, the higher the annual income in that occupation. But part of this higher annual income is necessary merely to offset the higher costs of entering that occupation, both the monetary costs of education and the income that could have been earned during the years of schooling. Once again, statistics on the inequality of incomes exaggerate the actual amount of inequality.

Besides considerations of the kind described above, figures on income do not include the in-kind benefits of public spending programs. Edgar Browning has shown that inclusion of such benefits raises the average income of those officially classified as poor in 1973 to 30 per cent more than the official poverty level.[4] In 1973, the 23 million people who were officially labelled poor had money income of $20.8 billion, while they would have required $30.5 billion to reach the poverty line. However, they received $18.8 billion in in-kind transfers, which increased their total income to $39.6 billion, 30 per cent above the poverty line.

The distribution of wealth is also subject to limitations of measurement that serve to exaggerate the actual degree of inequality. For instance, the standard measures of wealth exclude the wealth implicit in such pension schemes as social security. Yet social security membership can reasonably be conceptualised as a form of wealth. In fact, it is the most important source of wealth for most Americans and totals nearly two-thirds the amount of wealth as commonly defined.[5] An individual has a claim to future benefit payments, and this claim is as much a source of wealth as, for example, endowment insurance policies that might be expected to yield the same payments during retirement. Social security wealth is distributed with considerably more equality than other assets, so the inclusion of this form of wealth would reduce the degree of measured inequality.

Moreover, statistical measures of wealth are measures of the ownership of physical capital only. They exclude any meauure of human capital. Yet the human capital that is embodied in people as a result of education and training increases their income from what it would otherwise have been. The distribution of human capital is considerably more equal than that of physical capital, so inclusion of human capital would also reduce the degree of measured inequality in the distribution of wealth. The exclusion of human capital and social security wealth from common measures of the degree of inequality in the ownership of wealth operates to exaggerate the actual degree of inequality.

Egalitarian Rationalisations

Figures on the inequality of income and wealth, by themselves, provide no basis for judging the performance of an economy. Without some notion of an economically optimal or most preferred degree of inequality, there is no basis for saying whether more or less inequality is preferable to what currently exists. An early and prominent attempt to specify an optimal degree of inequality was Abba Lerner's argument that the optimal degree of inequality is zero.[6] More recently, much literature has carried forward the effort to formulate notions of optimal distributions of income and wealth.[7] This literature generally starts from the proposition that the optimal degree of inequality is zero, assuming that disincentive effects are absent; that is, the proposition holds only if the effort to promote equality does not reduce the total amount of production within the economy. Should the effort to equalise the distribution of income reduce the total amount of production, the optimal amount of inequality would be positive. An analogy to this situation would be cutting larger shares of a shrinking pie. The optimal inequality would occur when a further increase in the share of the pie that is given to those favoured by the state leads to a decrease in the absolute amount of pie they receive. This would result because of the reduction in effort on the part of those penalised by the state.[8]

The canonisation of equality has received a big boost from the veil-of-ignorance argument developed by John Rawls – or at least Rawls's construction has been interpreted to this effect.[9] Within the Rawlsian perspective, an optimal distribution of income or wealth is that which would be chosen by the individual members of the society if at the moment of choice, they thought that they had equally good chances of occupying each position within the distribution of income that might characterise the society. They could be asked to choose, for example, among distributions by quintile in which the shares were, say 10, 15, 20, 25, 30 in one case and 20, 20, 20, 20, 20 in another. The optimal distribution of income or wealth is simply that distribution that would be chosen by the participants under the conditions postulated. (This theory begs the questions of whether all participants would make the same choice or would even need to make such a choice, to say nothing of whether it is meaningful to speculate about how people with a historic existence would respond if they had no such existence.) In turn, according to Rawls, an optimal set of policies toward the transfer of income and wealth, including transfer taxation, would be that set of policies that would bring the distribution of income and wealth in line with the optimal distribution thus defined.

Optimal Inequality as Holistic Fallacy

The literature on optimal inequality, in assuming that the distribution of income and wealth must be chosen collectively, creates a problem where none exists. At any point in history, of course, there is a single observed distribution of income or wealth among a particular set of persons. It can be described by simple arithmetic. But simple arithmetic can be fallacious economics. This happens when one stumbles from arithmetic to statements such as '*the income distribution is a pure public good.* Each individual in society faces the same income distribution.'[10] This argument would hold for practically anything, the distribution of shoes, for instance. At any point in time, each member of society faces the same distribution of shoes. It hardly follows, however, that the shoe distribution must be chosen collectively. And it is no different for the distribution of income and wealth.

In a market economy the distribution of income and wealth, like the distribution of shoes, are products of personal choices by the participants in the economic process. These distributions are the *result* of choices, they are *not* themselves the objects of choice. It is not at all necessary to conceptualise a society as facing a choice among possible distributions, for such a distribution can be simply a product of the choices of the individual members with respect to the conduct of their economic activities.

There are various opportunities for making such choices, and changes in the attitudes generally held by citizens will change the resulting distribution. The choice among occupations is one instance of a choice that affects the distribution of income or wealth. Occupations differ in the distribution of returns they offer; teachers face a far less unequal distribution of returns among themselves than do lawyers. In choosing among occupations a person can take account of his distributional preferences; he can by himself decide whether he wants to take a chance at a large return even though he may fail and end up with a small return. A choice of whether to hire oneself to someone else or to become self-employed is similarly one that allows the individual to exercise preferences on distributional matters.

To say that one must participate in a collective choice over the distribution of rewards is to commit a holistic fallacy. It treats the pattern of distribution as something that must be agreed to and chosen by all for all. But such agreement and choice are unnecessary and would impose uniformity where none is required. The market economy allows persons to make their own choices, and these choices can vary from person to person. Those who want to try for the ecstasy of success even though they risk facing the agony of failure do not need to compromise their desires with those of others who wish to tread a middle road, Observed distributions emerge simply as a product of the choices of the participants in the economy. It is one of the prime virtues of the market form of social organisation that such questions as the distribution of income or wealth need never be put to collective choice in the first place.[11]

Redistributive Politics and Egalitarian Excess

While the distributions of income and wealth are the results of personal choices, not an object of collective choice, distributional considerations can influence the character of political outcomes. There are strong reasons for suggesting that prevailing political and fiscal institutions will produce an excessive amount of equalisation, excessive in terms of the logic used to construct the rationales for egalitarian policies.

Recall the use of the veil-of-ignorance framework for judging various distributive options. The norm within this framework is determined by the hypothetical choices that people would make if they were unaware of their particular position in the distribution of income and wealth. Political outcomes, by contrast, emerge within a context in which people *are* aware of their particular distributional positions. At present, the income or wealth of a majority of citizens is below the average. If these people could truly be placed behind the veil of ignorance, the possibility that they might receive above-average returns would temper their desire for redistribution. However, once they are aware of their distributive positions, they tend to support egalitarian measures. The reverse, of course, holds for that minority of the population with above-average income and wealth. Members of this group would be more willing to support redistribution under the veil of ignorance than if they were aware of their positions in the distributions of income and wealth. This is because, believing that their incomes might be below average, they might expect to gain from redistributive policies. In short, in a world where people are aware of their relative wealth and make choices through political institutions, redistribution will exeed that which would be chosen from behind the veil of ignorance.[12]

Albert Dicey suggested in 1914 that democracy might be unable to withstand the pressures that would be created if the recipients of government transfers were permitted to vote for members of Parliament.[13] Because it is the members of Parliament who choose whether or not to enact the program in the first place, as well as choosing the size of the transfer program, temptations and pressures would be created for the exchange of votes for government subsidies, with the subsidies being paid for by taxes inflicted on other citizens. Dicey expressed this fear in response to a newly enacted pension program in which the recipients, contrary to common practice, were permitted to vote for members of Parliament. Other authors have also expressed concern over the possible political irresponsibility that might arise under progressive income taxation because of the ability of a majority to impose tax rates on a minority that the majority themselves are unwilling to pay.[14] Recent developments in the literature on the political processes through which tax policy emerges do nothing to assuage these fears.[15]

Inequality in Dynamic Perspective

Perhaps the most damaging argument against perfect equality as an ideal, even if we are willing to ignore disincentive effects for purposes of discussion, is that it is an ideal under which few people would want to live. With rare exceptions, people seem to prefer to take a chance at earning an above-average income. One cannot win without taking a chance of losing, and few people play for ties. Individuals will differ in the intensity with which they aspire to win. But, once again, a form of social organisation based on a free market is one that gives expression to the whole array of attitudes on this matter.[16]

In gauging the extent to which a social order creates an environment in which its members can lead meaningful lives, the statistical distribution of income may have considerably less importance than the rate of mobility within the distribution, especially among generations. To illustrate, consider three individuals with incomes of $12,000, $8000, and $4000. Let us posit that the shape of this distribution will remain unchanged as time passes. One extreme possibility is that a child will come to occupy the same income position as his parents. Thus, children of parents with $12,000 incomes will themselves earn $12,000, and so forth. The other extreme possibility is that a child's income position will be wholly unrelated to his parents' income position. Thus, children of parents with $12,000 will have an equal chance of earning $12,000, $8000, or $4000. In either of these two extreme cases, however, the degree of inequality in the distribution of income will be identical. Yet the two societies would hardly be considered identical. This suggests that the focus of concern ought not to be the amount of inequality in the distribution of income, but the rate of mobility within the income scale. If one-half of the population received $5000 and one-half received $10,000, the distribution of income would be considerably more equal than the current distribution. Yet this clearly demarcated caste system would probably be rejected by about one-half of the populace.

A substantial amount of mobility seems to exist within the American distribution of income and wealth. In his study of income mobility over time, Lowell Gallaway found that 77 per cent of the difference between the average income in the United States in 1960 and the median income of the lowest income class was eradicated within one generation.[17] Table 13.1 shows that the occupational classification with the lowest income in 1960 was 'farm laborers and foremen', which had a median income of $1066. The median income of sons whose fathers belonged to this occupational class, however, was $4021. Thus, 77 per cent of the gap between their fathers' incomes and the average incomes of all fathers, $4097, was eliminated by mobility within the income distribution. The opposite effect occurred at the top of the occupational scale. The median income of 'managers, officials, and proprietors' in 1960 was $6664. But the median income of sons from this class was only $5747. Table 13.1 shows clearly that sons from the upper income classes tend to earn above-average income while sons from the lower income classes tend to earn below-average incomes. But Table 13.1 also shows that the income of sons from the upper income classes tends to fall toward the average

Table 13.1 Median income of Fathers and Sons by Father's Occupational Class, 1960

Father's Occupation	Father's Median Income	Son's Median Income
Managers, officials, and proprietors	$6664	$5717
Professional, technical, and kindred	6619	5737
Craftsmen, foreman, and kindred	5240	5195
Sales	4937	5608
Clerical and kindred	4785	5504
Operatives and kindred	4299	4834
Service, including private household	3310	4833
Laborers, except farm and mine	2948	4686
Farmers and farm managers	2169	4234
Farm laborers and foremen	1066	4021

Source: Lowell F. Gallaway, 'On the Importance of "Picking One's Parents" ' *Quarterly Review of Economics and Business*, Vol. 6 (Summer 1966). p. 12.

income while the income of sons from the lower income classes tends to rise toward the average income.

The evidence indicates that individual incomes have a strong tendency to regress toward the mean. While people in the upper income classes are likely to find their relative position worsening over time, people in the lower income classes are likely to find their relative income position improving. Children, in other words, are by no means locked into patterns set for them by their parents' place in life. On the contrary, the parents' place seems to exert relatively little influence over the circumstances that come to surround their children. This tendency for income to regress toward the mean seems attributable to two factors. On the one hand, random elements pervade all economic activities, so luck has much to do with one's economic fortunes.[18] On the other hand, biological inheritance, primarily intelligence, places constraints upon the options that one is likely to be able to exploit.[19]

It is well established that intelligence regresses toward the mean. While children of parents with above-average IQs tend to have above-average IQs, their IQs tend to be less than those of their parents. Table 13.2 illustrates this regression toward the mean for six occupational classes. While the mean IQ of parents in the higher professional class was 139.7, the mean IQ of their children was only 120.8 And while the mean IQ of parents in the unskilled class was 84.9, the mean IQ of their children was 92.6. From generation to generation, there is

Table 13.2 Mean IQ of Parent and Child, by Parent's Occupational Class

	Mean IQ	
Parent's Occupational Class	Parent	Child
Higher professional	139.7	120.8
Lower professional	130.6	114.7
Clerical	115.9	107.8
Semi-skilled	97.8	98.9
Unskilled	84.9	92.6
Average	100.0	100.0

Source: James E. Meade, *Efficiency, Equality, and the Ownership of Property* (London, 1964), p. 50.

mobility within the intelligence scale, even though the inequality in the distribution of intelligence remains constant. Thus, to the extent that high intelligence produces high income, biological inheritance will produce an intergenerational regression toward the mean income.

Luck also plays a strong role in the distribution of income from year to year. Any decision by an entrepreneur to create a new product or by an individual to train himself for a certain occupation is in part a gamble. In all cases an anticipated rate of return may be constructed based on an anticipation of future circumstances. But these anticipations will rarely be realised perfectly. Some people will gain by the discrepancy between anticipation and realisation, and some will lose. Some people will have runs of good luck, investing in areas that undergo unforeseeable increases in the relative demands for their output. Others will have runs of bad luck, investing in areas that suffer relative decreases in demand. There is a considerable, largely unappreciated, random variation in the distribution of income, recognition of which casts doubt upon the presumption of cumulative inequality.

Compound Interest and Cumulative Inequality: An Erroneous Analogy

Much of the support for transfer taxation has been stimulated by the belief or fear that a market economy tends naturally to produce a cumulative concentration of wealth. The rich are supposed to get richer and the poor poorer. Estate taxation is viewed as a means of offsetting this cumulative process. This belief is based largely on the arithmetic of compound interest and is epitomised by Carl Shoup's statement: 'Our existing social values insist upon some limit, or some restraining force, on the accumulation of wealth through gift or inheritance. (*If anyone thinks this is not so, let him keep doubling an amount that he considers acceptable for any one person to control.*)'[20] This line of argument, as fallacious as it is prominent, is worthy of a few observations.

Assertions about the cumulative inequality of wealth are usually derived from a line of argument based upon the arithmetic of compound interest. And the arithmetic of compound interest is truly inexorable. If a capital sum grows at 5 per cent compounded annually for thirty years, the terminal value will be 4.32 times the initial value. Under these circumstances, it would take an average rate of tax on estates of 77 per cent to prevent the accumulation of wealth from generation to generation. Five per cent per year is a very modest rate of return once one allows for inflation. Yet if $1000 had been invested 200 years ago at 5 per cent compounded annually, the present capital value would be $17.3 million. If $1000 had been invested 200 years ago at 10 per cent, which is about the average return on common stock, the present capital value would be $189.7 billion. If wealth actually grew this way, any ten families that had had $1000 each 200 years ago would together now own practically all of our stock of privately owned wealth.

Although reasoning about wealth based upon compound interest is tempting because of its simplicity, it is contradicted by the evidence. Fortunes do not accumulate at the average rate of return of the economy. Instead, there is a process of growth and decline. Fortunes may grow for a while, but either incompetence or bad luck will ensure their eventual dispersal. The heirs to a fortune are not necessarily as competent as its creator, and even the most competent will eventually come up against bad luck.[21]

The unsustainability of wealth holdings is, of course, contrary to the customary argument based on compound interest. The Crusonia plant is the illustration par excellence of compound interest: the more you have the more you get, and that is all there is to it. Life is not so simple once it is recognised that wealth must be consciously and wisely managed to maintain its productive capacity. Wealth is always dissipating, so it must be replaced. It requires the continual application of conscious economic calculation, along with some good fortune, to offset the ever present tendency toward dissipation. According to the compound-interest analogy, the wealthy inexorably become cumulatively wealthier, just as a Crusonia plant becomes cumulatively larger. Obviously, this type of reasoning, even if widely accepted, is inadequate, and some alternative framework is called for.

The problem of 'the gambler's ruin' is another model for examining certain facets of the accumulation of wealth over time. In its simplest form, the problem of the gambler's ruin states that the probability that a gambler will lose his fortune varies inversely with the size of his fortune relative to that of his opposition. If the gambler, whose fortune is χ, and his opposition, whose fortune is γ, face equal likelihoods of winning, the probability that the gambler will eventually lose his entire fortune is $1 - \chi/(\chi + \gamma)$. If the gambler and his opposition are equally rich, 0.5 is the probability of the gambler's eventual ruin.[22]

Especially relevant is the case of the enormously rich adversary. As the wealth of the adversary increases relative to that of the gambler, the probability of the gambler's eventual ruin approaches certainty. In an economic system, an individual striving to accumulate wealth can in certain respects be regarded as similar to a gambler playing against an enormously wealthy adversary. Although acting upon anticipations of such phenomena as demands and technologies is descriptively distinct from playing poker or shooting craps, the uncertainty of outcomes and the repetition of play characterise both settings. These similarities make the analogy helpful as a reasoning device, although the differences between gambling and entrepreneurial activity should also be kept in mind.

Of even greater interest than the probability that any given fortune will be exhausted is the expected length of time it will take to exhaust the fortune. It is relatively uninteresting by itself to argue that any fortune will eventually disperse, for the process might take 50 years or 500. The expected length of time it will take for the gambler to become ruined can be quite important: it makes a difference whether the expected duration is 50 years or 500.

The entries in Table 13.3 show the probability of ruin in a two-person game and the expected duration of play for several values of p, q, χ, and γ. The general outlines of the table are unmistakably clear.[23] Even when he has a 0.5 chance of winning, the gambler's chance of ruin is 0.9 when he has 10 per cent of the total wealth and rises to 0.99 when his share of the wealth falls to 1 per cent. When the probability of the gambler's winning falls below 0.5, his eventual ruin is practically certain, even when he initially possesses 10 per cent

Table 13.3 Probability of Gambler's Ruin and Expected Duration of Play

Initial Fortunes of		Probability of		Probability of	Number of Plays
Gambler (X)	Opposition (Y)	Gambler's winning (p)	Gambler's losing (q)	Gambler's Ruin (P_r)	Expected Until Ruin (D_r)
10	90	0.5	0.5	0.9	900
10	90	0.4	0.6	1.0[a]	50[a]
10	90	0.33	0.67	1.0[a]	30[a]
10	990	0.5	0.5	0.99	9900
10	990	0.4	0.6	1.0[a]	50[a]
10	990	0.33	0.67	1.0[a]	30[a]

[a] These values are extremely close approximations. The exact entry for P_r in the second row is 0.999999. Similarly, the exact value for D_r in the second row is 49.999999.

Source: Author's computations. For formulae, see text p. 309 and footnote 23.

of the wealth. The expected duration of play is highly sensitive to the probability that the gambler will win. When the gambler initially has 10 per cent of the wealth, the expected duration of play before ruin is 900 trials. The expected duration falls to 50 when the probability of winning falls to 0.4 and falls to 30 when the probability of success falls to 0.33.

We can now examine the role that confiscatory rates of taxation play in the process of the accumulation and dissipation of wealth over time. An entrepreneur makes investments in alternatives whose future payoffs are uncertain. Sometimes he will win; sometimes he will lose. Other things being equal, the more progressive the rate of tax on winnings, the less willing an entrepreneur will be to take risks. The greater the rate of progressivity, the higher the excess tax on gains vis-à-vis losses. Under a proportional income tax, for instance an income of $100,000 one year and zero the next will pay the same tax as annual incomes of $50,000 for two years. Under progressive taxation, however, the tax on $100,000 will be more than twice as large as the tax on $50,000.

Whereas an individual might be willing to make an investment with a probability of success of only, say, 0.40 under proportional taxation, he might require a probability of success of 0.45 under progressive taxation. And the higher the rate of tax on winnings, the more favorable the odds must be before an entrepreneur will make the investment. And the more favorable the odds, the slower the expected disintegration of the entrepreneur's fortune. The use of progressive rates of tax to penalise those with high income and large wealth will tend to promote a conservatism that reduces the rate of personal mobility within the distributions of income and wealth.

In the absence of inflation, government bonds would be a riskless investment. And if investments were truly riskless, the arithmetic of compound interest would exert itself. The higher the rate of tax on the accummulation of wealth, the more numerous will be the number of people who settle for lower, more certain returns. Fortunes are much less likely to erode under such circumstances. And the fortunes that do erode will erode at slower rates. On the one hand, high tax rates will encourage safe investments, which reduce the probability of ruin and lengthen the duration of time before ruin. On the other hand, by reducing the rate of mobility among wealth positions, high rates of tax also reduce the ability of newcomers to enter the high-wealth brackets. On both grounds, then, high rates of tax promote the retention of large amounts of wealth by those who already possess them.*

The progressive taxation of incomes and estates produces results that are clearly inconsistent with the desire to make it possible for all individuals to have reasonable opportunities to become wealthy. Present policies protect holders of previously accumulated wealth, both from themselves and from the competition of others who might otherwise amass new wealth. Some penalty is placed upon existing wealth holders, but a more severe obstacle is thrown in the path of those who are not wealthy but who might be inclined to attempt to become

---

* It is noteworthy that, in the post-war period of confiscatory taxation, capital gains have been the primary route by which new private wealth has been amassed. Earnings taken in this form, of course, are subject to lower tax rates. Rather than being looked upon as a loophole, however, the capital gains provision should be looked upon as a second-best provision in our tax system, with considerably lower tax rates being first best.

wealthy. In consequence, there is a tendency for wealth to beget wealth in a manner that would not take place if efforts to penalise high incomes and wealth through taxation were relaxed.

14

Can inequality be cured?

NATHAN KEYFITZ

≠

CHRISTOPHER JENCKS has raised in a novel and original form the old question of inequality. Underlying his book *Inequality: A Reassessment of the Effect of Family and Schooling in America* (1972) is the assumption that successive additions to a person's income provide diminishing returns in happiness, and hence that the simplest and most efficient way to increase total happiness is for the rich to give to the poor. No empirical data are likely to prove or disprove this statement. Everyone believes it in some degree; no one accepts it absolutely. Jencks knows that his data cannot decide such matters, and he is straightforward enough to tell us at the outset that equality is what he, personally, favors. We shall return to this basic point later. Meanwhile, there is much in Jencks's study that does have a substantial relation both to empirical data and to social policy in specific areas.

1. Using the large amount of research now available on income differences among individuals, to which he has added some research of his own, Jencks and his seven co-authors examine the extent to which those differences are traceable to schooling, to intelligence, and to home environment. Applying modern statistical techniques, they establish what part of income variation can be attributed to each of these three antecedents – and they find the part attributable to each to be

First published in *The Public Interest*, Vol. 33 (1973), pp. 91–101.

small. In particular, they find income little affected by schooling.

High income may be *correlated* with schooling, but simple correlation is not what we and Jencks want; we need to know how much of income is *due* to schooling. After all, when we find a rich man with good schooling we may suspect that his wealth is more closely related to his father's wealth than to any independent effect of his own schooling. The well off buy more education for their children, just as they buy more automobiles for them; in so far as education is merely a consumer good, it cannot cause the higher incomes of the next generation any more than sports cars can. Jencks seeks the part of individual income variance genuinely attributable to schooling, and he estimates it to be only about 12 per cent.

The result is puzzling and makes us ask how we ever got the impression that schooling is a chief means to upward mobility. Since intelligence and home environment are not easily manipulable as instruments of social action, schooling has been the hope of salvation for deprived individuals and groups. Can it have been such a means in earlier times, but be one no longer? Can schooling benefit the income of the community as a whole at all times – as most of us believe – even though no longer enabling individuals to rise in relation to their fellows? Oddly enough, both sets of propositions could be true and still be consistent with Jencks's correlations.

A parable will show one way of reconciling these seemingly contradictory relations. Once there was a nation, few of whose citizens went to school, in which those who did happen to be educated had high incomes while the rest were poor. Aware of this relationship, the more ambitious among the poor demanded that their children be admitted to the schools. The state yielded to this pressure and began to subsidise education. Now larger numbers went to high school and college, average income rose as education raised the general level of human capability, and variation in incomes declined. Subsidised schooling and other policies brought about a transition to the modern era. During the transition, educated people were in demand, and schooling was a means of social ascent for many individuals. But once subsidised education became widespread, the individuals who were more schooled could no longer capture for themselves much of the benefit of that schooling, and the correlation between income and education went down. Variation in years of schooling diminished, and a time eventually came when nearly everyone had a college degree. Long before that time, schooling differences among individuals had become small enough so that they could not possibly affect income.

This shows how education could become less effective as a means of reducing income inequality without being less useful to the community. The poor by definition are still those at the bottom – but they are at the bottom of the income distribution of a *rich rather than a poor country*, thanks in large part to the better education of themselves and others.

2. Income variation is an important enough matter to be considered by many sciences, each from its own viewpoint. In free market economics, everyone has the incentive to make his contribution as great as possible; his effort is added to a joint process; under competition he can appropriate to himself only the marginal contribution that he makes. Each of us is better off *just because* some of our neighbors are more productive than we are. If we accept the perspective of the free market, we reflect, when we see our neighbours' imposing houses, that their affluence comes from their higher productivity, and moreover that their productivity overflows and adds something to our income as well. This applies to minor differences between more and less skilled workmen, as well as to major differences between workmen and owners. There is not the slightest room for *ressentiment* or petty trade union spirit in this generous approach.

Opposed to it is the political view, associated especially with Marx, whereby the major variations of income are associated with class differences. Groups whose income derives heavily from property are in a position to appropriate large shares of economic output while producing little or nothing. They use what they take to improve their position further, until they have so concentrated power in their own hands and reduced themselves to so small a minority that they can be easily expropriated in their turn; thus inequality comes to an abrupt end just as it reaches its highest peak. This view assimilates the wealthy under capitalism with power holders of all epochs who maintain their incomes only by the continued exercise of force; it is an attack on inequality that lumps the chiefs of modern business together with colonial rulers, Roman emperors, the Pharaohs, and other such unpleasant people.

In contrast to both of these is Jencks's probability view of the present system. It disregards the free enterprise argument that by virtue of the force of competition the rich contribute more than they withdraw; it disregards also the Marxist charge of exploitation. High income ceases to be morally positive as in the former view or negative as in the latter; it is morally neutral.

Finding that only about 20 per cent of variation in income is accounted for by schooling, IQ and home environment, Jencks seeks the cause of the remaining variation – and fails to find it. Like the agronomist trying to assess the effect of the fertiliser he has applied to some plots and not to others, Jencks takes residual variation to be random, and he ascribes the remaining 80 per cent of variation in income to luck or chance.

Bridge players know that skill is important, but that there are cards with which the most skilled player can do nothing, and that luck sometimes gives him such cards; skill in bridge is therefore estimated by *average* performance. Engineers know that the most precise instrument has a margin of error, so that the measurement on a particular occasion is in effect randomly selected from a distribution of possible measurements. The agronomist designs his experiment so that he can make probability calculations afterwards, and he can properly do so provided he has allocated at random the plots to which the fertiliser or other treatment was applied. The allocation puts randomness into the experiment, and enables him to estimate with a specifiable degree of assurance just how much increase of yield was due to the treatment. He never denies that other causes of variation are there, and that these could be ascertained in further experimenting if it were useful to do so. But usually he does not care about these; if one variety of potato has five per cent higher yield than another and no disadvantages, he will recommend its use; his experiment was successful, even though it has failed to explain 98 per cent of the variance among plants.

More broadly, the randomness in any statistical analysis is relative to the variables that are identified; it is *a randomness for the purpose of the particular analysis* – for finding out whether the identified variables have an effect that stands out above 'noise'. The concept of randomness has the negative use of stopping us from publishing a result on the identified variables that could have arisen by chance. But 'chance' in this sense is a way of comprehending unidentified variables that we might take as clear and distinct causal agents if only we knew what they were. Neither in agronomy nor in social science is it to be assumed that the residual random variation of a particular analysis is inherently untraceable – only that it has not so far been traced.

To suppose that the portion of income variation not explained by the identified variables of schooling, IQ and home environment is *objectively* random, is to adopt the statistical model with a wholehearted literalness that embarrasses statisticians. Even those who think that randomness can be a property of the real world will demand infinite persistence in uncovering assignable causes of variation before they concede that any residual variance is really beyond all possible breakdown. They will be astonished at how positive a policy conclusion Jencks draws from his null result.

Thus, schooling the poor has been looked to as a means of increasing equality, as a mechanism that would retain and even augment the dynamism of American society. Jencks's analysis touches not dynamism but equality, and for this even the best existing schools give disappointing results. He pays little attention to whether the large unexplained variance of income may not be caused by some other variable that could be operated on to equalise incomes: newer educational techniques, childrearing practices, nutrition, vitamins. Having shown that schools make insufficient difference, he takes the direct approach: The *only* way to improve the lot of the poor is to give them money. That assertion could be true, and it is consistent with his data – but it does not follow from his data, and it could be false.

3. One of the refreshing features of the book is its

concentration on individual rather than group differences. Much previous writing is concerned with incomes of blacks as against those of whites or of women as against men. If only the opportunities for the several groups could be equalised, we have been told, their average incomes would be equal; what we want is that all have a fair chance in the competitive race. Different mean incomes of recognisable groups are taken to prove that opportunities are not equal, and this is what bothers most of us who have been concerned about the matter. Once the inequality of opportunity is removed and the *averages* become the same for blacks and whites, men and women, then *individual* differences in actual incomes obtained become tolerable.

But they are not tolerable for Jencks. He wants to see us equal, not only in opportunity, but in actual income received and spent. Equalising opportunity might make the statistical mean income for blacks and for whites identical, but it would leave half the individuals above the median and half below, and some by very large amounts. Schooling will at best equalise opportunity and may do little for actual receipts. School gives us a hunting licence and it trains us to shoot; Jencks wants to see us come back with equal amounts of bear. His way of achieving his objective is to divide the bears shot among all the hunters. Whatever the sport, we are not merely to go into the game with no handicap, but we are all to emerge with the same score.

In Jencks's model of the business world, everyone contributes to production, whether in manual or mental labor; instead of being paid fairly for his labor, he is given a lottery ticket; when the wheel stops, some draw millions, others barely enough to live on. This view relieves us of the charge of viciousness; no one would say that the winner of a church lottery is 'exploiting' the losers. Nonetheless, the proper policy, as Jencks sees it, is to reverse the effect of the lottery by recalling the larger prizes and redistributing them. Through such redistribution, the state would provide a kind of insurance that no private company has thought of offering; it would insure the child just born against the hazard of an unsuccessful career. Surely a life of poverty is a worse misfortune than having one's house burn down, and the case for income insurance is therefore even stronger than for fire insurance.

Jencks recognises that such a redistribution policy represents a value judgment. It appears to be morally supported by his finding that income differences are due to luck. But redistribution could be supported by many other explanations of income difference. Two examples are offered below.

It has been said that a large part of the population is suffering in varying degrees from a debilitating ailment that causes, among other symptoms, great loss of earnings. The ailment is the more insidious in that those who suffer most from it are least aware that they have it. Though partly incurable, it is rarely a direct cause of death. I refer to stupidity. Now we no longer think it humane to punish people for their personal defects, and low income is certainly a punishment. Cure of the underlying condition may be difficult, but we can readily eliminate the punishing symptom by giving money to those affected. However, Jencks does not use this argument, since his correlations show incomes to be about as little related to IQ as they are to schooling.

Suppose, alternatively, that one's income is determined by one's parents. An expensive school may not do much besides making the youth and childhood of the wealthy young more pleasant, but many other devices are at the disposal of the rich to ensure the advantage of their children. Their knowledge of the system enables them to advise their children on career choice, especially on how to avoid a dead-end job. By influencing their children to seek favored points of entry into the system, and by influencing the system to give special treatment to their children, as well as by directly bequeathing their wealth, they generate a partly hereditary class. The various ways, both direct and devious, in which those at the top can influence the incomes of their children have bothered critics not only in capitalist countries but in socialist ones as well. That a privileged class can arise and perpetuate itself even after the abolition of private property has been made clear in the Soviet Union and Eastern Europe since World War II. Inequality arising in such a fashion could indeed be eliminated by redistribution; but the resistance is great.*

We have given three arguments for redistribution, each based on a different cause of inequality: bad luck, stupidity, or poor parents. Jencks's luck model is not unique in leading to the policy he favors. The accounting for poverty that his data reject – i.e., low IQ and poor homes – would support redistribution just as well as attributing poverty to bad luck.

That income differences are not imputable to differences in the quality and amount of schooling leads Jencks to advocate redistribution. Since he could have been led to it by other considerations, the low correlation of education with income is not, as he seems to think, a necessary condition of his argument.

4. More important, it is not a sufficient condition either. Many useful personal qualities are not measured by IQ and would fall outside even a much wider definition of intelligence. Suppose that success in business was somehow the result of being able to think more persistently about problems rather than to think quickly. Then, those would succeed who had the ability to focus their thought for long periods on a single issue, rather than those who could produce the best quick solution. Isaac Newton once said that he was not more clever than other men, but only that he could hold his mind longer on one point. This quality of concentration could be responsible for high incomes, whether achieved by legitimate or other means, as well as for scientific discovery.

A quite different component of personality is the disposition to look critically at existing methods of production, to be

---

*The classical Marxist analysis is different from this and too radical to provide a case for redistribution. For it, inequality is one among many other bad features of capitalism, among them inefficiency in production, loss of creativity, and failure to hold the allegiance of its members, all of which are becoming progressively worse. To reform the capitalist system by dividing up incomes might indeed save the bourgeoisie for a time, but the bourgeoisie nonetheless oppose such division, drawn as they are to their own destruction by the tide of history. On this romantic Marxist view, redistribution is a petty notion of lower-middle class people envious of those above them.

willing to reject them and replace them with new methods when that will increase the effectiveness of an organisation. Much attention has been given to the role of innovation in the economic progress of nations, but not much headway has been made in testing for it in individuals. Jencks's 'competence' could include such elements, but the concept requires further analysis.

A society that wants production must find some way to give power to those of its members who are innovative or otherwise competent. If the competent person is allowed to retain the profit on his first venture, then he can start a second one on a larger scale; a natural selection results by which capital comes to be commanded by those who can make the most profitable use of it. This self-selection of the competent has drawbacks, and in some parts of the world more direct ways of assigning power are preferred. But if we have to wait for production until the competent producers can seize power directly, then we may have long to wait; those who are skilled in seizing and holding power may or may not be those who are competent in managing production.

Unequal incomes may not be able directly to generate desirable qualities of innovation, which could be inborn or determined in early childhood. But under suitable laws and regulations, larger-than-average incomes, saved and converted into capital by those who possess them, can be a means by which those competent in production are self-selected to exercise power.

More obvious than either concentration or innovation, and similarly difficult to measure, is effort. Those persons whose incomes are higher could be those who want more income badly enough to drop other objectives. To bring effort, innovation, and concentration into our empirical study, we would have to measure the presence of these qualities in individuals independently of income. And if such qualities are desirable and are spurred by income differences, then the whole problem is altered. The model assumed by Jencks will then no longer serve. It must be replaced by a more dynamic model, one that takes account of the determinants of *production*, not merely of inequalities of income.

5. Insofar as the distribution of income affects the amount of production, redistribution could be disastrous. If there is a feedback from income to production, so that the prospect of higher income induces a person to work harder and more intelligently than he would without such inducement, then society's mean income is a function of the variation in individual incomes. This is a mechanism governing the system as a whole.

Can we not study the mechanism by measuring the output of individuals and correlating this with their incomes? Recent experiments on the negative income tax, an idea first presented by Milton Friedman in 1962, suggest that the disincentive effect of redistribution is not as great as had been thought, and Jencks relies on this. But the known results apply simply to job-*holding*; statistics on the *intensity* of work are less easy to come by. If such experiments could be pursued and their many logical and practical difficulties somehow overcome, we might arrive at a curve relating production on the vertical axis to inequality on the horizontal; one point on such a curve would be the amount of inequality now existing in the United States and the present disposable national income of one trillion dollars. Suppose that with half the inequality (say, taxing away half of all incomes exceeding the average and distributing the tax so as to bring those below half-way up to the average), we would have an income of $900 billion; with one quarter the inequality, similarly defined, we would have $700 billion; with one tenth, $400 billion; and so on. At a certain point in the reduction of inequality, the incentive to produce could fall so low that even the poor would have lower incomes than they do now; the most devoted advocate of equality would presumably stop short of this. If we had such a curve, the electorate could vote intelligently on redistribution; they would know how much inequality would buy how much total income.

But the hope that we can immediately obtain such a curve is only a little less naive than the hope that the electorate would be able to agree on a particular point on the curve, or that the point would be one sacrificing income to equality. Professor Jencks fears that attitudes prevailing in the United States are such that people would choose a good deal of inequality, perhaps as much as now exists. He deplores this, and he may have a good case. On the one hand, the reduction of inequality by half may not greatly lower output. And on the other, we may not need all that output anyway. Many have called American output an unjustified expenditure of limited minerals and other non-renewable resources at the expense of the rest of the world.

6. The present system can be attacked in a quite different way by seeing income as subsidiary to social stratification. People don't primarily seek high incomes; money as such, and the physical pleasures that money can buy, are not their major aim. They want high incomes so that they can live like upper-class people. Much of the history of Europe over two centuries has been marked by the efforts of the bourgeoisie to behave like aristocrats; it was incidental to their struggle for upward mobility that they achieved material progress.

On this view, income above subsistence is not sought for hedonistic purposes, but so that the earner can assert and concretely symbolise his social ascent. Suppose that $25 worth of clothing permits a man to preserve decency and protect himself against the elements; if he actually spends 10 times as much, then nine tenths of the custom-made suit and other textiles on his back are chargeable to social ascent, or at least to factors other than need, which accounts only for one tenth. I am not asserting that we are now so rich that we could dispense with nine tenths of our incomes if we were willing to live comfortably but plainly; no one knows what the fraction would be. Certainly, if we were satisfied with the uniformity of the Chinese in their blue denims, most of our tailors and designers could be put to work doing other things and the work week could be reduced for everyone.

The last two paragraphs say that *much of our high GNP serves to mark social differences*; earlier paragraphs say in effect that *the purpose of the social differences is to give people an incentive to work hard and so to raise income*. To decide which is the means and which the goal is not as easy as social scientists used to think.

From one viewpoint, the preference for equality becomes a preference for a society whose members are less differentiated by style of life. With more equal incomes, we would live more nearly in the same way. Status differences would be less visible. There would be less incentive to produce on the part of individuals if they got little higher income for producing; on the other hand, with the lessened social competition a lower average income would suffice.

Jencks is right when he says that Americans do not at present want change in this direction. For a long time into the future the social competitive game will be the chief entertainment of most people. Such inexpensive alternatives as religion and touch football cannot match the seriousness of owning a Cadillac. One interpretation of the 1972 election is that McGovern was rejected because he stood for equality; in the trade-off between income and equality the electorate favored income. This preference is shown even by many whose incomes are below the average. I predict a continuation of the process by which visible social inequality will increase effort and hence production and hence income, and the income will be used to purchase the symbols of social inequality.

7. Jencks's *Inequality* is a scholarly book, largely made up of data and their interpretation. These data, whose difficulties are fairly confronted, all have a bearing on the question of whether schooling or something else accounts for income inequality. Jencks is humane; he regards the amount of inequality now existing as unjust. Having shown the impossibility of removing it through education, he seeks an alternative and more direct way.

After the thickets of statistical cross-classifications, multiple correlations, and path coefficients, what a relief to come out of the woods and find the simple answer – redistribute! The arithmetical formula he suggests is easily understood. If Jones has an income of $10,000, Smith of $20,000, and Brown of $30,000, then the average income is $20,000, and half the departure of Brown from this average – i.e., $5000 – is to be transferred to Jones, whose departure from the mean will also be halved. The same perfect balance will be found however many persons are involved; it can be shown to be a property of the arithmetic mean that the total departures above are equal to the departures below.

After redistribution, the incomes will be $15,000, $20,000, and $25,000 respectively. This is the degree of altruism that Jencks recommends, and it may be indexed by the fraction one half or 0.50 by which the departures are multiplied. One who was in favor of allowing more incentive might only redistribute one quarter of the departure from the average, and his index of altruism would be expressed by 0.25. Thus, everyone has a personal index of altruism, varying from 0.00 for those satisfied with the present distribution to 1.00 for those who want all incomes to be identical. One purpose of *Inequality* is to raise the public's index of altruism, which Jencks complains may now be close to 0.00.

When we look back to the origin of the graduated income tax we find somewhat the same simplicity. The object then was redistribution, and the argument for it was that a marginal dollar is of more use to the poor man than to the rich man, so a net gain in satisfaction results from transfer. But the simple idea was modified along lines that we all know: Municipalities have to be aided, so they were allowed to pay tax-free interest; farmers have a hard life, so they were permitted special definitions of income; oil exploration needs encouragement by double depreciation. These modifications drew wealth into municipal bonds, farming, and oil. The tax schedule at first was unambiguously graduated from zero to 60 per cent of income, but now many volumes of law books and administrative regulations have come to be needed for defining income. And the definitions are such that some individuals who live like millionaires turn out to have zero income for tax purposes, while office clerks and assembly-line workers pay tax on every dollar that goes through their hands. As inflation proceeds, nominal tax rates remain unchanged, so that higher and higher rates are paid on a given real income (this is not called raising taxes). Beyond a certain point in its evolution the graduation aspect of taxes disappears – the incidence becomes similar for all income levels.

Inequality does not compare the equalising effects of education with those of the income tax as both have actually operated to date. If it did, the chances are that education would emerge as a relatively effective agent. Instead, it compares the actual performance of education with a redistributive ideal, saying in effect: Let us get away from the complexity that has come to surround the gospel of redistribution, and restore the clear vision of the first prophets of the graduated income tax.

8. Reflection upon the fate of earlier equally pure ideas fills one with foreboding. Fifteen years ago, in 1958, John Kenneth Galbraith told us that in an affluent society we had practically all we needed to eat and to wear, and that our further individual wants were mostly created by the production process. Beyond a certain minimum, the market persuaded people to buy those goods it wanted to produce, and failed on collective goods like parks and schools. Government could spend our money for us better than we could ourselves; since we did not really want the goods bought with our marginal dollars, we would hardly miss what we gave up in the form of higher taxes.

The idea had appeal, and it was acted on. In 1958, when *The Affluent Society* was published, the federal budget was about $80 billions per year; now it has passed $250 billions. No one can say that intellectuals are without influence, especially when they are just slightly ahead of their time. Galbraith softened up the public, helped break down its resistance and reduce its squawks at the plucking that was in store for it. That this was not his intention, that much of the money was used by government for purposes against which he has spoken loudly and courageously, does not alter the direction of his influence.

Jencks could well attain the same eminence and have a similar effect. Governmental arithmetic may faithfully follow one half of the Jencks recommendation – taking away from the rich half of the excess of their income above the mean (always with the proviso that it would allow the more astute rich to define themselves as poor). But it would uncouple the other half of the Jencks recommendation – that the take be divided among those with below average incomes. It would explain that what with welfare payments, social security, and the like, much was already being done and to do more would be inflationary. Those who wanted to carry through the Jencks recommendation to the end and actually redistribute to the poor would indeed have their say, but so also would those who thought that fine pile of money would be better spent on interplanetary travel or on doubling our stock of strategic weaponry before the Russians doubled theirs. At best there would be a compromise based on the balance of forces at the time.

This is the long-range distortion to which the Jencks proposal is liable. In the short term, it has removed some of the justification for support to education. Jencks does not intend this any more than Galbraith was pushing for increased defense spending. But an idea, forcefully and attractively presented, assumes a life of its own. It is no longer under the control of its author, but is subject to capture by any power that can make use of it.

15

The charity of the uncharitable

GORDON TULLOCK

≠

IF I understand the common view among modern intellectuals, income redistribution is considered to be a rather simple and almost entirely ethical matter. There are, basically, two theories. The first is that those of us who are well-off use the state as a mechanism for making gifts to the poor. This is well represented by James Rodgers and Harold Hochman in their article, 'Pareto Optimal Redistribution'.[1] The second view, which I shall call the 'Downsian', is that in a democracy the poor are able to use their votes to obtain transfers from the rest of society (Anthony Downs [2, esp. pp. 198–201]). These two views are sometimes combined into the view that the bulk of the population takes money from the rich and gives it to the poor by use of the democratic process.

Although I have presented these two points of view very briefly, I think nevertheless that they sum up the standard justification for redistribution. Unfortunately, these essentially

First published in *Western Economic Journal*, Vol. 9 (1971), pp. 379–92:

For References, see page 392 below. The numbers *within square brackets* relate to these References.

1. Hochman and Rodgers, of course, are much more sophisticated in their handling of the problem that I have indicated in this single paragraph. Nevertheless, the point of view outlined above is espoused in it. The article has attracted a large number of comments, many of which are markedly less sophisticated than the original work.

ethical approaches cannot explain the bulk of the redistribution in our society. It is true that they *do* explain a small amount of it, but most of it comes from other motives and achieves other ends. Since these two ideas are probably fairly firmly engrained in the mind of the reader, I should like before I begin formal analysis to briefly discuss the facts of redistribution.

Firstly, the poor vote, and the amount of redistribution that they receive, in part, is a function of the extent to which they vote [5].[2] Thus, to at least some extent, the money received by the poor must represent the use by the poor of their political power, rather than a charitable gift from the rest of society. This would seem to indicate that the first of the explanations given above cannot, at the very least, be the entire explanation.

Secondly, anybody examining the status of the poor in the modern world must realise that democracies do not make very large gifts to them. If we consider the United States, the federal government officially lists its welfare expenditures as about $100 billion a year. This would be enough to give the bottom one-fifth of our nation an income of $10,000 per family of four, even if they had no other source of income. Clearly they do not receive benefits of this sort. Another calculation carried out by the Institute for Research on Poverty at the University of Wisconsin shows the total welfare deliveries to the poor as $40 billion [6].[3] This would, once again, if delivered to the poor in cash, work out to about $4000 per family of four in the bottom one-fifth of our population. Once again, it is clear they are not doing anywhere near this well.[4] US Senator Abraham Ribicoff, commenting on HEW, said: 'In fiscal 1972, the projected $31.1 billion for poverty programs would provide $4800 for every poor family of four, almost $1000 above the poverty line, if directly distributed to these families.'

If we turn to actual relief and assistance payments to the

2. See also Frey [3] for a discussion of the reasons why the poor exert less political influence than their per capital voting strength would appear to give them.

3. The figures in Lampman's study are for 1967.

4. The reasons why this particular calculation overestimates transfers to the poor will be discussed below.

poor, it turns out that they add up to much less than 1 per cent of the national income. This amount could clearly be more than explained simply on the assumption that the poor make use of their votes to obtain the transfer. Indeed, the amount they receive would appear to be less than the amount that they *would* receive if the federal budget were simply divided among the taxpayers in accordance with their voting potential.

Nor is the situation greatly different in other democracies. Webb and Sieve in comparing incomes in England in 1937 with 1959 come to the conclusion '. . . *the estimate of inequality of final incomes remains constant over the period of twenty years which saw the establishment and growth to some stability of the "welfare state"* [12, p. 109]'.[5] Granted the massive amounts of income that are transferred back and forth through the population by the British government, it is evident that the major effect and probably the major purpose of this transfer cannot be to help the poor. With well in excess of 30 per cent of the average individual's received income being taxed away in one way or another and the defense burden much lower as a part of GNP than it was in 1937, it is clear there are massive resources available for aiding the poor if that was indeed the objective of the British government.

Leaving aside for the moment any further discussion of the empirical facts about redistribution, let us turn to what has been done in the way of more formal theory of redistribution in a democracy.[6] The first of these in point of time is the argument of Anthony Downs that democracy will always lead to transfer of income from the wealthy to the poor. Indeed, he regards this as a major justification of democracy. We may contrast this with Benjamin Ward's view that redistribution in democracy would be essentially indeterminate.[7] Finally, there is the view

---

5. This comment is particularly revealing, since both Webb and Sieve are vigorous advocates of the British welfare state, and the subject matter of their book is the improvement of statistics on its effects.

6. This paper is entirely concerned with redistribution in democracies because this is the area where our knowledge of politics is best. I should not like to leave the implication that I am convinced that redistribution operates better in despotisms.

7. Note that Ward actually demonstrates that there would be cyclical majority in all such cases. Since the process must stop, however, and in

expressed in *The Calculus of Consent* (J. M. Buchanan and G. Tullock [1, pp. 144–5]) that the nature of the voting process in democracy is such that real resources will be transferred away from the rich, although it is not specified who will receive them. It will surprise no one that I espouse the Buchanan and Tullock view, but the Ward model will be used to supplement it by indicating that the actual output of the political process is not predetermined.[8]

The essence of the difference between the Downs model and the Ward model is simply that Downs implicitly assumes that redistribution must take place along a one-dimensional continuum in which people are arranged from the poorest to the wealthiest. At first glance, there would seem to be no obvious reason why the bottom 51 per cent of the population, using their majority to take money from the wealthy, would be more likely than the top 51 per cent using their majority to take money from the poor. Indeed, the 2 per cent of the population lying at the middle line would be the determining factor in such a choice, and hence we might anticipate that money would come from both ends to the middle.

In practice, of course, the wealthy have more money, and hence can be subject to heavier taxes. Thus the cost of admitting a wealthy person into a coalition, which proposes to transfer money away from the 49 per cent of the population not members, is higher than the cost of permitting the entry of a poor person. Following William Riker, one would therefore anticipate that voting coalitions would be made up in such a way as to minimise the number of wealthy members. This is, indeed, the element of truth in the Down model, is part of the Buchanan-Tullock model, and must be admitted as a modification of the Ward model.

If the dominant coalition is likely to be made up of the bottom 51 per cent of the population, this tells us nothing very much about how that coalition will divide the spoils. Further, it is obvious that this coalition must contain a good many

observed reality *does* stop at some point, the statement that he proved indeterminancy of the process is not an unjust summary.

8. The two models may be reconciled by use of the apparatus presented by Tullock [10].

persons who are not poor by any ordinary definition. If we accept the bottom 10 per cent of the population as poor, then they make up only 20 per cent of this coalition of the bottom 51 per cent. If we are more generous and count 20 per cent of the population as poor, then they make up 40 per cent. Clearly, this minority cannot dominate the coalition. If they received more per head than the other members of the coalition, they would do so because the lower middle class was generous.

Turning to formal bargaining theory, it is obvious that any transfer mechanism must provide at least as much for the top portion of this bottom 51 per cent coalition as for anyone else in the coalition because if it does not, the 49 per cent who are not members can very readily purchase the top 2 per cent for a coalition that transfers a small amount from the top income groups to this small 2 per cent group and to no one else. Indeed, such a coalition might take the entire transfer out of the bottom part of the population instead of out of the top. The reasoning so far would indicate that the people toward the top of the bottom 51 per cent might receive much more than the people at the lower end. The only restriction on a delivery of the bulk of the resources transferred from the wealthy to the upper end of the bottom coalition (other than charitable instincts on the part of the members of the upper end) would seem to be the possibility that the wealthy would attempt a coalition with the very poor.

If we look at the real world, we do see some signs of such coalition attempts. Among those persons who argue that all transfers should be strictly limited to the very poor by way of a stringent means test, it is likely that wealthy persons predominate. This is, of course, sensible from even a selfish standpoint. They could arrange to give to the present-day poor considerably more money than the poor are now receiving, in return for a coalition in which transfers to people in the upper part of the bottom 51 per cent are terminated, and make a neat profit. This particular coalition has so far foundered largely because of miscalculations by the poor. The poor realisé that the interests of the wealthy are clearly not congruent with their interests, but they do not realise that the interests of people between the twentieth and the fifty-first percentile of the income distribution are also not identical with theirs. They therefore tend to favor a coalition with the second group rather than the former.

The situation is interesting, and we may pause briefly to examine it by way of a three-person model. Suppose we have wealthy Mr A, middle-class Mr B, and poor Mr C. B and C form a coalition for the purpose of extracting money from Mr A, and let us begin by assuming that the money is to be equally divided between them. Suppose, further, that Mr C's income is $1000 per year before transfer, Mr B's is $2000 per year, and Mr A's is $3000 per year. Clearly, if the amount of transfer were somehow externally fixed at $500 but Mr A were permitted to decide how it was to be allocated, he would give all of it to Mr C.[9] He would reason that not until Mr C's income had risen to $2000 per year was it sensible to supplement Mr B's income. Mr B receives his payment simply because he wants it, not because there is any charitable motive involved on the part of anyone.

Under the circumstances, it is clear that Mr A would be willing to enter into a coalition with Mr C under which a transfer of $300 was made from A to C and none was made to B. This would be to the advantage of Mr C, and it seems likely that only the generally bad information and low IQ and/or motivation which we observe among the poor prevents such coalitions. Indeed, it is possible the poor would do better if they depended entirely on the charitable motives of the wealthy. It might be that Mr A, if left entirely to himself, would be willing to give Mr C more than $250, although he objects to spending $500 for $250 apiece to B and C. Most persons, after all, are to some extent charitable and it may well be that the very poor would do better than at present if they depended on the charity of the wealthy.

For example, an organization of society in which all transfers were made by a special electorate composed of persons in the top 10 per cent of the income stream who tax themselves for the purpose of benefiting other persons might lead to larger transfers to the genuinely poor than they now

9. Such a decision might be made available to taxpayers by allowing them to 'earmark' on their income tax returns a portion of their tax for alternative transfer programs.

receive. Certainly, if we fixed the total amount of transfer away from the upper income groups at its present level but gave them complete discretion as to how it was to be spent, they would spend far more of it on the very poor.

So far, however, we have unrealistically assumed that transfers must be made between different income groups along a unidimensional continuum. If we look at the real world, we observe that the bulk of the transfers are made to groups not defined by income. Farmers, college students, owners of oil wells, owners of private aircraft, older people regardless of their income, and, in all probability, the intellectual class are the major recipients of transfers, even though the bulk of the members of these groups are by no means poor.[10]

If we accept the real world situation as being one in which transfers are made to organised groups and these organised groups receive their transfers largely in terms of their political power (which seems to be a correct statement about the real world), there is no reason why we should anticipate that the poor would do particularly well. For one thing, they are hard to organise. Thus, the very large transfers that we do observe in the world are essentially demonstrations of the Ward proof, supplemented by the Buchanan-Tullock logrolling process, which only rather accidentally benefit the bottom 10 to 15 per cent of the population. For the reasons given above, we would anticipate that the top income groups would do rather badly from these transfers, and indeed they do. The Lampman study shows a transfer away from the upper income brackets of about 13 per cent of their income. The beneficiaries of these transfers, however, we would anticipate would not be particularly concentrated among the poor and, indeed, granted their general political ineptness, one might expect that they would do rather badly, which is what we observe in the real world.

---

10. The inclusion of intellectuals is essentially a subjective guess, based on general knowledge. It seems to me likely that the principal beneficiaries of those changes in our society that originated with the New Deal have been the intellectuals who, through their control of both the educational process and the media, have been able to divert very large resources into their own pockets. So far as I know, however, there is no statistical evidence for or against this point of view.

A somewhat cursory examination would seem to indicate that the actual percentage of income derived from wealthy people in democracies is an inverse function of the ease with which they can migrate. Very small countries, such as Switzerland, Sweden and Luxembourg, make no serious effort to collect taxes on the wealthy which are even as large in percentage terms as those they collect from the rest of the population. Medium-sized countries, like England, Germany, France and Italy, are in a better position for taxing the wealthy, and the United States is able to implement substantial *effective* progression in top income brackets. In no case, so far as I know, is the actual amount of progression in the taxes collected as high as the progression in the tax tables, but it is nevertheless real in the larger countries.

When we turn to expenditures, a quite different picture emerges. Any individual's vote is worth as much as any other individual's vote in getting expenditures. Indeed the wealthy, well-informed person who is capable of making sizable campaign expenditures may well be able to receive a considerably larger portion of the total tax collections than is someone without these advantages [3]. If we subtract tax payments from receipts, we would anticipate some negative amount to turn up from a wealthy person and perhaps, although not certainly, a positive amount for the rest of the population. The reason the second sum is not necessarily positive is because of certain intrinsic inefficiencies in the transfer system. It is to be expected that expenditures that actually cost more than the net total benefit will be made [7]. Under the circumstances, it is possible that, although the rich are injured, the rest of the population make very small or negative profits.

Thus, to repeat, we would anticipate that in democracy there would be some transfer of money away from the wealthy, but there is no obvious reason that this transfer would go to the poor. If we look at the real world, we do find this pattern. This pattern is, however, a relatively minor part of the redistribution of income as seen in the modern state. Economists frequently point out that confiscation of *all* the income of the wealthy in a typical modern state would pay only a tiny part of the routine expenditures of the existing government. On the other hand, there can be no doubt whatsoever that massive redistributions of income do occur by way of the political process. These redistributions, however, are not in the main transfers of funds from the wealthy to the poor, but transfers of funds among the middle-class. The bulk of these transfers come from people who lie between the twentieth and the ninetieth percentile of income, and the bulk of them go to the same income classes. This is, of course, the area with the largest taxable capacity, and also the area where political power is concentrated in a democracy.

These transfers do not meet any egalitarian criteria. Basically they are transfers from groups of people who, for one reason or another, are not politically powerful to people who are. Always and everywhere in democracies, the farmers do very well. As a matter of practical fact, the United States probably wastes fewer resources in supporting its farm program than almost any other Western country. This may surprise Americans, accustomed to our massively inefficient method of transferring money to some people who are, on the whole, about as well-off as the people from whom the transfers come; but examination of what is done in the Common Market will convince them very quickly that Americans are fortunate in this respect.

The farm program is not the only example; the Social Security Administration transfers money from the young to the old, regardless of income. Indeed, in this particular case, the very poor are badly damaged by the institution. Due to the method in which the taxes to pay for Social Security are collected, the poor pay a very substantial part of their tiny wages to the Social Security Administration. If, however, they are very poor, i.e., require public assistance when they are old, then the local authorities will subtract their Social Security payment from the amount they receive. The result from their standpoint is that they pay taxes, but receive no net benefit. This must lead to a significant transfer of resources away from the very poor.

The urban renewal project is another obvious, even scandalous, example of the type of redistribution we observe, and another major example is, of course, the subsidised public education system. The latter is particularly obvious as a redistribution to the well-off at the university level. In general, students who can get into a unversity, particularly those who can get scholarships, have enough natural talent so that they enter the university with a lifetime income well above average. At the expense of the taxpayer, they are then given an even higher lifetime expected income. But even if we turn to lower-level schools, somewhat the same problem exists. To begin with, these are clearly transfers from those in society who do not have children to those who do – to say nothing, of course, of the transfer to the children themselves.

Secondly, however, it is fairly certain that the payoff to education, even at the elementary level, is greatly varying, depending on both the inherited genes and the home environment. Thus, the return in real terms to education is vastly higher to the person who both has the natural talent and the background to have a good income all his life than to the person whose natural talent and background are such that he probably will be poor. We would, if we were interested in relatively egalitarian measures, make direct payments to these two parties which could then be invested in a manner that would be most suitable in each case. By compelling the transfer to be taken in a form that is of maximum benefit to people who are going to be well-off anyway and of minimum benefit to people who are going to be poor, we make the average citizen richer and the poor poorer.

These examples are merely a small part of a wide universe. It is clear that in most democracies the poor receive relatively minor transfers – in any realistic sense – from society, although *not* zero transfers. Although very large amounts of money are redistributed by government action, the bulk of this redistribution is composed of transfers back and forth within the middle income brackets. It is obvious why these transfers occur. Obtaining such a transfer is a rational investment of resources, and people do put their resources into it. The only thing which is in any sense astonishing about this phenomenon is that it is so little noted. Almost all standard discussions of redistribution imply that it is normally from the rich to the poor. Some such redistribution does indeed go on, but it is a trivial phenomenon compared to the redistribution within the middle class. I find the concentration of discussion of redistribution upon the very minor phenomenon of redistribution from the wealthy to the poor and the general ignoring of the major phenomenon – redistribution back and forth within the middle income groups in terms of political organisation – most remarkable.

This remarkable concentration on the minor part of this activity and ignoring of the major part requires, I feel, some explanation. Unfortunately, the only explanation I can offer is basically psychological. It will be outlined below, but I should begin by apologising to the reader for introducing a nonrigorous discussion of personal psychology, instead of something more satisfying.

We must begin by talking a little bit about a well-tested psychological phenomenon: 'reduction of cognitive dissonance'. It is well established that individuals' perception of the world is, to some extent, affected by a subconscious desire to reduce internal dissonance. Thus, an individual will, without any dishonesty, believe that certain activities which are in accord with motive A are also in accord with motive B, even if objectively they are not. The reason for this is that he does not wish to admit, even to himself, that he is disregarding motive B. Needless to say, this phenomenon occurs only when motive A and motive B would, in objective terms, lead to different actions and where the individual in fact regards motive A as more important than motive B.

Most of us have been trained in such a way that we are presented with a problem of this nature. All of us from the time we were small have been told that it is our duty to be charitable, to help the poor, and to do various other good acts. On the other hand, most of us have strong selfish drives. Clearly the injunction that if a man takes your coat, you should give him your cloak also, is not descriptive of the ordinary behavior of most human beings. It is, however, descriptive of what they say. Indeed, if we observe our colleagues in the unversity, we shall find that their expressed opinions are largely in accord with the ethically-given drive toward 'loving thy neighbor' and 'giving all you own to the poor'. If we look at their actual behaviour on the other hand, it turns out that they make few sacrifices for the poor.

It is clear, then, that they find these two drives – spending your own income yourself and helping the poor – in conflict, and that this should cause some internal tension. I should say, perhaps, that in my classes I commonly tell my students that if they really want to help the poor what they should do is get two jobs, work as hard as they possibly can, and then give all their income except that minimum amount that they need to stay alive to the inhabitants of India. They normally object to this pattern of behavior, but are normally not willing to admit that the reason they object is simply that they do not *really* feel that charitable.[11]

Indeed, if I ask my students or my faculty colleagues how much they personally give to the poor, it often turns out to be a small amount – in many cases zero. They very commonly explain their attitude by saying that they prefer governmental charitable activity. They seldom give any explanation as to why they should use the government channel for this activity and, in particular, never turn to the perfectly genuine externality arguments that do exist for this purpose.[12] They sometimes allege, however, that it is more efficient for them to vote for charity than to make a charitable contribution themselves because this brings in other people's money, too.

Suppose that it is suggested that I give $100 to the poor. Suppose further that this proposal is in the form of two options. Option 1 is that I take $100 out of my pocket and give it to some charity. Option 2 is that we vote on whether I should be taxed $100 for the purpose of making this charitable payment. The cost to me of making the direct payment is $100. The cost to me of voting for the tax, however, is $100 discounted by my estimate of the influence my vote will have on the outcome. Granted the constituency is 100,000 or more, the discounted cost to me of voting for this special tax on myself is vanishingly small. Thus, if I feel just a little bit charitable, I would not

---

11. I should say that in general the farther to the left the individual student, the more incoherent he becomes in dealing with this particular problem. It is not that the people on the right are willing to admit that they act selfishly, but simply that they are much less embarrassed by the question than the members of the New Left. Being less embarrassed, they are less likely to sputter.

12. For a statement of these reasons by a man who cannot possibly be accused of socialism, see Milton Friedman [4].

make the $100 payment but I would vote for the tax. I would make this vote in full awareness of the fact that many other persons are also voting on the same issue and that my vote will make very little difference in the outcome. Thus the cost to me of casting my vote is small. Putting it differently, the act that I am called upon to perform in voting is very low cost, even though it refers to a $100 gift; the private gift is high cost. Under the circumstances, one would predict that I would be more likely to vote for charitable activity than to undertake it myself.

Here, also, our phenomenon of reduction of cognitive dissonance comes in. If I am possessed both of selfish desires to spend my own money and a feeling that I must be charitable, I am wise to vote charitably and act selfishly. I should also tend, in discussion, to put much greater weight upon the importance of my vote than is actually justified, and to resent people who tell me that the vote makes almost no difference. At this point, the rationale for the ethical rule that private charity is bad and that all redistribution should be public becomes apparent. It provides a rationalisation for 'ethical' behaviour in urging government redistribution while actually making almost no sacrifice. It permits one to have the best of both worlds.

Some further implications can be drawn from this phenomenon. As the size of the constituency in which I am voting increases, the likelihood that my vote will have any effect on the outcome decreases. Consider my paying $100 to charity, voting on a tax of $100 to be levied on me by my local government for charitable purposes, voting on a similar tax for similar purposes for the state government, and finally voting on a similar tax for similar purposes by the national government. Clearly, the cost to me is monotonically decreasing through this set. I would be more likely to vote for the tax by the national government than for the state government, for the tax by the state government than for the local government, and more likely to vote for the tax by the local government than to make the direct payment myself. It is quite possible that this phenomenon explains the tendency to transfer charitable activity from local governments toward the national government. Looked at from the standpoint of the voter, he can obtain the satisfaction of 'behaving charitably' in a national election much cheaper than he can in the local election.

Note, however, that there is the possibility of a prisoner's dilemma here which might lead to the voting decision being the one which is binding. Suppose a proposal is made to tax everyone in the United States, who has more than $6000 a year income, $100 for the purpose of distributing it to the poor. Each person might feel that his vote carried practically no weight and that he could gain some pleasure from voting for charitable activity, and hence vote for it. This would mean that the act would pass and everyone would in fact be charged $100. Note that there is no miscalculation here. As in the usual prisoner's dilemma, the individual would be correct in his assessment of the cost to him of voting for or against this tax. The aggregation of the votes would mean, however, that he would find himself in the lower right instead of the upper left hand corner of the prisoner's dilemma matrix, and would put out more money for charity than he really wants to. He is attempting to buy at a discount the feeling of satisfaction which comes from a 'charitable act', and finds that he has to pay the full price.

Thus this line of reasoning would indicate that voting on charitable issues might lead to vast over-investment in charity. I doubt that this is so, however. Firstly, the particular pattern of drives that leads to the type of internal cognitive dissonance reduction which I have been describing is limited pretty largely to the upper classes. We intellectuals are the primary holders of these attitudes and we, together with our colleagues among the WASPs and upper-class Jews, make up only a minority of the population. The blue-collar majority are much less prone to this type of thinking, and hence we are free to cast votes in this way without its actually costing us very much.

There is, however, another phenomenon that might conceivably put us in the prisoner's dilemma. Intellectuals, for reasons I shall explain below, may not actually vote for charity, but they certainly talk about it a great deal. In the average university community the individual who said flatly that he is opposed to charity because he likes to spend his money himself would be subject to very large private costs. On the other hand, being in favour of various charitable activities and engaging in political activity in their behalf will normally have a distinct private payoff. Thus the average intellectual who might or might not be inclined to vote in the way we have described is certainly inclined to engage in political activity in favor of government charity. Over long periods of time this might change the general opinion of society, so that the government would become more charitable, and hence the prisoner's dilemma might exist in the long run by way of the opinion-forming process. I think that it does not, but my reasons for so thinking require a little more elaboration on the structure of our electoral system.

So far the model I have been using has assumed that there are direct votes on charitable transfers. We do not observe this in the real world. The actual situation in our democracy is that we vote only periodically, and that our vote conveys relatively little information in the technical sense to the politician. The politician offers a whole collection of issues and proposals to the electorate, and is elected or not elected in terms of the whole complex. Thus the weight of his stand on any given issue in determining his election is hard to determine. In general, however, it seems fairly clear that most politicians regard transfer of funds by government process as *mainly* a way of purchasing the votes of the people *who receive the funds*, not of those people who might be charitably interested in the well-being of such people.

Thus a politician soliciting the vote of university professors will normally make a number of remarks about how we must help the poor. This is, however, merely an effort to reduce the 'cognitive dissonance' in the professor's mind. What actually counts is his emphasis on how important he thinks it is that research be stimulated, that education receive larger funds, that the income tax law be provided with even more loopholes than it now has for academics, etc. The academic is normally quite capable of rationalizing all these things into a charitable activity, particularly if the candidate also makes some remarks about helping the poor. The end product is not that the prisoner's dilemma which I have been describing leads to an over-investment in charity, but that the various pressure groups – including the pressure group of the intellectuals – get very large transfers.

This phenomenon has led me to speculate on whether the poor might not do better if they depended on pure charity, rather than on an attempt to use the weight of their votes to acquire funds. It seems to me conceivable that if *all* persons who receive a significant part of their funds from any government unit were deprived of any vote in electing that government unit, the poor would do better than they do now. However, this is mere speculation.

So far this paper has been descriptive and not normative. I fear, however, that the bulk of my readers will feel that it is essentially a denunciation of what I have described. They probably expect me now to provide a remedy. In fact I am not at all sure the situation requires a remedy. Individuals who are obtaining a feeling of being charitable without much real cost through their use of the political process are maximising their individual preferences, and would be injured, i.e., have a lower level of satisfaction, if they were compelled to make a more objectively accurate calculation of the real effects of their behavior. It is not obvious to me that democratic government should not provide this type of satisfaction to the voters.

For those, however, who are disturbed and wish to 'do something', I can suggest three possible courses of action. The first course of action – and the one which I am sure most persons who are disturbed by the paper will take – is simply to deny that it is true and go on happily reducing cognitive dissonance by the combination of being selfish in private expenditures and 'generous' in politics. For most, I think, this is the utility maximising course of action.

For those who find this impossible, there are two remaining possibilities. They can take action to bring reality into accord with what is said, i.e., they can try to make people be as charitable in their actions as they are in their language, or conversely, to make people talk as they act, i.e., change people's statements so that they are in fact descriptive of what they *do*, rather than mere expressions of loyalty to the prevailing ideals. I myself would prefer the latter and, indeed, I suspect that if we could somehow carry it out, the poor would actually get rather more money than they do now. Granted that transfer to the poor is now muddled up with truly massive transfers to other people, the voter quite rationally tries to restrict the total volume of the transfer. I think if permitted to vote on direct payments to the poor, he would probably choose to give them more. This, of course, is a guess.

Thus, if it is thought that it is desirable to do something about the situation which I describe, I suggest that it is easier to change the way we talk than to change the way we behave. Further, if we do change the way we talk, we shall be better informed about the real world (including the preferences of ourselves and our friends), and hence likely to behave in a more effective manner. The poor, along with the rest of us, would benefit from the change.

16

Economic justice and the economist

RICHARD A. POSNER

≠

IN a recent issue of *The Public Interest* (vol. 31, Spring 1973), Lester Thurow, an economist at the Massachusetts Institute of Technology, argued that economic justice requires radical changes in the distribution of income and wealth in this country, and proposed specific redistributive measures. I shall argue three points here:

(*a*) The measures proposed by Thurow are highly questionable.

(*b*) There is no basis in economics for the concept of economic justice from which these measures are derived.

(*c*) The economist has an important role to play in a study and discussion of the distribution of income and wealth, but it is not the role that Thurow set for himself.

Thurow's specific proposals are as follows:

(1) The federal minimum wage (now $1.60 an hour, with a number of exemptions) would be increased to $2.50 an hour, the level at which every fully employed worker would earn at least $5000 a year. Presumably the exemptions in the present minimum wage law (for domestic workers, some farm workers, employees of very small businesses, and a few other groups) would be eliminated.

(2) The federal government would offer employment at the minimum wage to anybody who wanted to work full time and could not find a job in the market.

First published in *The Public Interest*, Vol. 33 (1973), pp. 109–19.

For Notes and References, see page 393 below.

(3) A tax on 'wealth and/or inheritance' would be imposed, designed to bring about the same distribution of wealth (i.e., property) as found in the earnings of white, male, fully employed workers. Thurow considers this distribution an appropriate 'interim equity goal'. The brackets and rates of the tax would be set so as to reduce the wealth of the wealthiest 14.5 per cent of American families, who according to Thurow now have between 60 and 70 per cent of the nation's wealth, to 28.5 per cent of that wealth, because this is the percentage of the annual earnings of white, male, fully employed workers that goes to the highest-paid 14.5 per cent of those workers.

These proposals would, if implemented, create costly dislocations in the economy, and in the society as a whole. As of April 1970, fully 43 per cent of all private non-farm, non-supervisory workers were earning less than $2.50 an hour, while the *median* wage of farm workers was much less than $2.50 an hour. A large number of studies of the employment effects of minimum wage laws have found, not surprisingly, that increases in the minimum wage cause unemployment.[1] And these were studies of much smaller increases than those proposed by Thurow. Moreover, the minimum wage law has always exempted the occupations in which the adverse effect on employment of imposing a minimum wage would be most serious. Thurow's proposal would eliminate these exemptions. One does not know just how many of the more than 20 million workers affected by the proposal would lose their jobs. But the number could be substantial – would almost surely be in the millions – and would be concentrated among the marginally employable, such as black teenagers and middle-aged women first entering the labor force; for we know from previous studies of the employment effects of the minimum wage that these groups are especially vulnerable.

Thurow, a labor economist, must know all this, which is presumably why he also proposes to require the federal government to offer jobs to all those who cannot find work. But he seems oblivious to the practical difficulties of implementing such a proposal. Once the Thurow proposal for a universally applicable $2.50 hourly minimum wage became effective, all sorts of people, all over the country (and especially in the South, where wages are lowest), would find themselves without work – farm workers, domestic help, dishwashers, sales clerks, soda jerks, delivery men, elevator operators, charwomen, rest-room attendants, and so on. They, together with people able to obtain only part-time employment at the minimum wage, would present themselves to the nearest federal office and demand work. How would the government respond? It could buy and operate restaurants, grocery stores, fruitstands, home-maintenance services, and farms in order to be able to offer workers made jobless by the minimum wage (or unable to find full-time employment at that wage) the same kind of work that they had previously done, and in the same places. This seems a highly inefficient, indeed an impracticable alternative. Then again, the government could offer these people jobs as postmen, clerks in army commissaries, orderlies in Veterans Administration hospitals, and the like. This latter alternative – a massive expansion in distinctively 'public-sector' jobs – seems to be what Thurow actually has in mind. All other objections aside, the huge costs of relocating large numbers of workers from private-sector to public-sector jobs, often in different localities, seem a decisive objection.

Alternatively, the government could simply pay the employers of workers now paid less than the statutory minimum the difference between their wage and the minimum; but this approach is also open to serious practical objection. The employer of such workers would have a powerful incentive to maintain wages at the lowest possible level (or even to reduce them) in order to maximise the government's subsidy of his labor costs. Clearly, he would never raise the wage of a worker whose competitive wage was lower than the statutory minimum, so the government's subsidy would rise over time as increases in general wage levels required increases in the statutory minimum. And the incentive for employers to upgrade the skills of their working force would be reduced, since if the market wage rate of the workers rose above the statutory minimum the employers would cease to receive any subsidy. The approach would assure the continued existence of a sizable class of marginal workers.

A related but more general criticism of Thurow's proposal is that it would reduce the incentive of marginal workers to improve their skills. The worker who today earns $3000 a year has a stong incentive to upgrade his skills to the point where he can earn $5000. Under Thurow's proposal he would have no such incentive, because his reward would be zero.

Thurow's proposal would have other consequences. Firms that employ workers at wages less than the proposed minimum would react by (*a*) increasing their wages, (*b*) discharging workers and either curtailing output or substituting capital for labor inputs, or (*c*) doing a little of each. Whichever course was followed, the cost of production would rise. At least part of the increase would be reflected in higher prices to consumers. And taxes would have to be raised in order to defray the costs to the federal government of employing all those made unemployable by the increase in, and extension of, the minimum wage.

1. At a guess, the wealth tax proposed by Professor Thurow would be even more dislocating. Assuming that the average size of wealthy families is not much different from the size of other families (actually it is slightly smaller), the 14.5 per cent wealthiest American families must comprise about 30 million people. Very few of them are really wealthy: A survey conducted in 1963 showed that, as of December 31, 1962, only 6.7 per cent of US households had a net worth of $50,000 or more. In the $50,000-$99,000 bracket, where two thirds of these 'wealthy families' fell, 23 per cent of the average family's net wealth was accounted for by home and automobile ownership.[2] Most such families are not what we have in mind when we speak of 'the rich', yet all of them would be forced to surrender to the government 50 per cent of their net worth.*

A by-product of the tax would be a change in spending patterns. Since people would not be permitted to accumulate

---

* Thurow does not indicate how the burden of the wealth tax would be allocated among people subject to it, but he implies that it would be allocated evenly, since he indicates a concern with possible Constitutional objections to taking away more than half of a person's wealth. If the group as a whole must reduce its wealth by one half, and no member is to be forced to give up more than one half of his wealth, then obviously every member's wealth must be reduced by exactly one half.

much money, they would have an incentive to substitute expenditures on consumption for savings. An extravagant style of living would be encouraged and the apparent inequality of income and wealth thereby increased. To encourage extravagance by the rich seems an odd way to promote economic justice.

By labeling his tax a wealth 'and/or inheritance' tax, Thurow implies that the desired redistribution of wealth could perhaps be accomplished by an inheritance tax alone. But even a 100 per cent inheritance tax would not achieve Thurow's purpose, since only a small fraction of the wealthiest 14.5 per cent of American families owe their wealth to inheritance. The Projector and Weiss study found that, even among families with $500,000 or more in wealth, only 34 per cent reported that inheritance accounted for a substantial portion of their wealth; for the $50,000-$99,000 bracket, the figure was only 12 per cent. A very steep inheritance tax would also create the undesirable incentive, just noted, to substitute consumption for savings. (A corollary is that the tax would yield little revenue.)

A striking feature of Professor Thurow's program is that it contains no provisions designed to benefit the millions of people who are incapable, for whatever reason, of full-time work. The program he proposes would actually make them worse off than they are now, since the higher minimum wage would, as mentioned earlier, increase the cost and hence prices of goods.

The subordination of the interests of the non-working poor and of consumers to the interests of workers, and the preoccupation with expropriating property, place Professor Thurow's proposals in the Marxist tradition. Marxists do not want to solve specific social problems; they want to turn society upside down. His proposals would do that. And these are only 'interim' proposals!

2. Thurow's program of redistribution is offered as the fruit of an economic analysis of the problem of the just distribution of income and wealth. However, in presenting and justifying the program, Professor Thurow is not speaking as an economist, and his proposals have no support in economic theory.

The opening pages of his essay suggest that economic theory does not yield a definition of the just distribution of income and wealth. This is true, and might well have served to end the essay, since Thurow's professional competence is as an economist. But he does not stop there, because he regards the unwillingness of the economist to define the just distribution of wealth as both a source of reproach to the profession* and a 'cop-out', since in his view economic analysis rests ultimately on postulates concerning just distribution. It does not.

For example, when an economist says that monopoly is less 'efficient' than competition, he means that the value of an industry's output, as measured by the willingness of consumers to pay for that output, is greater under a competitive than under a monopolistic organisation of production, since a monopoly price will induce some consumers to substitute a product that costs society more to produce than the monopolised product. If you happen not to like the consumers who are hurt by the monopoly price – the product may be yachts and the consumers rich people – you may prefer the less efficient to the more efficient organisation of yacht production. There is no inconsistency in having such a preference: 'More efficient' is not a synonym for 'better'. Economics is a science of means; it does not prescribe ends. An economist who declares that efficiency should be the paramount value of society steps out of his professional role. Thurow is thus incorrect in saying that efficiency 'ceases to have any meaning' unless certain 'ethical' postulates such as 'more is better' are accepted. Even if we were to stipulate that less is better, and the optimum output of the economic system zero, it would still be true that monopoly is inefficient because it reduces the value of output. Efficiency would still be a meaningful term, and its meaning would be, in fact, unchanged. To be sure, we might wish to define a new term, 'efficiency', having the opposite property to efficiency: It would be maximised when the value of output was minimised,

* The essay begins, 'Modern economics springs from the search for a definition of economic justice, but has largely abandoned that search.' This is an eccentric definition of the springs of modern economics. Modern economics is rooted in the interest of Smith, Ricardo, Marshall, and others in the operation of economic markets.

and vice versa. And we might be more interested in 'efficiency' than in old-fashioned efficiency. Efficiency is a widely used criterion in discussions of public policy because most people still believe that the maximisation of value is an important goal of society. But even if no one believed this, no part of economic theory would be invalidated as a result.

Thurow's deep confusion between facts and values is evidently responsible for such statements as that it is 'necessary for a market economy to start with a "just" distribution of economic resources', and that 'there is no way to avoid the problem of specifying economic equity'. Let us stipulate that the distribution of economic resources is unjust: The economic properties of the markets in which the unjustly endowed buyers and sellers meet would be unaffected. Of course we could not say that the outcomes of their interactions are 'just', but it is not the economist's business to characterise the justice of various outcomes.

Although Thurow holds that economics cannot escape from having to grapple with the problem of the just distribution of wealth, he apparently thinks it proper for the economist, in grappling with the problem, to escape from economics. His definition of the just distribution of wealth owes little to economics but much to an unspecified mélange of public opinion polls, introspection, and political hunches.

The key to his analysis is the concept of 'individual-societal preference'. This is an individual's preference for how the wealth and income in the society should be divided up, and is to be distinguished from the individual's 'personal-private preference', which determines what goods he buys, where he works, and so on. The just distribution of income and wealth is determined by adding up people's individual-societal preferences. Unfortunately, this is difficult to do. An advantage of economic markets is that they enable preferences to be determined in a generally reliable manner. If I say that I prefer a cheap foreign import to an expensive American car, but then buy the latter, the purchase speaks louder than the words. Willingness to pay provides more credible evidence of preference than willingness to say. It also provides a means of weighting preferences by their intensity: Scarce goods are assigned to the people willing to pay the most for them. The ascertainment and weighting of preferences in the absence of markets is extraordinarily difficult. The democratic political process is the normal alternative in our society – and a growing literature documents its numerous and serious deficiencies as a method of revealing the preferences of the electorate. Its use in place of the market should be carefully circumscribed.

Professor Thurow does not identify the mechanism by which 'individual-societal' preferences are authoritatively determined. We are left to infer his idea of the appropriate mechanism from such language as: 'socially, we simply decide . . .'; 'an act of social judgment'; 'studies in this area indicate that individuals have a very strong feeling . . .'; 'popular beliefs'; 'many societies – including ours – seem to think . . .'; 'my interpretation of our society's revealed preferences'; 'a general perception'. Formulations that personify society, such as 'societies . . . seem to think', obscure the problem. It is precisely because society is *not* a sentient, articulate individual that 'social choice', outside of economic markets, remains so elusive a concept.

3. It does not appear that Thurow looks to the democratic political process to reveal our individual-societal preferences. Plainly, the preferences revealed by that process are for a good deal less economic equality than Thurow believes just. Yet political feasibility is mentioned frequently. I note in this connection, unkindly, that Thurow was one of Senator McGovern's principal economic advisers in the 1972 Presidential campaign – not very good credentials for a political seer. The lesson Thurow draws from the 1972 campaign débâcle is in any event a peculiar one: The voters were unwilling to support massive redistributions, by means of taxes and subsidies, to the non-working poor; *therefore* they could be induced to support a more drastic redistribution of income and wealth accomplished through a combination of stiffer minimum wage laws and more extensive federal government employment with heavy wealth taxes. This view reflects a certain contempt for the thinking processes of American voters. Anyone who resents using taxes to support people who do not work should, as a matter of consistency,

also resent using taxes to pay someone $5000 a year for work worth only $1000 or $2000 in the market, and will view massive federal employment programs as boondoggles for the unproductive.

Thurow's discussion of 'wage contours' is relevant here. If it is true, as he says, that 'different groups of workers expect . . . to have a fixed structure of wages with respect to other groups', then it follows that a sharp increase in the wages of the lowest-paid workers, as proposed by Thurow, would lead the next tier of workers to insist on a wage increase that would maintain the 'historic differential' between their wages and those of the workers below them on the wage ladder. The demand for higher wages would travel upward through the entire ladder, leading to a general increase in prices, which in turn would require a further increase in the minimum wage, which then would kick off a new cycle of wage increases.

Thurow has also forgotten that Senator McGovern was forced by popular pressure to back off from proposing higher death taxes. The real lesson of the McGovern campaign is that most people do not believe that the distribution of income and wealth in this country is fundamentally unjust and they are unwilling to incur heavy costs to bring about a substantially more equal distribution. I think that Thurow realises this, and that when he says 'society thinks', he does not mean that his views would be supported in a public opinion poll or at the ballot box. Thurow must believe, rather, that our individual-societal preferences are authentically determined not by democratic political processes but by the opinion of an elite. Popular opinion is to be consulted only to assure that the goals of the elite are not so far in advance of popular opinion as to be wholly unattainable. The aim of his essay is to repackage the redistributive program of Senator McGovern in a form more palatable to the average person. But his approach can be effective only if the average person is easily deceived.

Because 'society's' preference for massive redistribution rests ultimately on the views expressed by the small minority of educated and well-to-do people who dominate the Left in this country, it is important for Thurow to reassure the reader that there is no contradiction between wanting to maximise one's personal wealth (the usual personal-private preference) and wanting to have society changed in a way that will significantly reduce that wealth. The difference between a 'personal-private' and an 'individual-societal' preference is clear enough in principle. But I, at least, would have difficulty identifying the authentic preference of someone whose personal-private and individual-societal preferences were not merely distinct, but opposite and indeed mutually exclusive. Imagine an individual who is grasping, ungenerous, and ruthlessly acquisitive in his personal and business dealings but who, if asked, will say that he supports a restructuring of society that would result in a drastic reduction in his relative and absolute wealth and income. Does such a person *really* prefer an egalitarian society? Do not his actions speak louder than his words? Is it not likely either that he is a hypocrite or that deep down he believes that in the restructured society his wealth and income (not necessarily pecuniary) would be greater than they are now?

Thurow's program rests on a weak foundation: the avowals, which only the credulous would take at face value, of a small and unrepresentative segment of the American people. He would be on firmer ground if he abandoned the pretense that his program is founded on people's preferences. He is telling people what they should think, not what they do think (which is again in the Marxist tradition). In any event his proposals owe nothing to economics.

4. The two gravest weaknesses in Thurow's essay are ones that he shares with most proponents of redistributing income and wealth, and therefore deserve special attention. They are the failure to define economic equality correctly and the failure to weigh the costs of redistribution against its benefits.

Thurow assumes that the distribution of annual money incomes among household units constitutes a reasonable measure of economic equality. It does not. Consider first the problem of the intertemporal distribution of earnings. Two workers, a carpenter and a baseball player, have the same lifetime earnings, but the first has a steady income every year while the lifetime earnings of the second are bunched in a few years. In any given year the earnings of the two will be highly unequal; and in a table of annual earnings, they will contribute to an impression of inequality. But there is no meaningful inequality between them. A related point is that a table of annual earnings will include the earnings of a young worker just starting out and a worker in his prime. The earnings of the two will be highly unequal; yet again, their lifetime earnings may be identical.

Consider next the differential investment in human capital (earning capacity). A dentist has higher lifetime earnings than a plumber. But the dentist may have borrowed money to go to college and dentistry school, and the difference between his lifetime earnings and the plumber's may be merely equal to the amount required to repay the loans with interest, plus the dentist's forgone earnings while in college and dentistry school. Differential investment in human capital may explain much of the difference between male and female earnings. If most women prefer to remain at home while their children are young, it follows that they will spend less time in the work force than men. Their lower potential lifetime earnings will induce them to invest less in their earning capacity, so their annual earnings (which include repayment of, as well as return on, investment in human capital) will be lower. Their shorter time in the work force will also lead employers to invest less in training them, with similar results.

Another important factor is uncertainty of earnings, and taste for or against risk. Suppose that a successful inventor has an average income of $100,000 a year but only one out of ten inventors is successful (the rest have zero incomes from inventing). Then the average earnings of inventors will be only $10,000 a year and this is the correct figure to use in comparing inventors' incomes with those, say, of civil servants. Suppose, in addition, that people are 'risk-averse', preferring the certainty of earning $10,000 a year, for example, to a 10 per cent chance of earning $100,000 a year. If so, it will be necessary to compensate people for bearing risk. Society may have to pay successful inventors $150,000 a year before inventing becomes as attractive a career as civil service. The civil servant with his $10,000 income and the successful inventor with his $150,000 income will contribute to the statistical impression of economic inequality; in fact, their incomes are not unequal in any meaningful economic sense.

Still another very important factor is attitude toward deferred income. A high school graduate must choose between continuing in school, thereby deferring the production of income for several years, or beginning to work immediately. The additional education will enable him to obtain a higher income; but the additional income, as we saw earlier, is not pure gravy – it includes the repayment, with interest, of his investment (chiefly in the form of forgone earnings during the period of education) in earning capacity. If he attaches a very high time value to money – if a dollar today is worth much more to him than a dollar tomorrow – the return on such an investment may not compensate him for the present earnings that he will have to forgo. He will prefer to begin work immediately, even though his lifetime earnings will be lower. Income inequality is thus partly a matter of choice.

5. Finally, money income does not adequately measure real income. Consider two families, one where both husband and wife work and earn $10,000 each, and the other where only the husband works, and earns $10,000. The real income of the first family may be lower, not higher, than the real income of the second. The wife in the second family may be staying home because her services in the home are thought to be worth more than the income she would receive in a job outside the home. Suppose she could earn $12,000 in such a job. Then her services in the home (ignoring the tax advantages of non-market income) must be worth at least $12,000, making the family's real income $22,000. Or consider two construction workers, one of whom receives higher wages but has a more dangerous job. His higher wage is simply compensation for the higher expected accident costs in the more dangerous job, but it contributes to the statistical impression of economic inequality.

Income to the economist is a different concept from *monetary earnings*. It includes leisure and all sorts of other non-pecuniary yields from activity that are excluded in measures of pecuniary earnings, and it excludes repayment of human capital, compensation for risk, interest or deferred earnings, and other items that the statistical aggregates count as income. It is the economic concept of income that is relevant in appraising economic equality. The economic concept is poorly approximated by the kind of measure that Thurow uses.

Thurow treats the distribution of wealth as a measure of economic equality distinct from and coequal in importance to the distribution of income. This procedure would be defensible if he defined wealth properly, but he does not. A person's wealth is the present value of all of his future earnings, pecuniary and non-pecuniary (less the costs involved in the production of those earnings). The value of a home is the present value of its imputed rental income; the value of jewelry is the present value of the non-pecuniary income, in the form of pleasure, that the jewelry yields; the value of a share of stock is the present value of its expected dividends and capital gains. These forms of wealth are included in the statistics on which Thurow relies – but the most important is excluded: human capital or earning capacity. Were it included, the distribution of wealth would not be, as Thurow asserts, much more unequal than the distribution of income.

If income and wealth were correctly measured – as an economist would measure them – we could evaluate Thurow's premise that there is serious economic inequality among people who work. He has failed to establish this premise. And he considers only one type of cost associated with altering the distribution of income and wealth: the reduced incentive to work associated with heavy income taxes. He wholly ignores the costs of the redistributive measures that *he* proposes – the extension of the minimum wage, the expansion of public employment, and the tax on wealth. All of these are costly measures. His minimum wage proposal would, by raising the price of much labor far above market levels, reduce the efficiency with which labor is used in production. Employers would substitute methods of production that were cheaper to them, given the artificially high price of labor, but more costly to the society than the methods that had been displaced. Workers would be shifted from private-sector to government jobs, in which their labor would probably be less productive (otherwise the shift would presumably have taken place already). The heavy tax on wealth would induce costly adaptations designed to reduce its impact. It would also weaken the incentive to engage in various high-risk activities – such as starting new companies – that are economically feasible only because success is highly rewarded. True, the entrepreneurial role could be taken over by the government, but the experience of the Communist countries suggests that this would be highly inefficient.

The fact that the redistribution of income and wealth along the lines proposed by Thurow would have very high costs is not a decisive objection against his proposals. But in measuring those costs, Thurow would have contributed to an understanding of the issues involved in distributive policy.

6. The last point suggests the essential failing of Thurow's essay. He has refused to respect the division of labor between economists and other students of society. Economics is a positive science. The economist has an important contribution to make to the debate over the appropriate distribution of income and wealth, but it is descriptive rather than normative. He can measure economic equality, or at least point out the limitations of the conventional indices; he can attempt to explain the real inequality that he finds; he can assess the distributive effects of various policies; and he can estimate the costs of various redistributive measures. Thurow does none of these things. He attempts instead to prescribe the just distribution; and this is a matter outside of his competence as an economist.

Finally, I am puzzled by the fact that nowhere in his essay does Thurow suggest a reason why a much greater equality of income and wealth would be a good thing for our society. He does not claim that society would be wealthier, happier, or politically more stable as a result – and none of these conclusions is self-evident. He does not claim that the well being of the people who would benefit from the redistribution is more important than that of the people who would lose from the redistribution. He takes for granted the desirability of redistributing income and wealth, and discusses only methods and tactics. While I have concentrated on what seem to me to be serious errors in his analysis, I am above all struck by his having ignored the fundamental question of what society would gain by achievement of his 'interim' redistributive goals.

17

The grail of equality

PETER BAUER

≠

WHY, in free and open societies such as those of Western countries, are some people better off than others: not necessarily wiser, nicer, happier or more virtuous, but better off? The causes of differences* in income and wealth are complex and various, and people will always disagree on how they apply to particular societies, groups or individuals. But, in substance, such differences result from people's widely differing aptitudes and motivations, and also to some extent from chance circumstances. Some people are gifted, hard-working, ambitious and enterprising, or had far-sighted parents, and they are therefore more likely to become well-off.

But whatever the causes of the economic differences in an open and free society, political action which deliberately aimed to minimise, or even remove, these differences would entail such extensive coercion that the society would cease to be open and free. The successful pursuit of the unholy grail of economic equality would exchange the promised reduction or removal of differences in income and wealth for much greater actual inequality of power between rulers and subjects. There is thus an underlying contradiction in the declared objective of egalitarianism in open societies.

For the Reference, see page 393 below.

* I use the term 'differences' rather than 'inequalities' – except in the context of political power – for reasons I shall go into later. Also, I use 'differences in income and wealth', or more simply 'income differences', interchangeably with 'economic differences'.

1

When social scientists talk of social problems, they usually mean discrepancies between social reality and what they assume to be norms. Because they are largely preocupied with discerning, announcing and emphasizing discrepancies between the norms they assume and reality, social scientists tend to generate social problems rather than solve them. This way of looking at social situations and reading problems into them is evident in the persistent and extensive concern of egalitarians with economic differences.

In recent years, there has been a vast upsurge of interest in the subject of these differences: witness, in Britain, the Standing Royal Commission on the Distribution of Income and Wealth (Diamond Commission, 1975–79), and, throughout the West, the research activities and publications of academics, the contents of university curricula, and the preoccupations of journalists, broadcasters, and other popularisers.

The appeal of egalitarianism is likely to persist. As Tocqueville observed, when social differences diminish – as they have diminished in the West – those which remain appear especially irksome and objectionable; and as he also pointed out, material advance is apt to engender discontent over failure to have achieved some other objective. The contemporary predilection for numbers and quantification, and also the emphasis on material conditions, have further helped to focus attention on economic differences.

The pervasive influence of the machine and of mass production points in the same direction. The criterion of uniformity for judging the efficiency of the machines used in mass production reinforces any philosophical appeal which egalitarianism may have. An efficient lathe, mould or press is designed to turn out identical products. Even small differences give grounds for criticism. This attitude may have had a powerful, if unconscious, influence on our attitudes to social matters

Once the moral and political case for egalitarian policies is taken for granted, the movement for egalitarianism feeds on itself. If the results of egalitarian policies are deemed favourable, it is evidence that still more could be achieved by further and sterner measures; if on the other hand the policies are deemed to have failed, it is evidence that they were not drastic enough. Such reactions are fostered when it is widely assumed that the economic positions of people are properly the concern of official policy.

Political power enables rulers forcibly to restrict the choices open to their subjects. Possession of wealth, on the other hand, does not confer such coercive power in this crucial sense. Wealth can sometimes secure a degree of political influence, although the likelihood and significance of this possibility are apt to be much exaggerated. In any case, wealth as such does not imply coercive power. Indeed, those who are rich are vulnerable to envy and to criticism founded on an unreasoning presumption in favour of economic equality. These attitudes have at times led to the persecution and even destruction of productive or prosperous groups, often ethnic minorities. Possession of wealth offers no sure protection against such dangers. Moreover, the effort usually required for economic success is apt to divert the attention of the rich from political affairs; and ability to accumulate wealth is often accompanied by an indifference to political opportunities, or a failure to recognise political dangers.

In an open society, income differences normally reflect the operation of voluntary arrangements. The absence of coercive power in most forms of successful economic activity is recognised in Samuel Johnson's familiar observation that 'there are few ways in which a man can be more innocently employed than in getting money'. This conclusion is particularly evident in a modern open society. In these societies the accumulation of wealth, especially great wealth, normally results from activities which extend the choices of others, as is clear from the fortunes acquired in, say, mass retailing or the development of the motor car.

2

People differ in economic aptitudes as they do in artistic, intellectual, musical and athletic abilities. In particular, they differ in their ability to perceive and utilize economic opportunities. Readiness to take advantage of economic opportunities is of great significance in explaining economic differences in open societies. This should be evident on a little reflection. The opportunities seized by such men as Thomas Edison, Henry Ford, Lord Northcliffe or Sir Isaac Wolfson were open to most people in their countries. The same applies elsewhere; witness the many Chinese and Japanese *nouveaux riches* in the East. Income differences resulting from readiness to benefit from economic opportunities will be especially wide if there is rapid social, economic and technical change, including the development of new products and the opening up of new markets.

Chance often plays a part in economic life, and thus in the emergence and perhaps persistence of income differences. But this is no different from other fields of human endeavour. Pasteur's celebrated observation that chance visits the prepared mind applies as much to economic life as it does to scientific activity.

An unfounded belief in the basic equality of people's economic faculties has coloured the language of the discussion. If people are assumed to be equally endowed and motivated, then wide economic differences suggest that some undefined but malevolent force has perverted the course of events. Of course, people are not equally motivated or endowed in their economic attitudes and attributes, and this explains substantial economic differences between them in open societies. This discrepancy between the unfounded belief (or assumption) and reality may partly account for the almost universal practice of describing differences as inequalities. Difference is plainly the more appropriate expression since it is neutral. It does not prejudge the issue – unlike the term inequality, which clearly suggests a situation that is unjust or otherwise objectionable. In recent years, inequality has come to be used interchangeably with inequity, and equality with equity. That difference is a more appropriate term than inequality is also suggested by the accepted practice of referring to people's physical characteristics, such as height and weight, as differences rather than inequalities, and under no circumstances as inequities.

On the other hand, the term inequality is appropriate in discussing political power because that power implies a relationship of command between rulers and subjects. As I suggested above, those who have political power can coerce others by restricting their choices, while wealth does not by itself confer such powers on the rich.

In contemporary parlance, social justice has come to mean substantially equal incomes. Why should this be so? It is not obvious why it should be just to penalise those who are most productive and contribute more to output, and to favour those who produce less. This conclusion is reinforced when it is remembered that relatively well-off people have often given up leisure, enjoyment and consumption, and that these past sacrifices have significantly contributed to their higher incomes. This is but one instance of a wider issue. Income differences or changes in income and the nature of poverty cannot be discussed seriously without examining how they have come about. Although this matter is central to an analysis of egalitarian ideas and proposals, further discussion of it is left until section 8 below, after other matters which are more prominent in the espousal and presentation of egalitarianism have been considered.

Advocates of redistribution propose that results of economic processes should be separated from the processes themselves, that people should share the fruits of economic activities in which they have not participated. The idea of equality over the past two centuries has progressed, or declined, from equality before the law, through equality of opportunity, to equality of result (or even equality of one quantifiable aspect of the result).

The demands to divorce the results of economic activity from the processes leading up to them are one facet of the contributory preoccupation with situations and the neglect of the antecedent sequences. Such practices reflect the unhistorical approach of much contemporary discussion of social issues, the amputation of the time dimension from our culture, to borrow from Sir Ernest Gombrich.

A given degree of concentration of income and wealth at a particular time has a very different meaning if the societies are fluid, such as, say, those of Malaysia or Western Europe, or more nearly stable or static as, for example, that of rural India.

This rather basic consideration rarely enters into egalitarian rhetoric. Moreover, for a rounded view of income differences, incomes have to be considered beyond one generation. Economic differences may be extended or reduced, or rankings of individuals or families maintained or reversed, over a span of a generation or two.* Again, this consideration is rarely reflected in discussions of income differences.

Egalitarians often suggest that the incomes of the rich, or property incomes, have been received at the expense of other people, rather than earned by supplying valuable resources. A familiar instance is the use of the term unearned income, when in fact such income is no less earned than is any other income.

Incomes, including those of the relatively prosperous or the owners of property, are not taken from other people. Normally they are produced by their recipients and the resources they own; they are not misappropriated from others; they do not

---

* A full assessment of changes in income differences over time is a complex exercise which requires examination of inter-generation as well as intra-generation changes, that is, changes in income differences between generations as well as those within a generation. The introduction of more than one generation into the analysis also implies that the income-receiving group must be thought of as extending beyond the family. (Otherwise consideration of more than one generation would imply marriages between brothers and sisters.) Take the case where group A and group B are drawn from the same generation; and let us assume that, whatever the relative position of A and B in any single year, the aggregated lifetime income of A exceeds that of B. In other words, there is a clear intra-generation difference. Now let us contrast two opposing situations; in the first, group A descendants have larger incomes than group B descendants but in the second the reverse is the case. We need not concern ourselves at this stage with the reasons why differences in incomes between specified groups may continue between generations or be reversed. But we can already note certain consequences. Taking first and second generation circumstances together, we clearly have a far less unequal income situation in the second case than in the first. Or, putting the same argument in another way, it is not sufficient to confine oneself to lifetime income comparisons: one needs also to know whether such differences are perpetuated or reversed over generations if we are to have a fully rounded view of income differences or inequalities in a society. (In the same way, unemployment statistics mean very different things if they relate to two people being out of work for short periods rather than to one for a long period.)

deprive others of what those others had, or could have had, or should have had.*

The misconception that the incomes of the well-off are somehow obtained by exploitation rather than earned has often had disastrous consequences: for instance, it has led to spurious justification of the expropriation, and even destruction, of economically productive groups to which I have already referred. The same misconception is behind the familiar references to shares (usually unequal shares) of different groups in the national cake, and behind assertions that certain groups have not shared in national or international prosperity – assertions which do not ask how much these groups may have contributed to it.

The terminology of the economic theory of distribution has a long history and a reputable ancestry. It has come to be accepted so generally that it is almost impossible not to use it. Nevertheless, the terminology is misleading. Distribution of income suggests a pre-existing income which somehow is parcelled out. But, as I have just noted, recipients of income normally produce their incomes: there is no distribution of income divorced from its production. Distribution also has a technical meaning in statistics (as, for instance, a normal distribution), which is quite different from the meaning of the term both in the theory of income and in egalitarian discourse. These different uses of the term should not be confused.

In a market economy, the production and distribution of income are two sides of the same process. Income will be equally distributed when people's contribution to it will be equal. The term redistribution is especially misleading because what is being 'redistributed' is not a pre-existing income. What happens in fact is that part of the income is removed from those who have produced it, and transfered to other groups.

The general proposition that incomes, including those of the well-to-do or of producers of services, are generated, produced and not taken from others, is subject to partial qualification. The incomes of some groups are often

---

* Certain specific exceptions which do not affect the substance of the argument are noted later in this section.

augmented by the exercise of monopoly power, which in most instances reflects barriers to entry, or other forms of restriction, erected or supported by the state. It has even been argued that state-supported restrictions have contributed materially to the extent of income differences in some Western societies, a contribution which would be eliminated if market forces were allowed freer play.

It is difficult to tell just how important a factor this is. In any event, it does not mean that the incomes of these favoured groups (other than the recipients of straight state subsidies) are not generated by their members; what it means is that restrictions enable these groups to charge more for their services than they could otherwise. But such a situation does not mean that high incomes are usually achieved at the expense of the rest of the community. The levels of income of particular groups do not by themselves indicate the presence or absence of restriction on entry. Successful businessmen, entertainers and athletes, for instance, can earn very high incomes even when they do not curtail their output, and when there are no contrived barriers to entry into their activities. Similarly, an expansion of demand can greatly increase the incomes of certain groups even when, again, there are no such barriers. On the other hand, even modest incomes of professional people, trade unionists, or farmers may be inflated by barriers to entry.

3

The policy termed redistribution benefits some people by confiscating part of the incomes of others. The beneficiaries may be poor, but this is by no means always so. Major beneficiaries of redistribution include its advocates, organisers and administrators, notably politicians and civil servants. This outcome promotes the self-perpetuation of the process. And once the notion is accepted that economic differences are somehow reprehensible, the door is opened to forcible intervention on any number of different and shifting grounds and criteria; these include differences in income or wealth, differences in their rate of change, and many others besides.

On the national level, the operation of the welfare state

comprises two quite different forms of redistribution: wealth transfers between groups, and redistribution of responsibility between the agents of the state and private citizens. Welfare state policies do not always redistribute income between the rich and the poor. They do not necessarily redistribute income even among individuals. The same people may be taxed at some times and subsidised at others.

The substantial taxes, including direct taxes, paid by the poor in the welfare states of the West make clear that, contrary to what is widely believed, the welfare state is not simply an agency of redistribution from rich to poor. In Britain in 1978 a single man earning £25 a week (less than one-half of the average unskilled wage) paid direct taxes. Those who earn the average wage of manual workers and have two children pay substantial direct taxes. Both categories also pay heavy indirect taxes.

The substantial taxation of the poor in countries which have extensive provision of social services is one facet of the confusion of redistribution of income with redistribution of responsibility just noted. By now, egalitarians and other supporters of social services often recognise explicitly that state-financed old-age pensions, health care, education, subsidised housing and food, welfare and unemployment payments and other social services do not represent solely or even primarily transfers from rich to poor. Heavy taxation of the poor, together with extensive provision of welfare services, reflects the self-perpetuating character of redistributive policies. The case for these continues to be taken for granted, even after it has become plain that to a considerable extent they benefit people other than the supposed beneficiaries.

Old age, ill-health, the bringing-up of children, housing, interruption of earnings, these are contingencies of life to be paid for out of one's income, and for which adults can be expected to provide by saving or insurance. In many Western countries, provision for these contingencies has come to be taken over largely by the state. Because the provision cannot be adjusted to the widely differing circumstances of individuals and families, it is apt to be both expensive and unsatisfactory. Such provision is necessarily financed by taxation. As a result, many people's post-tax income becomes like pocket-money, which is not required for major necessities and hazards of life, because these are paid for by taxes largely levied on themselves. This policy treats adults as if they were children. Adults manage incomes: children receive pocket-money. The redistribution of responsibilities implied in the operation of the welfare state means the reduction of the status of adults to that of children.

There is a further result of large-scale redistribution of responsibility between the agents of the state and private individuals, a result which acts as an anomalous and even ominous force for perpetuating and extending the policy. Prudent people, even if poor, can normally provide for the contingencies of life by saving and insurance, but only if the value of money is stable. They are unable to do so when this condition does not hold. The heavy state spending on the welfare state promotes inflation, the erosion of the value of money, a risk against which many people cannot protect themselves, certainly not by saving and insurance. The difficulty, or imposibility, of protecting themselves effectively leads them to accept or to demand that tax-financed provision for these contingencies should be maintained or extended, even if this is recognised to be unsatisfactory. The result greatly reinforces political, administrative and other sectional interests in perpetuating and extending the welfare system.

Many people receive in subsidies or government services broadly the same amount as they pay in taxes. But the two transfers do not simply cancel out, leaving things unchanged. People subject to them are still unable to escape certain adverse consequences of redistributive policies. First, taxation usually has some disincentive effects, and so may eligibility for subsidies. Second, people's ability to dispose of their incomes has been shifted from themselves to the politicians and officials who design and carry out such policies, and this reduces their range of choice in the disposal of their income.

Proposals for redistribution, supposedly in order to reduce differences in incomes, are also often pretexts for measures for the political or economic benefit of some persons or groups at the expense of others, with no certainty, or even presumption, of a reduction in conventionally measured differences in income. That they do not ensure even approximate economic equality is suggested by the experience of Communist countries. International comparisons of the distribution of incomes are fraught with conceptual and statistical problems, some of then intractable. But there are evident wide differences in income in Communist countries after decades of Communist rule. And in the Soviet Union (a country often thought to be dedicated to the removal of economic differences), the differences in income and living standards are quite as pronounced as in some more market-oriented societies – and this after more than half a century of mass coercion.

4

Equality of opportunity was until recently the principal theme of egalitarian ideology. For example, many Fabians, notably Tawney, thought that equality of opportunity would result in substantial equality of income; that any remaining differences would reflect merit, and would therefore be widely respected and readily accepted. These ideas by-pass the fundamental and intractable problem behind the central dilemma of egalitarianism: granted that equals should be treated equally, how shall we treat those who are unequally endowed, motivated or placed? For instance, loving parents and a cultivated background benefit those fortunate enough to possess them. Good looks and other such advantages result in unequal opportunities.

An open society, one with *la carrière ouverte aux talents,* is the most familiar interpretation of the ambiguous concept of equality of opportunity. The concept is then certainly and obviously incompatible with substantial equality of income and wealth. This is so because individuals and groups differ in economic aptitudes and motivations. These differences are evident in the rise from poverty to prosperity of countless individuals and groups the world over. They are evident also in the wide and persistent differences in prosperity between religious and ethnic groups in different areas and societies. Instructive examples include the economic success of certain communities in the face of adverse official discrimination, such as Nonconformists, Huguenots and Jews in the West, and the Chinese communities in South-East Asia. An open society may well bring about greater economic and social equality than a closed or caste society, but wide economic differences are bound to emerge and persist in it.

Only the belief that everybody's aptitudes and motivations are the same – a belief which can have sinister consequences – supports the notion that an open society is practically synonymous with economic equality, or at any rate promotes or ensures it. It is extraordinary that this notion should have been entertained for so long, and is often still entertained, when the evidence to the contrary is both overwhelming and obvious.

The idea that the economic aptitudes and motivations of all people are the same derives from the doctrine of the natural equality of man. According to this idea, we are all the same except for differences in money and education; the poor are like the rich except for having less money; and the peoples of the Third World, themselves all much the same, differ from those of the West only in being poorer.

This scheme of things envisages economic differences between people as being the only difference of any significance. At the same time, it is assumed that the differences can be removed without changing people's behaviour and without affecting their economic performance significantly. The continued belief that the persistence of economic differences in open societies is abnormal or accidental then leads to proposals and measures which go counter to equality before the law or to the maintenance of equality of opportunity – witness educational quotas on a racial basis in the United States and elsewhere.

The champions of equality in the sense of *la carrière ouverte aux talents* used to argue that income differences would be readily accepted once it became clear that they reflected achievement. This assumption, too, is facile. Lack of economic success is apt to be keenly felt and resented when economic achievement is thought to be important, and when failure is thought to result from inadequacy rather than from, say, an accident of birth. When faced with differences of economic achievement in an open society, many people react by denying that success reflects a contribution to society, let alone that it reflects merit. Such reactions have contributed to the denigration of market economies in open societies, because economic differences have persisted in them.

5

The adverse effects of redistributive policies on economic performance are implied in such expressions as trade-off between efficiency and equity, or between social justice and efficiency. These formulations recognise to some extent that economic activity is not a zero-sum game. But they still disguise the extent to which the outcome of economic processes depends on the performance of people – performance which can be promoted or obstructed by official policy.

I have already noted that it is by no means obvious why it should be unjust that those who produce more should enjoy higher incomes. And attempts to prevent them from doing so will affect adversely the average level of income. It will do so cumulatively because if everybody can expect to receive only something like an average of all incomes, this average itself will fall. A neat example of this process emerged from an experiment designed a few years ago by a teacher in an American university. The students demanded much greater equality in all walks of life, including the grading of their papers. In response to these demands, the teacher announced that from a given date the students would be given equal grades for their weekly papers, and that the grades would be based on the average performance of the class. The experiment brought about a rapid decline in average performance and thus in average grade, because the incentive to work declined greatly.

Because wide income differences have not disappeared in open societies, pressures for their further reduction or elimination have also continued. Hence the demands for increasing the scope and level of what is misleadingly termed redistributive taxation. It is misleading because, as I have noted earlier, it is not a pre-existing income that is being redistributed; rather, part of the incomes produced by some people is confiscated for the benefit of other people, including those who derive political or personal advantage from advocating or administering these arrangements. This last point, that the organisers and administrators of redistribution benefit from it, deserves attention. These beneficiaries are not poor and are indeed often prosperous, so that here also redistribution works in a fashion very different from what is usually assumed.

The imposition of more specific disabilities (additional to progressive taxation) on groups and individuals with cultural and personal characteristics favourable to economic success is now widely advocated and even practised. Special taxation of talented persons has been proposed on the argument that their talents should be regarded as communal property. Such proposals mean conscription of abilities, which is to some extent implicit in progressive taxation as well. The removal of children from their parents, and even attempted manipulation of the genetic code, have also been suggested as instruments for the promotion of equality, though dismissed at any rate for the time being. Quotas handicapping the ambitious and the gifted have already been widely adopted in higher education and in certain areas of economic activity in the United States.

There may be a further reason for the attempts to control and standardise the social and personal determinants of economic differences, as distinct from the attempts to equalise net incomes. An income serves two functions. First, it enables its recipient to buy goods and services. Second, it is an indicator of achievement, and a mark of recognition and status. The former rôle depends on net income. If differences in recognition or status are considered objectionable, this sets up pressure for equalising incomes before tax, and thus for controlling and standardising the factors behind them.

6

Attempts to minimise economic differences in an open and free society necessarily involve the use of coercive power. They politicise economic life: economic activity comes to depend largely on political decisions, and the incomes of people and their economic *modus vivendi* come increasingly under the control of politicians and civil servants. The extent of these consequences will depend on the degree of economic equality the rulers wish to achieve; and also on the capacities, ambitions and circumstances of the groups and individuals between whom economic differences are to be curtailed or abolished.

Extensive politicisation of life enhances the prizes of political power and thus the stakes in the fight for it. This outcome in turn intensifies political tension, at least until opposition is effectively demoralised, or forcibly suppressed. And because people's economic fortunes come to depend so much on political and administrative decisions, their talents and energies are diverted from economic activity to political life, sometimes from choice and often from necessity. These consequences are manifest in many societies, especially in multiracial societies.

In numerous countries, politicisation of life, often pursued in the name of equality, now means that the question of who are the rulers has become a matter of the greatest importance. The effect on people's fears, feelings and conduct is observable in many countries where there is some ethnic diversity, including the United Kingdom. It stands out starkly in the heterogeneous societies of the Third World, where the conduct of the rulers is often a matter of life and death for millions of people. The ferocity of the political struggle in many Third World countries cannot be understood without an awareness of the politicisation of life there. This process has been helped along by the slogans of equality, and reinforced by the idea that high incomes, especially of minorities, have not been earned but have been taken by them from other people.

When the inequality in political power between rulers and subjects is pronounced, conventional measurements of incomes and living standards cannot even remotely convey the substance of the situation. Such measurements greatly understate the realities of inequality in the society, in which the rulers can command the resources available practically at will. They may use their power to secure for themselves large incomes; or they may choose austere forms of life. They still have vast power over the lives of their subjects, which they can use to secure higher living standards for themselves whenever they wish. Dzerzhinski, Nasser and Nyerere have been among rulers whose relatively simple mode of life has elicited sycophantic adulation from their admirers. But their simple mode of life has not prevented them from combining it with the ruthless exercise of their virtually unlimited power over their subjects.

It is now widely urged that differences in income and living standards should be reduced or eliminated not only within countries but between them, and indeed even globally. There are the proposals for a New International Economic Order approved by the General Assembly of the United Nations. Because of the enormous and stubborn differences between peoples, policies designed to equalise their living standards would require world government with totalitarian powers. Such a government, to be equal to its ambitions, would be even more coercive and brutal than the totalitarian governments of individual countries.

The various adverse and often sinister consequences of the politicisation of life promoted by egalitarianism are widely ignored or swept under the carpet, even when they are both pronounced and evident. A major reason for this neglect is that egalitarians, including many academics, are more interested in advocating the removal of economic differences than in enquiring what is behind them; that is, how they have come about. Yet the background is indispensable for an understanding of the situations to which egalitarians address themselves, and for an assessment of the implications and results of egalitarian policies.

7

Economic differences are largely the result of people's capacities and motivations. This is evident in open societies, and also where societies are not open, nor yet completely closed or caste-bound. A disproportionate number of the poor lack the capabilities and inclination for economic achievement, and often for cultural achievement as well. Weak members of a society need to be helped. But large-scale penalisation of productive groups for the benefit of the materially and culturally less productive, and for the benefit of those who administer wealth transfers, impairs the prospects of a society. This outcome is especially likely when the less productive receive support without stigma and, indeed, as of right; and even more so when those who are more productive are made to feel guilty on that account. These are precisely the stances and attitudes prominent in the advocacy and practices of redistribution.

The terminology of the negative income tax reflects the acceptance of the principle of support without stigma. The payment of income tax is a statutory obligation. A negative income tax is the inverse: the right to an income regardless of performance, simply by virtue of being alive and poor.

Personal and group differences in economic aptitudes and motivations are likely to disappoint the expectation that guarantee of a cash income would make it possible to abolish specific welfare services. These services will still have to be supplied to the many recipients of cash payments who will nevertheless fail to provide for the contingencies of life. Such people are likely to be disproportionately represented among the recipients of negative income tax. In Britain this is suggested, for instance, by the prevalence of avoidable ill-health and dental decay among children of unskilled workers who own television sets.

Many recipients of both domestic and international wealth transfers are paupers, in the traditional sense of persons dependent on official charity. But because the support is given as of right and even envisaged as restitution for past wrongs, the paupers can not only insist on these transfers, but can attempt also to prescribe the political conduct of the donors. This is evident in the advocacy of international wealth transfers from the West to the Third World.

8

Some modern egalitarians seem readier than their predecessors to recognise personal and group differences in economic endowment and in motivation. This acknowledgement brings into the open previously ignored dilemmas. The recognition of such differences has also induced these egalitarians to advocate the elimination not only of economic differences but also of differences in aptitudes and motivations; that is, the causes of economic differences. Hence some of the policies and drastic proposals noted above.

Although acknowledgement of the determinants of economic differences has helped to clarify some central issues and dilemmas of egalitarian policies, in other ways the level of discourse has remained unsatisfactory. Indeed, in recent decades the standard may even have deteriorated.

The uncritical reliance on statistics in egalitarian discourse and policies provides a major illustration. There is, for instance, the familiar practice of expressing the income or wealth of a small proportion of the population of a country as a percentage of the income or wealth of the whole population. The misleading, even meaningless, nature of this practice should be evident. Thus children have no incomes, or very low incomes; people normally cannot make appreciable savings until well into middle age; and many married women have no cash incomes or only low cash incomes. Income differences need to be expressed on a basis which separates the different age groups, and also men from women. In technical language, the differences have to be expressed on an age or sex-standardised basis.

Further complexities and ambiguities ensue if we compare family incomes. A childless couple is likely to have a higher per capita income than a family with children. But it does not follow that the former is better off. The conventional method of calculating the national income implies that children are simply an unavoidable cost or burden, and assumes that people do not enjoy the generation and possession of children sufficiently to outweigh any differences in income per capita. It also results in paradoxes, such as the recording in many conventional national income calculations of the birth of a calf or the survival of a cow as an increase in per capita income, while the birth or survival of a child is registered as a diminution. Further problems arise over the definition of 'capita'. For example, should a child be treated as equivalent to half an adult? Moreover, conventional income comparisons do not distinguish adequately between income and the cost of securing income, for instance in such contexts as the cost of training, or of enjoyment forgone in training, or in long hours of work, or in the cost of travel to and from work. And professional people who have invested heavily in training which has enabled them to earn high incomes are disadvantaged in terms of real income compared with those who have used their time to learn to do things such as household repairs for themselves – a consideration of some significance when direct taxation and the cost of labour-intensive services are high.

State-provided or guaranteed pensions represent another example of the intractable conceptual difficulties behind assessment of economic differences. Such pensions can be very valuable to particular individuals, and they represent the equivalent of large capital sums, notably when they are index-linked. But they are unmarketable and thus cannot be turned into capital. And their value depends on the ability and willingness of future governments to honour them.

Finally, we now come to a wide issue, mentioned briefly earlier in this essay, which is crucial to an examination of income differences and changes. Even when income statistics are free of problems of concept and measurement, which is unusual, by themselves they tell us nothing about the background of the situation they reflect. It is indispensable for sensible assessment and policy to know why people are poor and how income differences have arisen. For instance, those who are poor through crippling disease or unavoidable or uninsurable accident, or erosion of savings through inflation, need to be treated differently from those people whose poverty has resulted from persistent overspending of large incomes. Again, incomes can become more equal as a result of more people dying or being forcibly sterilised. Yet conventional terminology describes the result as an 'improvement in income distribution'. Conversely, if more very poor people live longer, this registers as a so-called worsening of income distribution.

Some policies, popular beliefs and mores affect income differences between societies so greatly that they are central to any sensible discussion on such differences. The many obvious examples include the persecution of productive groups in Asia and Africa; the subordination of economic advance to egalitarian objectives as in Britain; the refusal to take animal life as in South Asia; or to let women work outside the home as in many Muslim countries. These pertinent matters are freely ignored by advocates of global redistribution who focus entirely on conventionally measured income differences. Altogether, we have become so preoccupied with quantifiable matters that even such an obvious distinction (and one formerly well-recognised) as that between sturdy beggars and needy poor has come to be neglected or even derided by egalitarians.

Disregard of such basic matters reflects the naive belief that statistics denote facts more effectively and more exactly than does qualitative description, or even that statistics alone objectively depict social facts. These habits of mind are of a piece with Mr Gradgrind's attitude in Dickens's *Hard Times*.*

Neglect of the time dimension of historical processes frequent in contemporary discourse (which I have briefly mentioned earlier) in references to international income differences is another highly misleading practice. Incomes and living standards in the West are the outcome of many centuries of cultural and economic progress; they have not come about in one or two generations. It is therefore not surprising, abnormal or reprehensible that many Third World countries (notably in Africa) which do not have centuries of progress behind them should have much lower incomes than the twentieth-century West. The pertinence of this long period of antecedent development is ignored in the advocacy of global redistribution. It is ignored also in the insistence that Third World countries should promptly reach Western levels of income by a process of virtually instant development. This insistence is apt to issue in coercive policies in these countries, which not only inhibit a rise in living standards but also provoke social tension, or even upheaval, as well as political conflict.

9

Redistribution of income and reduction of poverty are often thought to be interchangeable concepts. Indeed, it is often taken for granted that egalitarian policies necessarily improve the condition of the poor. This is not so. The promotion of economic equality and the alleviation of poverty are distinct

---

* 'Now, what I want is, Facts. Teach these boys and girls nothing but Facts. Facts alone are wanted in life. Plant nothing else, and root out everything else. You can only form the minds of reasoning animals upon Facts: nothing else will ever be of any service to them. This is the principle on which I bring up my own children, and this is the principle on which I bring up these children. Stick to Facts, sir!'

and often conflicting. To make the rich poorer does not make the poor richer.

The advocates of egalitarian policies focus on relative income differences, or the relative positions of different groups. They thereby divert attention from the causes of poverty, especially the causes which underlie real hardship; and from the possibilities of effective remedial measures. Relief of poverty, especially the improvement in the position of the very poor, has nothing to do with the pursuit of equality. Egalitarian policies often ignore the poor, especially those who are self-reliant and enterprising.

Except perhaps over very short periods, redistributive policies are much more likely to depress the living standards of the poor than to raise them. The extensive politicisation brought about by large-scale redistribution diverts people's energies and ambitions from productive economic activity to politics and public administration, and also to attempts to benefit from politically-organised redistribution, or to escape its consequences. An even more evident result is that these policies systematically transfer resources from people who are economically productive to others who are less so. Thus, such policies inhibit the rise in incomes and living standards, including those of the poor.

Besides these results of wide egalitarian policies, many specific measures thought to be egalitarian often benefit middle income groups at the expense both of the rich and the poor. This is the likely result of such policies as, for instance, the granting of privileges to trade unions, official prescription of minimal wages, the imposition of rent controls, restrictive licensing of enterprises, legislation for the promotion of so-called equal opportunities, and heavy direct taxation of persons and of enterprises.

In sum, the pursuit of economic equality is more likely to harm than to benefit the living standards of the very poor by politicising life, by restricting the accumulation and effective deployment of capital, by obstructing social and economic mobility at all levels, and by inhibiting enterprise in many different ways. Continued poverty, whether resulting from soi-disant egalitarian measures or from other causes, then serves as plausible argument or rationalisation for further and more stringent egalitarianism. These repercussions are necessarily ignored when the promotion of equality and the alleviation of poverty are regarded as identical.

10

Disregard of the restriction of the opportunities of the poor brought about by such policies is promoted by a curious asymmetrical application of that environmental determinism which underlies so much contemporary discourse of social affairs. The poor are seen as helpless victims of their environment, as people at the mercy of external forces and without wills of their own. The implication is that they are without the primary human characteristic of responsibility. This determinism, however, does not extend to the rich. They are seen as having wills of their own which are, however, deployed for selfish and even villainous ends. Poverty is thus a condition caused by external forces and not by personal conduct. Wealth, on the other hand, is the result of conduct which is purposeful but reprehensible. The poor are seen as passive but virtuous, the rich as active but wicked.

This picture is painted by certain groups who regard themselves as standing apart from rich and poor, and perhaps as above both. They are, in the main, politicians, social reformers, welfare administrators, social scientists, writers, artists, media people, churchmen and even entertainers. As noted in the introduction, they now form much of what was once called the political nation. In the advocacy of redistribution and its altogether misleading identification with the relief of poverty, a significant section of this new political nation operates in a manner which has been termed (I believe, by Dr R.M. Hartwell of Oxford University) the redistribution industry.

Many members of these groups, especially politicians, academics and media men, have in recent decades done much to articulate, institutionalise and organise envy and resentment against economically effective people. Envy and resentment may be as old as mankind;[1] but especially in the West and in the Westernised Third World countries, these sentiments seem nowadays more insistent, persistent and extensive than they had been formerly. Politicians and intellectuals have supplied articulation and a veneer of intellectual respectability to envy and resentment. They have argued that economic differences are abnormal and reprehensible, and also that they result from exploitation. And they have also advanced the cause of more esoteric arguments such as that of the diminishing marginal utility of money, and also by encouraging preoccupation with quantifiable matters, especially conventionally measured income differences. Also, the confirmation of spurious legitimacy on envy and resentment has been made easier by the wide-spread feeling of guilt. Unless arguments and rationalisations, which have played such a part in the articulation of envy and resentment in the name of equality, are exposed effectively, they may do irreparable damage to the prospects of a free and open society.

Notes and references

1 THE CASE AGAINST EQUALITY *William Letwin*

1. Some authors, other than those whose work is represented in this collection, who have recently challenged the egalitarian position are: Keith Joseph and Jonathan Sumption, *Equality* (London, 1979); G. Lowell Field and John Higley, *Elitism* (London, 1980); and Antony Flew, *Libertarians versus Egalitarians* (Berkeley, Cal., 1980).

2. Historical explanations recently offered for the rise of egalitarianism are: Gerhard Emmanuel Lenski, *Power and Privilege* (New York, 1966); and Earnest Gellner, 'The Social Roots of Egalitarianism', *Dialectics and Humanism*, 4 (1979), pp. 27–43.

3. For a recent compendium of critical essays on John Rawls, see N. Daniels (ed.), *Reading Rawls* (New York, 1976).

4. For a systematic analysis of income redistribution programmes in the United States and of their tendency to reduce incentives, see Martin Anderson, *Welfare* (Stanford, Cal., 1978).

5. An excellent critique of egalitarian theories of education is in David E. Cooper, *Illusions of Equality* (London, 1980). A useful compendium of American views is given in Donald M. Levine and Mary Jo Bane, *The 'Inequality' Controversy* (New York, 1975), which takes as its point of departure the study by Christopher Jencks et al., *Inequality* (New York, 1972; London, 1973, 1975).

6. A most thorough study of equality before the law, in the constitutional practice of the United States especially, including an admirable bibliographical spread, is given in P. G. Polyviou, *The Equal Protection of the Laws* (London, 1980).

7. An ingenious analysis of American statistics reaches a similar conclusion: see Morton Paglin, 'The Measurement and Trend of Inequality', *American Economic Review*, 65 (Sept. 1975), pp. 598–609. For a survey of statistical techniques, see F. A. Cowell, *Measuring Inequality* (London, 1977).

8. For the effect of chance on the outcome of investments and thus on the distribution of wealth, see E. Schwartz and J. A. Greenleaf, 'A Comment on Investment Decisions . . .', *Journal of Finance*, 33 (1978), pp. 1222–7.

2 AGAINST EQUALITY AGAIN *J. R. Lucas*

(References are reorganised and renumbered from the original.)

1. J. R. Lucas, 'Against Equality', *Philosophy*, 40 (1965), pp. 296–307; reprinted in Hugo A. Bedau (ed.), *Justice and Equality* (Englewood Cliffs, NJ., 1971), pp. 138–51.

2. I have given an essentially similar but fuller account in 'Equality in Education', in Bryan R. Wilson (ed.), *Education, Equality and Society* (London, 1975), pp. 40–3.

3. S. I. Benn, 'Egalitarianism and Equal Consideration of Interests', in J. Rowland Pennock and John W. Chapman (eds), *Nomos,* IX: *Equality* (New York, 1967), pp. 64–5; reprinted in Bedau (ed.), *Justice and Equality*, op. cit., p. 155.

4. Hugo A. Bedau, 'Radical Egalitarianism', in *Justice and Equality*, op. cit., p. 173; or his 'Egalitarianism and the Idea of Equality', in *Nomos*, IX: *Equality*, op. cit., p. 19.

5. Lucas, 'Against Equality', op. cit., pp. 302–3; and reprint, op. cit., pp. 145–6.

6. Benn, 'Egalitarianism and Equal Consideration of Interests', op. cit., pp. 65ff.; and reprint, op. cit., pp. 156ff.

7. Ibid., p. 60; reprint, p. 159.

8. J. C. Davies, *Human Nature in Politics* (New York, 1963), p. 45.

9. See more fully my 'Justice', *Philosophy*, 47 (1972), pp. 229–48; or my *Democracy and Participation* (Harmondsworth, 1976), ch. 7, pp. 108–13.

10. B. A. O. Williams, 'The Idea of Equality', in Peter Laslett and W. G. Runciman (eds), *Philosophy, Politics and Society*, series II (Oxford, 1962), pp. 114–20; reprinted in Bedau (ed.), *Justice and Equality*, op. cit., pp. 121–6.

11. F. A. Hayek, *The Constitution of Liberty* (London, 1960), chs 2, 3 and 8; and Quintin Hogg (Lord Hailsham), *The Case for Conservatism* (Harmondsworth, 1947), chs 16 and 26.

3 THE IDEA OF EQUALITY AS A SUBSTANTIVE PRINCIPLE *John Charvet*

(References inserted for this volume.)

1. John Rawls, 'Justice as Fairness', in Peter Laslett and W. G. Runciman (eds), *Philosophy, Politics and Society*, series II (Oxford, 1962), pp. 132–57.

2. B. A. O. Williams, 'The Idea of Equality', in ibid., pp. 114–20.

4 THE PURSUIT OF EQUALITY *Robert Nisbet*

(Reference inserted for this volume.)

1. John Rawls, *A Theory of Justice* (Cambridge, Mass., 1971; Oxford, 1972).

5 THE PROCRUSTEAN IDEAL *Antony Flew*

1. For a study of the background beliefs of the Founding Fathers on these issues, see: Wilhelm Sjöstrand, *Freedom and Equality as Fundamental Educational Principles in Western Democracy from John Locke to Edmund Burke* (Stockholm, 1973), ch. II.

2. Both these fallacies (and 'racism' in the sense implicitly defined above) are in fact totally repudiated by Arthur Jensen and H. J. Eysenck, two psychologists who have in recent years been ferociously abused for daring to question the assumption that there are no such average differences. Compare 'The Jensen Uproar' in my *Sociology, Equality and Education* (London, 1976; New York, 1976).

3. Kant, *Groundwork of the Metaphysic of Morals,* in *The Moral Law*, ed. & trans H. J. Paton (London, 1948, 1966; New York, 1967), pp. 90–1: 1948 edn cited.

4. D. M. Levine and M. J. Bane (eds), *The 'Inequality' Controversy* (New York, 1975), pp. 5, 198 (italics added); but compare and contrast p. 11.

5. *The Analects of Confucius*, ed. & trans W. E. Soothill (London, 1910), p. 399 (VIII, 2).

6. Jean Floud, essay in P. R. Cox, H. B. Miles and J. Peel (eds), *Equalities and Inequalities in Education* (London, 1975), pp. 37, 41.

7. Lars Ericsson, *Justice in the Distribution of Economic Resources* (Stockholm, 1976), p. 130 (inverted commas added).

8. In C. H. Firth (ed.), *The Clarke Papers* (1891), I, p. 301.

9. Milton Friedman, *Capitalism and Freedom* (Chicago and London, 1962); F. A. Hayek, *The Road to Serfdom* (London, 1944: new edn 1976; Chicago, 1944) & *The Constitution of Liberty* (London, 1960: new edn 1976; Chicago, 1960); and Keith Joseph, *Stranded on the Middle Ground* (London, 1976).

10. Quoted in *The Economist* (17 June 1972), p. 23. I possess a photocopy of the complete Russian text.

11. A recent National Opinion Poll revealed a four-to-one majority in favour of the legalisation of voluntary euthanasia.

12. J. S. Mill, *On Liberty* (Everyman edn, London, 1910), p. 67.

13. These two quite different ideals are clearly confounded in the publisher's puff for Mr Frank Field's *Unequal Britain* (London, 1977): 'As Director of the Child Poverty Action Group, he draws together evidence from all the major social reports to ask if there is a cycle of inequality in which a large number of people are trapped.' Seeing not scarcity but inequality as the evil, Field is, like most of the ideologues of social justice, understandably unconcerned about wealth creation. But it should be remarked that both that unconcern and any commitment to impose and lower a ceiling are, in different ways, incongruous with the stated aims of the organisation which he heads. For it claims, surely, to be concerned with a floor, not a ceiling, and with absolutes more than relatives.

14. The original suggestion, which would surely have won the instant support of J. S. Mill, came from Milton Friedman. But it seems to have been developed for a British context first in A. T. Peacock and J. Wiseman,

Education for Democrats (London, 1964, 1970). Compare: E. G. West, *Economics, Education and the Politician* (London, 1968, 1976); Ralph Harris and Arthur Seldon, *Choice in Welfare* (London, 1970); and A. K. Maynard, *Experiment with Choice in Education* (1975).

15. *Daily Telegraph* (25 Nov. 1975): sneer-quotes original.

16. Christopher Jencks et al., *Inequality* (New York, 1972; London, 1973, 1975).

17. On 'equality and social justice' as the ideology of the New Class, see Robert Nisbet, 'The Fatal Ambivalence', *Encounter* (Dec. 1976); compare my 'Equality *or* Justice', in P. A. French (ed.), *Studies in Ethical Theory*.

18. Anthony Quinton, *Utilitarian Ethics* (London, 1973; New York, 1973), pp. 75–6.

19. These two quotations are borrowed: the first from Terry Arthur, *Ninety-Five Percent is Crap* (New York, 1975), p. 183; and the second from F. A. Hayek, *The Constitution of Liberty*, op. cit. (note 9), p. 518.

20. *New Society* (20 Nov. 1975), p. 424.

21. H. Stretton, *Capitalism, Socialism and the Environment* (Cambridge, 1976), p. vi.

22. Ralph Harris and Arthur Seldon, *Not from Benevolence . . .: 20 Years of Economic Dissent* (London, 1977), ch. IV.

23. Printed in *The Listener* (5 May 1974), p. 566.

6 EQUALITY OF OPPORTUNITY *Charles Frankel*

1. R. H. Tawney, *Equality* (New York, 1929; London, 1931), p. 127.

2. Ibid., p. 124.

3. Aristotle, *Nichomachean Ethics*, 5.

4. Isaiah Berlin, for example, writes: 'In so far as some minimum degree of prevalence of rules is a necessary condition for the existence of human societies . . ., and in so far as morality, both personal and political, is largely conceived of in terms of rules, the kind of equality with which obedience to rules is virtually identical, is among the deepest needs and convictions of mankind. . . . A plea for equality in this sense is therefore a plea for life in accordance with rules as opposed to other standards, e.g., the *ad hoc* orders of an inspired leader, or arbitrary desires.' – 'Equality as an Ideal', *Proceedings of the Aristotelian Society*, 56 (1955–56); reprinted in Frederick A. Olafson (ed.), *Justice and Social Policy* (Englewood Cliffs, N.J., 1961), p. 132. But the last sentence quoted appears to rest on a distinction that is not a distinction, unless we can say what the difference is between *rules* and *standards*. If we wish to say that inspired leaders may not issue *ad hoc* orders, this is to establish a set of rules superior to the sovereign's will. But if no such rules are established, and if it is generally understood and accepted that what the ruler says is equal *is* equal, then people are living in accordance with a rule – a most troubling and frightening one, admittedly, but a rule nonetheless. Nor is this a purely hypothetical possibility: consider Nazi Germany and Stalinist Russia at certain long moments in their history.

5. Henry Sée, *Les origines du capitalisme moderne* (Paris, 1926), p. 183.
6. Berlin, op. cit., p. 131.
7. Brian Barry, *Political Argument* (New York, 1965), p. 120.

7 EQUALITY OF OPPORTUNITY AND EQUALITY OF RESULTS *James S. Coleman*

1. Barry R. Chiswick and Jacob Mincer, 'Time Series Changes in Income Inequality in the United States from 1939, with Projections to 1985', *J. of Political Economy*, 80 (May–June 1972), pp. S34–S71.

8 THE IDEA OF EQUALITY RECONSIDERED *Andrew Ward*

1. Bernard Williams, 'The Idea of Equality' in P. Laslett and W. G. Runciman (eds), *Philosophy, Politics and Society* (Oxford, 1962).
2. Ibid., p. 123.
3. I am grateful to Professor H. B. Acton for suggesting this objection.

9 EQUALITY UNDER THE LAW *Geoffrey Marshall*

(Renumbered from the original.)

1. J.-J. Rousseau, *Social Contract*, Bk 2, ch. iv.
2. John Morley, *Life of Gladstone* (London, 1908), I, p. 569.
3. A. V. Dicey, *Introduction to the Study of the Law of the Constitution* (1885) 10th edn ed. E. C. S. Wade (London, 1961), p. 202.
4. Lon Fuller, *The Morality of Law* (1964), rev. ed. (New Haven, Conn., 1969), ch. ii.
5. 22 Henry VIII c. 9: 'It is ordained and enacted by authority of this present Parliament that the said Richard Rose shall be therefore boiled to death . . .'
6. War Damage Act, 1965. See *Burmah Oil Co.* v. *Lord Advocate* [1964], 2 All E.R.
7. *Entick* v. *Carrington* (1765), 19 State Trials 1030 *per* Lord Camden CJ.
8. See *Ridge* v. *Baldwin* [1964], A.C. 40. H. W. R. Wade, *Administrative Law,* 2nd edn (Oxford, 1961), pp. 185–98.
9. A point conceded by Dicey in 'The Development of Administrative Law in England', 31 *Law Quarterly Rev.* 148 (1915).
10. G. N. Joshi, *Aspects of Indian Constitutional Law* (London, 1965), p. 80.
11. Frankfurter J in *Morey* v. *Doud*, 354 U.S. 457 at 472 (1957).
12. 336 U.S. 106 at 115 (1949).
13. 335 U.S. 464 (1948).
14. *Aziz* v. *State of Bombay*, 1954 S.C.R. 930.
15. 6 B. Verf G.E. 389 (1957). Article 3 of the Basic Law states that

'(1) All persons shall be equal before the law; (2) Men and women shall have equal rights; (3) No one may be prejudiced or privileged because of his sex, descent, race, language, faith, homeland, and origin, or because of his religious and political views.'

16. *Patsone* v. *Pennsylvania*, 232 U.S. 138 at 144 (1914).

17. *Plessy* v. *Ferguson*, 163 U.S. 537 at 550 (1896).

18. *Skinner* v. *Oklahoma*, 316 U.S. 535 at 541 (1942).

19. *Syed Mohammed* v. *State of Andhra*, 1954 S.C.R. 1117.

20. *Report on the Constitutions of Rhodesia and Nyasaland* (HMSO, London, 1960), Cmnd. 148, p. 78.

21. Cf. Warren CJ's remarks in *Curtis Publishing Co.* v. *Butts* and *Associated Press* v. *Walker*, 388 U.S. 130 at 163 (1967) on the blurring of 'public' and 'private'.

22. Shelley v. Kraemer, 334 U.S. 1 (1948).

23. For example, *Peterson* v. *South Carolina*, 373 U.S. 244 (1963).

24. 378 U.S. 226 (1964).

25. 379 U.S. 241 (1964)

26. 379 U.S. 294 (1964).

27. *Reitman* v. *Mulkey*, 387 U.S. 369 (1967), held an amendment to the California state constitution protecting the right to sell, lease or rent property at the individual's absolute discretion to be in violation of the Fourteenth Amendment.

10 HOW UNEVENLY IS WEALTH SPREAD TODAY? *George Polanyi & John B. Wood*

(Renumbered from the original.)

1. *Labour Party Manifesto* (London, 1974), pp. 9, 15.

2. J. R. M. Willis, Institute of Fiscal Studies Conference, Feb. 1973.

3. *Inland Revenue Statistics 1972* (HMSO, London, 1973), p. 156.

4. Viz., there has been no comprehensive survey of personal wealth among the living since the sample surveys of income and savings by the Oxford University Institute of Statistics in the 1950s.

5. Less than half of all deaths: cf. p. 240.

6. *Inland Revenue Statistics 1972*, Appendix, Table A.

7. In practice, the Inland Revenue tries to correct for this source of error by some averaging of mortality multipliers and wealth totals, but this cannot wholly remove the sampling errors.

8. A. B. Atkinson, *Unequal Shares: Wealth in Britain* (Harmondsworth, 1972), Table 5, p. 21.

9. H. F. Lydall and D. G. Tipping, 'The Distribution of Personal Wealth in Britain', *Bulletin of Oxford University Institute of Statistics* (Feb. 1962), noted (p. 99) a tendency to exaggerate upwards in the recording of social class in death registers.

10. For reservations on the estate duty method, where this point is mentioned, cf. J. Whalley, 'Official Estimates of the Size Distribution of

Wealth in Great Britain: Some Reservations', mimeographed, 1974. We are grateful for permission to use material from this paper.

11. Raised to £12,500 in March 1971, and to £15,000 in March 1972.

12. Based on the analysis of estates for which duty began to be paid in 1970–71.

13. J. Revell, *The Wealth of the Nation* (Cambridge, 1967), pp. 170–4. Cf. below, p. 236 and Table 10.2.

14. E. Victor Morgan, *The Structure of Property Ownership in Great Britain* (Oxford, 1960), pp. 74, 80.

15. Revell, op. cit., pp. 147–60.

16. A. B. Atkinson, 'The Distribution of Wealth and the Individual Life Cycle', *Oxford Economic Papers* (July 1971), p. 251.

17. After allowing for the effect of administrative concessions in force until 1958, providing for deliberate under-valuation in some cases (Lydall and Tipping, p. 102).

18. *Inland Revenue Statistics 1972*, p. 156.

19. Ibid., Appendix, Table B (Cash and Bank Deposits).

20. Ibid., p. 156.

21. T. P. Hill, 'Incomes, Savings and Net Worth: The Savings Surveys of 1952–54', *Bulletin of Oxford University Institute of Statistics* (May 1955), p. 155. The proportion of owners is quoted gross (before deducting liabilities) to correspond with Inland Revenue estimates which show the same number of owners before and after deducting liabilities.

22. *Inland Revenue Statistics, 1972*, p. 156. Since the sample surveys of income and property of households made by the Oxford University Institute of Statistics in the 1950s (references in Lydall and Tyndall, op. cit.) are 20 years out of date [i.e., in 1974, when this essay was written – Ed.], the IEA hopes to be able to organise a major survey of personal wealth in 1974.

23. See below, p. 254.

24. D. Projector and G. Weiss, *Survey of Financial Characteristics of Consumers*, Federal Reserve Technical Papers (Washington DC, 1966), p. 30.

25. See our Table on p. 17 [of the original publication excerpted here – Ed.]. The estate duty information on wealth distribution is adequate to establish trends over time, although not for giving an absolute measure of the degree of wealth concentration at a point of time (see above, p. 230).

26. Alan Day, "The Nation's Wealth: Who Owns It?', *Observer* (20 Jan. 1974). This estimate was for adults aged 25 and over in Great Britain, and is therefore comparable with Professor Atkinson's estimates.

27. P. T. Bauer and A. R. Prest, 'Income Differences and Inequalities', *Moorgate and Wall Street Review* (Autumn 1973), p. 43.

28. T. W. Schultz, *The Economic Value of Education* (New York, 1963), p. 51.

29. J. E. Meade, *Efficiency, Equality and the Ownership of Property* (London, 1964), p. 32.

30. Ibid., p. 30.

31. Kathleen Langley, 'The Distribution of Capital in Private Hands' *Bulletin of Oxford University Institute of Statistics* (Feb. 1951).

32. Lydall and Tipping, op. cit., note 9, above (1961).

33. On 25 Jan. 1974, in a BBC programme called 'Wealth and People', the presenter (Peter Donaldson) commented: 'How little the pattern of wealth has changed in the last 50 years.' The programme was part of a series called 'The Economics of the Real World' (sic!).

34. Atkinson, op. cit., note 16, above, p. 244. Cf. the discussion of age differences, above pp. 243–5.

35. Dorothy S. Projector, *Survey of Changes in Family Circumstances,* Federal Reserve Technical Papers (Washington DC, 1968), p. 14.

36. Ibid., pp. 9, 10.

37. Ibid., p. 14.

38. The prevalence of envy in every type of society, and throughout the ages, is well documented by Helmut Schoek in *Envy: A Theory of Social Behaviour* (London, 1970; New York, 1970). Professor Schoek argues that, for economic progress and well-being, societies must come to terms with envy, but cannot assuage it by egalitarian measures.

11 THE STABILITY OF INEQUALITY *Kenneth E. Boulding*

Works cited:

Irma Adelman and Cynthia Taft Morris, *Economic Growth and Social Equality in Developing Countries* (Stanford, Cal., 1973).

Kenneth F. Boulding, *The Economy of Love and Fear: A Preface to Grants Economics* (Belmont, 1973).

Hollis Chenery et al., *Redistribution with Growth* (London, 1974).

Milton Rokeach, *Beliefs, Attitudes, Values: A Theory of Organisation and Change* (San Francisco, 1968).

Milton Rokeach, *The Nature of Human Values* (New York, 1973).

Adam Smith, *Theory of the Moral Sentiments* (1759); new edn (New York, 1966).

13 THE EGALITARIAN IMPERATIVE *Richard E. Wagner*

1. Lester C. Thurow, *Generating Inequality* (New York, 1975), pp. 3–19.

2. Adam Smith, *Wealth of Nations* (1776), Bk I, ch. 10. See also Milton Friedman, *Price Theory* (Chicago, 1976), pp. 238–50.

3. For documentation to the effect that failure to consider the relation between age and income overstates the degree of inequality by about 50 per cent, see Mortin Paglin, 'The Measurement and Trend of Inequality: A Basic Revision', *American Economic Review*, 65 (Sept. 1975), pp. 598–609. A related analysis is developed in Edgar K. Browning, 'The Trend Toward Equality in the Distribution of Net Income', *Southern Economic Journal*, 43 (July 1976), pp. 912–23.

4. Edgar K. Browning, *Redistribution and the Welfare System* (Washington DC, 1975), p. 24.

5. Martin S. Feldstein, 'Social Security, Induced Retirement and Aggregate Capital Accumulation', *Journal of Political Economy*, 82 (Oct. 1974), pp. 905–26. See also the same author's 'Social Security and Saving: The Extended Life Cycle Theory', *American Economic Review*, Proceedings, 66 (May 1976), pp. 77–86.

6. Abba Lerner, *The Economics of Control* (New York, 1944), pp. 26–32.

7. See, for instance, the following articles in the *Quarterly Journal of Economics*: Ray C. Fair, 'The Optimal Distribution of Income', 85 (Nov. 1971), pp. 551–79; Edmund S. Phelps, 'Taxation of Wage Income for Economic Justice', 87 (Aug. 1973), pp. 331–54; and Lester C. Thurow, 'The Income Distribution as a Pure Public Good', 85 (May 1971), pp. 327–36.

8. This point comes across especially clearly in Phelps, op. cit., note 7 above, p. 334. In his Figure 1, the absence of incentive effects would yield a linear opportunity locus *FF*, in which case optimality would lie on the 45-degree line, indicating perfect equality.

9. John Rawls, *A Theory of Justice* (Cambridge, Mass., 1971; Oxford, 1972).

10. Thurow, op. cit., note 7 above, p. 328. (Thurow's italics.)

11. This point is developed clearly in Milton Friedman, 'Choice, Chance and the Personal Distribution of Income', *Journal of Political Economy*, 61 (Aug. 1953), pp. 277–90.

12. See the development of this argument in Richard E. Wagner, 'Politics, Bureaucracy and Budgetary Choice', *Journal of Money, Credit and Banking*, 6 (Aug. 1974), pp. 370–1. I do not intend to suggest that equalisation can be explained wholly by the disparity in the size of above-average and below-average income groups. It surely cannot, for then it would be impossible to explain why full equalisation does not result. Rather, the analysis merely suggests that an increase in the size of the below-average group will increase the amount of equalisation. For a more complete treatment of equalisation within this framework, see the same author's *The Public Economy* (Chicago, 1973), pp. 168–71.

13. A. V. Dicey, *Lectures on the Relation Between Law and Public Opinion in England in the Nineteenth Century* (1905); 2nd edn (London, 1914), p. *xxxv*.

14. See, for instance, Walter J. Blum and Harry Kalven Jnr, *The Uneasy Case for Progressive Taxation* (Chicago, 1953), pp. 19–21.

15. Indeed, a considerable amount of inequality is itself a product of legislation. There is a tendency for legislation to produce adverse distributional outcomes, on the one hand, and a proclivity, on the other hand, to call for further legislation to promote contrary distributional outcomes.

16. For a discussion of this point and many others in the contemporary literature on material equality, see Leland B. Yeager, 'Can a Liberal be an Egalitarian?', in F. A. Hayek et al., *Toward Liberty* (Menlo Park, Cal., 1971), pp. 422–40.

17. Lowell E. Gallaway, 'On the Importance of "Picking One's Parents" ', *Quarterly Review of Economics and Business*, 6 (Summer 1966), pp. 7–15. For a presentation of alternative evidence in support of the same

theme, see Christopher Jencks et al., *Inequality: A Reassessment of the Effect of Family and Schooling in America* (New York, 1972).

18. Recall that ancient Hebrew wisdom: 'Speed does not win the race nor strength the battle. Bread does not belong to the wise, nor wealth to the intelligent, nor success to the skilful; time and chance govern all.' *Ecclesiastes*, IX 11 (New English Bible translation).

19. James Meade relates differences in income and wealth to differences in luck and inheritance, with inheritance containing four components: genetic, educational, social and economic. See James E. Meade, *The Inheritance of Inequalities: Some Biological, Demographic, Social and Economic Factors,* Proceedings of the British Academy, 59 (London, 1973).

20. Carl S. Shoup, *Federal Estate and Gift Taxes*, Brookings Institute (Washington DC, 1966), p. 108. (Italics added.)

21. On these points, see George J. Stigler, *The Theory of Price*, 3rd edn (New York, 1966), pp. 307–9.

22. The problem of the gambler's ruin is surveyed in William Feller, *An Introduction to Probability Theory and its Applications*, 2nd edn (New York, 1957), I, 311–13.

23. Let p denote the probability that the gambler wins and q the possibility that he loses. If $p = q$, the probability that the gambler will become ruined is:

$$P_r = 1 - \chi/(\chi + \gamma). \text{ If } p \neq q,\ P_r = \frac{(q/p)^{(\chi+\gamma)} - (q/p)^{\chi}}{(q/p)^{(\chi+\gamma)} - 1}.$$

If $p = q$, the expected duration before ruin will be:

$$D_r = \chi\gamma. \text{ If } p \neq q,\ D_r = \frac{\chi}{q-p} - \frac{\chi+\gamma}{q-p} \cdot \frac{1-(q/p)^{\chi}}{1-(q/p)^{(\chi+\gamma)}}.$$

15 THE CHARITY OF THE UNCHARITABLE *Gordon Tullock*

1. J. M. Buchanan and G. Tullock, *The Calculus of Consent* (Ann Arbor, Mich., 1962).

2. A. Downs, *An Economic Theory of Democracy* (New York, 1957).

3. B. Frey, 'Why Do High Income People Participate More in Politics?', *Public Choice*, 11 (Fall 1971), pp. 101–5.

4. M. Friedman, *Capitalism and Freedom* (Chicago, 1962).

5. B. R. Fry and R. F. Winters, 'The Politics of Redistribution', *American Political Science Review*, 64 (June 1970), pp. 508–22.

6. R. J. Lampman, 'Transfer and Redistribution as Social Process', mimeograph.

7. W. A. Niskanen, *Bureaucracy and Representative Government* (Chicago, 1971).

8. W. Riker, *The Theory of Political Coalitions* (New Haven, Conn., 1962).

9. J. Rodgers and H. Hochman, 'Pareto Optimal Redistribution', *American Economic Review*, 59 (Sept. 1969), pp. 542–57.

10. G. Tullock, 'A Simple Algebraic Logrolling Method', *American Economic Review*, 60 (June 1970), pp. 419–26.

11. B. Ward, 'Majority Rule and Allocation', *Journal of Conflict Resolution*, 5 (Dec. 1961), pp. 379–89.

12. A. L. Webb and J. E. B. Sieve, *Income Distribution and the Welfare State*, Social Administration Research Trust (London, 1971).

13. US Congress, Senate: Senator A. Ribicoff speaking about Amendments to the President's Welfare Program – Amendment no. 318, 92nd Congress, 1st session, 22 July 1971: *Congressional Record*, S11783.

16 ECONOMIC JUSTICE AND THE ECONOMIST *Richard A. Posner*

1. See, for example, John M. Peterson and Charles T. Stewart Jnr, *Employment Effects of Minimum Wage Rates* (Washington DC, 1969), and studies cited therein; Marvin Kosters and Finis Welch, 'The Effects of Minimum Wages on the Distribution of Changes in Aggregate Employment', *American Economic Review*, 62 (1972), p. 323.

2. See Dorothy S. Projector and Gertrude S. Weiss, *Survey of Financial Characteristics of Consumers*, Federal Reserve Technical Papers (Washington DC, 1966), pp. 151, 22.

17 THE GRAIL OF EQUALITY *Peter Bauer*

1. The antiquity and ubiquity of envy is the major theme of Helmut Schoek's massive treatise, *Envy: A Theory of Social Behaviour* (London, 1970; New York, 1970).

Index of names

Index of subjects